The Pathetick Musician

The Pathetick Musician

Moving an Audience in the Age of Eloquence

BRUCE HAYNES AND GEOFFREY BURGESS

OXFORD
UNIVERSITY PRESS

OXFORD
UNIVERSITY PRESS

Oxford University Press is a department of the University of Oxford. It furthers
the University's objective of excellence in research, scholarship, and education
by publishing worldwide. Oxford is a registered trade mark of Oxford University
Press in the UK and certain other countries.

Published in the United States of America by Oxford University Press
198 Madison Avenue, New York, NY 10016, United States of America.

© Oxford University Press 2016

All rights reserved. No part of this publication may be reproduced, stored in
a retrieval system, or transmitted, in any form or by any means, without the
prior permission in writing of Oxford University Press, or as expressly permitted
by law, by license, or under terms agreed with the appropriate reproduction
rights organization. Inquiries concerning reproduction outside the scope of the
above should be sent to the Rights Department, Oxford University Press, at the
address above.

This volume is published with the generous support of the Margarita M. Hanson Endowment
of the American Musicological Society, funded in part by the National Endowment for the
Humanities and the Andrew W. Mellon Foundation.

You must not circulate this work in any other form
and you must impose this same condition on any acquirer.

Library of Congress Cataloging-in-Publication Data
Haynes, Bruce, 1942–2011, author.
The pathetick musician: moving an audience in the age of eloquence/Bruce Haynes
and Geoffrey Burgess.
pages cm
Includes bibliographical references and index.
"Bibliography of the writings of Bruce Haynes": pages
ISBN 978–0–19–937373–4 (hardcover: alk. paper)
1. Music—17th century—Philosophy and aesthetics.
2. Music—18th century—Philosophy and aesthetics.
I. Burgess, Geoffrey, author. II. Title. III. Title: Pathetic musician.
ML3845.H39 2016
780.9′032–dc23
2015029319

To Susie and Leon, the vibrant inspirational figures in the lives of the two authors.

CONTENTS

Foreword: Aus der Tiefen (*Geoffrey Burgess*)   xi
Preface: Pipe Dreams (*Bruce Haynes*)   xxi
Acknowledgments   xxvii
About the Companion Website   xxix

PART ONE   BACH AND THE RHETORICAL HERITAGE

INTRODUCTION: THE ELOQUENT MUSICIAN (BH)   3

The Truth in Eloquence   3
   Rhetorical Music   6

The Pathetick Musician   7

Ut pictura poesis   9

The Officers of Rhetoric   11

Style Coaches   14

Further Reading   16

1. IN THE REALM OF THE PASSIONS (BH)   18

Humanism and the Rhetorical Ethos   18

Seconda prattica   19

The Romantic Revolution   25

Of Æsthetics and Beauty   28

Autonomous Music: "Art for Art's Sake"   31
   Personally Expressing Passions or Passionately Expressing Persons?   33

Afterword by Geoffrey Burgess 35

Further Reading 36

2. THE PRINCIPLES OF ELOQUENCE: THE ARTIST'S TOOLBOX (GB) 38

The Offices of Rhetoric 38

Structuring Rhetoric 41

The Sense of Music 42

    Figures of Speech, Figures of Song 44

    Hypotyposis or Painting 49

    Pathopoia or Arousing Passions 50

    Topics: Intertextual Allusion 57

    Ethopoeïa: Musical Characterization 58

    Key and Character 59

On the Possibility of a *Figurenlehre* 65

Further Reading 66

3. BACH'S EXPRESSIVE UNIVERSE (GB) 68

Imitation: Portraying and Evoking the World 68

"Clear running water": Schweitzer's Legacy 69

Figuring Bach's World 70

    Bach the Poet, Bach the Painter 72

    Onomatopoeia 80

Landscape Painting and "Paintings of Life" 84

Further Reading 90

4. BACH'S INNER WORLD (GB) 91

General and Particular Expression 91

Reading Bach's Passions 93

    Fear and *Tremolo* 98

Antithesis: At Odds with Oneself 100

Polyphonies of Passions: Passions in Polyphony 105

    Laughing at Death: The Proximity of Opposites 114

Further Reading 117

PART TWO   PERFORMING ELOQUENCE

5. ENHANCING ELOQUENCE IN PERFORMANCE (*ELOCUTIO*) (GB)   121
- The "Intentional Fallacy" Fallacy: Whose Intention?   121
- *Elocutio*: The Essence of Performance Practice   127
- "Humouring" the Score   128
- Tempo and Affect   134
- Light and Shadow   137
- Further Reading   138

6. FIGURES: SPINNING STRAW INTO GOLD (GB)   139
- Public Speaking, Public Musicking   139
- Declamation as Figurative Speech   141
- Figures as Ornamental Glosses   146
    - Essential Graces   149
    - Graces as Glosses   151
    - The Salt of Music, the Spice of Dissonance   153
    - Graces as Passionate Expression   154
- Structuring Ornaments: *Passaggi* and Paraphrase   160
- Ornaments in History   162
- Further Reading   167

7. THE EXPRESSIVE GESTURE (GB)   168
- Audible Architecture   168
- Articulating the Musical Gesture   171
- The Breath of Life   175
- Agogics   181
    - The Agogic Accent (prolonged beat)   181
    - The Agogic Pickup   182
    - The Agogic Placement   182
    - The Hesitation   183
- Finding the Poetry in the Notes   183
- Pause to Reflect   186

Gesture and Character   189

Gesturing toward the Phrase   195

Further Reading   199

8. *KAIROS:* EXPRESSIVE TIMING (GB)   200

Chronos and *Kairos:* Two Kinds of Time   200

The Metronome and the Modern Tendency toward *Chronos*   202

The Beat, or Pulse in Baroque Music   204

"The true motion of the Bass"   207

Tempo Fluctuation   211

Borrowed Time   221

Kairos: Isolating Musical Events   225

Timing in Dance Music   228

Further Reading   232

9. TO KINDLE THE HEART: ENGAGEMENT IN PERFORMANCE (GB)   234

The Sovereign Audience   235

Authentic Ears   241

Music in the Body   243

The Meaning of *Vortrag*   249

"The unutterable ravishing Soul's delight"   250

Dance: *Une poésie muette*   252

Sincerity in Performance   254

Mental Multitasking   260

Further Reading   261

10. ANALYZING EXPRESSION IN PERIOD RECORDINGS OF BACH'S CANTATAS (BH)   263

Appendix Bruce Haynes: List of Publications   275
Notes   283
General Bibliography   297
Index   311

FOREWORD
Aus der Tiefen

GEOFFREY BURGESS

In 1984 I heard Bruce Haynes play live for the first time in a concert of music by J. S. Bach. The program, directed by Gustav Leonhardt at the Oude Muziek Festival in Utrecht, included the Sinfonia from BWV 152, *Tritt auf die Glaubensbahn*, and Cantata 131, *Aus der Tiefen*. I was already familiar with Bruce's playing from recordings and had met him briefly a couple of months prior, but in concert I found Bruce's special blend of poise and eloquent spontaneity at once compelling and moving. Afterwards I was eager to talk with him about the concert and his views on the music, but there were time constraints. With his generous smile Bruce assured me we would have plenty of time for future conversations. Little did I suspect how long our dialogue would last, and how true the theme of the final work on that concert would hold. Thirty years later, after an intensive study period, the release of our co-authored book *The Oboe*, our dialogue continues with Bruce's voice calling *aus der Tiefen* through the draft of this book.

A child of the 1960s Dutch early music school, Bruce Haynes (1942–2011) was mentored by Alan Curtis in Berkeley, California, and then studied recorder with Frans Brüggen and chamber music with Gustav Leonhardt in The Netherlands. He went on to play a leading role in the early music movement as one of the pioneers of the twentieth-century revival of the Baroque oboe, which he taught at the Koninklijk Conservatorium in The Hague for ten years from 1972. Even more than his exceptional qualities as a performer, Bruce will be remembered as the early music movement's spokesman—and whistleblower. After dedicating years to playing eighteenth-century oboe (which he preferred to call by its historical name *hautboy*) and researching its history, in his last years he turned to more general questions of interpretation. His ideas and basic tenets owe much to the teaching of his mentors, and his polemical stance was very much in line with the

Dutch school's principles, not only regarding the technical aspects of their particular brand of performance practice but also the ethos of questioning that they promoted. Haynes was guided by advice given years earlier by Frans Brüggen:

> We are *not* the same musicians, mentally *nor* the same human beings, and not being the same, it *is* very difficult to read an old music treatise in its proper meaning and context. The solution, of course, is to read less about music and more about context.[1]

Building contexts took an increasingly central place in Bruce's work. Research was necessary not just to understand music from the "foreign land" of past centuries but also to question the inevitable outgrowth of the divide between modern sensibilities and Baroque esthetics. The adoption of period instruments in the 1960s represented a paradigm shift. Later, after Bruce had retired from playing, he found himself asking what had motivated him, midcareer, to take the radical step of changing instruments from oboe to hautboy (then a virtually unknown instrument that for lack of experienced masters or an established tradition, he taught himself to play). Among preliminary jottings for the present book he wrote "If we cannot place music, painting, or writing in a context, that art would be devoid of meaning. No object could be identifiable as a work of art. It would become sheer noise, or indecipherable marks or stains on unidentifiable material." The quest to decipher the signs of Baroque music on instruments of the time alongside visual art, theater, and above all the art of verbal eloquence of the same period became central to his thinking and teaching. Equally important was the recovery of the spirit of discovery and revolution that had been such a decisive force behind the early music movement as it took shape in the 1960s.

Bruce was nothing if not an idealist, and his revolutionary spirit was undying. While other practitioners were eager to push the boundary of early music forward into the nineteenth century, he held to Baroque music in order to delve deeper into its riches and complexities. The bombast of Romantic art repelled him, and when Frans Brüggen shifted the focus of his Orchestra of the Eighteenth Century to late Classical and early nineteenth-century music, he was openly skeptical and felt that Brüggen would compromise his art by turning away from what he did best. "It is just possible," he wrote to Brüggen in 1982:

> that this turn towards later music will channel the early music movement back into the mainstream of established "concert" music, and it will be seen as an aberration of a half-generation rather than a great turning-point in the basic aesthetic assumptions of concert music. I still see "early music" as a protest, a reaction to the concept of music as ritual ceremony, and I am alarmed to see this tendency to bring it back to the establishment, to make it together and in tune at the expense of expressive and new.[2]

Haynes's predictions have proven largely accurate, and by now the professionalization and institutionalization of early music are virtually irreversible. Its mainstream status has made much possible, but to pioneers like Bruce, the compromises are only too apparent.[3] Over the course of the past decades, early music has become instated into the mainstream, and in the process it has been bought out. As much as period musicians have come to rely on regular work with established groups and growing audience bases, these same institutionalized performances have spawned entrenched traditions that have stymied creative experimentation. This is no more true than with the Bach Passions and with classical music's number one institution: the inevitable Christmas *Messiah* performance, the single most significant employer of period-players around the world. The enthusiastic rediscovery of HIP (Historically Informed Performance) of Handel and Bach that rejuvenated the tradition in the 1970s has since lapsed into unthinking convention. Period instruments are now standard. Early music had sold its heart and soul to the establishment.

But, while critics like Richard Taruskin took the view that early music had from the beginning been of a modern disposition and saw its progress in an inevitable fusion of mainstream and alternative, Haynes was not ready to acknowledge defeat.[4] With its means becoming its end, technique taking over from vital spirit, and economy controlling artistry, he saw its end in sight. Despite his disillusionment, Bruce still acknowledged optimistically that the hard-won acquisition of a sophisticated and nuanced understanding of the instruments, techniques, and styles of the past could enable early musicians to reach the goals and purposes of music as they were originally understood. As long as early music could be protected from the contagion of modern intervention, it could retain its value. *The End of Early Music* set out his philosophy for a musical elocution that prioritized expressivity above technical aspects. *The End* was not a swansong: quite the contrary, it was a provocation for period musicians to reawaken the early music movement's founding principles and end goals.

From the 1990s Bruce had moved progressively away from being an active performer, finding his métier as a writer. After publishing *The Story of A*, a history of performing pitch, *The Eloquent Oboe* brought together his extensive research on the instrument's history, much of which was synthesized in *The Oboe* that we co-authored. Then with *The End of Early Music* his writings reached a broader, international audience, stimulating much discussion on the nature and goals of HIP: not the Historically Informed Performance of early music but, as Bruce insisted, Historically *Inspired* Performance.

Almost as soon as *The End of Early Music* appeared in print in 2007, Haynes began work on a supplementary volume that would elaborate some of the topics that warranted more detailed treatment. His first sketches, with titles including *Implementing Eloquence, Paradigm Lost,* and *Music on the Cartesian*

Model: Arousing the Passions with and without Words, show him grappling with the divide between the Modernist aesthetic and what he coined the Eloquent (or Rhetorical) style. He also toyed with the idea of a book on singing, believing that as the natural musical instrument was an ideal to which all seventeenth- and eighteenth-century musicians aspired, singing would gather a wide range of topics of importance to the Rhetorical style. Simultaneously, he started to collect material for a book on the Bach cantatas, with a provisional title of *Persuasive Bach: Learning Musical Rhetoric from the Cantata*. Over time, these three streams merged into *The Pathetick Musician*, a study of the significance of rhetoric and particularly *pathopoeia*, or passionate eloquence, in musical performance centering on the works of J. S. Bach. Portions of the manuscript were given as lecture series, individual workshops, and papers, and in the Spring of 2011, a draft of the book served as course readings for Bruce's last graduate seminar at McGill University. In each incarnation, his central agenda was to critique the present state of early music and above all, to re-implement what he sensed was crucially undervalued—eloquent performance and passionate expression. By redefining the goals of performance practice, he hoped to equip performers with the materials to create moving, even provocative, performances that get to the heart of the matter.

A book on the rhetorical and passion-based interpretation of Baroque music could have focused on the music of any seventeenth- or eighteenth-century composer—Monteverdi, Purcell, Lully, Handel, or Vivaldi—but given Bruce's lifelong dedication to the music of Johann Sebastian Bach, it seems appropriate that he grounded his final work in Bach's sacred vocal music. His involvement from the 1970s in the first recording of the complete cycle of Bach cantatas with the Leonhardt Consort led to an extensive study of Bach's music and a range of attempts to rediscover lost works for oboe. Later, he indulged in two projects that exemplified the type of (re)creative play with history that he called for in *The End of Early Music*: an arrangement of movements by Bach into six concertos for varied instrumentation modeled after the Brandenburg set (completed by his partner Susie Napper, and recorded posthumously by the Montréal Baroque Band), and *Althea of Tarsia* an *opera pasticcio*, based on an exacting study of the entire corpus of Bach's cantatas, that matched arias and recitatives to an imaginary scenario. Both served as the groundwork for this book.

For Bruce, Bach's music was the ultimate vehicle for musical eloquence. This stood in stark opposition to earlier attitudes. The mid-twentieth-century Bach revival had focused on motoric rhythms, terraced dynamics, and exacting details of interpretation: double-dotting, execution in place of expression and more than anything "freedom from feeling." It had treated Bach's music with its mathematical calculation and intellectual grounding as the ultimate "pure" music absent of subjectivity and easily appropriated into the same postwar objectivism that had spawned formalism in literary studies and the brutalist style in architecture. But the early music movement of the late 1950s and '60s staged a revolution, and injected this repertoire with revitalized expressivity, and while performance was based on intellectual and historical study, the pioneers—Nikolaus Harnoncourt, Gustav Leonhardt, Frans Brüggen, Luigi Ferdinando Tagliavini, and the Kuijken brothers—reached new audiences with vivid, novel approaches.

As it stood at Bruce's death *The Pathetick Musician,* although broad-ranging in its coverage and insightful on many levels, still lacked a clear focus. Bruce had mapped out the general plan of the book and amassed a substantial quantity of source material, but he had not fully developed the supporting narrative. Although he had established the direction of the argument, his conclusions were not always in sight. Undoubtedly much was clear in Bruce's mind, ready to be committed to paper in the final stages of writing. Of course, we will never know exactly what the book would have looked like if he had had the opportunity to bring it to completion, but I doubt that it would have been what this pathetic(k) musician has been able to create. At the same time I feel confident that Bruce would not have objected to what I have done. For him, researching and questioning were only valuable if they stimulate dialogue, and so *The Pathetick Musician* as it now stands takes up the challenge of responding to his provocations.

Preparing the book for publication has borne an uncanny resemblance to the process of creating eloquence out of a composer's jottings (which, after all, is the central topic of the book). All I had to fashion a coherent narrative from was a draft, sometimes near-complete, at others frustratingly cursory, and a jumble of notes, commentaries to recorded performances, correspondence with members of his circle of colleagues and experts, and accounts from students who took his seminars at McGill. The closest to a "How to" guide was the table of contents, and while the book's general *inventio* and *dispositio* had been laid out, many of the details still required elaboration, embellishment, and eloquent articulation. Making sense of a dead man's thoughts is always a daunting undertaking, but having worked closely with Bruce on *The Oboe* (which we wrote collaboratively between 1998 and 2004), I was perhaps better qualified than anyone to disentangle the threads of his *Nachlass*. As an oboist and researcher, my career would have been unthinkable without Haynes's pioneering work. Since studying with him in the late 1980s, and performing major works of Bach and French opera with Bruce in the 1990s, I have been continuously engaged in the performance of the eighteenth-century repertoire and the education of musicians in the Rhetorical style.

An early plan to reproduce Bruce's text as it stood, with commentary in the form of marginalia, annotations, and bibliographic guidance proved too cumbersome to be of general use. I realized that my role would have to evolve from that of editor to co-author. I then set out not only to complete Bruce's work but to complement it with more detailed examples. A large part of my task was to supply connective tissue that could both clarify and reinforce Bruce's points. Those sections that were closest to fully written—what became the preface, introduction, and chapters 1 and 10—I left largely intact and, apart from light emendations and revisions, are as he drafted them. They retain his voice and serve as bookends, framing the rest of the book. While the remaining chapters required more editorial intervention and reorganization of the material, the basic tenets remain Bruce's.

In the form he left it, the book was closer to a set of readings than a developed monograph. In order to give it a more logical sequence and progressive flow, I reduced the quotations to a manageable number based on relevance. While all references have been verified, given their volume, there will inevitably be inaccuracies that have escaped my attention, and for which I take full responsibility. To enhance usefulness to English readers and to reduce space, all quotations are given in translation. Wherever possible, I have followed Bruce's practice of quoting from contemporaneous English translations of the foreign-language texts. Retaining original spelling and punctuation both preserves the spirit of the original, and exemplifies the connection between early reading practices and the interpretation of musical scores. In this way it serves as a lucid reflection on the subject matter of the book. Where no period version exists, the translations are our own.[5]

The End of Early Music set a new benchmark in music publishing by being one of the first books produced with a companion website with audio examples. It won an ASCAP Deems Taylor Media Award for this. Bruce's concept for *Pathetick* likewise relied heavily on sound clips, and I recognized that it was an essential element to the total product. In the belief that the music could speak for itself, Bruce rarely provided more than a few words to guide users' listening, preferring to leave it to his audience to make connections between his text and the recordings. Without diminishing the importance of direct musical experience, I felt it was worth providing users with more detailed guidance on what to listen for. This also means that if the website is unavailable while reading, the essential points can still be grasped from the text alone.

Bruce's search for answers never ended. His last words were "I am questioning . . ." Forever probing for new ways to envision music and deeper levels of understanding, his mus(ick)ing probed the core and meaning of the music to which he dedicated his life. The way he continually reworked material, toyed with arguments, examining them from different angles like through a kaleidoscope (one of his favorite images), encouraged me in my role as co-author to take a liberal hand with the manuscript. So, as well as being consistent with his philosophy as musician and historian, I have been inspired to amplify his groundwork with my own research. Developing his points further has allowed me, in some instances, to provide a more nuanced picture. Knowing his time was limited, Bruce was forced to take some economical shortcuts in *The Pathetick Musician*. He filled out some topics by alluding to and even quoting verbatim from *The End of Early Music*. Instead of repeating this material I have continued the thread of the argument by introducing fresh material that supports the same general claims.

In his quest to open lines of discourse and incorporate different perspectives, Bruce took delight in trying out different arguments. Rather than hold blindly to received wisdom, he would break a path through the undergrowth of fresh information, leaving it to others to work out the details and draw their own conclusions. To that end, he took an almost perverse delight in pushing lines of reasoning to breaking point before abandoning them and starting afresh. He was apt to completely rethink his position and even flip arguments on their heads from one draft to the next. I felt sure that in *The Pathetick Musician* he was at times consciously playing the devil's advocate, and where his position is unsustainable, I have retained his musings as *confutatio* to the basic *argumento*.

This book (both as Bruce conceived it and as I have reworked it) is aimed primarily at practicing musicians—professionals, students, performers, and historians committed to gaining a deeper understanding of early music performance. That said, readers seeking clear-cut rules ready to apply in a "just-add-water" recipe for eloquent performances will be disappointed. Modern-trained musicians are often hesitant to approach early music because they lack the rules—the game plan—as it were. But the quest for foolproof style guidelines confuses interpretation with correctness and accuracy. Likewise, the 'rules' of Classical rhetoric are no sure recipe for a successful performance: they can only serve as guidance in the process of achieving eloquence.

Expecting that there is some clear and simple set of rules reflects a popular misconception that there is some particular template that one can cut the music to that will make it Baroque, or transform a mundane performance into a piece of eloquent rhetoric. That misconception—as prevalent in HIP circles as with modern symphonic players—is worrying because it indicates a perception of period performance as representing rules, as a limit setter. David Boyden's observation that "what everyone knew then, no one knows now" humbles us in our quest for the elusive seventeenth- and eighteenth-century "good taste."[6] It would be irresponsible for us to advocate that by simply turning to history for solutions we could magically perfect the art of affective performance. We can be informed and inspired by the practices of past artists, but every decision we make is rooted in the world in which we live and work. The advent of a new style does not threaten the existence of an old one; it merely adds an option. Period performance is one manifestation of the paradigm shift to the view that there is more than the one set way, and that there can be choices and alternatives. It also provides the perspective to see differences between performing styles (whether Modern, Romantic, or HIP) in sharper relief.

Consequently, none of the opinions voiced here should be taken as definitive. Our criticisms of recorded performances should not be taken as damning judgment. They remain the opinions of a particular viewpoint. No one can get everything right, and our goal is to foster further growth. Our intention is to demonstrate how vital it is for all involved in early music—performers, scholars, programmers, and audiences—to continue to think about what performing this music means—as much to the culture that created it as in today's world. Examining how it came about and by what means it contributed to its own time will also enrich our understanding of the place of early music in modern culture. The supportive evidence enriches that perspective but should also allow others to explore new paths.

In his recent book *Bach: Music in the Castle of Heaven,* John Eliot Gardiner argues persuasively that while musicologists can dither, performers cannot sit on the fence but, in the heat of the moment, must take sides and present a persuasive reading of the score. As much as Bruce would have concurred with this attitude, and as a performer he asserted clear and often controversial readings, he was aware of how dangerous it can be to hold onto entrenched opinions. Dangerous because, no matter how closely our interpretations are based on reliable authorities and sound reasoning, we can easily get it wrong, and also because—whether right or wrong—we can nullify the work's potential to take on new meanings and to continue to have a life. Likewise, even the prospect of recovering the single finite idea of originary inspiration in the hope that the work would unfold in a truer, more meaningful way is the worst sort of authenticity: it restricts rather than enriches our options. Ongoing discovery, acquisition, and experiment with new techniques and refinements are necessary to keep period performance from stagnating, from becoming an unthinking default "automatic pilot" setting, or from gradually drifting back to a one-style-fits-all approach. Applying new ways of viewing what may have become routine—whether as superficial as renaming the Renaissance and Baroque as the Rhetorical period, or contemplating the significance of calling the *da capo* the *conclusio* in a musical oration—should bring out more of the music's meaning, not less.

While much of the historical evidence and recent scholarship Haynes and I have drawn from will be familiar to widely read scholars and curious musicians, our aim has been to bring together ideas from disparate sources and shed new light on their essential meaning in the cultural ethos of the time. Many of the technical aspects of *pronunciatio* and *actio* have been treated in modern performance-practice manuals that lose sight of eloquent performance as the ultimate purpose of rhetorical study. Our goal is to reinvoke the fuller meaning of these texts, and thus promote eloquent performance.

The central message of Haynes's late work is that it is only through affective performance that music's message can reach its audience, and to that end he emphasized the importance of going back to the models of Classical rhetoric that had inspired the music in the first place. Other studies of musical rhetoric by writers such as George Buelow, Dietrich Bartel, and Mark Evan Bonds have focused on the adaptation of rhetorical principles to musical composition, but they have not adequately addressed the importance of rhetoric to performance. The tacit assumption lying behind their approach is that as long as the score is replicated faithfully, the rhetoric of the music will be self-evident. We find this inadequate—both as an explanation for how music operated in the past and how it can be given relevance in today's culture. As important as mastering the technical aspects of their craft, performers need to understand the rhetorical elements of composition in order to take them up and breathe life into a composer's notes. Judy Tarling's perceptive synthesis of treatises on rhetoric relevant to musical performance in *The Weapons of Rhetoric* (2004) is an important starting point for this approach, and it has been implemented as a textbook in advanced performance studies around the world. Building on her work, *The Pathetick Musician* attempts to provide a practical and deeper study by looking more closely at the operation of rhetorical principles in musical performance.

In the 1960s and '70s "rhetorical performance" was highly valued by many early music practitioners, most notably Harnoncourt, and the Dutch school led by Brüggen, and Leonhardt. Haynes held to it as a guiding principle throughout his career as a performer. Others were more circumspect about this approach, and of late its importance has diminished as a defining characteristic of the movement. The Belgian traverso player Barthold Kuijken, for instance expressed his misgivings:

> We cannot expect musical rhetoric to be identical to language-based rhetoric. . . . It is my opinion that this might function to some extent, but it can lead us away from purely musical matters. . . I would rather look at the individual characteristics of performing arts: poets, actors, dancers, conductors, singers, and instrumentalists all have their own sets of rules and conventions.[7]

While Haynes would doubtless have agreed about the differences in modalities of expression in the arts, and his preference for literal readings of the texts of vocal music may have in some instances oversimplified his view of the interplay (or even tension) between musical and textual elements, he would probably have disagreed that "purely musical matters" have an independent existence in a culture where the dominant model was the rhetoric of language.

As it takes up and develops many of the themes in Haynes's earlier work, *The Pathetick Musician* will be of particular interest to those already familiar with *The End of Early Music*. In this sense then, *The Pathetick Musician* is Beyond the End of Early Music; but in another, more fundamental way, it is a means toward an End—the eloquent contemplation and enjoyment of Rhetorical music.

The two parts of the book fall into three subject areas:

Part I: Bach and the Rhetorical Heritage
1. Introduction, and chapters 1 and 2 define the Rhetorical period when Classical eloquence was applied directly to the composition and performance of music, and the defining characteristics of musical eloquence.
2. Chapters 3 and 4 consider various rhetorical strategies at the compositional level (or *dispositio*) in Bach's cantatas.

Part II: Performing Eloquence
3. Chapters 5 through 9 comprise case studies on eloquent performance and the pragmatics of *elocutio* and *actio*.

By way of conclusion, chapter 10 takes the form of Haynes's critique of recorded performances of selected case studies from Bach's cantatas, and synthesizes much of the discussion. At the same time as it supplements Part I, this final chapter provides material for further discussion.

Searching though Bruce's files, I came across a note to an anonymous addressee, which I imagine could have been written to the future editor of *The Pathetick Musician*. Keeping these words at hand as I worked, they were a constant reminder that beyond any sense of personal or egotistical attachment, Bruce would have wanted his ideas disseminated for their value to others.

> Well, I'm not here to be grateful to you for this, but I'm certainly feeling it as I write now. Use your judgement, maybe it's not worth the trouble. What I mean is, I hope you won't feel obliged to get this out for sentimental reasons.

I trust that the chapters that follow demonstrate that the material that Bruce had assembled are indeed worthy on their own right, and that the greatest tribute that any of us can pay to Haynes's work is to engage with it actively and, pursuing his lines of reasoning, never give up the search for eloquence.

—*Philadelphia, 2015*

PREFACE
Pipe Dreams

BRUCE HAYNES

So oft ich meine Tabakspfeife,	*When for pleasure and diversion*
Mit gutem Knaster angefüllt,	*I take my pipe*
Zur Lust und Zeitvertreib ergreife,	*And fill it with good shag,*
So gibt sie mir ein Trauerbild–	*It often offers me a lesson in life,*
Und füget diese Lehre bei,	*Reminding me*
Daß ich derselben ähnlich sei.	*How similar I am to it.*

"Erbauliche Gedanken eines Tobackrauchers" BWV 515 from the notebook for Anna Magdalena Bach (1725)

I've just loaded my 9BC with Balkan Sasieni and lit up. What a pleasure! My first pipe since last week. Years ago I stopped bringing pipes with me on trips, since the likelihood of finding a place to smoke where I won't disturb others was so small, and smoking stops being a pleasure if you worry that it may be giving someone else the opposite feeling. I've pretty much stopped smoking my pipe anywhere but in my studio. The last few years, I've found one of the medicines I take tends to cause drowsiness, but smoking a pipe counteracts it, so I'm actually smoking more than I used to. In fact, I wouldn't have been able to have written what I have over the last years without my pipes.

The pipe is said to draw wisdom from the lips of philosophers, and stifle the voices of fools. I hope that works for me, whichever category I'm in! I'm in good company, because Sebastian Bach was a pipe smoker, too, and even left us with an aria called "Erbauliche Gedanken eines Tobackrauchers." (Edifying Thoughts of a Tobacco Smoker) with a delightfully philosophical text on the inspirational aspects of smoking.

This book began as my attempt to sort out for myself the issues of expression and the passions in Baroque performance. My premise has been that we have been so concerned by the mechanics of music production that we have lost touch the spirit, the real music, the musicking.

Music and emotion are associated in most, perhaps all, human cultural activities with the theory of the passions, which as foreign as it may seem to us today, was a forebear for our modern psychology. My hope with this book is to confirm and reinforce our growing appreciation for the emotional side of music before the Romantic revolution. It's difficult to isolate emotion as expressed and experienced in art from one's life in general, but since I have begun to think of music as rhetoric, as I read more about these topics, and as it becomes evident that the music was originally conceived for the primary purpose of evoking emotion, I find myself gradually becoming more affected by what I hear. This is something I am glad to share with anyone who reads this, and it is also what makes it worth writing.

The notion that music is primarily emotional communication may seem, at first, like a small element in the craft of being a musician. Perhaps it is self-evident, but when I think of my own experience playing music from before 1800, I wish I had known from the outset what I know now. I was sometimes aware (even very conscious) of a piece's emotion, but it never dawned on me that my job was to awaken that emotion in the hearts of my listeners. Nor did I know that virtually all the music I was performing was intended to convey passions. There were times when it would have made an overwhelming difference to me as a player to know that this music was never conceived to be merely beautiful and enchanting to listen to, but that it almost always had an ulterior motive: some kind of point to make. That would have affected my playing (quite literally!) because musicians who do not have that information (and most do not) inevitably tend toward the fast lane, or simply the efflorescence of beauty. It's easy, you just put your fingers on the right keys at the right time, and the music plays itself . . . or does it?

We are so used to beauty as an obligatory attribute of any artwork—something that needs to be consciously and deliberately expressed—that it's difficult to imagine any other view. I catch myself sometimes describing a work of art as "beautiful" when what I really mean is that it has touched my heart. I've found enough substance in the idea of music as an expressive art that goes beyond "mere" beauty to fill a book, and to be worth devoting several satisfying years to its study. I hope, if you read on, you'll see what I mean about the vital and fundamental effect this idea can have on contemporary music in general, and especially on modern performances of music from the seventeenth and eighteenth centuries, as well as new music written in that style.

I believe this subject goes right to the heart of Baroque Performance Practice. I myself used to think that if I played by the rules, I could somehow get it right, and there are many musicians who continue to think that way. But if we don't touch our listeners, what is the point? I hope this book will convert them, thereby energizing a new vitality that will afford us musicians an even deeper understanding of our art and a more gratifying experience of music in performance—for the performers as much as the listeners. Even after I find it no longer possible to participate as a performer, this meditation has done this for me.

It would be easy to dismiss this book as biased: as presenting the existing historical evidence in a selective way, of quoting what agrees with my argument and ignoring the main bulk of sources who either disagree or ignore the subject of musical eloquence for the simple and obvious reason that it didn't really exist. More than once I have had such thoughts, discouraged by the lack of a major, systematic historical study, and the obvious absence of a rhetorical element in the visions of music proposed by our greatest historical thinkers. But now I am certain it is *their* visions that have shown us only part of the picture: they have turned our eyes to music as the product of a single creative genius—the composer—and ignored the vital role that the performer plays in the life of any piece of music, and indeed of any musical style.

I feel that I have accumulated enough sources to back up my case, but all the same, it has become harder to judge the difference between insights and platitudes. I hope you will be lucky, and the contents of this book will turn out to be the former. Eight years ago, I wrote in the preface to a book on the history of the hautboy:

> This is not a "how to" book... it is meant to be a report on the hautboy in the past. But if you happen to believe (as I do myself) that the history of a "historical instrument" is a guidebook for how to play it, then it might possibly give you ideas about not only how the hautboy *was* played, but how it *should be* played. That, however, is a decision each player and listener makes alone. "That was then, this is now," and it is not the humble mandate of this book to establish the relation between the two.[1]

Now, three books later, I find myself thinking differently. First of all, I wanted to sort out an issue for myself. For me, that means writing it down, for the reasons explained in an engaging comment by Roger North that has stood by me through the years:

> I have ever found I did not well know my owne thoughts, till I had wrote and reviewed them; and then for the most part, mists fell away, and fondness and failings appeared in a clear light.[2]

Second, why not share this with others? That means presenting a convincing, persuasive case. Third, there is wisdom in taking the past as a guide for the present. After all, historically inspired performance (HIP) has always sought enrichment of current practices by returning to history.

As you may have gathered from the title of this book, it is meant to operate along the lines of Quantz's or Emanuel Bach's. Not that I claim parity with those sages of Parnassus; quite the reverse: I hope they would have been complimented by my imitation of their style. Like them, I wish to record my own ideas of what is good musicking, based on a healthy respect for the performing traditions described in their books and others, as well as my own experience as a professional performing musician (I joined the musician's union in 1961). This is not intended to be a book for an exclusive market: the self-styled specialists of early music, the HIP (no matter how historically informed or historically inspired), the authentic brigade. These categories are walls that exclude many very good ideas from what is simply "performance," or inform what is otherwise simply "music." I can quite happily quote Quantz to voice my approach:

> It may seem at times that I speak rather dictatorially, basing my arguments on nothing more than a simple *one must*, without offering further evidence. . . . I can only say that anyone who doesn't wish to trust my taste, which I have attempted to purify over the years and which I have carefully considered, is welcome to try the reverse of that I teach, after which he can choose that which seems to suit him best.
>
> I don't wish to claim infallibility. If I am shown with reason and moderation something that's better than what I've said, I will be the first to accept and publicize it. I continue to investigate the issues I have treated here.[3]

Wenn nun die Pfeife angezündet,	When my pipe is smoking well,
So sieht man, wie im Augenblick	It produces a great quantity of smoke,
Der Rauch in freier Luft verschwindet,	Which, however, immediately vanishes into thin air,
Nichts als die Asche bleibt zurück.	Leaving nothing but ash.
So wird des Menschen Ruhm verzehrt	Thus also worldly fame is consumed
Und dessen Leib in Staub verkehrt.	And, like one's body, eventually turns to dust.

Before I launch into the details, let me reinforce that rhetoric is not "merely" a theory. As one writer put it, "rhetoric *was meant to be done*, not contemplated."[4] It is not just the compositional basis of much music of the seventeenth and eighteenth centuries, it is also an essential part of the way it was performed. Rhetoric is the performing artist's toolbox, the lore of "playing an audience," a set of techniques and skills, practiced for many centuries, that can be drawn from to produce specific results. That is not to say that playing by the rules of rhetoric will guarantee results: those rules remain guidelines that performers need to absorb so that they can "feel" the music and get on with the business of communicating effectively and eloquently. I agree entirely with Joshua Rifkin who argues that performers in the seventeenth and eighteenth centuries did not have recourse to the rules because they "did it all intuitively." But that is no reason to throw out the rules.[5] We are, as Frans Brüggen once observed, not the same people and our instincts are not these of the musicians of the Rhetorical era, so we need to cultivate rhetorical instincts by absorbing the rules.[6] Because, in the end, a musical composition, a play, a ballet, or a public speech is not eloquent of its own. Each needs musicians, actors, dancers, or orators to bring forth its eloquence.

As presented here, rhetoric is a practical collection of basic techniques of communication, described from the point of view of the performer. To conceive of music in these terms influences performance in a fundamental way, because it assumes the existence of a central message—the movement's passion—which is what gives it meaning or sense. And to understand the meaning of a piece is to know a great deal about how to play or sing it, and what listeners may expect when they lend it their ears. This is, surely, the heart of the project of reviving lost performance traditions.

Ich kann bei so gestalten Sachen	*So in this way, each time I load my pipe,*
Mir bei dem Toback jederzeit	*It is not only the tobacco that is kindled,*
Erbauliche Gedanken machen.	*But my thoughts as well.*
Drum schmauch ich voll Zufriedenheit	*And puffing contentedly*
Zu Land, zu Wasser und zu Haus	*In a reflective mood,*
Mein Pfeifchen stets in Andacht aus.	*I smoke my pipe and contemplate life.*

—Montréal, 2011

ACKNOWLEDGMENTS

I am deeply grateful to Bruce Haynes's long-time partner Susie Napper for her perennial support throughout the process of bringing *The Pathetick Musician* to press. Beginning with her invitation for me to take on the project, her support included countless hours of enlightening talk over tea and cake where we jointly brought clarity to the task ahead, and providing me with free access to the contents of Bruce's studio and computer files. Susie patiently witnessed me dismember Bruce's prose, tugging it out of shape in order to reconfigure it in its present form, always ready with a cheerful reprimand if I strayed from the book's focus to educate "simple-minded" musicians. Bruce's and Susie's eldest daughter, Anaïs Haynes, also took an active role in the editing.

I wish to thank those who read the manuscript at various stages and offered insightful advice. Stephen Zohn, Michael Marissen, Stephen Stubbs, and Kate van Orden, all experienced scholars as well as eloquent performers, were sympathetic readers who came with practical guidance, and astute observations on the shortcomings in my work and the occasional factual error. Conversations with Joshua Rifkin served to keep me on track and honest to the book's purpose, while reminding me of the need to be vigilant in the use of historical sources and logical in the treatment of evidence. It was also reassuring to have votes of confidence from several of Bruce's closest collaborators and intellectual interlocutors: Judy Tarling, fellow McGill University professor Tom Beghin, former student Karim Nasr, and long-standing friends and musical colleagues including Ton Koopman, Scott Metcalfe, and Nathaniel Watson. My contributions benefited from the opportunity to teach material from the book at the Brussels Conservatoire, and the Royal Danish Academy of Music, Copenhagen, and I have also implemented many of the concepts in my ongoing teaching at the Eastman School of Music, the Curtis Institute of Music, and Temple University.

The typesetting of the musical examples and editing of the audio clips on the companion website were funded in part by a grant from the Margarita M. Hanson Endowment of the American Musicological Society, supported by the National Endowment for the Humanities and the Andrew W. Mellon Foundation.

Finally, this book would never have seen the light of day were it not for the expert professionalism of the production team at the New York office of Oxford University Press under the guidance of Suzanne Ryan, whose unwavering belief in the project enabled me to push through its complexities, and the patience and loving support of my husband Leon Schelhase.

ABOUT THE COMPANION WEBSITE

www.oup.com/us/thepatheticmusician

The audio examples indicated in the text with Oxford's symbol ⊙ are available online at the accompanying website. Readers are encouraged to consult them as they read the text. While audio examples should constitute the centerpiece of a book about musical performance, for technical reasons most excerpts have had to be kept short, in most cases around thirty seconds in duration. To allow listeners to take fullest advantage of the clips, the text provides listening context and guidance. Still, hopefully the few seconds allowed for each excerpt will prove more eloquent than prose.

The Pathetick Musician

PART ONE

BACH AND THE RHETORICAL HERITAGE

Introduction: The Eloquent Musician

BRUCE HAYNES

> When a musician ... does not have the ability to bend the souls of listeners to where he wishes, his skill and knowledge may be considered null and vain.
> —Vincenzo Galilei, 1581[1]

> In rhetoric more than anything else the continuity of the old European tradition was embodied. [Ignorance of rhetoric] is the greatest barrier between us and our ancestors.
> —C. S. Lewis, 1962[2]

The Truth in Eloquence

I still remember my surprise some years ago when I opened a Chinese fortune cookie and found the following message inside:

> The object of rhetoric is not truth, but persuasion.

This deceptively simple statement (itself so fiercely dedicated to truth) is auspiciously sincere compared to the banalities that most fortune cookies doom us to. And, as I would later discover, is right in line with the concept of rhetoric in the sixteenth to the eighteenth centuries. The humanistic thinkers of the Renaissance and Baroque based their thinking on Aristotle's definition of rhetoric as "the art of finding, in a particular case, the available means of persuasion,"[3] and elaborated many times over the complementary relationship between persuasion and truth. To François de Fénelon, the French cleric and classics scholar who tutored Louis XIV's grandson, the process of persuasion did not exclude truth; on the contrary, it helped the listener to accept it not only "by placing the Truth in so clear a Light as to gain Attention and Assent," as he wrote, "but likewise by moving all the secret Springs of the Soul, to make it love that Truth it is convinc'd of."[4]

In this way, rhetoric was thought of not merely as elegant speaking but as speech used to produce a desired effect. Eloquence is the measure of effectiveness at achieving that goal. To quote Plato: "an oration is eloquent to the degree that it affects the hearer's mind."[5] We can thus say that expression is eloquent when it succeeds in persuading—that is, touching or moving—the listener, and the degree to which it moves is a measure of its effectiveness. Fénelon commented on this, and the following quotation demonstrates both how much the authorities of Classical Greece and Rome held sway over him and his contemporaries and the importance they placed on the audience's response:

> Plato says that the Eloquence of a discourse is measured by the effect it has on the listener's soul. This can serve you as a guide in accurately judging any discourse you hear. If a discourse leaves you cold and merely amuses your mind but does not enlighten it, nor move your heart, it is not truly eloquent, no matter how beautiful it may be. Do you want to know what Cicero says on this point, echoing Plato? He'll tell you that the whole force of the text should be bent to moving those secret springs that Nature has placed in the hearts of men. Consult, then, your own heart to know whether the orators you hear are good speakers. If they make a lively impression on you, and cause your soul to attend with sensitivity to what they say; if they move and animate your Passions, so as to raise you above yourself, be assured that they have achieved the goal of Eloquence.[6]

Recognizing the importance of rhetoric allows us to understand the style of any performance art of the seventeenth and eighteenth centuries—whether oratory, acting, music, or dance—more fully and accurately. Rhetoric was the basis of a large part of the education curriculum. It described composing, writing, performing, and how passions could be elicited from readers, viewers, and audiences. As a methodology, a process of making art, rhetoric was so accepted and pervasive that critics, philosophers, and aestheticians assumed everyone knew and accepted its purpose, terminology, and the description of the process of composition. Consequently, as Walter Ong has noted:

> Until the modern technological age, which effectively began with the Industrial Revolution and Romanticism, Western culture in its intellectual and academic manifestations can be meaningfully described as rhetorical culture.[7]

Up to that time rhetoric was the science of sciences, the one by which all the others could be explained. A concept passed down through the ages, rhetoric was invented by the Greeks, developed by the Romans, safeguarded in Arabic culture from the middle of the eighth century, and then enthusiastically revived in Europe in the Humanistic climate of the fifteenth and sixteenth centuries.

The three centuries from about 1500 to 1800 have a strong coherence in their rhetorical paradigm, and in this sense the work of Mozart's generation can be said to be built on the same fundamental principles as Monteverdi's. With the rise of Romanticism, rhetoric was virtually expunged from the arts. The beginning of its fall can be traced to about the mid-eighteenth century, and its reputation was in decline by 1800. It was, of course, at this point that Western society took a sharp turn with the revolutions in France and America and the social upheavals resulting from the Industrial Revolution. Rhetoric is still present in modern culture, although it has been appropriated by newly invented fields with scientific-sounding names like semiology, discourse analysis, and hermeneutics. These disciplines are products of a different ethos and have more limited and specific perspectives than rhetoric. Even though they reawakened interest in musical rhetoric and helped to elucidate the meaning of expression in pre-Romantic art, they were conceived outside the influence of a living rhetorical tradition and are often based on issues arising from the Romantic tradition. Consequently they can misrepresent the art of communication as practiced in the sixteenth to eighteenth centuries. For this reason I have found it more pertinent to adhere to the ideas of writers from the same time that the music was composed.

To the extent that the arts embody concepts of reality, they offer insight into how the world was perceived at the time they were made. And for that reason, if we are able to understand what the arts of the past have to say, they are very effective tools for studying human history.[8] Many of our choices as musicians are made without great thought; they simply "feel right." And the results of those choices have produced the art we see, hear, and think about today. So to revive a historical artform, a knowledge of the assumptions and beliefs that were available in a given period is essential for making choices that do indeed "feel right" for that period. This is not the only factor, to be sure. There are economic, educational, and social influences as well.[9]

It was in the early twentieth century when the entire discipline of rhetoric, once the common property of every educated man, was rediscovered. During the intervening decades, rhetoric has been reconstructed, and only now are we beginning to understand how much Western music depended on rhetorical concepts.[10] From around the 1960s, a number of performers took the lead to put these ideas into practice: Nikolaus Harnoncourt wrote and taught on the topic, and his performances are eloquent demonstrations of what is possible. My mentors Gustav Leonhardt and Frans Brüggen also took leading roles, as did Reinhardt Goebel, Rinaldo Alessandrini, and William Christie in the next generation. It is now time to step back and take a broader account of the phenomenon and also to recover what might have been lost since the pioneering endeavors of over a half century ago.

Rhetorical Music

> The main accent has to lie on diction, narratorship, not of course in a modern sense ... but in an old Quintillian-based sense.
> —Frans Brüggen[11]

When is music rhetorical? Always. In various degrees and different ways. It can be rhetorical when it is built of figures, or when it tells a story, or when it is inflected with gestural intent (a rhetorical pause). But in this book when I speak of Rhetorical music with a capital *R*, I refer to music belonging to a particular historical period that cultivated a specific predisposition and ethos in the arts governed by the principles of rhetoric handed down from Classical Greece and Rome. The reign of Rhetorical music in this sense coincides roughly with the late Renaissance, Baroque, and Classical periods. It had its origins in sixteenth-century Humanism, and the principles of Classical eloquence remained embedded in the practice of musical composition and performance up to approximately 1800. (Chapter 1 takes a more detailed look at the rise and demise of rhetoric in Western music.)

As long as we understand the language of the speaker, we can follow the logic of an oration and judge its persuasive powers. But how does this work in music? Rhetoric is usually taken to be synonymous with oratory, and rhetoric's original mode, as invented by the Greeks, used words as its medium. Speech has always been of fundamental importance in Western culture, and when the rhetorical approach was revived from the late fifteenth century, the Humanists immediately saw other applications, especially in the performing arts, which (like oratory) are essentially systems for communicating ideas.

"Persuasion" takes on a particular meaning when applied to the arts and music where truth has a more subjective or abstract sense. Charles Batteux explained the idea particularly well in his friendly little book published in 1746 with the apt and intriguing title *Les Beaux-Arts reduits à un même principe* (which could be rendered in English as "The Fine Arts Distilled into a Unified Principle"):

> Now to persuade men, it is necessary to prove, to please, and to move. Sometimes one of these means alone is sufficient, sometimes it is necessary to join all three. We prove by arguments, we please by morals, and we move by the passions.[12]

By arguments, I presume Batteux is referring to *dialectics*, the technique of critical examination into the truth of an argument by means of words and logic. Batteux divided the art of persuasion into three categories: giving proof, producing a pleasurable experience, and moving the audience. These reflect the three principal places where oratory was practiced in his day: the law courts, the church, and the theater. The lawyer proved by arguments, the preacher pleased through morals, the actor and musician moved audiences through evoking the passions. While each of these activities had its own specific context, range of subjects, purpose, and set of corresponding techniques, at base their goal was the same: to persuade through eloquent performance.

To some seventeenth- and eighteenth-century thinkers there was in fact very little difference between the orator's and musician's crafts. This forms the basis of advice given by the eighteenth-century flute player Johann Joachim Quantz:

> Expression in music can be compared to that of an orator. The orator and the musician have the same goal, both in the composition of their productions and in their expression. They want to seize hearts, to excite or calm the movements of the soul, and transport the listener from one passion to another. It is in their interests to have some idea of each other's abilities.[13]

Likewise, Batteux wrote that one need not be a trained musician to know if one is moved by a musical performance. Confessing that he was no expert on the technical aspects of music, Batteux still felt that he was enough of a connoisseur to

> enter into the merit of a piece of music that has been worked up with the greatest care ... for the business of music is to move and, as music speaks to me in tones, the language is natural to me.[14]

This serves as a cardinal reminder that as musicians, our powers of persuasion reside far less in technical execution than in our ability to move listeners at a more fundamental level. Batteux's point is that each listener is the ultimate authority on this subject, being the only one who is able to say if he has been moved, and thus whether a performance is eloquent. This, of course, introduces the dilemma that judgment rests on the subjective perception of the listener. What might have been eloquent on one instance, or to one listener might have no effect when repeated for a less responsive audience.

The Pathetick Musician

> Sighs of pleasure deeply fetched, so pathetically expressed.
> —John Cleland, 1749[15]

Persuasion in the sense of moving the passions is what the ancient Greeks called *pathopoeia*, a word that derives from παθος (*pathos*, or passion), and ποιειν (*poiein*, to make). Pathos is of course the root of the word "pathetick," which means—and has meant for centuries—"producing an effect upon the emotions; moving, stirring, affecting."[16] A Pathetick Musician is one who is capable of feeling and expressing passions or strong emotions, and of convincing his audience to share the experience. The current derogatory meaning of "pathetic" ("miserably inadequate; of such a low standard as to be ridiculous or contemptible") dates from about the middle of the twentieth century.[17]

Descriptions of *pathopoeia* from the sixteenth to eighteenth century speak of the passions or, as they are often known today, the affects. Henry Peacham's *Garden of Eloquence* (1577), for instance, describes *pathopoeia* as "when the Oratoure mooveth the mindes of his hearers . . . to indignation, anger, feare . . . the Oratour [himself] being moved with any of those Passions."[18]

The passions represent the extreme end of the emotional scale. They are intense, controlling, even overpowering conditions, as contrasted with milder feelings, sentiments, and transient emotional states. As Batteux wrote in 1746, "When the impressions are lively and violent, then it is that they are properly called passions. They are impetuous motions carrying us away towards an object, or averting us from it."[19] Passions are thus suited to the art of persuasion in oratory where, in the words of Quantz, they "seize hearts, to excite or calm the movements of the soul, and transport the listener from one passion to another."[20] Passions had to be deliberately evoked by the performer, who could also still them and, with the aim of commanding the listener's constant attention, introduce a constantly varying palette of emotional states.[21]

Passions were not thought of as fleeting personal emotions but as absolute states, aroused by an external force rather than being self-induced. The subjects treated by Baroque artists were drawn from a commonality of experience that transcended individual experience. This is why Handel's epitaph described his compositions as having "surpassed the power of words in expressing the various passions of the human heart." In other words, it did not celebrate Handel for his ability to express his own personal emotions and feelings, but rather for being able to capture generic states that his audiences could also relate to.

This is quite different from the model that emerged in the Romantic period when the emotional content of a work was identified with the creative artist—whether painter, composer, or author—and when performers, actors, and musicians were classed as reproductive artists who brought art to life, but who were ultimately not responsible for the work's eloquence. Holding on to those same Romantic values today, we base our judgment on how realistically artists are able to show emotions as they relate to a modern psychological framework. To fully understand how the older concept of passions worked, we have to put aside the desire to identify a composer's music with his personal psyche. We will never know what emotions Bach felt the day he wrote the aria "Erbarme dich" from the St. Matthew Passion; nor are his personal experiences necessarily relevant to understanding the passions of sorrow and regret that he managed to crystallize in his setting of that text.

In the Rhetorical era, there was a belief in the power of the passions and it was above all the responsibility of the performer to bring them forth. Directly or indirectly, many of the authors I have been quoting hark back to Cicero, the great Roman orator of the first century BC, who wrote:

> It is by the help of the passions that eloquence triumphs, and exerts its empire over our hearts. He who has the art of raising these properly, is at any time master of our minds; and can at his pleasure make us pass from sorrow to joy, from pity to rage, vehement as a tempest, penetrating as lightning, and rapid as a torrent; he surmounts all obstacles, and the flood of his eloquence carries all before it.[22]

To illustrate my case, most of the time I will draw from the vocal music of Johann Sebastian Bach. His observation and imitation of the passions is insightful and sensitive. Like a good poet, he reminds us of the truly important things in life. His portrayals of the passions are moving, subtle, and profound, and often fill our hearts to overflowing. That is because his settings are more than vehicles for the text; they complement it and participate in the message, and furthermore, as Michael Marissen has shown, in numerous cases his setting supplies missing elements that strengthen the theological message of the text and justifies the popular identification of Bach as the Fifth Evangelist.[23] Rarely is there any doubt which passions Bach is evoking: our challenge is to put them into words. Naturally, it helps to have the texts of his pieces as confirmation. But it is just as important to treat instrumental music in the same vein. Without a text to guide us, the passions may be more difficult to recognize, and the ideas more difficult to pinpoint, but the music nevertheless functions as wordless rhetoric.

Ut pictura poesis

At the height of its powers, rhetoric was seen as a synthetic art that brought together knowledge in various fields with audiences of various kinds. There was common belief that the arts shared similar guiding principles. The abbé Dubos expressed this in 1719 when (quoting Cicero) he observed that "all the liberal arts seem to have one common chain of agreement, and to be connected together by a kind of *mutual affinity*."[24] Most authors explained the principle of mutual affinity by pointing to the ancient practice of *mimesis*—or the imitation of the passions—and each artistic medium took nature as its primary point of reference and of imitation. This principle was identical regardless of the expressive medium. As Dubos put it:

> Wherefore as the painter imitates the strokes and colors of nature, in like manner the musician imitates the tones, accents, sighs, and inflexions of the voice; and in short all those sounds, by which nature herself expresses her sentiments and passions.[25]

The arts, then, were seen as parallel in effect, purpose, and means. *Ut pictura poesis* (literally "As in painting, so in poetry") was the expression commonly used to allude to this concept.[26]

To call the arts parallel is of course a truism. Parallel lines never meet; each art, while related to the others, had its own path, its own techniques, materials, and limitations. They coalesced most evidently in opera, which was a synthesis of poetry, music, painting, architecture, acting, and (often) dance. Here the dialogue of different arts provides copious models of how artists operated across different media to express the same subject. Still, even in contexts where arts functioned more autonomously, their parallels are of great service. When we talk about music, it helps to know something of how the same subjects are treated in painting, poetry, and novels of the same culture and period. In that way it is easier to enter into the language that a particular art used to communicate ideas and construct its view of the world. Such comparisons will guide our discussion in the following chapters.

Closely allied to the idea of *Ut pictura poesis* is the concept of *synonymy*. This refers to how different artistic media express the same concept. It is one thing to express a passion like despair or joy in words—in poetry, for instance—and another to translate it into the medium of music, where feelings may be just as strong but are differently circumscribed and proportioned. An actor can express a great deal in the way he intones the single word "despair," but to communicate as much in music can take considerably longer, but once said, may be more affecting.

The kind of information that can be communicated in words as compared with music often entails a difference between denotation and connotation. As an example, a description of two people falling in love—what they look like, the color of their hair, their ages—is pretty straightforward with words, but difficult to convey in music. On the other hand, a portrayal of the feelings that lovers experience as their love opens and blooms is just what music does well, whereas expressing such things with words is a challenge to any writer or poet. This process of translation, of exchangeability of meaning in different media, seemed self-evident to artists, including poets and musicians, from at least the early sixteenth century right through to the end of the eighteenth century.

Putting words and music together can be very gratifying, as it combines the best potentials of both. It is, I imagine, what d'Alembert meant when he wrote that music is "nothing more than a translation of the words which are set to an air."[27] As we will see in chapter 1, the emergence of the *seconda prattica* in the early Baroque resulted in a new way of combining poetry and music, which meant that music was not simply subservient to the text but was given its own emotive powers, and that over time it accrued greater expressive force. As a result, in vocal music of the Rhetorical period, the sum is always greater than the parts. The eloquence of the text is elaborated, compounded, and nuanced by the expressive capabilities of the musical setting.

The Officers of Rhetoric

The classic sequence of the rhetorical process—the five stages, or *offices* as they were called—apply as much to a musical performance as an oration.

- *Inventio:* Invention.
- *Dispositio*: Organization.
- *Elocutio*: Technique and Style.
- *Memoria*: Memory.
- *Actio/Pronuntiatio*: Expression and Delivery.

The rhetorical process is the backbone of what we undertake in this book and which will be discussed in more detail in chapter 2. For now, let us address the question of who does what.

Three agents or officers are vital to the creation of any eloquent experience: creator (author, composer, or playwright), performer (orator, actor, or musician), and audience (reader, listener, or viewer). For effective communication to take place, each must hold the relationship to the others in mind and understand his or her responsibilities for the different stages in the process. The composer starts what the performer finishes. Mozart once said that a musician should play a piece in a way that makes listeners believe he composed it, and this reflects the complementary nature of composing and performing.[28] That is why in the past the composer and performer were often the same person (just like orators usually write their own speeches). Bearing this in mind, the differences in the roles of composer and performer are technical. They constitute a division of labor rather than two separate activities, and in the ideal performance their individuality becomes fused.

Likewise, the five offices are facets of a single unified sequence of actions. The performer finishes what the composer started. A performer cannot perform without a thorough and sympathetic understanding of the compositional elements that went into a particular piece—the *inventio* and *dispositio* that, in turn, give rise to the structured sequence of rhetoric—*exordium, narratio, propositio, confirmatio, confutatio,* and *peroratio*. Nor could a composer imagine a work without keeping in mind the stylistic conventions of his performing colleagues, and their ability to touch an audience: *elocutio* and *actio* formed the matrix in which his composition operated. This is also why Quantz admonished musicians to familiarize themselves with the rhetorical art, implying an understanding of composition.

Instructions on the rhetorical workings of music may predominate in composition treatises, but this does not mean that it is irrelevant to the performer's art: we have to keep in mind how much overlap existed between these activities, and how both had as a final goal to move the audience. As we will examine in case studies throughout this book, the approximate nature of musical notation means that the expression of an affect or passion often depends even more on the performer than on the composer. This also means that musical meaning is as much the responsibility of the performer as the composer.

If the essence of any kind of rhetoric, including music, is the message it delivers, that is, the specific passion it expresses, then the performing artist must guarantee that the message is received and produces a response. In other words, if the player doesn't take responsibility for expressing a passion, it won't happen of its own accord. Even if rhetorical principles are followed in all the processes up to *elocutio*, if they are not instilled with eloquence in performance, the music will neither generate interest, nor convey meaning (or at least anything like the meaning it might have originally represented).

Within the period bounded roughly by 1600 and 1800, music that was rhetorical and eloquent did not belong to a special category: it was how music was performed, and it was the goal that all musicians aspired to. This is not to say that there weren't unpracticed, or inexperienced musicians who, despite technical proficiency, rarely achieved eloquence. In 1676, Thomas Mace decried the emptiness of those who "drudge, and take much Pains to Play their Lessons very Perfectly," but whose performances contain little "Life, or Spirit." He attributed this to a

> want of the knowledge of this last Thing, I now mention, viz. They do not labour to find out the Humour, Life, or Spirit of their Lessons: Therefore I am more Earnest about It, than many (It may be) think Needful: but Experience will confirm what I say.[29]

The same idea recurs in literature throughout the eighteenth century. Batteux, like many of his contemporaries, often repeated the idea that "all music should have a sense, a signification."[30] Johann Mattheson also repeatedly insisted that "not a single melody should be without meaning, without aim, or without affection,"[31] and Rousseau found it "a trifle to read exactly the music by the notes," and insisted that musicians "enter into all the ideas of the composer, [and] feel and render the fire of the expression."[32] To this end, discovering this sense and signification should be a performer's first priority. If there were an oath that young musicians take as they enter the profession, like doctors who take the Hippocratic oath, its first clause would be the imperative to touch and move the hearts of listeners by discovering and expressing the music's passion. This is a recognized priority in popular music, jazz, and other vernacular genres, but classical musicians can only too easily become like Thomas Mace's drudges. Many rehearsals would be more effective if the first subject discussed were the expressive goals. Sadly, in my experience, it is rarely discussed at all.

One of the students in a seminar I taught recently took great exception to the opinion that performers need to take into consideration the level of knowledge and taste of their audiences. She felt it was not the musician's job to pander to ignorance. As a player, her choice of repertoire or manner of playing were decisions that she felt should be based on her own sensibilities, not those of her listeners. I sympathize with her feeling because it is one felt by most artists today: that we are the experts. But in rhetorical terms, not to be eloquent is to fail as a performer. And eloquence means above anything else, moving your audience—any audience.

This, it seems to me, is an issue of historical authenticity in its most basic and urgent sense. To repeat Plato's advice: "an oration is eloquent to the degree that it affects the hearer's mind."[33] That is the litmus test of musical eloquence. It creates a connection between listeners and musicians, a connection that is too often missing in concerts today, because performers (historically inspired performers as much as anyone) do the "Romantic aloofness thing," showing indifference to how their music is received. Others argue that historically inspired performance should be a faithful replication of the score and should create a transparent interpretation that does not interfere with the music's ability to speak for itself. But Rhetorical music doesn't work that way. The idea of the autonomous work of art that exists outside of performance is a product of Romantic aesthetics. As we will see in chapter 5, Rhetorical music is designed for the performer to participate in the creative process in meaningful and concrete ways.

The early music movement started out as a reaction against tradition and forged new paths to re-imagine the music of lost traditions with the help of historical documentation and musical techniques on rediscovered instruments. But in many cases, adhering to the letter means that the music is deprived of its spirit. We may pay heed to Quantz's advice on playing trills, adding dynamic nuance, or articulating notes in rapid passages, but what of his warning to the musician who "sings or plays without warmth," or "tries to contradict the original passions, or performs everything in general without sensitivity, without passion, without being moved one's self, so it seems as if he is singing or playing as an agent for someone else"?[34]

There have been significant advances in technical proficiency on early instruments, but currently, in my view, there seems to be a corresponding unwillingness and even a lack of personal commitment to confront the core of the matter: to move audiences. In the eighteenth century a performer might go his entire career without playing music beyond that of the local (and living) Kapellmeister, but today musicians are expected to master a range of styles by many distant (and dead) composers. The present situation would seem to encourage variety and curiosity to learn about and appreciate the centuries of musical styles that we encounter, along with a certain level of risk taking; but it seems that so often quite the opposite is the case. Performers have little understanding of the real value of what they do. Proficiency too often substitutes for a performance that breathes new life into the musical language of a former age by speaking it with eloquence.

Style Coaches

Before embarking on the study of the music of J. S. Bach we need to find a guide or "style coach." Writers from the 1680s to 1750 shared basic tenets of musical performance, but when it came to details, their opinions could vary considerably. We need to find a historically appropriate and culturally relevant informant who is also reliable. If we were to imagine the perfect witness to how musicians performed the music of J. S. Bach and his contemporaries, our "man on the scene," we might well look for a professional musician from Leipzig or a nearby town or court, a singer, orchestral player or chamber musician of the same age or a little younger than Bach, interested in all forms of music, a regular churchgoer but also at home at the opera, a composer himself, well-traveled but sympathetic to German music, thoughtful, and perhaps even an instrument maker.

It is our good fortune that such a person did actually exist and that he wrote an insightful, detailed book about how musicians make music. This was Johann Joachim Quantz, the son of a country blacksmith born in 1697 in Lower Saxony to the west of Leipzig. Twelve years Bach's junior, Quantz was a self-made musician and, for the first part of his career, a member of the Dresden court Capelle, the most prestigious musical establishment in Germany at the time. In 1728 he became flute teacher to Prince Frederick, and in 1740 when Frederick ascended the Prussian throne, he followed as one of the key members of the new monarch's musical retinue. Dresden was not only the capital of Saxony but its largest city. Saxony's second city, Leipzig, where Bach worked, was 112 km (about seventy miles) to the west. Bach's son Wilhelm Friedemann was organist at the St. Sophia's Church in Dresden from 1733, and three years later Johann Sebastian was appointed Royal Composer at Dresden. As a gesture of thanks, he performed a concert there, choosing to play on the magnificent new Silbermann organ at the Frauenkirche. Quantz, along with other members of the Capelle, may well have heard his concert.

Quantz's *Versuch einer Anweisung die Flöte traversiere zu spielen* (Essay of a Method for Playing the Transverse Flute) was written primarily for his royal pupil Frederick, but in the introduction he set out its more general functions as: "Instructions for playing the flute, and for becoming a good musician at the same time." He published his book at the age of fifty-five, toward the end of a long and successful career. The *Versuch* became famous almost immediately, and (though many of its precepts are virtually ignored) has had a considerable influence on players from then up to the present time. The British music critic Charles Burney met Quantz in Potsdam in 1770, just three years before Quantz's death, and remarked that his taste was "that of forty years ago."[35] Burney could have been pulling the number out of his hat, but it does seem to be meaningful. Forty years before 1770 would have been 1730, at which point Burney was reaching adulthood and developing his awareness of musical taste. It was also almost exactly the midpoint of Quantz's career at Dresden. Musical style wasn't identical in Dresden and London, but both cities were rich cosmopolitan centers open to foreign influence, and so there is reason to think that Burney knew what he was saying.

Bach had arrived at Leipzig seven years before 1730, by which time he had performed most of his cantatas. He was more conservative in his musical taste, and it might be argued that his style was another forty years older than the fashionable galant style with which Quantz was associated. But the differences are not at the level of *inventio*. They apply more to *elocutio*—the foreground detail that is the main concern of a performance practice manual like Quantz's. Still, for Bach's music, the match seems about as good as it can get. Even if he couldn't bring himself to compose like them, Bach knew and respected the Dresden composers of Quantz's generation. Quantz's book is steeped in competence and practical common sense told from the point of view of a performing musician. It is one of the most informative guides, and most suitable to apply to the study of Quantz's own music as well as that of J. S. Bach. For that reason it is one of our main sources of inspiration.

Other German musicians of Bach's generation were neither as detailed nor as broad in their purview of musical practices. Even the *Versuch über die wahre Art das Clavier zu spielen* (Essay on the True Art of Playing Keyboard Instruments), published just one year after Quantz's by Bach's son Carl Philipp Emanuel who also worked at the court of Frederick the Great, doesn't give such a well-rounded account of *elocutio*. C. P. E. Bach's and Quantz's careers overlapped when they both held posts at the Prussian court from 1740 to 1768, and even if they disagreed on some points, their basic premises were largely similar. Emmanuel Bach's *Versuch* may be more forward-looking in musical style than Quantz's, but it is still an important corroborative source.

Johann Mattheson would also be a close runner-up in the search for a style guide. Born four years before Bach (the same year as Telemann, 1681), Mattheson lived all his life in Hamburg, a thriving cultural metropolis in northern Germany where he spent equal parts of his career in opera, church music, and as a music theorist. A singer rather than an instrumentalist (taking soprano parts before his voice broke and he became a tenor), Mattheson was also an experienced composer. He served as cantor up to 1728 when his deafness led to his retirement. From then he applied his experience to writing practical guides and theoretical treatises on music. Born to privilege, Mattheson was more erudite and better educated than Quantz. Hamburg was a more open cultural environment than any cities in Saxony, and this allowed him to develop wider ranging and more cosmopolitan interests than either Quantz or Bach. Through his appointment as secretary to the English ambassador, Mattheson came into contact with recent currents in international philosophy. In fact Bach probably envied Mattheson's situation, and aspired to be part of Hamburg's music cultural life. He made two visits there at the height of the city's golden age as an opera center, and in 1720 he would probably have taken the post as organist at the St. Jacobi Church if he had been able to make the obligatory financial contribution to the church. The musical world of Hamburg was by no means estranged from Leipzig's. So, even if he never met Bach, Mattheson was also eminently qualified to serve as a guide to the Leipzig cantor's music, and his *Vollkommene Capellmeister* finds an important place in our discussion.

Further Reading

This book can provide no more than a brief description of this vast, time-honored system of public communication and persuasion. A good introduction is Ong's *Rhetoric, Romance, and Technology*. Much work has already been done to describe the principles of rhetoric and how they apply to music. In addition to Buelow's articles in the *Grove Dictionary* and his article "Johann Mattheson and the Invention of the Affektenlehre," Judy Tarling's *Weapons of Rhetoric* is essential reading and a vital supplement to this book. I do not intend to duplicate that work. My aim is more closely aligned with providing practicing musicians with the means of putting rhetoric into practice.

Because of the affinity of music to the other arts, insight into making music and the goals of musicians can be found in many different sources. Loquacious and prolific, Humanist musicians and writers evidently loved to tell others what they thought music was supposed to achieve. It is in this sense that Tarling's comment strikes a chord: rhetoric's many treatises, going back to the Romans and Greeks of antiquity, are the musician's "ultimate performance practice manuals."[36] Besides Aristotle, Quintilian (ca. 95 AD) and the *Ad Herennium* (first century BC; formerly attr. Marcus Tullius Cicero), there is an abundance of literature from the sixteenth through the eighteenth centuries.

The reference to flute playing in the title of Quantz's magnum opus has been partly responsible for his *Versuch* being passed over as a source of musical cultural practice for general musicians. Reaffirming the relevance of Quantz's *Versuch* to the music of J. S. Bach is, in part, my response to Frederick Neumann's objection (voiced in "The Use of Baroque Treatises") that it reflected different musical fashion in performance than Bach's.

Along with the treatises of Quantz, C. P. E. Bach, and Mattheson, other key performance-practice manuals and aesthetics treatises include Bacilly's *Art de bien chanter*, and Mace's *Musick's Monument*. These are books written by practicing musicians; other more general writings on the arts include Jean-Baptiste Dubos's important *Réflexions critiques*, first published in François Couperin's time (1719), which discusses poetry, painting, and music interchangeably, and *Les Beaux-Arts reduits à un même principe* by Charles Batteux, which appeared a generation later when Rameau was writing his operas.

Amy Schmitter provides a useful discussion of the philosophical differences between passions, emotions, and moods in "17th and 18th Century Theories of Emotions." See also Jensen, *Signs and Meaning*, 238–62. On the theory of mimesis, see Auerbach, *Mimesis*, Gebauer and Wulf, *Mimesis: Culture–Art–Society*, Juslin "From Mimesis to Catharsis," and Neubauer, *The Emancipation of Music from Language*. See also Leisinger, "Affections, Rhetoric, and Musical Expression," which defines affects and passions as states influenced by external agency rather than internal psychology.

Harnoncourt's teaching on musical rhetoric is documented in two volumes: *Der musikalische Dialog* (translated as *The Musical Dialogue*), and *Musik als Klangrede, wege zu einem neuen Musikverständnis* (*Baroque Music Today: Music as Speech: Ways to a New Understanding of Music*).

1

In the Realm of the Passions

BRUCE HAYNES

> As we must now admit unanimously that our *finis musices* is to stir the affections and to delight the ear, the true *objectum musices*, it follows that we must establish all our musical rules according to the ear.
> —Heinichen, 1728[1]

Humanism and the Rhetorical Ethos

In this book I use the term Rhetorical music (with a capital R) to designate works composed during the seventeenth and eighteenth centuries, a span of time bounded roughly by the careers of Monteverdi and Mozart. In stylistic terms there is clearly a world of difference between the music of these two composers, but in terms of their understanding of music and its purposes they were remarkably close. Both left statements regarding the practice of text setting that identify turning points in the philosophy of music in relation to language, and demarcate the Rhetorical period. When Monteverdi explained in 1607 (in the words of his brother Giulio Cesare) that the text should be the master of the music—"*orazione sia padrone dell' armonia e non serva*," he went against a long-held tradition that music and text were essentially autonomous.[2] Toward the end of the eighteenth century, Mozart overturned Monteverdi's position when he indicated that in opera the poetry must be the obedient daughter of the music—"*muß schlechterdings die Poesie der Musick gehorsame Tochter seyn.*"[3] Even if these opposing views on text setting show significant shifts in opinion, Monteverdi and Mozart shared the underlying idea that music was a vehicle for expressing concrete ideas, and therefore a communication system closely related to eloquent speech.

The Rhetorical period, then, was a window of time during which musical composition was dominated by text, and musical expression was embedded in concrete concepts. Opera and vocal music dominated the musical landscape and served as a testing ground for passionate musical expression in other genres. The creative process was grounded on the principles of Classical rhetoric; the five offices and rhetorical structure served as models for form in musical composition. A sophisticated array of musical figures was developed to give music the potential to "speak" to audiences, even when it was not directly responding to a text.

Up to the fifteenth century, music and rhetoric had led parallel but separate careers. It was through the intellectual movement known as Humanism that rhetoric was established as the prime model for communication, and instead of being related to mathematics, music came to be aligned with rhetoric. Taking inspiration from the teachings of Classical Greece and Rome, the Humanists set out to revive the ethical and emotional power of music reported in ancient sources. Composers and performers began to imitate human passions by mirroring the imagery of the poetic texts they set. So instead of music's value being invested in its proportional harmony and its place within a divinely ordered universe, emphasis was increasingly placed on its ability to awaken emotional responses in the listener. In that way, the Humanists sought to unlock the secrets of ancient musical practices.

It may seem strange that prior to this, expression was of secondary importance. Music was considered a science, aligned with the cosmic order and the universal laws of proportion. In that system, the highest part of the soul was seen as governed by reason, while the lower parts (being amoral and similar to those of animals, desiring sensual and material gratification) were in perpetual conflict with it. When reason was in control, the soul was in harmony and the person would act "reasonably." From this point of view, passions were seen as anomalies, like storms that disturbed the cosmic harmony; they were not encouraged, but instead they had to be managed and limited.[4] This viewpoint did not vanish immediately, particularly in writings from authors with religious agendas. Well into the seventeenth century Athanasius Kircher (1602–80) upheld the concept of musical harmony as a reflection of the proportions of divine creation.

Seconda prattica

Music built on the principles of rhetoric was profoundly different from music of previous periods. Paradigm shifts of this magnitude have such big repercussions that it is nearly impossible to date them without creating black-and-white dichotomies where artists take extreme and opposing stands. In music, one of the best known of these dichotomies is the division between the older *prima prattica* and the developing *seconda prattica* that effectively turned the tables on traditional attitudes to music and its goals.

The term *seconda prattica* was first defended by Claudio Monteverdi in 1605 in the brief preface to his Fifth Book of Madrigals, but the principles it stood for had already been in use for much of the sixteenth century. In 1504, Vincenzo Calmeta wrote that "the best singers are those who are able to express the text well and more importantly, are able to convey the sense behind those words."[5] Samuel Quickelberg explains that Orlando di Lassus's five-part settings of *Penitential Psalms* (composed about 1560) were considered so affective and impassioned because they exemplified the ideal match of music and poetry:

> Lassus expressed these psalms so appropriately in accommodating, according to necessity, thoughts and words with lamenting and plaintive tones, in expressing the force of the individual passions, and in placing the object almost alive before the eyes, that one is at a loss to say whether the sweetness of the passions enhanced the lamenting tones more greatly, or whether the lamenting tones brought greater ornament to the sweetness of the passions.[6]

These goals were not confined to singers and to vocal music. Sylvestro di Ganassi's influential instruction books, *Il Fontegara*, published in Venice in the 1530s and '40s testify that instrumentalists worked just as much to "give an appropriate spirit to the instrument for every kind of musical passion" even without the support of specific words. And in 1555, Pontus de Tyard wrote this description of Francesco da Milano playing the lute:

> He made the very strings to swoon [*mourir*] beneath his fingers and transported all who listened into such gentle melancholy that one present buried his head in his hands, another let his entire body slump into an ungainly posture with members all awry, while another, his mouth sagged open and his eyes more than half shut, seemed, one would judge, as if transfixed upon the strings, and yet another, with chin sunk upon his chest, hiding the most sadly taciturn visage ever seen, remained abstracted in all his senses save his hearing, as if his soul had fled from all the seats of sensibility to take refuge in his ears where more easefully it could rejoice in such enchanting symphony.[7]

We could hardly ask for an account of a more passionate performance, echoing the fabled power of music in ancient Greece. Another story that attracted particular attention was the story of King Alexander's challenge to the lyre player Timotheus to prove his boast that through music he could make sad men happy and peaceful men angry. As Timotheus took up his lyre, he began with a grave sound, causing the king to be melancholy, then suddenly changed to a joyful tune he made the king dance. Changing the mode once again, he "provoked such a rage in Alexander that guards had to be called to restrain him from attacking his guests."⁸ The story became a commonplace in musical literature, and late Renaissance and Baroque musicians strove to emulate Timotheus's performance.⁹ In 1736 Handel composed an oratorio based on this story. Typical of the age, the text (written by John Dryden in 1697) reconfigured the legend to demonstrate that the music of the ancients, as powerful as it was, was no match for the works of modern composers. Dryden's and Handel's version Christianizes the pagan story with an apparition of St. Cecilia, the patron saint of music. The Orpheus myth, taken from Ovid's *Metamorphoses* became an even more enduring trope for the human singer who could make stones weep, and withstand the torments of Hades through the power of his musical delivery. In the numerous Orpheus operas that were written in the Rhetorical period, here too the ability of modern musicians to outdo the music of the ancients became a frequently revisited theme.

The *seconda prattica* was closely associated with the inception of monody and the birth of opera. The *stile rappresentativo* (also called *cantar recitando*, or *stile recitativo*), a form of recitative developed in the Florentine Academies around 1600, was part of a radical project to re-create a modern, completely sung drama comparable in expressive intensity to ancient Greek theater. In this rhythmically free style of singing, poetic accents were marked with harmonic changes, and affective words reinforced with dissonances. It was accompanied by a simple continuo line comprised mostly of long notes, which in the absence of a strict beat allowed the instrumentalists to follow the spontaneous rhythms of the singer. *Euridice* by Jacopo Peri and the poet Ottavio Rinuccini, performed in the Pitti Palace in Florence in 1600, is written entirely in *stile rappresentativo*. Cavalieri used it in his *Rappresentatione di Anima, et di Corpo* of the same year, and Monteverdi also made much use of it in his operas and madrigals.

Monody was considered the perfect vehicle to accomplish music's true purpose: expressing passionate states. The Classical philologist Girolamo Mei (1519–94) went as far as to declare that it was the only medium capable of achieving this goal, and called contrapuntal music "a product of corrupt taste and the vanity of musicians."¹⁰ His justification for focusing on monody is telling:

> What chiefly persuaded me that the entire chorus [in Greek drama] sang one and the same air was observing that the music of the ancients was held to be a valuable medium for moving the passions, as witnessed by the many incidents related by the writers.¹¹

Mei's argument was not unreasonable, but it was only speculative. He had next to no evidence for how ancient Greek drama was actually performed. Attempts to reconstruct it were based on evidence of its effect rather than on how it actually sounded. But, like so many other occasions in history, the utopian past was pressed into service to justify new practices.

Monody may have been the prime medium of the new passionate style, but it was not the only one. The *seconda prattica* originated in polyphonic composition, and the madrigal was, before the invention of monody, the privileged genre. Polyphonic madrigals by De Rore, Vicentino, De Wert, Marenzio, and Luzzaschi treated the words with heightened sensitivity. The music served as settings for the poems: "setting" in the sense of a frame around a painting, or a jewelry setting that carries and displays a precious stone. These composers employed polyphony's full richness to enhance and elucidate the ideas expressed in the poetry. To reflect the intensity of the poem, they stretched the traditional rules governing voice-leading and the treatment of dissonance, and amplified the level of chromaticism.

In effect, two independent systems were at work here: on the one hand, the imperatives of musical composition grounded in the rules of polyphony as codified by the sixteenth-century theorist Gioseffo Zarlino (1517–90), and on the other hand, the exigencies of the poetry, including its material characteristics—accent, quantity, emphasis, and cadence, and rhetorical and expressive elements such as figures and imagery. One of the accomplishments of a master musician was the ability to superimpose one set of rules over the other, and thereby reconcile them into a coherent whole. The concept of parallel systems is also seen in the writings of Christoph Bernhard (1628–92) whose *stylus luxurians* involved *figurae melopoeticae* (musico-poetic figures) and different rules of dissonance treatment, and was similar to the *seconda prattica*.[12]

There was a move to eliminate polyphony altogether and replace it with monody, but the mono(dy)mania did not prevail. Neither Monteverdi nor his predecessors who had written in *seconda prattica* wished to discard polyphony and the *prima prattica*. The whole point was that there were two systems. This meant that a musician like Claudio Monteverdi, who knew how to respect the rules of counterpoint, as well as break them for rhetorical effect, could feel comfortable using either system as a consistent practice on its own terms. His operas juxtapose monody with polyphonic textures, each used for distinct rhetorical effects, and his Eighth Book of Madrigals (published in 1638) includes examples of both the old polyphonic and new monophonic treatments. In "Hor che'l ciel e la terra," five singers plus an instrumental ensemble express one man's nocturnal musings. Here, instead of the singers representing different characters, they each contribute to a corporate image of a single individual. The newer theatrical style is exemplified in the "Il combattimento di Tancrede e Clorinda" where a narrator recounts a scene and the two protagonists sing dialogue in *stile rappresentativo*. It is unclear if this madrigal was intended for dramatic performance like an operatic scene, but recent attempts have proven effective.

Musical philosophers stressed the ethical value of the arts and the expression of passions as a means of building and maintaining a healthy, balanced society. Writing in 1635, the Frenchman Marin Mersenne believed that all art "should arouse and control passions, inculcate and preserve virtue, even cure disease and ensure the stability of the state."[13] Operas based strictly on the Florentine Academy's model of ancient Greek drama continued to be written for the next couple of decades, music's ethical power to affect the audience's emotions remaining the central guiding principle. In Italy the balance gradually shifted from strict text-dominance and monody to freer interplay between musical and textual components and the increased use of varied musical textures. Gradually over the course of the seventeenth century the fluid interchange between sections where text dominated (recitative) and more musically-driven forms (arias) became polarized, and by the end of the century the *da capo* aria emerged as the prime form of passionate outpouring in opera. The aria is where, through the art of persuasion, singers win over their audience and is thus a prime candidate for the application of rhetorical procedures. The structural makeup of the *da capo* aria owed as much to musical as to rhetorical elements.

The new musical style and doctrine of musical rhetoric spread from Italy to other areas of Europe. Italian opera was exported to German-speaking areas, where it influenced both Catholic and Lutheran sacred music, and it was also adapted to Spanish theater. Inroads were slower in France. A national opera was finally institutionalized in the 1670s. When Jean Baptiste Lully and his librettist Philippe Quinault began composing *tragédies en musique*, they held fast to Aristotelian conventions of dramaturgy which, grounded on credibility and the semblance of reality (verisimilitude), provided cues for appropriate passions.

Over time, homophony emerged as the predominant texture of Baroque music. Whereas in monody the focus was on a vocal line following speech-like rhythm and intonation with the rudimentary support of a simple bass line, homophony allowed for a more varied interaction between melody and bass. Within the expressive potential of this harmonic skeleton, there was also room for independent melodic bass lines, idiomatic instrumental writing, and fully developed inner parts. Indeed, the tension between the horizontal, onwards motion of melody and vertical harmony emerged as an essential ingredient that distinguished Baroque polyphony from earlier forms. Counterpoint never disappeared from the Rhetorical style, and various polyphonic devices were recognized as powerful resources for the effective communication of affects.

Musical practice from conceptual composition to realization in performance was seen as an unbroken continuum, so it was only natural that the principles of rhetoric should have been applied to all aspects of music making from *inventio* to *pronuntiatio*. The early seventeenth century also saw the elaboration and codification of musical figures and topics—musical *decoratio*. As interest shifted from the rhetoric of musical performance to that of composition (i.e., from *elocutio* and *actio* to *inventio* and *dispositio*), the structure and organization of musical compositions drew increasingly on a rhetorical model.

The rhetorical model was not static but was adapted to changing aesthetics. In the 1730s, for instance, Mattheson was one of the first writers to consider *da capo* aria form as the elaboration of a single theme and consequently comparable to the principles of Classical oratory.[14] He admitted that the musical *exordium* and *peroratio* were identical, and *confutatio* and *confirmatio* were reversed from their traditional sequence. But as an Enlightenment thinker, he did not hesitate to uphold the musical practices of his own age over the conventions of traditional wisdom. From the conceptualization of *da capo* aria form in terms of *exordium—narratio—confirmatio—confutatio—perorartio*, it is not hard to see how the same principles would in due course serve for the elaboration of larger stretches of instrumental music, and more complex structures such as sonata-form movements.

One of the main reasons why rhetoric exercised such a pervasive influence from the sixteenth to the nineteenth century was its use in education and its presence in everyday life. In Leipzig in Bach's day as in many other European cities of the time, rhetoric played a crucial role in three principal domains: the law courts, the church, and the theater. It formed an important part of specialized instruction in Latin and legal studies; the principles of Classical rhetoric were familiar to a broad cross-section of the population through sermons preached in church services, and through theatrical declamation. Johann Christoph Gottsched (1700–66), professor of rhetoric at the Leipzig University, instigated important reforms to the format of sermons. Instead of constructing sermons as concordances of biblical quotations, he called for preachers to develop arguments along the lines of Classical rhetoric. Leipzig was also known as the cradle of German theater, and during Bach's lifetime the city was an important center for drama. Gottsched and the actress and theater manager Caroline Neuberin (1697–1760) were concerned to elevate the moral reputation of the theater and actors, and they modeled their work on French plays by Racine and Corneille. It was reasonably common for musicians to study law at university. G. P. Telemann and J. S. Bach's eldest sons Wilhelm Friedemann and Carl Philipp Emanuel gained firsthand experience in rhetoric and the art of persuasion. Johann Sebastian himself had not benefitted from such training. His schooling at St. Michael's Choir School in Lüneburg was no match for the university educations of Telemann, Mattheson, or Heinichen. His job description in Leipzig included teaching Latin and the rudiments of rhetoric at the Thomasschule, but he passed on these duties to substitutes. Likewise, when he defended himself against Johann Adolf Scheibe's accusations of composing bombastic and confusing music, Bach employed the services of the Leipzig rhetoric professor Johann Abraham Birnbaum (1708–76).

Scheibe turned this against Bach and denounced him as deficient in essential skills for his trade, including rhetoric and letter-writing. But Scheibe apparently lacked the requisite musical perception to recognize that Bach's music more than adequately demonstrated his ability to not only respect the rhetorical formulas of poetic texts but also to respond instinctively to them with music of a complementary rhetorical nature.

The late eighteenth century saw a gradual decline in the study of rhetoric, and by the end of the century the terms *affect* and *passion* had all but disappeared from writings, replaced with a vocabulary relating more to individualized emotional states. Musical practices reflected the gradual disappearance of Classical rhetoric as the governing principle of communication and the arts. The basic response to the art of persuasion remained in place, but the way rhetoric was formulated and how it was manifest in musical contexts changed. Still, there was no sharp division between Rhetorical and Romantic periods. What has been called the "emancipation" of instrumental music in the late eighteenth century did not result in the so-called "pure" music freed from the anchor of language, concrete concepts, and passionate expression.[15] Composers continued to conceive music that could "speak" to audiences even without the aid of a text.

The Romantic Revolution

In both intensity and universality, the Romantic revolution can be compared to the paradigm shift initiated by the Humanists at the beginning of the sixteenth century. Reflecting profound changes in social infrastructure in economics, politics, philosophy, law, and the arts in general, Romanticism saw "the birth of many if not all of the central discourses of modernity: natural science, politics, and economics as well as art."[16] While it is often dangerous to draw arbitrary lines in shifting cultural sands, the French Revolution serves as a convenient watershed. Its causes and the conditions that led to it crystallized much of the parallel revolution in the artistic arena. The Romantic revolution set out to overturn and replace the Humanist doctrines that looked back to antiquity. The success of that break with tradition can be measured by how poorly rhetoric is understood today, and how little is generally known today about its significance and influence prior to the rise of Romanticism.

Still, revolutions don't happen overnight. Rhetoric and the imitation of the passions were deeply embedded in European culture, and they could not simply vanish without trace. While the assumptions of Romanticism were in many instances opposite to those of the Rhetorical period, the roots of Romanticism grew in Rhetorical soil, and the two systems co-existed for some time. Certain elements of rhetoric were never abandoned; many of them survive to this day.

In chapter 5 we will see how in 1800 Giuseppe Cambini was still able to translate ideas from traditional rhetorical and passion-based expression into the new Romantic idiom. And other writers, like Johann Nepomuk Hummel, continued to emphasize the importance of rhetoric in eloquent performance: "As in speaking, it is necessary to lay an *emphasis* on certain syllables or words, in order to render our discourse impressive, and the meaning of our words intelligible to the hearer, so in music the same thing is requisite."[17] The system of figures also remained largely in place, and its conventions were versatile enough to continue to evoke specific meanings. Thirty years into the nineteenth century, even as the place of rhetoric as the governing principal of human communication was waning, the pictorial qualities of a work as quintessentially Romantic as Héctor Berlioz's *Symphonie fantastique* (1830) still relied on figures and topics formulated in the previous century (sighing gestures, dance topics, the pastoral, and a quotation from Gregorian chant).

Nor did nineteenth-century writers and speakers abandon the tradition of eloquence in public speaking, but the Classical rhetorical heritage ceased to be their prime point of reference. More importantly, rhetoric was no longer the cornerstone of expression across all the arts; it was viewed as a hindrance to the free expression of personal emotion. By the twentieth century, rhetoric took on a more negative connotation. It became *mere* rhetoric: all talk and no truth, hollow promises, chicanery, the lubricant that oils the machine of politics. These connotations still hold true for us today where rhetorical display often makes up for a lack of content, particularly in the political arena where "rhetoric" is too frequently a cover-up for "deception" or "obfuscation."

To illustrate the rise and fall of rhetoric in the arts, it might be useful to consider an analogy with the natural sciences. It took centuries for the medieval doctrine of the divine Order of Being to give way to the Baroque idea of the fixity of species, and to transition with the rise of modern science over the course of the eighteenth and nineteenth centuries to the more fluid concept of evolution where all creatures were seen to be in a constant state of change. Likewise in the arts, the Renaissance concept of fixed humours developed slowly into the more sophisticated mixture of affects and the creation of distinctive passions in the Rhetorical period, and from there progressed toward the Romantic notion of individual expression grounded in modern psychology.[18] The difference is that while we recognize that modern notions of science explain nature more satisfactorily, the different paradigms of understanding emotions cannot be graded objectively according to correctness: each is a product of its culture, and when we play music from earlier periods, we need to be cognizant of the different ways people thought about how emotions could be expressed.

The following passage, taken from Pierre Baillot's cello method of 1804, illustrates the emerging Romantic sensibility, and how the theory of imitating nature and evoking the passions gradually left the rails and were transformed into a generalized, quasi-religious intensity of expression often overlaid with a nostalgic longing for a lost golden age. The author situates the music of Boccherini within the Renaissance grace of the paintings of the Italian religious artist Francesco Albani (1578–1660) and the rustic landscapes of the Swiss Romantic painter and poet Salomon Gessner (1730–88):

> Should one seek to make the Violoncello sing, it is a touching and majestic voice, not of those who paint and illuminate the passions, but of those that moderate them, in raising the soul to a higher region.
>
> But it is in the Adagio that the violoncello has the greatest means of moving us: nothing can surpass the charm which it has in the music of this great master [Boccherini]; if he makes it sing alone, it is with a sensibility so profound, a simplicity so noble, that one forgets all art and imitation, and, penetrated by a religious sentiment, one imagines one hears a celestial voice, whose expression is a stranger to all that wounds the heart; one could say rather that it seeks to console; if all five instruments are made to speak at the same time, it is with a full, august harmony which invites one to recollection, which casts the imagination into a sweet reverie, or which fixes it upon enchanted tableaux; it is the grace of Albani, it is the naive sensibility of Gessner; and when changing style, it takes on a sombre and melancholy tint, it goes directly to the heart by means so sweet, that tears fall without one being aware; if he saddens, it is to touch us the more; if he seems to strip the soul of all its strength, it is to reconcile it with itself, to appease the tumult of passions, and to make a delicious calm follow; to transport us into a better world, there to taste the pleasures of the golden age.[19]

Baillot's prose recalls passages from the poet Ludwig Tieck (1773–1853) that depict listening to a piece of music as a furtive search for meaning in an art considered beyond the grasp of verbal expression:

> Like magical seeds, how rapidly the sounds take root within us, and now there's a rushing of invisible, fiery forces, and in an instant a grove is rustling with a thousand wonderful flowers, and with incomprehensibly rare colors, and our childhood and an even more distant past are playing and jesting in the leaves and the treetops. Then the flowers become excited and move among one another, color gleams upon color, lustre shines upon lustre, and all the light, the sparkling, the rain of beams, coaxes out new lustre and new beams of light.[20]

Three general aspects of Romanticism stand out as strikingly different from the artistic values and assumptions of the centuries prior to 1800:

- Beauty as a unique artistic standard
- Autonomy or Absolute music: self-contained works of art
- Emphasis on individual expression

Although these tenets were not new, the way the Romantics adapted them to musical expression was very different from how they were treated by previous generations. Consciously or unconsciously, Romantic values still permeate our thinking about art. Later artistic movements have reacted to and qualified these overriding principles, but none has succeeded in obliterating the underlying tenets of Romanticism. Our present attitudes are still governed to a large extent by these notions, and they affect our ability to perform pre-Romantic music in historically appropriate ways.

Of Æsthetics and Beauty

Style studies oblige us to come to terms with the taste of different periods and how concepts of expressivity have changed over time. The quest for beauty in and of itself took on greater importance over the course of the eighteenth century. Eventually it became the subject of the new category of thought called Æsthetics, a designation given by German writers to a branch of inquiry that had as its object the "philosophical theory of the beautiful."[21] The Æsthetic of Beauty does not set easily with a rhetorical mindset because beauty is not in itself an emotion. It is a by-product of eloquent expression, an abstract condition or state, often achieved by chance rather than design. This is not to say that moments of sheer beauty and instances where listeners felt themselves transported to a state of ecstatic reverie were totally absent from pre-Romantic music. In 1668 Samuel Pepys wrote about being touched on both a sensual and a transcendental level by incidental music in a play:

> That which did please me beyond anything in the whole world was the wind musique when the Angell comes down, which is so sweet that it ravished me; and indeed, in a word, did wrap up my soul so that it made me really sick, just as I have formerly been when in love with my wife; that neither then, nor all the evening going home and at home, I was able to think of anything, but remained all night transported, so as I could not believe that ever any music hath that real command over the soul of a man as this did upon me.[22]

There are pieces by Bach—"Welt, ade! ich bin dein müde," in the cantata *Wer weiß, wie nahe mir mein Ende?* (BWV 27); "Mache dich" from the St. Matthew Passion; and the Agnus Dei from the b-minor Mass come to mind—that are inherently beautiful but they also express more specific passions like serenity, resolution, and gratification. Mozart also crafted movements that could be described as "pure" beauty and have a less clearly defined passion. Take the Adagio from the *Serenade for 13 Winds*, K. 361, or the slow movements of his piano concertos. Like Salieri in *Amadeus* (an unashamedly Romantic film), we may find ourselves filled with awe at Mozart's inexplicable talent to express transcendent beauty.

The euphoric contemplation of beauty became a Romantic preoccupation, the goal being the attainment of the Sublime: a transcendent, quasi-religious state beyond emotions, passions, or subjectivity. Romantic painters routinely depicted musicians and audiences lost in reverie or a state of rapture, pondering an unattainable or lost state of pleasure. Again, this was not new. We encountered a similar description in de Tyard's account of melancholia induced by the lute playing of Francesco da Milano, but in the nineteenth century the highly personal, introspective experience of music became a pervasive image and was recognized as the normal state rather than an exceptional condition of artistic creativity as in previous periods. Modern aesthetics are governed to a large extent by Romantic concepts and likewise prioritize beauty above what specific emotions the music might convey.

Æsthetics comes with subliminal baggage we all picked up when we first learned the word: the "fairy tale" implication that art has always been about beauty. We are so used to beauty as an obligatory attribute of any artwork—something that needs to be consciously and deliberately expressed—that it's difficult to imagine it any other way. One of the residual manifestations of the beauty cult is the way modern musicians emote. Their behavior while playing, their facial expressions and body carriage indicate that they are going through an extreme emotion, but the same indulgence is applied indiscriminately for any emotion. Passions, by contrast, are specific emotions and will trigger specific bodily gestures. Some eighteenth-century musicians were not immune to inappropriate body language. Pietro Locatelli, for example, was apparently given to grimacing as he played. This had no rational connection to his musical expression, but was cited as evidence of a lack of self control, and of a state of inspired possession.[23]

It is sometimes said that the line between heaven and hell is very thin. Does thinking on the other side of the thin line that divides the beautiful from the ugly offer a useful perspective? Ugliness and unpleasantness played a part in artistic creation in the days before the Romantic exaltation of the beautiful. For those of us raised on the Romantic premise of art-as-beauty, this idea is less intuitive, and some modern philosophers express their unwillingness to experience anything other than "nice" subjects in music.[24] It should not surprise us that writers who lived three or more centuries ago had different ideas and assumptions from the ones we hold today about music and what it can express. There was, however, a long tradition dealing with the appropriate use of ugliness in art. Grégoire Huret, in a book published in 1670, thought that negative passions like despair and rage "should never be expressed in pictures, etc., since this can only injure the health of beholders."[25] This goes back at least as far as Aristotle who commented that

> Tho' we should be loth to look at monsters, and people in agony, yet we gaze on these very objects with pleasure when copied by painters; and the better they are copied, the more satisfaction we have in beholding them.[26]

Unpleasant or shocking subjects were not shunned in Baroque art. As Mattheson remarked:

> The business of music, though it should mainly strive to be charming and pleasing, still serves occasionally with its dissonances or harsh variations to some measure and with suitable instruments to present not only something of the unpleasant and disagreeable, but also something of the frightening and horrible.[27]

Roger North speculated that if musicians attempted to equal the work of poets and painters, then they should also not shun disagreeable emotions. This passage from North's writings alludes to Raphael's famous depiction of death during the plague:

> A composer of Musick ought to look upon himself to be in a parallel state with painters or poets. . . . Whoever saw the famous Pest House of Rafael, and felt not sorrow? Imagine that a skillfull master of musick were required to compose a symphony proper for the spectators at that time. Would not he strive by some dolorous ayre, consentient with their minds at that time, to excite parallel ideas?[28]

Music and the arts have the ability to neutralize negative passions. It was thought that by experiencing disagreeable passions in controlled doses through art or cultural rituals, they could be purged, and emotional and rational stability reestablished in both the individual and society. Aristotle spoke of the pleasure of gazing on the artistic representation of ugliness, and North responded to the unpleasantness in Rafael's image with sorrow. Elsewhere, North spoke of how music "makes the passions sublime and noble, so that in such sweetness wee envy even the miserable, and would rejoyce to enter their condition."[29] Batteux later rounded this idea off with the following observation:

> Nothing is so irregular as the motion of the passions of love, anger, and discord. Oft-times to express them, the voice must suddenly become harsh and unmusical; now if art does but a very little soften these discords in nature, *the justness of the expression* makes up for the harshness of it.[30]

We need to distinguish between music that represents ugliness and music that is itself ugly. Mattheson warned musicians that when representing "anger, ardor, vengeance, rage, fury, and all other similarly violent passions," it is not enough to "make a lot of noise"; each particular passion requires its own attributes and, significantly, he noted that in order to remain "musical" and regardless the strength of the expression [*Ausdrucks*], a musical representation must have a "singing quality." The overriding principle was one of pleasure, and Mattheson believed that "whatever is not pleasing to the hearer, is explicitly and without exception bad; be it ever so understandable."[31]

Other writers warned not to overstep good taste. An artistic imitation of unpleasant and negative passions still needed to be agreeable. Speaking of warlike passions, Charles Avison wrote in 1753, that the "martial Sounds are of the *social* Kind: They may excite Courage and Contempt of Death, but never Hatred or Cruelty."[32] Wolfgang Mozart said something similar later in the century when he wrote in more general terms:

> Passions, whether violent or not, must never be expressed in such a way as to excite disgust, so music, even in the most terrible situations, must never offend the ear, but must please the hearer, or in other words must never cease to be *music*.[33]

Autonomous Music: "Art for Art's Sake"

The Romantic revolution also saw a major paradigm shift regarding music's relation to other arts. Music was progressively regarded as a transcendent art beyond all others, an autonomous medium beyond words, concrete ideas, and the specifics of culture and time. The mid-twentieth-century historian Carl Dahlhaus called this the "autonomy principle" and saw it as *the* crucial development in nineteenth-century music: the right of absolute music to be listened to for its own sake rather than functioning within an overriding extra-musical process (such as setting a text or accompanying a religious service). Dahlhaus was concerned primarily with the origins of abstract instrumental music, and he downplayed the presence of opera and text-based music in the nineteenth century.

There has always been a sense that even if it functioned like a language, music is capable of going beyond words. In 1676 Thomas Mace confessed that

> *Musick* speaks so transcendently, and Communicates Its Notions so Intelligibly to the Internal, Intellectual, and Incomprehensible Faculties of the Soul; so far beyond all *Language of Words*, that I confess, and most solemnly affirm, I have been more *Sensibly, Fervently,* and *Zealously Captivated*, and drawn into *Divine Raptures,* and *Contemplations,* by Those *Unexpressible Rhetorical, Uncontroulable Perswasions,* and *Instructions* of *Musicks Divine Language,* than ever yet I have been, by the best *Verbal Rhetorick,* that came from any Mans Mouth, either in *Pulpit*, or elsewhere.[34]

But the Romantics fetishized music's transcendent quality to an unprecedented degree. To philosophers and poets like Johann Wolfgang Goethe, Jean Paul Richter, Novalis, Ludwig Tieck, and Friedrich Schlegel, instrumental music was no mere mortal language but was a way for mortals to intercede with higher realms. *Absolute Tonkunst* was "the art of arts, just because it is indefinite [and] innocent of reference to the external world."[35] "All art," Walter Pater wrote in 1877:

> constantly aspires towards the condition of music. For while in all other kinds of art it is possible to distinguish the matter from the form, and the understanding can always make this distinction, yet it is the constant effort of art to obliterate it.[36]

Felix Mendelssohn-Bartholdy, who stood with one foot in the Romantic camp and the other in the Rhetorical heritage, put a slightly different spin on this. For him it was language, whether in the form of an entire speech or individual words, that was ambiguous and vague, and could be

> so easily misunderstood in comparison to genuine music, which fills the soul with a thousand things better than words. The thoughts which are expressed to me by music that I love are not too *indefinite* to be put into words, but on the contrary, too *definite*.[37]

With Absolute Music came the idea that Art (with a capital *A*) had no utilitarian function, no external point of reference, and no extramusical meaning. This was far removed from the role music had played in the Rhetorical era, where it was rarely separated from the pragmatics of performance and its associations with other forms of communication and social interaction. The notion of autonomous music was perpetuated in the middle of the twentieth century with the emergence of Formal Analysis. This approach to music takes the notes in the score to the exclusion of other factors, including technical aspects of performance and reception history, as both its start and end point. It may be appropriate for music current with the rise of Formalism itself—abstract serial music, or music founded on Stravinsky's doctrine that music is "essentially powerless to express anything at all"—but it doesn't work for most other styles.[38] The following strategy outlined by John Burkholder is typical of a residual Formalist approach. Writing about dramatic music by Monteverdi and Mozart, he reasoned that "when music does not make sense on musical terms alone, we are forced to look outside—to the words, character, or dramatic situation—for an explanation."[39] As should already be clear, seeing the words, character, and dramatic intent of a musical work as being removed from or *outside* the music turns Rhetorical art on its head. First, the word: *Prima la parole*. In most instances, it makes greater sense to start with the text in order to unravel the logic of the music. By reinstating the original understanding of Rhetorical music as based on concrete ideas and the imitation of nature and human passions, the difficulties of making sense of it dissolve.

Personally Expressing Passions or Passionately Expressing Persons?

In the mature Romantic paradigm, a work of art emerges from the part of the mind we now call the unconscious. Art is not an imitation of predefined passionate conditions, but a unique personal state. "Creativity" and "originality" in the Romantic vocabulary stem from the attitude that the inspirational basis of art is formed from an artist's personal feelings and experiences. Instead of art reflecting the world around, as in the Rhetorical era, the Romantics looked within and foregrounded the individual artist as prophet. The composer's work was then a sort of autobiography in notes, worthy of elevating the creator to quasi-godlike status. Here is Baillot again:

> The composer who has entered into his subject extends or restrains his ideas within a circle more or less great; like Mozart, he may raise himself almost to Heaven to plead with a merciful god for favor to

the dead on Judgment Day; like Haydn, he may embrace all creation in one glance, painting the genius of Man emanating from the divine, or brought toward the earth; like Gluck, he may present the picture of the passions which agitate us upon the stage of the world; or, finally, he may choose a less vast theatre, and turn in upon himself; like Boccherini, he may seek to return us to our primitive innocence.[40]

The reverence of the artist and the rise of Absolute Music weakened not only the traditional bond between composer and performer (up to that time, often one and the same) but also the connection between artist and audience. The elevated status of Romantic artists meant that they could afford to be less concerned with public taste and opinion than were their counterparts in previous centuries. Musicians could now follow their own caprice knowing that if presented convincingly as an accessory to their personal artistry, even their most eccentric behavior would win public acceptance. Claude Lévi-Strauss provided an interesting interpretation linking the reverence of the Romantic artist with the changing understanding of the meaning of music. Arguing that as musical expression in the Romantic imagination was at once intelligible and untranslatable, it approached the status of divine utterance, and thus led to the veneration of the masters of that language—the composers—as demigods in a pantheistic Parnassus.[41]

Baroque musicians were quite serious about reaching their audiences through expressive performance, but they did not draw inspiration exclusively from personal feelings. In a society where patronage controlled art and where creative artists were expected to conform to social convention and established codes of expression, musicians could not afford to be indifferent to the reaction of their audiences. After all, in the Rhetorical period musicians were servants; they provided unique musical experiences for specific occasions and were unlikely to ever repeat a given performance. (Chapter 9 returns to this topic.)

When comparing Rhetorical and Romantic art in his book *Signs and Meaning*, James Jensen understandably explained the rhetorical process from the perspective of the model that we are most familiar with today—the Romantic vision. When he declared "the rhetorical process is not expressive art," what he seems to have meant was that the rhetorical process does not involve an artist expressing personal feelings in the same way that we are used to in Romantic art.[42] The point is well taken, but rhetoric is inseparable from expression. What is at issue is not the expressive potential of either Rhetorical or Romantic music: the point is more that the subject, nature of expression, and artistic goals of each are quite different. Evoking passions in Rhetorical music does not preclude describing private or individual feelings, but the main focus is on passions that can be recognized, understood, and shared between audience and performer. So when we hear an aria by Bach or Handel, we do not think how tortured their souls were. Instead we are drawn to how effective they were as imitators of nature and human passions.

Rhetorical art is often described as art that disguises itself, where the performer retreats from view. Put in abstract terms, the artist should, in the words of Fénelon, fill his audience's minds "entirely with his Subject," rather than "paint his own Character, and amuse others with his Wit."[43] Batteux likewise instructed the artist to hide his effort to please:

> Eloquence and architecture would deserve the greatest reproach, if the design of pleasing appeared strongly in them. 'Tis in these that art blushes if it is discovered. Every thing that is only ornamental is vicious, since it is use and not pleasure we require of them.[44]

These recommendations are based on a much older tradition stemming from Quintilian, who wrote in the first century AD "never use art, if you have not the art to conceal it."[45]

This is of course 180 degrees from the aspirations of Romantic artists who did their utmost to project themselves (and audiences expected that too), and where the rules and formulas of Classical rhetoric were no longer considered appropriate to most artistic expression. They were too generic, too unbending, and interfered with direct and unmediated expression of personal emotions.

Afterword by Geoffrey Burgess

It might be useful to conclude this discussion with a perceptive observation from Nikolaus Harnoncourt that crystallizes many of the issues addressed in this chapter:

> I like to say that music prior to 1800 *speaks*, which subsequent music *paints*. The former must be *understood*, since anything that is spoken presupposes understanding. The latter affects us by means of moods which need not be understood, because they should be *felt*.[46]

Since the publication of these remarks in 1982, rhetoric has played an increasingly central role in the HIP movement, and at the same time historically *inspired* performance has made its mark on the interpretation of Romantic music. Together, these developments have coalesced to increase our awareness of how unwise it is to draw a clear demarcation between musical speech and painting. We have learned to identify how Rhetorical music paints, just as we have discovered how Romantic music can tell a story. In chapter 3, we will find that "painting" was commonly used by eighteenth-century writers to describe expressing or imitating passions in all the arts, but that landscape painting was held in low esteem when it did not engage the viewer on an emotional level. Still, as foolhardy as it may be to insist on an emphatic separation between Rhetorical and Romantic approaches—even if they stand on opposite sides of a cultural revolution—in broadest terms it can be said that much Baroque music is closely aligned with language and that it speaks through a narrative that unfolds over time, while Romantic music generally steps back from a detailed account to create an impression or mood with bolder brushstrokes. (This comment refers primarily to the Romantic ideal of "absolute" music autonomous of programmatic and "extra-musical" associations.) The Romantic masterpiece is laid out as if an entire symphony can be heard as a single snapshot; the Rhetorical work is more like a succession of frames in a moving image.

By admitting that post-1800 music appeals directly to the senses while Baroque music calls for a more intellectual, and consequently a less emotionally conditioned response, Harnoncourt revealed just how compelling the Romantic paradigm is for twentieth- and twenty-first-century musicians. Even if, as he suggested, Romantic music is more immediate in its appeal, the design of Rhetorical music is equally dependent on emotional expression and response. But in order to recover its expressive qualities, we have to engage in the intellectual exercise of relearning its passionate language. When we gain mastery of its eloquence, we will find that Rhetorical music can speak just as directly and paint in equally vivid tones as later, more familiar music.

Further Reading

Claude Palisca's extensive studies *The Florentine Camerata, Music and Ideas*, and his translation of Galilei are essential starting points for any investigation of Humanism and the emergence of the *seconda prattica*. Ossi's *Divining the Oracle* is a more critical recent study. Smith's book *Performance of 16th-Century Music* is highly informative, and Robert Toft's *Tune Thy Musicke to Thy Hart: The Art of Eloquent Singing in England, 1597–1622* provides a valuable practical guide for English repertoire.

On rhetoric in education during Bach's lifetime, see Butt's *Music Education and the Art of Performance*. Haynes's fundamental assumptions about Romantic aesthetics and how they differed from Rhetorical and modern art are discussed in *The End of Early Music*, ch. 4. Dahlhaus's influential interpretation of nineteenth-century musical practices is outlined in *The Idea of Absolute Music*. More studies on the transition from Rhetorical to Romantic ideologies are found in Neubauer's *Emancipation of Music from Language* and Abrams's *The Mirror and the Lamp*. The work of these writers has been reevaluated by Jensen in *Signs and Meaning* and by Monelle in *The Sense of Music*. Richard Leppert's *Sight of Sound* provides a stimulating exposé on the aesthetics of listening in the nineteenth century.

2

The Principles of Eloquence: The Artist's Toolbox

GEOFFREY BURGESS

> Music: at once intelligible and untranslatable.
> —Claude Lévi-Strauss[1]

> What passion cannot music raise and quell?
> —Dryden, *A Song for St. Cecilia's Day*, 1687

The Offices of Rhetoric

The rhetorical process, the backbone of eloquent expression, comprises five stages or offices:

- *Inventio:* Invention. The Message. The original inspiration, argument, or idea.
- *Dispositio*: Organization. Arrangement, form, structure, and decorum.
- *Elocutio*: Technique and Style. *Vortrag* (or expression), the figural elocution of the musical blueprint. Physical and technical aspects of performance practice.
- *Memoria*: Memorization. Also involves style memory and recognition, improvisation, composition, essential graces, and extempore *passaggi*.
- *Actio/Pronuntiatio*: The Act of Performance. This is another aspect of *Vortrag*. As well as expression, and delivery, *actio* involves all aspects of communication between performer and audience.

The first office, *inventio*, is the work's raison d'être. It is an abstract concept that in theory could serve as the basis for expression in any medium. Once the *inventio* has been set, the other offices translate and shape the raw concept to give it a form suitable for the chosen medium. The *inventio* is not just the theme of a musical composition, it is the guiding concept and inspiration that has an ulterior purpose and a message beyond the notes on the page.

In the Rhetorical era, *inventio* was not only the spark of inspiration that led to a work of art. It also required intelligence and application to recognize how an idea could serve as the kernel for musical elaboration. Johann Mattheson attributed *inventio* to the mysterious processes of artistic creation:

> [*Inventio*] depends mostly upon an innate quality of the mind and the fortuitous disposition of the cells in the brain. It also depends not a little on the time and on a good mood . . . [it] does not always depend on our will . . . occasionally a notion which is incomparable comes without much reflection and in a completely innocent and natural way. One must not let such a moment pass idly by but should put it to good use.[2]

This quotation makes it clear that *inventio* was, at least for this eighteenth-century artist, quite different from the fickle notion of genius that the Romantics glorified. The creative process has always been viewed as inexplicable and mysterious, but the eighteenth-century Enlightenment sought a rational explanation that would enable *inventio* to be harnessed for practical application. In Mattheson's and Bach's day, "the hectic pace of production," as Robert Marshall has reasoned, "obviously did not tolerate passive reliance on the unpredictable arrival of Inspiration."[3] There was a job to be done, and the craft of composition involved the skill of organizing material efficiently and effectively as much as the good fortune of stumbling on an ingenious idea. There wasn't the same sense of ownership connected with an *inventio* as with, say, a theme of a symphony. Pre-Romantic composers often borrowed material—whether from a common pool of material, the work of other composers, or from themselves. Theoretically, the same popular song, harmonic schema, chorale tune, or motif could form the inspirational basis for countless works. It was up to each composer to make something of it and so craft it into a unique composition.

Ultimately, musical meaning concerns both composer and performer. The whole point of the rhetorical process is that the *inventio* is shared, and everyone involved in the production is dedicated to its end. An essential step in the process is when the performer grasps the *inventio*; without this realization the music will be without purpose, and there will be nothing to communicate to the listeners. Rhetorical music, then, demands more than a subservient hireling musician who "executes" the will of the genius-composer.

The second office, *dispositio*, has several facets. In music, it involves conceiving of the musical ingredients (themes) and organizing them into a composition (meaning to arrange orderly). All decisions about form, the appropriateness and congruity of ideas and their arrangement (also known as *decorum*) come under *dispositio*. According to Mattheson, the first considerations in composing a piece of music are to set the sequence of ideas, and establish the key and meter.[4] The text of vocal music usually has its own *dispositio*, which will influence how the composer organizes the musical setting. Chapter 7 examines some applications of these procedures, including musical punctuation and the articulation of musical gestures (phrasing units), pauses, and various techniques of "humouring" the different sections of a musical work to clarify the *dispositio*.

Elocutio is the third office and covers the physical and technical aspects of performance, including performing style and technique, instruments, musical sources, and so forth. Most of what we now call performance practice comes under this category.

The fourth office of rhetoric is *memoria*. This means more than just memorization. In music, *memoria* deals with the elements that are gathered from experience and acquired through habit or cultural memory: all the unwritten aspects of improvisation, composition, and extempore ornamentation. That is why Joshua Reynolds spoke of invention as "little more than a new combination of those images which have been previously gathered and deposited in the memory."[5] Our knowledge of music today would serve the same purpose if we were not so concerned with being original. The relevance of memory to all musical creation is explained in a passage from Roger North's writings when he speaks of improvisation:

> It is not to be expected that a master invents all he plays in that manner [i.e., while improvising]. No, he doth but play over those passages that are in his memory and habituall to him. But the choice, application, and connexion are his, and so is the measure ... These passages which a voluntiere [i.e., improviser] serves himself of are (by transitions of his owne) so interwoven as to make one style, and will appear as a new work of a good composer, of whom the best (as I will venture to say here) useth the methods of a voluntere, and more or less borrows ayre from those that went before him, and such as he hath bin most conversant with ... for no man is an absolute inventor of art, but comonly takes up and adds to the inventions of predecessors.[6]

Memoria, then, plays an integral part in both composition and performance, and covers anything that the performer adds to the *dispositio* as well as the ability to make written music sound spontaneous. Improvisation acts as a conduit from *inventio* to *dispositio*, and an indispensible part of composing is remembering what one has just improvised long enough to write it down.

Improvising and playing from memory correspond to what good comedians do off the script when they spar off each other and engage in witty banter to complement their lines. Musicians continue to be bound to the text. "Just play what's on the page!" the conductor demands, but for most Rhetorical music that is a death sentence. There was much more open acceptance that musical notation was only a small part of the story. Playing less literally and using part books instead of scores, as was done in the past, sharpened memory skills. Even the rehearsal process was markedly different from modern practices. Often with no more than a single run-through before the performance, and no access to writing implements, musicians had to rely on oral transmission and memory. (Ink and quill were impractical, and there is scant evidence that musicians used pencils, even after 1660 when they were widely available through mass-production.) There was no room for playing on automatic pilot. Musicians had to be attentive and responsive listeners, and use memory as much as their sight-reading abilities. If the Kapellmeister altered a rhythm or corrected an accidental, the rest of the ensemble needed to follow and remember what decisions were made in the performance. If one player improvised graces, the others needed to either remember them long enough to duplicate them, or to substitute them with others from their own stock of memorized ornaments.

Finally, the fifth office of rhetoric—*actio*, delivery, or expression (*Vortrag* in German) covers all aspects of performance not addressed by *elocutio*. Fundamentally, *actio* is concerned with how the artist interacts with the audience. It involves the performer's deportment, and how he wins over the public; it also addresses the performer's duty to integrate all the elements of the work. Together with *elocutio*, *actio* forms the primary focus of what we have to say in the rest of this book. (Refer in particular to the discussion of Quantz's comments on "good *Vortrag*" in chapter 9.)

Structuring Rhetoric

In the Renaissance and early Baroque, musical rhetoric focused on how musical figures could enhance the imitation of poetic ideas. As attention shifted to the formal procedures of musical composition in the eighteenth century, the principles of rhetorical structure assumed greater importance. Classical treatises on rhetoric outlined the following sequence for the organization of an eloquent presentation:

Exordium (introduction),
Narratio (factual account),
Propositio (the proposed argument or point to be made),
Confirmatio (supporting arguments),
Confutatio (rebuttals), and
Peroratio or *Conclusio* (concluding comments)

Completely or partially, this six-part rhetorical structure can be found as the basis of musical compositions. Several writers adapted and modified this basic framework to the particular concerns and the musical style of their age, but their starting point was the structure as outlined here. The rhetorical analogy was a pervasive image and not only reflected actual practices, but shaped them as well.

At first, rhetorical structure might appear to pertain only to the *inventio* and *dispositio* and thus be of relevance only to composers, but it is also of great service to performers. In his book *Wordless Rhetoric*, Mark Evan Bonds considers whether rhetoric provided a meaningful basis for composers and a satisfactory explanation for the origins of Classical musical forms. In a similar vein, Joshua Rifkin concluded that because the majority of writers mention rhetoric in connection with composition, it was of little or no concern to performers.[7] This is misguided on two counts. Many writers encouraged performers as well as composers to participate in the rhetorical process, and even if it were true that writers applied rhetoric primarily to composition, composers and performers were so often the same person that the distinction is untenable. Where they were not the same, it was even more important for the performer to understand the *inventio* and *dispositio*. When, for instance, Mattheson analyzed an aria by Marcello, his primary function was to show composers how to apply rhetorical structure to musical composition.[8] But he subscribed to the general principle that effective musical communication was the shared responsibility of composer and performer. Familiarity with the underlying structure can only help the performer bring clarity to the sequence of different ideas, whether in an aria, instrumental sonata, or operatic scene. Indeed, the performer provides the vital link that can make or break a composition's eloquence.

The Sense of Music

> All kind of music and dancing should have a determinate sense [*un sens*] and meaning [*signification*].
> —Batteux, 1746[9]

Musical symbolism is most obvious when it involves imitations of music: there is no mistaking a trumpet call, a bagpipe drone, or dance music. The imitation of nonmusical sounds is also effective—birdsong, thunder, or the ticking of a clock. And music can be very successful at imitating motion—up, down, fast, slow. That is why waves, storms, and galloping horses were stock in trade for Rhetorical composers. The following chapters contain an abundance of examples of this type of musical symbolism. Music can also imitate motions associated with specific human passions. An example is the *pianto*, a descending second, originally associated with weeping in sixteenth-century laments but later generalized as a sigh and used as a metaphor for lamentation (Ex. 2.1).

Example 2.1 The *Pianto*

The *pianto* is an onomatopoeia because it imitates the sound of a sigh. Downward figures like this are found with similar emotional connotations in cultures around the world. As an onomatopoeia, the *pianto* relies on direct imitation and is effective the closer it approaches a genuine sigh. In Rhetorical music the sigh motif took on myriad forms, and over time and through familiarity, it was "indexed" as a code for grief, pain, regret, and loss. The *pianto* thus evolved from a neutral gesture or a meaningful figure, into a musical metaphor. That is, it came to be recognized as meaning something beyond a stepwise descending interval. Example 2.2 is an instance of where Bach used a chain of *pianti* to build phrases in an instrumental lament.

Example 2.2 Phrases built on *pianto* gestures in the Lament from J. S. Bach's *Capriccio sopra la lontananza del fratello dilettissimo*, BWV 992.

Some objects, motions, states, and concepts are beyond the direct imitative capabilities of music but can still be alluded to through less direct means. In 1753 Charles Avison doubted the effectiveness of music to imitate cold:

> It is one Property of Frost to make Persons shake and tremble; yet, a tremulous Movement of Semitones, will never give the true Idea of Frost: though, perhaps, they may of a trembling Person.[10]

This quotation pinpoints the nature of imitation in the Rhetorical era. The premise was that although art cannot substitute for all natural states (music, for instance, cannot *make* listeners feel cold), it can portray the emotional response to different states and, if expressed eloquently, can elicit a sympathetic response from the listener that emulates (imitates or represents) the original condition. This type of imitation often works through either suggestion or stylized exaggeration. Henry Purcell's Frost Scene in *King Arthur* and Winter in Vivaldi's *Four Seasons* suggest cold not with Avison's tremulous semitones but with repeated notes as a graphic emulation of chattering teeth. In order to represent a reaction to cold, the repeated notes do not need to be an accurate imitation of the physical state: the music uses its own means to elicit an emotional reaction that is similar to being cold.

Related to this is the concept that in order to emulate nature, art does not have to be realistic: it only needs to be credible. Artistic truth is verisimilitude—the semblance of truth dictated by the medium of expression and stylistic convention. It would be ludicrous (not to say embarrassing) if in Handel's *Messiah*, the tenor's voice really cracked when he sings "Thou shalt dash them in pieces like a potter's vessel," but if he gives the impression that his voice is breaking while remaining vocally in control, the result can be a powerful representation. Likewise, in the fourth movement of *Ach wie flüchtig, ach wie nichtig*, BWV 26, where the text speaks of how the "towering floods rush and rend, / until everything crashes into heaps in destruction" (*Wie rauschen und reißen die wallenden Fluten, / Bis alles zerschmettert in Trümmern zerfällt*), it would be very easy for the three oboes to fall apart on their unison sixteenth-note descending passages. That would not be a musical representation of chaos; such a loss of decorum amounts to chaos itself, and the result would be both ridiculous and embarrassing. The artistic representation of chaos here, as in other places like the overture to Jean-Féry Rebel's *Éléments*, or the introduction to Haydn's *Creation*, still demands control.

Figures of Speech, Figures of Song

> The most excellent ornaments, exornations, lightes, flowers, and formes of speech, commonly called the figures of rhetorike.
> —Henry Peacham, 1577[11]

In the Rhetorical period, musical symbolism was largely bound up in discrete musical units. Gestures like the two-note *pianto* are the building blocks of musical eloquence. They constitute the raw materials of figures—the musical equivalent to figures of speech in language—and topics (more extended and compound techniques of symbolism). (We will say more about these terms and how they differ in usage in chapter 3).

Figures are any devices or strategies that enhance expression. Also called tropes, they illustrate, emphasize, and elaborate the *inventio*. They are (to use a figure of speech) what spins straw into gold.[12] Like a musician who crafts a difficult passage into brilliant virtuosity, figures transform a sequence of notes into a meaningful eloquent statement. In Rhetorical music, there is no essential difference between a musical gesture and a figure: figures are simply gestures invested with meaning.

Figures can be ornamental elaborations that transform mundane "talk" into heightened declamation or ecstatic revelation. Here is the definition from the first edition of the *Dictionnaire de l'Académie française* (1694):

> *Figure*, used in rhetoric to mean a certain passage of thoughts and words [*un certain tour de pensées & de paroles*] that create beauty and ornament in the oration.... The most common figure in an oration is the metaphor.[13]

To show how figures work in language, I will take an example from Shakespeare. This is the gist of King Richard III's speech to his troops as they prepare for battle:

> My heart beats with excitement. Move our flags forward. Attack our enemy. Let the traditional motto of our patron saint instil anger in us. We will win if we attack!

Of course, these plain and matter-of-fact words are not what that paragon of Elizabethan spin doctors, gave him in *Richard III* (act 5, sc. 3).

> A thousand hearts are great within my bosom:
> Advance our standards! set upon our foes!
> Our ancient word of courage, fair Saint George,
> Inspire us with the spleen of fiery dragons!
> Upon them! Victory sits upon our helms.

The powerful images (dragons, spleen, St. George ...) and poetic variants ("standards" in place of "flags," "bosom" for "heart") elevate the message from a military order to an inspiring plea.

Figures are just as important in the eloquent performance of music. In 1728 the influential eighteenth-century German rhetorician, Johann Christoph Gottsched, called figures "the very language of the passions [*Leidenschaften.*]"[14] Dietrich Bartel explains how, according to Gottsched, figures could, "like the actions of the swordsman,"

> be used to startle, distress, delight, enrage, and elicit approval from an audience. The figures thus assumed a dual purpose: like facial expressions or the work of a painter, they could be used to portray the reigning

affection; and like the combative endeavors of the fencer, they could arouse various affections in the listener.[15]

As musical styles changed, the exact "meaning" of specific figures mutated and evolved. Even in the course of a composition, a skillful composer can play with the potential for a single figure to stand for more than one idea. Take, for instance, the symbol of the cross. This is a complex abstract concept involving several layers of meaning: it can be the image of a crossroads, the X of negation or contradiction, or the cross of the crucifixion. This figure elicited more esoteric musical symbolism than the *pianto* or shivering. Bach used various musical figures to mirror this poetic figure—crossing vocal or instrumental lines (referred to by the rhetorical terms *metabasis* or *transgresso*), or in the relationship of different sections in a musical form. In other places he used a visual analogue of the cross (*Kreuz*): the sharp sign. Sharps are not only seen but are heard when they result in dissonance. In BWV 56, *Ich will den Kreutzstab gehne tragen* (I would gladly carry the cross), Bach placed a sharpened note on the first syllable of the word *Kreutzstab* (crucifix), a painful major seventh above the gesture's starting point. The resulting dissonance is cancelled out when the note is lowered to its natural pitch on *gerne*—"gladly carry." The falling gestures on *tragen* are not so much sighing *pianti* as a graphic depiction of the heavy, shuffling steps of someone struggling under the burden of the cross. Ex 2.3. This phrase, then, is a musical pun that nevertheless carries serious intent: an allegory in microcosm for the pain of Christ on the cross that resolves in the salvation of the faithful.

Example 2.3 BWV 56/1. Autograph score, Berlin Staatsbibliothek Mus. ms. Bach P 118. NB *Kreuzstab* is abbreviated to *Xstab* and set to a C♯.

Other musical figures may not be the same on each occurrence. That is the case with what might be called the "knot untied." Fairly frequent in Bach's music, this figure involves dense and complicated harmonies that seem to have no possible resolution but is not associated with a specific harmonic sequence. A succinct example is Bach's setting of the chorale "Solls ja so sein" in the cantata *Ich elender*

The Principles of Eloquence

Mensch, wer wird mich erlösen (BWV 48). The text speaks of punishment and pain (*Straf und Pein*) and true repentance (*wohl büßen*). Bach responded with a harmonically intricate setting that sounds almost atonal before magically resolving to a consonant chord—like a knot untying. Another instance appears in the remarkable recitative section in the middle of the opening chorus of BWV 103 (*Ihr werdet weinen und heulen*), but here the harmonic progression is quite different (see Ex. 2.4).

Musical figures are many things, but one thing they are not easily definable. There is an enormous number of figures in Rhetorical music, and they take a myriad of forms, so no study can ever hope to address all of them. A figure can be a gesture, a trill, a technique of word painting, or a fugue. Dietrich Bartel, who made a thorough study of the primary sources, organized them into seven categories:[16]

- Melodic repetition
- Harmonic repetition; fugal figures
- Representation and depiction
- Dissonance and displacement
- Interruption and silence
- Melodic and harmonic ornamentation
- Miscellaneous

Example 2.4 Knots untying

(a) BWV 48/3

Example 2.4 (Continued)

(b) BWV 103/1

Bartel's system focuses on musical characteristics, rather than what they signified or how they were used. The following sections take up these topics in reference to two fundamental categories of figures that are particularly relevant to musical expression: *hypotyposis* or figures that paint vivid images, and *pathopoeia* or figures that evoke specific passions.[17]

Example 2.4 (b) (Continued)

Hypotyposis or Painting

In 1566 Johannes Susenbrotus defined *hypotyposis* as "when a person or thing is depicted through written or oral expression in such a fashion that it is perceived as though the described person were present or the event was personally experienced."[18] *Hypotyposis* is a perfect antidote to the dry, learned harangue. In the eighteenth century Dubos wrote:

> The very severest writer, who professes most seriously, that he intends to employ nothing but plain reason to convince us, soon finds, that to carry his point he must move us: and that, for the end, he must set before us the pictures of the objects he treats of.[19]

In the Rhetorical period the imitation of nature was usually just called "painting," regardless the artistic medium. Each art, by virtue of the concept of *ut pictura poesis* painted the same *inventio* using different imitative techniques. The first edition of the *Dictionnaire de l'Académie française* includes an example sentence as part of the definition of *peindre* and *peinture* ("to paint" and "painting"): "In painting the objects of nature, this poet/orator excels in painting passions and the weaknesses of the human heart." Likewise, in 1674 Fénelon wrote that "the lively *painting* of Things, is, as it were, the very Soul of Eloquence," and remarked that "to paint, is not only to describe Things; but to represent the Circumstances of 'em, in such a lively sensible manner, that the Hearer shall fancy he almost sees them with his Eyes."[20]

Music being a performance art is capable of particularly effective *hypotyposis*. The idea was that composers could be as much poets as painters. The German-Czech polymath Mauritius Johann Vogt (1669–1730) encouraged the composer to think like a poet, "not only so that he recognize the meter of the verse, but that his themes also be inventive, and like a painter, place the beautiful or frightful images lifelike before the eyes of the listeners through music."[21]

Pathopoeia or Arousing Passions

With *pathopoeia* we move from the external physical world to painting internal emotional states. In the Early Modern era, human nature was the subject of a number of systematic studies. Some, like La Bruyère's *Caractères* (1688), were based on Classical models. Others, like Charles Le Brun's *Conférence sur l'expression* owed more to modern Cartesian philosophy and attempted to create codified systems of figures to represent human emotions.[22] La Bruyère and Le Brun were at the forefront of theories of the visual depiction of emotion. Their careers coincided with the establishment of artistic academies in France that Louis XIV set up to oversee the formulation of artistic principles. Le Brun (1619–90) was not only the director of the French Académie Royale de Peinture et Sculpture but also a founder of the Gobelins tapestry workshops. As *Premier peintre du Roi*, he designed and supervised several important interiors at Versailles and other royal residences. *Les caractères* of Le Brun was widely read and served as a textbook of etiquette and courtly morals.

Both Le Brun's and La Bruyère's work related closely to French art, but they had important applications to art in other European cultures of the time. Across Germany the *Louis-quartorzien* style accrued particularly high cultural value. Saxon art collectors cultivated cosmopolitan tastes, and as Germany was not known for its painters, their collecting gravitated to the work of French and Italian masters.[23] In Dresden, Elector Friedrich Augustus II replaced Elias Gottlob Haussmann (1695–1774) as court painter with a student of Le Brun: Louis de Silvestre (1675–1760). From 1727 when he was appointed director of the Royal Academy of Arts, de Silvestre brought awareness of French style in the visual arts to Saxony. So even though it was Haussmann who painted Bach's portrait in 1746, French theories of art were not at all foreign to Bach's world, and it is worthwhile considering the emotional characteristics of Bach's music through the lens of French art theories.

In the late 1660s, Le Brun presented a series of lectures at the French Académie that summarized his thoughts on representing emotion in the visual arts. Later published as *Conférence sur l'expression générale et particulière* with a subtitle emphasizing its usefulness to those learning to represent the passions in visual art, Le Brun's work exercised considerable influence on art theory, both in his own time and over the next two centuries. Le Brun made a convincing and usable scheme of some two dozen of the most common passions. Figure 2.1 shows his character sketches for simple (or naïve) love and anger.

Striving to be definitive and systematic, Le Brun based his work on René Descartes's theory of human emotions built on six so-called primitive passions: wonder, love, hatred, joy, sadness, and desire as outlined in his *Observationes de passionibus animae/Les Passions de l'âme* of 1649. Descartes considered wonder the first and essential condition, because without registering wonderment or fascination, there can be no emotional engagement:

> When the first encounter with some object surprises us, this makes us wonder and stonish at it [*admiremur & eo percellamur/que nous l'admirons et en sommes étonnés*] and since this can happen before we know in the least whether this object is suitable to us or not, it seems to me that Wonder is the first of all the passions.[24]

Figure 2.1 Two character sketches by Charles Le Brun a) L'amour simple (simple or naïve love) b) La colère (anger).

Wonder is pre-rational, pre-passionate, and consequently is neither positive nor negative. It is the shiver that goes up our spine when the first rapturous sounds hit our ears before we recognize what they represent, or who created them and for what effect. The corollary to wonder is desire—the ability to extend wonder into the potential of future experience. Between these two, Descartes placed a further two pairs of opposites—love and hatred, joy and sadness. He reasoned that all other passions derived from these six conditions, either as qualifications or combinations, while acknowledging the primacy of love. Descartes's theory spelled the birth of the modern age and served as the groundwork for most later theories of artistic expression.[25]

Le Brun's scientific study of visual depictions of passion was not accepted without dispute, and as we might expect, it is rare to find unanimity among writers on the subject. In a book published just two years after Le Brun presented his *Conférence*, Grégoire Huret denied the possibility of "evoking the gentle passions in such a way that they can be distinguished," and claimed that "even the stronger emotions, if they are easier to represent, are also too closely related to be easily recognizable."[26] Even Le Brun was not able to avoid incongruities and confusion. His depiction of anger, for instance, is hardly distinguishable from jealousy.

Without going too deeply into these debates, let us consider what we can glean from Le Brun's work. Like other seventeenth- and eighteenth-century artists, Le Brun was confident in his ability to isolate the essential characteristics of each passion and held to these as absolute truths. Like other artists of his age, he considered art the imitation of nature not as it is, but as it was idealized in an abstracted sense: nature as it ought to be as ordained by a given cultural perspective. So in reality, Le Brun's paintings reflect a culturally specific view of the world. They were comprehensible to French academicians, but they may well have met with bewilderment from non-European (or even non-French) visitors to the royal palaces where they hung. Similarly, we should not underestimate the foreignness of late seventeenth-century French sensibilities to our view of nature and human emotions. We need a guide to interpret the body language and facial expressions depicted in Baroque art. Fortunately, there are contemporary written descriptions that do some of the translating for us.

Le Brun was the preeminent French exponent of historical painting, and rarely had cause to depict passions in the raw and simple form that he attempted to show in his *Conférence*. The purpose of historical painting was not simply to depict historical events but, much like of music, the end goal was to elicit emotional response from the observer.[27] By depicting each passionate state with sufficient force, Le Brun strove to draw the observer into the experience of the historical personages he depicted.

For his first painting commission from Louis XIV, Le Brun took as his subject the queen of Persia submitting to her enemy Alexander the Great (see Fig. 2.2). In 1703 André Félibien (1619–95), a renowned commentator on the fine arts, devoted a small book to this work. Believing that painting should show the visible signs of human passion, he provided a detailed description and interpretation of the facial expressions and physical demeanor of each of Le Brun's figures. His description begins with the queen at Alexander's feet, in whom "grief is most wonderfully express'd":

> We may see in her eyes and thro' her whole countenance, the manifest dissatisfaction she receives from the condition she is reduced to… And we may also discover in her eyes and all the features of her face, the Hopes she has in the clemency of so generous a conqueror.[28]

Of the queen's two daughters Félibien wrote:

> This princess is weeping, … nevertheless we may see the endeavours to restrain herself, and to conceal part of her affliction. … She keeps her eyes half closed, as if she endeavour'd to escape the sight of this conqueror, and to hide from herself the lamentable condition she finds herself in.[29]
>
> As to her younger sister, abundance of things are to be considered in her; grief, fear and admiration produce different effects in her looks: for grief appears in her eyes still wet with tears; her eye-brows advanced shew her Fear, and her mouth somewhat opened and drawn up express her admiration. … By her countenance and the disposition of her body, one may judge of the activity of her imagination, and the uncertainty of her thoughts. She would joyn her Hands and yet she does it not.[30]

In Félibien's reading, each figure embodies a constellation of passions: the queen's grief is mitigated by hope; the older princess's lamentation is colored by modesty and propriety, while her sister simultaneously portrays grief, fear, and admiration. These are no longer raw and bluntly defined conditions but refined passions matched to the specific circumstances.

This system of breaking down complex emotions into distinct passions was a widely accepted practice and can be useful when analyzing the passions expressed in other arts. The static poses of historical painting and sculpture along with abstract theories can all be translated into acting and oratory where facial expressions and physical gestures depict specific passions. It is equally easy to see how bodily carriage can be given motion in dance. But what about music?

Figure 2.2 Simon Gribelin, engraving (published 1707) after Le Brun, *The Queen of Persia at the Feet of Alexander* (1661).

We have mentioned the sigh motif as a musical emblem for sorrow, but which bodily movements or vocal expressions can a composer imitate to paint modesty or admiration?

Most of the time, it isn't particularly difficult to recognize passions in a purely visceral way. The problem is to identify them, to name them, and to distinguish similar passions. Naming and categorizing passions expressed in music is not a pointless intellectual exercise, nor does it necessarily diminish the mysterious power that we might sense in a piece of music. The reluctance to put words to music is another hangover from Romantic sensibility that elevated music beyond verbal description. Recognizing the passions in a musical work clarifies and reinforces our intentions of what should be brought out in performance. It also provides a means of communicating our intentions to our fellow performers and to our listeners.

Each artistic medium had a range of emotions natural to its mode of expression. Each art's potential was also directed by historical and cultural factors that dictated what was appropriate to the medium. In his study of musical psychology and perception, Patrik Juslin shows that the majority of twenty-first-century listeners and performers agree that happiness, anger, sadness, fear, and tenderness can be expressed through music, but that they differ about nuances within these categories.[31] We should not be surprised that this list differs from what Baroque music was called on to express. To most writers, music was capable of conveying a wide array of emotional states. In the late seventeenth century Roger North stated that "there is no end of the varietys of imitation in musick, so I leave that to imagination," and elaborated that a musician

> may put in execution all the various states of body and mind, by a musicall imitation . . . that his humour or *capriccio*, as well as good understanding and sence, shall in his fancy conjure up. He will be grave, reasonable, merry, capering and dancing, artificiall, melencholly, querolous, stately and proud, or submissive and humble, buisie, in haste, frighted, quarrell and fight, run, walk, or consider, search, rejoyce, prattle, weep, laugh, insult, triumph; and at last, perhaps, layd downe to rest of sleep.[32]

Closer to the time and culture of J. S. Bach, Johann Mattheson, a particularly rich source of wisdom and information, proposed a different list. Like Le Brun, Mattheson was also strongly influenced by Descartes, and there is good reason to believe that his study was intended as a musical elaboration of the Cartesian theory of the passions.[33] He cautioned that an exhaustive catalogue would be tedious, so presumably he considered these passions to be the most suited to musical treatment:[34]

Die Liebe	Love
Die Begierde	Lust
Die Traurigkeit	Sadness
Die Freude	Joy
Der Stoltz (der Hochmuth, die Hoffart)	Pride (including Haughtiness and Arrogance)
Der Demuth, Geduld	Humility (including Patience)
Die Hartnäckigkeit	Stubbornness
Der Zorn (Eifer, die Rache, die Wut, Grimm)	Anger (including Ardor, Vengeance, Rage, and Fury)
Der Lieben Eifersucht (die brennende Liebe, Mistrauen, Begrierde, Rache, Traurigkeit, Furcht, Schaam; unruhig, verdrießlich, grimmiges, kläglich)	Jealousy (a blend of seven passions: Ardent love, Mistrust, Desire, Revenge, Sadness, Fear, Shame Distress, represented in restless, vexatious, angry and distressing music)
Die Hoffnung, freudigen Verlangen	Hope or joyful longing
Die Furcht, Kleinmüthigkeit	Fright and Horror
Die Anmuth	Charm
Wiedriges, Unangenehmes; fürchterliches, entsetzliches	Unpleasant and disagreeable; frightening and horrible
Die Verzweifflung, grausame Furcht	Despair and cruel fear
Das Mitleid (Liebe und Traurigkeit)	Pity (combines love and sadness)
Die Gelassenheit	Composure

Like Descartes and Félibien, Mattheson thought of the more complex emotional states as composites of basic passions, and so it is possible to rationalize his list into logical groupings. At the most basic level, we can divide passions along the lines of positive and negative states. Not surprisingly, Mattheson viewed love as the fundamental passion and placed it "quite reasonably . . . at the top of them all; as it occupies far greater space in musical pieces than the other passions."[35] He did not list hatred; the closest opposite to love in his list is anger. We can now reorganize Mattheson's list as follows:

Positive:
  Love, Joy, Humility, Patience, Desire, Hopefulness, Courage, Pity

Negative:
  Anger, Sadness, Ardor, Vengeance, Rage, Fury, Jealousy, Mistrust, Stubbornness, Fear, Shame, Pride (including Haughtiness and Arrogance), Restlessness, Vexatiousness, Distress, Dejection, Failure, Fright, Horror, Despair

From this we can already see that Mattheson included more negative passions by a ratio of about three to one. This may relate to his observation that more people respond to sad music because they are generally unhappy. He did not say why people would want to be reminded of their misery. Perhaps it was because he believed that music could act as a palliative to life's sorrows.[36] (We might be reminded of the blues, a genre of sad music intended to alleviate sorrow.) Mattheson's ratio of passions compares interestingly with Bach's choices in the cantatas where there are almost twice as many positive passions as negative, and the largest category revolves around the related passions of joy, happiness, and bliss.

So, based on their similarity, we can further organize Mattheson's list logically (more or less) into three positive groups based around Love, Joy, and Pity, and five negative groups dominated by Anger, Sadness, Arrogance, Jealousy and Shame, and Fear (see Table 2.1). From here, it is much easier to approach a spe-

Table 2.1 **Passion Constellations based on Johannes Mattheson**

Positive:
Love/Humility/Patience/Desire
Joy/Hopefulness/Courage
Pity
Negative:
Anger/Ardour/Vengeance/Rage/Fury
Sadness/Dejection/Despair/Restlessness/Failure
Arrogance/Pride/Haughtiness/Stubbornness/Vexatiousness
Jealousy/Shame
Fear/Distress/Fright/Horror/Mistrust

cific description to match the feel of a musical piece.

"Passion Constellations" seems to be an appropriate term for these groups of terms with similar meanings. The constellations define passions in gradually more specific shadings, grouped around a generic center. Once the designation or label for the passion is discovered, its particular quality or character can serve as a guide for eloquent performance. In chapter 4 we will see how they can be applied to Bach's vocal music.

Topics: Intertextual Allusion

Meaning can be transmitted in music by referring to another work, style, or musical genre. As defined by Leonard Ratner, a topic is a reference or citation in music, the evocation of a style or a type.[37] Topics are established by convention and have broader cultural currency than figures. As they stand for more developed concepts, topics may involve a nexus of figures and can act as references to things already known, even clichés, like those seen in Example 2.5:

Example 2.5 Three Topics.

Citations like these are easy to make in music. Four notes brings the world of Beethoven's Fifth, five a Viennese waltz, and seven notes suffice for a birthday announcement. Eighteenth-century dance topics are easily recognized but take more than just a single gesture to establish. They are defined by a combination of elements involving meter, rhythmic profile, and phraseology and accompany unique combinations of choreographic steps. Some, like the chaconne and passacaille, are defined by specific harmonic progressions. The pastoral topic could be called up with one or more of the following: the drone bass of a shepherd's bagpipe, siciliana rhythms, cantabile melodic gestures, wind instruments, and imitations to birdcalls and babbling brooks. It goes without saying that topics don't work when divorced from their cultural context—heard in a vacuum as it were. There is still much to be discovered about this level of musical allusion in Rhetorical music.

Ethopoeïa: Musical Characterization

In its pure state, each passion is in essence abstract and does not constitute a balanced image of human nature. As we have seen, by combining passions in constellations artists could construct more realistic portraits of personalities or characters. In rhetoric this is termed *ethopoeia*. Stock character types and actual persons who exhibit specific character traits fall into this category. "Character" (like the French equivalent *caractère,* and the old-fashioned English term "humour") can refer to someone's general disposition—bold, angry, and courageous, or maybe capricious, jovial, and likable—or the artistic embodiment of such traits as in the characters in a play or novel. The most influential study of *ethopoeia* from the Rhetorical age was La Bruyère's *Caractères*. In this expanded translation of a treatise by the fourth-century BC Greek writer Theophrastus, La Bruyère discussed different categories of characters, some based on occupations and stations in life (sovereign, courtier, artist), others on personal markers (the honest man, the fop, the prude), or more general moral and behavioral characteristics. Drawing on the dual meaning of *caractère*, in addition to elaborating a catalogue of general character types, La Bruyère's book illustrates character traits through character sketches.

Musical pieces that describe a character rather than a passion in pure form are common in Rhetorical music. There is a good number in intimate genres where they could serve as conversation pieces in artistic *salons*. Character trait and personal portrait often coalesce in the solo keyboard *pièces de caractère* by François Couperin and Jean Philippe Rameau. (Couperin knew La Bruyère's work and may also have been personally acquainted with him.) Some of these pieces are based on actual people from the composers' circle of acquaintances; others are imitations of general character types; still others owe their identity to personalities interposed on the music in poetic parodies.

Ethopoeia was also practiced by eighteenth-century German composers, including Johann Kuhnau and Georg Philipp Telemann. C. P. E. Bach's trio sonata *Sanguineus and Melancholicus*, Wq 161.4 stands somewhere between *pathapoeia* and *ethopoeia*. The score is accompanied by the composer's own descriptive program explaining the dialogue between opposite "humours" who are gradually integrated into a mixed (*gemischtes*) style over the course of the work. The reference to sanguine and melancholic characters harks back to ancient and medieval ideas of physiology. In Hippocratic medicine the proportions of the four chief fluids, also known as the cardinal humours of the human body—blood, phlegm, yellow bile (or choler), and black bile (or melancholy)—were thought to determine a person's physical and mental disposition. Sanguineus and Melancholicus are not really characters; they are more like paradigmatic conditions. The piece's charm is in the way Bach has them engage in dialogue like real people.

🔊 AUDIO EX. 6.5. C.P.E. Bach, Trio Sonata *Sanguineus & Melancholicus*, Wq 161/4 Ensemble Florilegium (Channel Classics, 1997)
a) Allegretto–Presto
b) Allegro

Key and Character

> Euery key hath a peculiar ayre proper vnto it selfe,
> so that if you goe into another then that wherein you begun,
> you change the aire of the song.
> —Thomas Morley, 1597[38]

With the development in the seventeenth century of tonality from the earlier modal theory, theorists saw the modern key system as a way of emulating the affective properties that Classical Latin and Greek writers attributed to the ancient modes. Key characteristics are hard to categorize as figures or topics, but they are undeniably aligned with affect and passion. Despite Morley's confidence in the epigraphic quotation above, the subject of whether keys could be aligned with specific passions elicited vigorous debate. Numerous writers, including Jean Rousseau, Marc-Antoine Charpentier, Johannes Mattheson, and Jean Philippe Rameau, to name just the best known (summarized in Table 2.2), identified tonalities with corresponding passions, but their opinions do not fully agree.

Mattheson's description of the affective qualities of keys in *Das neu-eröffnete Orchestre* (1713) is frequently cited, but a thorough reading of his text indicates that he never intended it to be universally prescriptive.[39] On the contrary, he viewed tonality as just one parameter along with several others including meter, melody, tempo, and rhythm that can be used to depict different passions. Furthermore, Mattheson admitted that people of different temperaments would likely differ in their perception of tonalities.

Over time certain conventions emerged, and while there was still some disagreement, there was a good deal of common ground among the opinions of authorities. Quantz was aware that it was hard to establish a consensus "on whether certain keys have particularly individual effects," but held to his opinion. "As for myself, until I can be convinced of the contrary, I will trust to my experience, which assures me of the different effect of different keys," and he invited his readers to prove him wrong.[40] The four authorities quoted in Table 2.2 are in general agreement. They differ most markedly in their assessment of A and E major, for which their associations range from devotional to justing for A, and quarrelsome to tender for E. In fact, Mattheson was himself conflicted in his response to A major, which he found suited to both lamentation and play. F major and B♭ major also receive contradictory associations, most evidently between the German Mattheson and the two French opera composers who would have been familiar with the tradition of writing music for demonic scenes in flat keys. Most twenty-first-century musicians would find it hard to characterize E♭ major as cruel and harsh, or E major as quarrelsome and clamorous. These eighteenth-century responses probably resulted from unequal temperaments (more about that soon).

A number of theories were proposed to explain how tonalities acquired characteristics. Some argued that the associations arose from differences in pitch level; others attributed them to unequal temperament. The instruments associated with specific keys also played a role. The relative pitch level of different tonalities is meaningful only when considered in a closed system and at a standard pitch. The gradual rise in pitch may explain why, over time, certain keys changed their affective identity. Things get more complicated when we consider the differences between the same key at different pitch levels, when transposition

Table 2.2 **Key Characteristics according to Four Composers of Rhetorical Music***

	Jean Rousseau 1691	M. A. Charpentier 1692	J. Mattheson 1713–19	J. P. Rameau 1722
C maj.	gay, grand	gay, militant	rejoicing	for mirth & rejoicing
c min.	complaints, laments	gloomy, sad	lovely, sad	tender, for plaints
D maj.	gay, grand	joyful, militant	noisy, joyful	for mirth & rejoicing
d min.	serious	serious, pious	devout, grand, flowing not skipping	Sweet, tender
E♭ maj.		cruel, harsh	pathetic, serious	
d# min.		horrible, frightful		
E maj.		quarrelsome, clamorous	fatally sad	grand, tender
e min.	tender	amorous, plaintive	pensive, grieved	sweet, tender
F maj.	devotional	furious, quick-tempered	most beautiful, virtuous	for tempests, furies
f min.	for complaints, lamentations	dark, plaintive	calm but with deep despair	tender, for plaints
f# min.			languid, love sick	
G maj.	tender	sweetly joyful	persuasive, serious & cheerful	
g min.	sad	serious, magnificent	mostly beautiful, grace & kindness	sweet & tender
A maj.	devotional	joyful, magnificent	lamenting, sad, playful, jesting	for mirth, rejoicing
a min.	serious	tender, plaintive	honourable, calm	
B♭ maj.		magnificent, joyful	diverting, sumptuous	for tempests, furies
b♭ min.		gloomy, terrible		for mournful songs
B maj.		harsh, plaintive	offensive, hard, desperate	
b min.		lonely, melancholic	bizarre, morose	sweet, tender

*Based on a similar table in Tarling, *Weapons*, 77.

is involved, or when different pitch levels collided, such as in Bach's music where *Chorton* (choir pitch) and *Kammerton* (chamber pitch) were routinely juxtaposed. Here, even deciding how to name the tonality becomes something of a riddle: Should we talk of C major at *Chorton* or D major at *Tief-Kammerton*?[41]

Unequal temperaments result in small variations to the makeup of scales in different tonalities and have a decisive impact on the way music sounds. The two recordings of the Aria from J. S. Bach's *Goldberg Variations* (BWV 988) in Audio Example 2.1 have been adjusted so that they sound at the same pitch to facilitate comparison. The first, performed by Ralph Kirkpatrick, is in equal temperament; in the second, Pierre Hantaï uses a mean-tone oriented tuning. To listeners used to equal temperament, mean-tone will sound somewhat more "spicy;" it has the advantage of more sonorous triads in the home key, but increased dissonance on other chords.

🔊 AUDIO EX. 2.1. Aria from Goldberg Variations:
a) Ralph Kirkpatrick, piano (Archive, 1959). Pitch adjusted to match Ex. 2.1b.
b) Pierre Hantaï, harpsichord (Opus 111, 2000).

Listening to music that covers a wide range of tonalities, like Bach's *Well Tempered Clavier* (*WTC*), can be a very different experience when the keyboard is tuned in a mean-tone temperament to when it is in equal temperament. We know that Bach did not intend his set twenty-four preludes and fugues in all keys to be played in equal temperament, and there is a range of historically appropriate temperaments that provide plenty of opportunity to capture the character of each key without rendering any intolerably discordant. Recently, some harpsichordists have chosen to use the Bach-Lehman temperament, a hypothetical reconstruction of Bach's tuning system based on a decorative squiggle on the title page of Bach's autograph of the *WTC*.[42] Although controversial in its derivation, this temperament bears close similarities to tuning systems used in Bach's day. It is fairly mild compared to other temperaments, but it still provides distinctive patterns for each key. The effect is most obvious when comparing distantly related keys, such as offered by the sequence of the first major-key preludes (C, C♯, D, E♭, and E major). To make the experiment fairer, the pitches of the excerpts in Audio Example 2.2 have been adjusted so that they match C major. But still, any player will react to the music and the sonority resulting from the temperament to characterize the music with different registrations and touch that affect the way the listener responds to the temperament. A completely objective comparison would require eliminating these differences by, for instance, hearing the same music transposed to different keys in the same non-equal temperament played by the same performer on the same instrument.

🔊 AUDIO EX. 2.2. *Well-Tempered Clavier Book 1* Preludes 1, 3, 5, 7, 9 in C, C♯, D, E♭, and E majors, Peter Watchorn, harpsichord (Musica Omnia, 2006). Bach-Lehmann temperament; pitch adjusted so that each excerpt sounds at the same level.

Bach filled out the tonal gamut of the *WTC* by transposing preexisting works, and when assembling his harpsichord concertos BWV 1058, 1054, 1062, and 1057 he transposed the violin concertos BWV 1041–43 and 1049 down a step to accommodate the range of the keyboard.[43] Some of these concerto movements also found their way into church cantatas where the solo part was played on organ, again at a different pitch. That suggests that Bach admitted some degree of flexibility, undercutting a one-to-one equation between tonality and character. Nonetheless, his practical sense directed him to transpose between keys relatively close on the tonal wheel that would sound similar when played in a mean-tone tuning system. Transpositions between C and D major, or g minor and f minor are common, but those between E major and F major are rare. Among a longer list of likely candidates, the three clear instances of transposition of preexisting music in Book 2 of the *WTC* are exceptions, as each involves a distant relationship: the C♯ major Prelude and Fugue started life in C major, the E♭ major fugue was originally in D major, and the A♭ major Fugue in F.[44] Handel was equally practically minded, and like any good *opera seria* composer, obligingly transposed his arias to fit the vocal range and abilities of different singers as his works made the rounds of European theaters. This did not mean that the original character of the aria was lost. Some of the transposed versions may make it harder to project the emotion, but as Mattheson pointed out, tonality is not the only deciding factor in the definition of the character of music.

Instrumental associations are strong designators of key characteristics. C major and D major are tinged with the stately and majestic connotations of the trumpet. String instruments are more resonant when the open strings are in use, so D major will sound more confident than the covered sound of b♭ minor. This is consistent with the listing of key characteristics that equate D major with mirth and jubilation, and b♭ minor with gloom and mourning. Similarly, each woodwind instrument had a range of comfortable tonalities which composers knew about and used.

Baroque music rarely stays in one tonality for long: the character of a piece of music depends as much on what keys it moves to for contrast as the inherent quality of the central tonality. Just as a character is a blend of different passions, a tonality is made up of the intervals of the scale and the sonorous quality of its primary chords. The way a composition combined different keys was called "modulation"— that is, the way it delineated and defined its mode. Each musical composition put a unique spin on a tonality. Across the seventeenth and eighteenth centuries the definition of modulation changed and came to mean the movement from one key to another.[45] By 1728 this newer concept was winning currency and beginning to cast doubt on the usefulness of the theory of key characteristics. Heinichen, who was not inclined to the theory, commented wryly that "if these imagined [affective] properties [of the keys] had any inherent validity, shipwrecks would be occurring continuously with every small change of temperament."[46] With this in mind, modulations add to the overall impression of a tonality, but not every key visited in the course of a piece will be equally significant to the character of the piece.

In some instances composers seem to have made choices (conscious or otherwise) based on tonal characteristics. Charpentier's list is a useful guide to interpreting his music, but just as with other musical figures and symbols, the correspondence between tonality and character isn't always straightforward. In his opera *Médée* (1693) there is a reasonable level of agreement between his descriptions of key characteristics and the passions expressed in the text, but his aphoristic descriptions are hardly adequate to encapsulate the complexities of the musical drama. Take the heroine's agonized monologue (Audio Ex. 2.3) at the beginning of act 5.

🔊 AUDIO EX. 2.3. Marc-Antoine Charpentier, *Médée*, act 5, sc. 1
Lorraine Hunt, Les Arts Florissants, dir. Christie (Erato, 1995).

As Médée contemplates murdering her own children to avenge Jason's unfaithful love, her emotions oscillate between rage and tenderness. The music follows the vicissitudes of her emotions, traversing C major and e minor (the relative minor of the dominant). This unusual tonal juxtaposition was probably not accidental. For Charpentier C major was "bright and warlike" (*gay et guerrier*), and e minor was "effeminate, amorous, and plaintive" (*efféminé, amoureux et plaintif*). Appropriately, Charpentier uses e minor most often when Médée expresses her feelings toward her children, but she could never be said to be *gay* in this scene; it is the warlike aspect that comes to the fore. Charpentier may have chosen C major in combination with e minor to tinge her exultant jubilation with bittersweet revenge.

With Bach we are on less secure ground when it comes to considering his choice of keys because he did not leave any writings to explain his understanding of key characteristics. We can still learn a great deal through analyzing his tonal structures. The progression toward sharp keys in the St. John Passion was no doubt calculated to presage the crucifixion, and the flat keys of g minor and c minor in the opening and closing choruses color the music with feelings of anxiety, loss, and mourning.

On the Possibility of a *Figurenlehre*

The sheer number of potential figures and topics in Baroque music can be daunting. It is of course tempting to seek comfort from a system that decodes the plethora of devices used to enhance expression. Starting at the beginning of the seventeenth century with Joachim Burmeister, numerous writers borrowed Latin and Greek terminology from verbal rhetoric (*epanadiplosis, paronomasia, subsumtio, figura corta, suspirans, accentus,* etc.) to describe musical figures of analogous or similar meaning in an attempt to arrive at a single universal system. Constructing lists much like the taxonomies of plant species or insects, these writers attempted to name (after the fact) the profusion of figures that were already in use. In the end, their attempts were just the tip of the iceberg, and were neither consistent nor systematic. Even Burmeister acknowledged defeat and wrote that the mass of figures "is known to be so wide and great among composers that it is hardly possible for us to determine their number."[47] Different names were used for the same figure, and many new terms appeared, unknown to verbal rhetoric.[48] Vickers has gone as far as to criticize seventeenth- and eighteenth-century writers for playing fast and loose with the terms of Classical language-based rhetoric. In all, these theorists described only around ninety musical figures. Those that got documented have understandably taken on an air of canonic authority, but most figuration was evanescent and just the reverse of orthodox. Improvised once, new figures quickly vanished into oblivion. Bach's music draws on a wealth of figures—both documented and those that never made it to the treatises. The richness of his output and his use of figures has prompted more intensive study of musical symbolism than the music of any other composer. But Bach (being Bach) expressed figures and patterns imaginatively and differently every time he used them, and often with humor or irony (for further examples and discussion of the complexities, see chapter 4).

As well as realizing that a systematic codification of figures was virtually impossible, Baroque theorists probably concluded that their quest was irrelevant, because just like the figures of speech in spoken language, musical figures were in constant flux. This underpins George Buelow's belief that the idea of a fully worked-out *Figurenlehre*, or a system of "stereotyped musical figures with specific affective connotations" was "an invention of twentieth-century musicologists, and never existed in the Baroque composer's mind or in theoretical explanations."[49]

Nevertheless, it would be unwise to throw the baby out with the bathwater (to use another figure). Rhetoric is a tool, not a rite or dogma: its basic principles, including the use of figures, are essential; literal word choice and naming less so.[50] Rhetorical terminology is like a lexicon for an art like fly fishing or wine tasting that allows considerable personal discretion in its practice. Using rhetorical terminology should never become a secret language where each musical figure is labeled with a rhetorical term in the vain hope of being "expressive." That would make music into no more than "playing by numbers." For that reason, we have not found it necessary in this study to stress the identification of rhetorical terms, and sometimes we reserve the right to differ on terminology with some of the old sources. What *is* important is to recognize that music is a symbolic language and to understand the role figures play in the pursuit of eloquence.

Here we have been concerned mostly with the concept of musical figures and how they enhance the *inventio* or compositional skeleton. When we take up the topic again in chapter 6, we will have more to say about performance and ornamentation as figural elaborations of the musical text.

Further Reading

Buelow's articles in the *New Grove Dictionary* (*NGD*) and "Johann Mattheson and the Invention of the Affektenlehre" do a good job of explaining how rhetoric has been applied to music. As well as including practical advice, they give extensive references to the Classical writings on rhetoric and give insightful examples of musical figures. Beghin's and Goldberg's *Haydn and the Performance of Rhetoric* presents several detailed studies of rhetoric in late eighteenth-century music.

Dietrich Bartel's *Musica Poetica* reports on and discusses musical figures listed in writings from 1606 to 1788. This nuanced view compares *Figurenlehren* as developed by a number of individual writers and demonstrates beyond reasonable doubt the existence of a conventional framework governing the use of musical figures among practicing musicians of the seventeenth and eighteenth centuries.

On memory and rehearsal techniques, see "Memory as Art" in Ong, *Rhetoric, Romance and Technology*, and chapter 2, "Part Book vs. Score culture" in Smith, *Performance of 16th-Century Music*.

Leonard Ratner's *Classic Music: Expression, Form, and Style* is the standard text on the subject of musical topics. Since its publication in 1980, Ratner's theory has been the subject of critique and refinement. See Agawu, *Playing with Signs* (1991), Hatten, *Interpreting Musical Gestures, Topics and Tropes* (2004), and Monelle, *The Sense of Music* (2007).

In his *Vollkommene Capellmeister*, Johannes Mattheson, who had a particular interest in the passions appropriate to music, cited Johann David Heinichen's list of sixteen: rage, aggression, majesty, fear, playfulness, strife, unity, happiness, flightiness, sorrow, love, fieriness, yearning, sighing, flirtation, mystery [*schattenreichen*] (*General-Bass* §64). Although somewhat different to Mattheson's they, too, could be arranged systematically into constellations around love and rage.

Wessel provides a particularly thorough compilation of passions appropriate to musical expression in his dissertation, "The Affektenlehre in the 18th Century."

For the most recent studies on Couperin's *pièces de caractère*, see Clark and Connon, *The Mirror of Human Life*, and Moroney, "The 'Parodies' of François Couperin's Harpsichord Pieces."

Steblin's *History of Key Characteristics* is the most extensive study on the subject. Haynes's *History of Performing Pitch* also includes essential information on the complexities of matching pitch levels with tonalities in the Rhetorical period. See also Chafe, *Tonal Allegory*, and his 2014 study of tonality in the St. John Passion in chapter 5 of *J. S. Bach's Johannine Theology*. Bradley Lehman's website LaripS.com provides abundant information on his controversial Bach-Lehman temperament. For critiques and historical alternatives see O'Donnell, "Bach's Temperament," and Lindley, "Bach-Style Keyboard Tuning." In *How Equal Temperament Ruined Harmony*, Ross Duffin provides a layman's account of this complex subject. Haynes "Beyond Temperament" is an important discussion of nonkeyboard temperaments. In "The Temperament Police," a team of researchers led by Tidhar and Dixon presents recent research on digital recognition of keyboard temperaments.

There is a profusion of studies of Bach's of musical figuration and symbolism. One of the earliest was Karl Geringer's lecture "Symbolism in the Music of J. S. Bach"; Mellers, *Bach and the Dance of God*, and Tatlow's *Bach and the Riddle of the Number Alphabet* and *Bach's Numbers* provide important viewpoints. For a balanced overview of opinions, see Schulenberg "Musical Expression and Musical Rhetoric."

3

Bach's Expressive Universe

GEOFFREY BURGESS

I was taught by my teacher, Kapellmeister Bach (who is still alive), not to play Chorales just offhand, but rather following the passion [*Affect*] of the words.

—J. G. Ziegler, 1746[1]

If the mere words of an orator are capable of making our hearts cheerful or depressed, how much more is this true of music, which can depict affects in an even more lively and penetrating manner.

—G. Scheibel, 1721[2]

Imitation: Portraying and Evoking the World

The concepts of "expression" and "representation" were central to performance in Bach's day; both words had pedigrees going back well before the Baroque period and were close to inseparable—sometimes virtually synonymous. It was the same in French: the *Dictionnaire de l'Académie française* defined "expression" as "an effective and realistic representation of the passions."[3] "Representation" was also called imitation and was the key essential act in the mimetic tradition of the arts originating with Aristotle who wrote in his *Poetics*: "everybody when listening to Imitations is thrown into a corresponding state of feeling . . . when we listen to such representations we change in our soul."[4]

The basic strategy of all the arts, then, was to imitate nature (or an idealized concept of nature) and to move the audience by arousing the passions. In the seventeenth century, Bernard Lamy explained that the "common way of affecting the heart of man" was to give a "lively [that is, lifelike or vivid] sense and impression of the object of that Passion wherewith we desire he should be mov'd."[5] That is why an actor was said to be "representing" or "imitating" a passion. All the artist's experience and persuasive skills were bent to the purpose of expressing a particular passion, pleading his case much as a lawyer would in a court of law or a politician in parliament. The artist's case rested on his ability to convince the audience to accept the plausibility and relevance of each passion to the subject being expressed.

As elaborated in chapter 1, in the seventeenth and early eighteenth centuries it was commonly accepted that the passions were the point of interest, not the individual who was attempting to evoke them through his acting. In other words, "grief" was the issue, not the actor's personal anguish. So to separate "expressing" grief from "representing" it, as many modern writers have done, is misleading because, in terms of rhetoric, they amount to the same thing.[6] This is more an issue in modern English usage where "expression" reflects Romantic aesthetics and comes with a more personalized component.

"Clear running water": Schweitzer's Legacy

In 1911, when Albert Schweitzer published his remarkable book about J. S. Bach, the Romantic movement was at its zenith and had eclipsed the Aristotelian heritage of expression by means of imitation. Writing empirically and in the absence of an awareness of the Classical heritage of rhetoric, passions, or musical figures, Schweitzer found himself staring imitation in the face without an intellectual context to explain it. He could not ignore Bach's consistent use of imitation and offered many examples of both natural phenomena and physical conditions that he saw reflected in Bach's music like "clear running water."[7]

Schweitzer's contemporaries found it difficult to understand—much less accept—the idea that Bach had conceived music in terms of imitation. At the time Schweitzer was writing, Bach was valued as an intellectual composer, the creator of music of such structural perfection and spiritual richness that it transcended materialism. Many still view the literal imitations found in Bach's music as beneath his dignity, or at best inconsistent with the sublime qualities they hear in the B-minor Mass, "Erbarme dich," or the "Air on a G-string" from BWV 1068. Still, Schweitzer was determined to save Bach "from the suspicion of having done anything to pervert pure music into representative music" and challenged the view that Bach's pictorial writing arose from a "naïve materialistic conception of music."[8] But instead of denying it, or covering it up as Phillip Spitta had done in his monumental study of Bach, Schweitzer did quite the reverse and demonstrated that imitation was an essential part of Bach's compositional technique.[9] Recognizing that musicians, like poets or painters, take distinctive expressive paths, he viewed Bach primarily as a "poetic" composer and that his music was conceived declamatorily, driven by an intimate and inseparable connection to the poetic texts it sets.[10]

From an analysis of a large corpus of Bach's music, Schweitzer concluded that it was possible to arrive at a formula for the underlying principles of his expression, musical construction, and appropriate performance style. While he might have gone too far when he tried to define Bach's "complete musical language," what he demonstrated with both sensitivity and thoroughness was that Bach conceived music as imitation and evocation. Some of Schweitzer's remarks are now dated (e.g., his treatment of performance practice), but his musical analysis is insightful and has informed the approach taken here. Although we still have much to learn about applied eloquence, in the century since the appearance of Schweitzer's book we have reconstructed a context that lends plausibility to the principle of representing ideas and objects in Baroque music. Taking up the challenge of fathoming the depths of human expression contained in Bach's cantatas, we may well find ourselves humbled by Schweitzer's concluding remarks:

> We become conscious of how little of what can be observed has really been noted thus far, and how much is still to be revealed by comparative research into the whole of Bach's work, until the individuality and the perfection of the expression in his music are made clear enough to executants to influence their performances of the works.[11]

Figuring Bach's World

Having already described the function of musical figures and rhetorical tropes in chapter 2, here we will examine the way Bach operated within the Rhetorical musical language. There is an advantage to treating vocal music where the text usually provides the key to what the music is imitating. Concrete concepts served as points of departure for musical composition in the Rhetorical period. The following comment from Jean-Philippe Rameau in 1722 indicates this attitude held for both vocal and instrumental music:

> The words one sets to music always have a specific expression, either sad or happy, that one cannot avoid rendering; ... and he who does not take words for guides imagines instead a subject that holds him in much the same subjugation [*esclavage*].[12]

Significantly, Rameau implies that even where words are not involved, the composer still took a "subject" as his guide. In other words, for him there was no such thing as "absolute" music lacking what has since been labeled "extramusical" significance.

There are countless examples of where Baroque composers reused instrumental pieces in vocal works by simply adding a text to the music. These amplify the similarities between instrumental and vocal genres, and remind us that Rhetorical music, even if untexted, was conceived as Rameau indicated: a vehicle for specific ideas. In the cantata BWV 146 (*Wir müssen durch viel Trübsal*), Bach superimposed vocal parts over the unaltered instrumental parts to the second movement of the d-minor harpsichord concerto (BWV 1052). The text explains that much sorrow (*viel Trübsal*) must be endured before entering the kingdom of God. Bach obviously thought that the music was appropriate to the text, so applying the poetic idea to the concerto can help realize the meaning of the plodding repeated notes and expressive falling intervals of the opening ritornello. Still, music cannot be held down to a fixed single meaning. When he first wrote the overture to the Fourth Orchestral Suite (BWV1069), Bach may not have thought of jubilant laughter, but he must have thought that the character of what he composed lent itself to the opening line of the text of cantata BWV 110, *Unser Mund sei voll Lachens* (May our mouths be full of laughter). The same notes could represent a range of passions but usually only within a single constellation. We see this when Bach reset existing vocal pieces. The shift in connotation could be subtle, such as when he reworked the suffering and pain expressed in the first chorus of BWV 12, *Weinen, Klagen, Sorgen, Zagen*, to represent the agony of crucifixion and burial in the Crucifixus of the B-minor Mass. It could also be antithetical. Bach reworked an expression of confidence in God's promises in BWV 187 (*Es wartet alles auf dich*; aria mvt. 5, "Gott versorget alles Leben") into a prayer for God's mercy ("Qui tollis peccata mundi") in the g-minor Lutheran Mass, BWV 235/5. The meanings could also cover a wider range of passions. The music of the Agnus dei from the B-minor Mass began life in 1725 as a setting of a text about God's blessings (BWV Anh 1, 196); ten years later the same music was used for a sorrowful song of farewell ("Ach bleibst doch, mein liebster Leben") to the ascended Christ in the *Ascension Oratorio* (BWV 11, 1735), before its third incarnation as the final supplication for salvation in the late Mass setting (BWV 232, 1749).

In vocal music such as Bach's cantatas, the text is perhaps the most important, but not the only signifier of affect. Composers used the individual elements in Rhetorical music—key, tempo, melody, harmony, rhythm, text, instrumentation, etc.—in mutually supportive ways in their musical descriptions. The analyses that follow will show that for the most part, Bach followed this principle. He tended to depict joyful passions with fast music in major keys with a predominance of bright sonorities, and he set sad passions to slow tempi, minor keys, and lower timbres. Still, Bach also left many surprising, even paradoxical exceptions that seem to break from conventional usage and set challenges that continue to fascinate us and keep the performance of his music alive.

Let's first consider the general types of imitation that Bach worked with. These fall into the three categories discussed in chapter 2: *hypotyposis, pathopoeia,* and *ethopoeia*. Of these, *pathopoeia* is perhaps the most important in Bach's music and Baroque music in general. In combination with *hypotyposis, pathopoeia* constitutes the focus of this and the next chapter.

Bach the Poet, Bach the Painter

Although nowadays word painting in music is often preceded by the word "mere," in the eighteenth century, *hypotyposis* was a respectable concept. Even Hans David and Arthur Mendel in their *Bach Reader* disparaged word painting as "a kind of formula technique: a set of symbolic patterns to which Bach would recur whenever the textual situation required," and went to pains to prove that Bach's genius was never hindered by a lack of fertile imagination nor the need to fall back on convention.

> To ascribe to Bach a predominantly intellectual routine of this sort is to overestimate the importance of certain elements apparent in his music. He was neither so poorly endowed with imagination that he had to establish for himself a whole reservoir of ready-made patterns, to draw on whenever inspiration failed, nor so theoretically minded that he would heed the pedantic attempts of his contemporaries to establish music as a branch of rhetoric.[13]

Here David and Mendel are objecting to the idea that Bach used a "reservoir of ready-made patterns" that might suggest a prescribed or codified system of musical figures, or that his innate musical intuition could be reduced to an intellectual exercise. But Schweitzer's book is a clear indication of how Bach used figures very effectively, and more recently, Bartel has brought conclusive evidence to show that while the terminology for musical figures wasn't always uniform, there was both a reasonable level of agreement about their use, as well as consistency within the practice of single composers.[14]

All art, and particularly Rhetorical music, depends to some degree on convention. Potentially, passions are universally understandable. But music functions like a language and can be understood only from a specific cultural outlook. To expect modern listeners to instantly recognize the passions in Rhetorical music is much like expecting someone to understand a foreign language at a first hearing. As Schweitzer pointed out, "anyone who understands the language of a composition . . . perceives ideas in the music that do not speak directly to the uninitiated, though they are there all the time."[15] Undeniably, Bach's music operates in a very different world from ours. The difference has to do as much with the disparity between our worldview and Bach's cosmology, as changes to social organization and to the understanding of human emotions that have arisen in the intervening three centuries. A large part of the challenge of performing Bach's music today is knowing how to develop a way of rendering his imitation comprehensible and significant to modern audiences while remaining faithful to his mode of expression.

Perhaps the most essential difference between Bach's world and ours concerns spirituality and religion. Bach held to the long-standing belief in Western heritage that music was a reflection of the divinely ordered universe. He wrote that the study of thorough-bass was "to make a well-sounding harmony to the glory of God and the permissible delectation of the spirit—the aim and final reason of all music," and that when this is not observed, "there is no real music but only devilish hubbub."[16] Spiritual practice played a central role in Bach's world and influenced all his music, not just his sacred vocal works.[17] From what we know of his theology from his library and the annotations he made in his Bible, Bach was an orthodox Lutheran. The nature of his spirituality and the expression of his belief through music were specific to his Lutheran upbringing and cultural milieu. He quite literally followed in Luther's steps, living and working in some of the same places where Luther's activities, two centuries before, had led to the Reformation. As Robin Leaver has put it:

> The complex religious context and cross-currents within which Bach lived and worked, instead of simply being the external environment of his professional and personal activities, were in fact more fundamental: they formed the substance of his internalized world-view that undergirded all of his compositional output.[18]

The emotional imagery of the poetry prevalent in Bach's cantata texts was influenced by Pietism, a movement within the Lutheran church that rose in the 1670s. But at the same time as stressing the importance of personal devotion, hard-core Pietists tried to eliminate elaborate music from religious services; so rather than representing his central beliefs, Pietism for Bach formed a figurative overlay on top of traditional Lutheran theology. Many of Bach's principles (and, as we will see, some of the apparent paradoxes in his musical settings) derive from his religious basis. The principles of eloquence provide a means of bridging differences between our modern perspectives and Bach's. The rhetoric of the passions allows us to evoke enduring truths of human emotion that can inspire modern audiences and in this way approach the original meanings of Bach's music.

Bach does not seem to have disapproved of imitating natural events, nor does he seem to have felt that it was beneath his goal of composing music fitting to praise God. His imitations were often remarkably vivid and could be surprisingly worldly. Despite the long-standing suspicion that music's emotive tug could distract from devout spirituality, there was more overlap between the hedonistic world of opera and church music in the eighteenth century than pious Bach devotees care to admit. The strategies that Catholic and Protestant composers alike used to move a congregation were virtually the same as the stock of figures that charmed operagoers. As one theologian put it in 1721, "I do not understand why the opera alone should have the privilege to move us to tears, and why this is not also appropriate to the church."[19]

Word painting and *hypotyposis* can be literal. Bach's music abounds in both natural and man-made sounds. There are specific events, such as Judas discarding the silver pieces in the St. Matthew Passion imitated by the violinist "tossing off" strings of thirty-second notes, or Jesus knocking at the door painted with pizzicato string chords in movement 4 of the Advent cantata *Nun komm, der Heiden Heiland* (BWV 61), or the representation of God incarnate descending from heaven in the downwards arpeggios toward the end of the "Et in unum Dominum" movement of the B-minor Mass. Other cases of *hypotyposis* are less literal. In order to avoid producing a potentially comical effect that would have disturbed the solemnity of the Good Friday service, Bach refrained from onomatopoeia when setting the passage referring to the cock crowing in his Passion settings. The musical depictions are only barely realistic. In both St. Matthew and St. John Passion he writes angular lines outlining a seventh chord on the word *krähen* (*der Hahn krähen*) which do not sound too much like a cock's crow. They remain artistic emulations rather than exact mimicry and might better be thought of as markers rather than imitations. Bach's treatment of this movement makes the more graphic and extended imitation of Peter's tears in the agonized chromatic line that immediately follow in the Evangelist's accounts all the more moving.

Overall, Bach's painting of nature is less wide-ranging than that of some of his contemporaries. There is a total absence of barking dogs as in Vivaldi's *Four Seasons*, meowing cats (cf. Biber's *Sonata Rappresentativa*), and the birdlife that adorns the operas of Handel is, surprisingly, all but absent from Bach's vocal music. Furthermore, the depiction of the world is rarely an end in itself in Bach's music: pictorial images serve to illustrate particular passions. *Hypotyposis* helped support passionate eloquence by grounding listeners' responses in worldly experience and thereby giving them a concrete point of reference. Take for instance the aria "Bald zur Rechten, bald zur Linken" from BWV 96 (*Herr Christ, der einge Gottessohn*). The text is about indecision and the fear of going astray from the true path. Two paths are clearly etched in Bach's music. Rising phrases are answered by descending gestures; some are played by the wind instruments, others are given to the strings (Ex. 3.1).

A performance that passes over the intentionally divided nature of Bach's melodic writing in this ritornello would miss the point. A sense of confusion could be effectively conveyed with a slight hesitation between the two parts of the phrase. But indecision is only a part of this piece's message. The larger point being put across is the steadfast nature of God's guidance in the midst of human indecision. This is illustrated in the second part of the aria where the divergent motion of the instrumental parts is arrested and replaced with a series of static chords. It is instructive to compare the rhetorical strategies in this movement

Example 3.1 BWV 96/5, opening ritornello.

with another aria that represents the opposite condition—unwavering decisiveness. In the second aria in the St. John Passion, "Ich folge dir gleichfalls" (I follow you likewise), two unison flutes follow the soprano's lead in canon to represent the disciple faithfully walking in Jesus's footsteps.

Bach's *hypotyposis* could also be refined and subtle, a simple action to trigger an emotional response. In movement six in BWV 150, *Nach dir, Herr, verlanget mich*, a rising harmonic progression depicts the narrator's eyes being drawn heavenward. But more than this: each rising phrase set to the words "Mein Augen sehen stets zu dem Herrn" (My eyes always look to the Lord) takes the music into progressively distant and seemingly wondrous realms (Ex. 3.1, and Audio Ex. 3.1).

Example 3.2 Ravishing harmonies in BWV 150/6.

* *Bassoon part transposed from original notation a minor third higher than the sother parts.*

🔊 AUDIO EX. 3.1. BWV 150/6, Bach Collegium Japan, dir. Masaaki Suzuki (BIS, 1995).

From D major, the music moves through a set of remarkable progressions dwelling on F♯ major, b minor, C♯ major and f♯ minor before settling on G♯, a tritone away from the starting point, and a striking depiction of the otherworldly quality

Example 3.2 (Continued)

of the divine vision. The alluring quality of each chord is enhanced with rocking sixteenth-notes in the bassoon and hocketing violins. As we are attracted to these wondrous harmonies, we can imagine the narrator's eyes drawn to a shimmering brilliance. The harmonic movement from ♯iv back to the tonic in the second part of the aria also serves to represent the next image in the text: release from the snares of worldly trepidation.

The harmonies in BWV 150/6 bring to mind the portrayal of God's *Liebesstrahl,* or beam of love in BWV 164/4 "Ach, schmelze doch durch deinen Liebesstrahl" (Ah! Melt with Your ray of Love). This recitative is enshrouded in a harmonic instrumental halo, a device that Bach reserved for instances of profound solemnity or representations of divine presence, and specifically for the words of Jesus in his setting of the St. Matthew Passion.

The reverential heavenward gaze was a much-visited theme in Baroque religious art and shares features with the treatment of the amorous gaze of lovers in secular paintings. Le Brun's study of *ravissement* (rapture) in his *Conférence* (Fig. 3.1a) has strong resonances with two contemporary compositions. The earlier is Le Brun's own representation of Mary Magdalene, her eyes drawn upwards to inspiring rays of divine light (Fig. 3.1b). The other is a portrayal of eroticized rapture in the figure of Ariadne in Antoine Coypel's *Bacchus and Ariadne* (Fig. 3.2).[20]

Bach captured a similar transposition of a passion from a secular to a sacred context in the cantata *Komm, du süsse Todesstunde,* BWV161. In the fifth movement, "Wenn es meines Gottes Wille" (If it is my God's will), the music paints the rapture of religious ecstasy in unmistakably operatic tones. The vocal parts in this simple major-key triple-time movement are set against a backdrop of fluttering recorders (Ex. 3.3). The rest of the text refers to the poet's soul being transported to the sweet joy of heaven while his body occupies the earth. Bach's music paints the rapturous beauties of heaven with the familiar images of earthly charms. The result is a canvas of hedonistic bliss, a painting of a divine being unfurling her beauties to the world in much the same way that Handel would

Figure 3.1 a) Le Brun, *Ravissement* (ecstacy, or rapture) b) Jean Couvay, *The Penitent Magdalene,* engraving after a lost painting by Le Brun

Figure 3.2 Antoine Coypel, *Bacchus & Ariadne on the Isle of Naxos* c.1693 (detail) Philadelphia Museum of Art, Pennsylvania, PA, USA/Purchased with funds (by exchange) from the bequest of Edna M. Welsh and the gift of Mrs. R. Barclay Scull, 1990/Bridgeman Images (a color version of the entire painting can be found on the companion website).

Example 3.3 BWV 161/5, opening measures.

depict the spellbound rapture of those witnessing the apparition of a female seductress in his operas (such as "V'adoro pupille" in act 2 of *Giulio Cesare* during which Cleopatra disguised as the servant Lydia seduces the hero).

This is not the only reference to erotic and lustful topics in Bach's music. He was not above roguish behavior and raunchy humor (viz., his altercation with the bassoonist in Arnstadt), and even the Pietist poetry that he drew on for his sacred cantatas was not devoid of erotic innuendo.[21] The mystical union or marriage of the Soul and Christ was a favorite topic. This image had its origins in the Lutheran *ordo salutis* or doctrine of salvation, formulated in the second part of the seventeenth century.[22] When presented dramatically, as in a duet for soprano and bass, the mystical dialogue could take on erotic implications. The duet "Wenn kömmst du, mein Heil" in cantata *Wachet auf*, BWV 140 is an example of this tradition. This is about as close to the wind as Bach and his librettists ever dared sail in the religious cantatas.

Soprano: Wenn kömmst du, mein Heil?
Bass: Ich komme, dein Teil.
Soprano: Ich warte mit brennendem Öle.
Soprano & Bass: Eröffne den Saal
Ich öffne den Saal zum himmlischen Mahl.
Soprano: Komm, Jesu.
Bass: Ich komme, komm, liebliche Seele.

Soprano: *When are you coming, my Savior?*
Bass: *I am coming, your portion.*
Soprano: *I am waiting with burning oil.*
Soprano and Bass: *Open the hall*
I open the hall for the heavenly feast.
Soprano: *Come, Jesus!*
Bass: *Come, lovely soul!*

In this particular example, there is the added complication that both singers were male. During Bach's lifetime, prominent Lutheran theologians initiated a move to involve female singers in church music, but in all the churches where Bach worked women were still banned from participating. This meant that the soprano parts were sung by boy trebles.[23] To satisfy this convention, the love-couple in BWV 140 was represented by a boy and an adult man. Although intended to camouflage the music's erotic implications, it was not without its own complications.[24]

Onomatopoeia

In the previous examples, Bach paints by analogy: with *onomatopoeia* the imitation takes the form of a sound associated with the thing or action being depicted. In the previous chapter we gave the example of the *pianto* as a musical representation of sorrow; joy can also be expressed with the use of onomatopoeia. In *Unser Mund sei voll Lachens* (May our mouth be full of laughter) BWV 110/1, the chorus is made to laugh on an active melisma on first syllable of the word "lachens." In *Der Himmel lacht, die Erde jubilieret* (The heavens laugh, the earth rejoices) BWV 31/1, laughter is simulated instrumentally in the instrumental sinfonia that precedes another chorus where melismatic treatment results in jubilant chortling (Ex. 3.4a, b). These two choruses open cantatas written for the festivities of Christmas and Easter, so the laughter is not humorous but jubilant and celebratory.

Onomatopoeia can also involve instrumental sonorities and their associated references, such as the oboe band used to imitate shepherds' pipes in the Sinfonia to Part 2 of the Christmas Oratorio (BWV 248:II/1), or the horn calls that signal the hunt in Brandenburg Concerto 1 (BWV 1046). It can also draw from instrumental techniques. For instance, an aria from Bach's 1731 cantata *Schwingt freudig euch empor* (BWV 36) begins with the text "Auch mit gedämpften, schwachen Stimmen" (Even with muted, weak voices). Consistent with the word *gedämpften*, the violin part is marked *con sordino*.[25] Some of Bach's pictorial effects result from the coloristic qualities of combining specific tonalities and instruments. "Zerfließe, mein Herze, in Fluten der Zähren" (Melt, my heart, in floods of tears), the final aria in the St. John Passion, is in f minor. This is an extraordinary and difficult key for the two obbligato instruments—traverso and oboe da caccia. The large percentage

Example 3.4 Bach's laughter

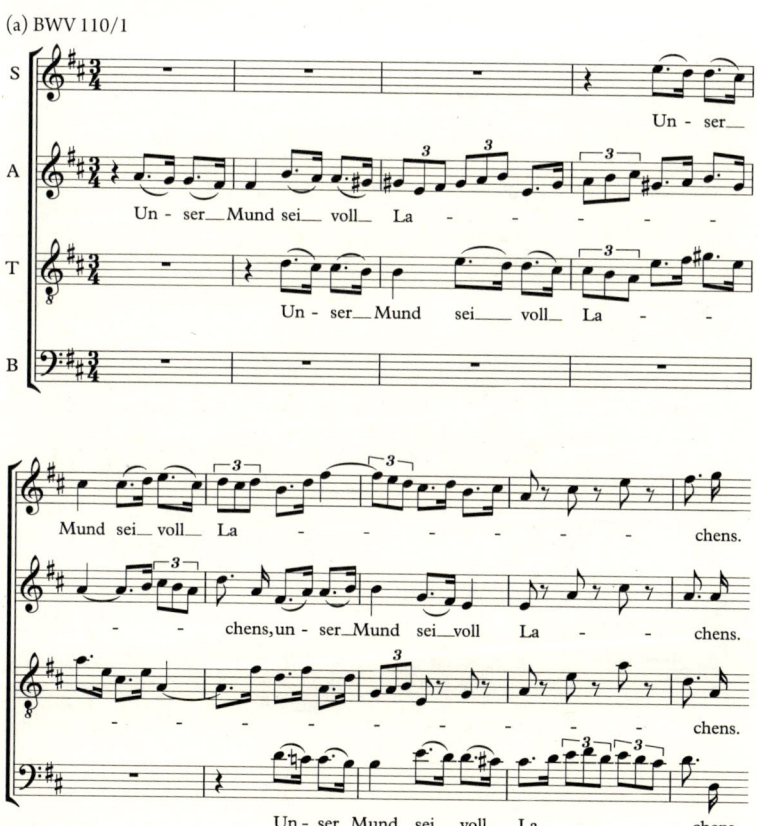

Example 3.4 (Continued)

(b) BWV 31/1

of cross-fingerings it requires the wind players to use in this key produces a covered, "tragic" sound that corresponds to the aria's desperate, almost stifled emotion.

Bach occasionally wrote disagreeable sounds by exploiting the technical limitations of instruments. In *Gott fahret auf mit Jauchzen* (BWV 43) he called for the trumpet to play notes that are normally avoided because they are not compatible with tuning systems used by other instruments. Here is the text of the first section of the bass aria:

Er ists, der ganz allein	*It is he who, quite alone,*
Die Kelter hat getreten	*Has trodden the winepress*
Voll Schmerzen, Qual und Pein.	*Full of anguish, torment, and pain.*

The trumpet's 14th harmonic (b♭2) is introduced in the ritornello, but later the almost unusably flat 7th partial (b♭1) coincides with the word *Qual* ("torment" or "agony"). If the player bends the pitch to match the other instruments, it takes on a dull and "pained" tone—an apt illustration of the agony expressed in the text (Ex. 3.5). The effect is almost nonexistent on modern trumpets equipped with valves to regulate the pitch of each note. Even in performances with "period instruments" it often sounds less extreme than it would have done in Bach's day because today most players use nonhistorical finger holes to bring this note and others like it more "in tune."

Example 3.5 Opening ritornello and use of 7th partial on "Qual" in BWV 43/7.

It might seem odd that Bach would use the preeminent instrument of majestic victory in an aria about pain, and it is understandable that he replaced the trumpet with a violin in later performances.[26] But the original instrumentation makes sense when we consider the text of the *confutatio* that uses the image of crowning the hero with garlands. Bach does not dwell on pain in the second part of the aria: rather, the sense is that pain has been victoriously overcome. In place of a complete reprise of the first section, the music ends with the reference to the triumphant crowning, and the abbreviated *confirmatio* comprises the opening instrumental ritornello that leaves behind the anguish of the 7th partial. In this way Bach was able to convey the idea of overcoming pain and also satisy the *da capo* convention.

Landscape Painting and "Paintings of Life"

There has always been a certain amount of disapproval of literal tone painting, stemming from a concern that painting every image in a text can undermine the impact of the piece's overall message. The question of what was considered worthy of artistic expression has also been the subject of continual debate. In the 1660s the French vocal authority, Benigne de Bacilly, found incessant and formulaic word painting entirely frivolous and puerile (*tout à fait badine et puerile*), while in the next century Dubos was adamant that the imitation of objects "may possibly amuse us some few moments, may even draw from us an applause of the artist's abilities in imitating, but can never raise any emotion or concern."[27] In a similar vein, Batteux divided music into two types: music that "imitates only such tones and sounds as are without passion, and answers to landscape-painting," and music that "expresses animated sounds, and such as belongs to the sentiments, and answers to paintings of life."[28] More than most other genres, landscape painting came under critical censure in the seventeenth and eighteenth centuries because, as Batteux hinted, it was often lacking in emotional content. The most highly regarded exponents, like Nicholas Poussin (1594–1665) and Claude Lorrain (ca. 1600–82), took care to bring human passion into their work. But, in much the same way that passions were seen as transpersonal emotions, the human figures these artists incorporated into their landscapes were not recognizable individuals but archetypes or allegorical figures. In Lorrain's depiction of Pysche outside Cupid's palace (Fig. 3.3), the female figure is dwarfed by the surrounding landscape. It is hard to make out any personal features, but the lone figure of Psyche gives meaning and elevates Poussin's work from an imitation of nature to a painting of life. Her posture and pensive expression are clear enough to register as emotional responses to the twilight landscape.

In line with the essential principle of imitation, music that describes inanimate objects and pieces that express passions (Batteux's "paintings of life") were both considered representations of the world—simply different aspects of the

Figure 3.3 Richard Earlom engraving from *Liber Veritatis*, vol 2, 1777 after the painting by Claude Lorrain, *Landscape with Psyche outside the Palace of Cupid*, 1664.

same reality. Descriptive painting in any medium is rarely without emotional content. Like their landscape-painter counterparts, painters in sound used the imitation of objects and natural phenomena to elicit emotional response, and the highest praise went to composers who, like Lorrain, were able to incorporate the painting of nature with the painting of life.

As we observed in the previous chapter, the imitation of movement comes more naturally to music than describing a rose, a landscape, or a facial expression. As well as painting motion, music can also imitate the effects that motion triggers (emotions), and thereby move the listener. Watching a wild sea, for instance, implies being on it, and would probably inspire strong emotions in most of us such as exhilaration mixed with unease or fear. The storm at sea was such a common trope in eighteenth-century art because it was easily understood as an illustration of internal turmoil. It was also adaptable to different contexts and could serve as an analogue to the lover in a sea of emotional distress, or to the soul of the faithful lost in a tumultuous world. Bach probably never experienced a sea storm himself (the only opportunity would have been during his visit to Lübeck in 1705, and even then he would have been a landed observer), but that did not prevent him from producing imitations using the artistic conventions of his time. Many of the same musical devices are found in musical depictions of sea storms in works from different composers and national styles. Audio Examples 3.2a and b are two instances from Leipzig and Paris.

🔊 AUDIO EX.3.2. Depictions of Storms at Sea
a) Bach, BWV 81/3, Gerald Finley with English Baroque Soloists dir. Gardiner (Soli Deo Gloria, 2009)
b) Marais, "Tempête" from *Alcyone*, act IV, Musiciens du Louvre, dir. Minkowski (Erato, 1990)

To paint these scenes, Bach and Marin Marais both used waves of rapid scales rising and falling over incessant repeated notes. Like masterpieces of landscape art, these musical paintings are peopled with passionate interest. Both are accompanied by commentaries from witnesses. In *Jesus schläft, was soll ich hoffen?* BWV 81, the tenor describes "die schäumenden Wellen von Belials Bächen/Verdoppeln die Wut" (the foaming waves of Belial's water redouble their rage), while the storm scene in Marais's *Alcyone* (1706), a model for numerous similar scenes in French opera, includes a chorus of sailors who recount their emotions in the midst of the raging sea. While Marais's chorus is unable to resist the force of nature as the opera's hero drowns, in the middle section of Bach's aria the tenor rises above the waves "like a rock" in islands of recitative.

In the end it seems that for these Baroque composers, imitating the foaming waves on a wild sea was not so different from imitating the feeling of anxiety. As soon as we start trying to isolate the outside physical descriptions from internal emotional states, the line between them starts to blur. Like other Baroque composers, Bach's paintings of the natural world often serve as external manifestations of an internal passionate world, and like the figures in a landscape painting, the vocalists in his works are not always identifiable individuals. His music dramas such as the Coffee Cantata (*Schweigt stille, plaudert nicht*, BWV 211) are populated by lifelike characters, and the Passions and oratorios narrate a sequence of events involving recognizable people. The sacred cantatas, on the other hand, draw from a stock of allegorical and mythological figures—the Daughter of Zion, Pan and Phoebus—symbolic entities like the Soul, or iconic figures of the Christian faith. But even where the singer portrays a specific identity, it is usually not crucial to identify the character. It is more important for the audience to be moved by the passions and the moral concepts aroused by the performance than to identify with the vocalists as individuals. As Gardiner put it, the singers in Bach's cantatas are proxies for human beings going through specific crises.[29] *Pathopoeia*, then, remained Bach's dominant rhetorical strategy, overshadowing the use of character studies, or *ethopoeia*. This is one important difference between Bach's cantatas and Baroque opera where the arias are assigned to characters in a fictitious drama and focus on the character as much as the passionate state she or he is going through.

Sometimes Bach used the same performer to negotiate different roles. This can be confusing for modern audiences because the conventions Bach followed are not always compatible with our sense of how drama works, and they consequently seem to undermine the work's credibility. In Bach's own performances of his

Passion settings, the same vocalist sang the role of Evangelist and the tenor arias. This distribution was not only a practical expedient required by the number of competent singers available, it has bearing on the work's message. The Evangelist starts out recounting the story in matter-of-fact recitative as a disinterested bystander, but at the end of Part 1 of the St. John Passion he becomes engaged in the plight of the drama's protagonists. Drawn into the drama, he breaks down in an extended chromatic melisma describing Peter's tears ("und weinete bitterlich" [and wept bitterly]). He then identifies further with Peter's distress in an aria. When he begins "Ach mein Sinn" (Alas my mind), it is unclear whose words he is singing, and which role he is playing. Does he become Peter, or is he singing a commentary on the Passion narrative? His identity is uncertain up to the last line of the aria text when Peter is referred to in the third person—"Weil *der Knecht* den Herrn verleugnet hat" (Since *the servant* has denied the Lord). This clarifies that it is not Peter expressing his personal pain. We then realize that the Evangelist-tenor stands in for anyone experiencing Peter's plight, and the aria is thus a meditation on Peter's condition, and that "*der Knecht*" could be anyone. This process of empathy, of being drawn into the drama, plays out the response that Bach solicited from his listeners, a process that is only partially realized when (as is usually the case today) the Evangelist's recitative and the aria are sung by two different singers. In this case, reviving the practice of one-to-a-part performance provides an opportunity to reevaluate Bach's sense of dramaturgy.

In the same way that visual artists created an affective painting by balancing landscape with passion, composers needed to maintain a balance between pictorialism on individual words and the overriding idea of the text that they were setting. In the late seventeenth century Roger North made the following observations, no doubt in response to the fashion for exaggerated madrigalisms and localized word painting that distracted from the central passion of a given piece:

> And that fancy of imitating the formes of things by sounds is very apt to run out too farr; as when anything is sayd to *rise*, the musick must needs advance in the scale, which comonly proves too short to reach the skyes, tho' a voice is made almost to crack, and the air is wounded almost to death, yet it will come short; and on the other side going downe into gloomy vaults, wee begin to grumble, and double DD is not deep enough to reach the pitt of Hell. All these humours corrupt the musick, and answer no reasonable intent.[30]

North lived at a time when the practice of setting individual words in sequence was giving way to a more integrated approach where one principal passion was taken as the main focus for an entire aria. There are situations where the earlier treatment remained in use. For instance, the painting of individual words continued to be a hallmark of mad scenes, where a breakdown of logic was used to depict insane leaps from one emotional extreme to another. To quote North again:

> When an unfortunate person says—"they laugh at my dolorous complaints," the composer, who ought to assume the caracter of greif, falls a laughing, *a. a. a. a.*, and so spins out a devision of divers measures upon that word *laugh*, and then falls abruptly into dolour, which he aggravates with some exotick flatt; whereas in truth the whole poem ought to have a malencholy and querolous cast, and that's enough.[31]

The more coherent style of text setting advocated by North was a consequence of the move from the last decades of the seventeenth century to create broader compositional structures with a greater sense of unity, which in turn allowed ideas to be developed more extensively. Bach's earliest cantatas written for Mülhausen and Arnstadt are backward-looking in this respect. Both of these towns were conservative and reforms to liturgical practices were slow to take effect. Salomon Frank (1659–1725), secretary to the council of Weimar, supplied the texts to at least twelve of Bach's cantatas composed between 1714 and 1716, including *Ich hatte viel Bekümmernis* (BWV 21). These are made up mostly of biblical quotations and hymns that Bach often treated in the older word-by-word style of text setting. Already in 1720 when Bach presented Cantata 21 for his audition in Hamburg, Mattheson ridiculed it as démodé.[32] From around that time, "textual myopia" and abrupt contrasts like the ones North complained about were to become increasingly rare in Bach's music. As well as following general trends in musical text setting, this shift was also in response to the reforms of the poet and theologian Erdmann Neumeister (1671–1756). Bringing the Lutheran cantata in line with his reforms in homiletic practice, Neumeister introduced aria texts that, like sermons, were glosses or mediations on the scriptures. When setting texts of this type, Bach would focus on one overriding idea, image, or passion in each clearly defined section. Where the text of an aria was built on *antithesis*, he created the means to explain the relationship of opposites in the music. (More about this in chapter 4.)

Hypotyposis can be so vivid that it obliterates the deeper significance of the text. Dubos detected this imbalance in the work of a "too considerable" number of musicians. In the following quotation he used "sentiment" to refer to "the first ideas which rise in the soul, upon its receiving the impression of some lively passion":

> If they set to music, for example, the verse of the psalm *The Lord said unto my Lord*, which begins with these words, *he shall drink of the brook in the way*, they dwell entirely upon the expression of the rapidity of the brook in its course, without attending to the sense of the verse, which contains a prophecy on the passion of Christ. And yet the expression of a word

can never affect us as much as that of a sentiment.... If a musician pays some regard to the expression of a word, he ought to do it without losing sight of the general purport of the phrase which he has set to music.[33]

Dubos's discussion of the image of the flowing brook (from Psalm 110 v. 7) matches numerous arias by Bach. In BWV 26/2 it is easy to hear a stream in the liquid sixteenth notes of the flute part, while the isolated notes in the bass might represent the drops of rain in the summer shower mentioned later in the text (see Ex. 3.6a, b).

So schnell ein rauschend Wasser schießt	As swiftly as rushing water shoots forth
So eilen unser Lebenstage.	Do the days of our life run by.
Die Zeit vergeht, die Stunden eilen.	Time passes away, hours run by
Wie sich die Tropfen plötzlich teilen,	Just as the drops suddenly divide
Wenn alles in den Abgrund schießt.	When everything shoots into the depths.

Example 3.6 BWV 26/2 a) opening ritornello b) bars 33-36.

However, looking closer at the text, we realize that the aria is not only about rushing water. That serves as a metaphor for the speed of passing time. The "general purport" or "sentiment" of the text, the thing to which the performer must draw the listener's attention, is a cautionary message on life's fleeting nature: in the words of the opening line of the cantata *Ach wie flüchtig, ach wie nichtig* (Ah, how fleeting, ah how insignificant). In this light, the performer approaching this first aria should make sure that the tempo is brisk enough to illustrate swift running water, but also find a way to convey the idea of transience. The fleeting quality of life takes time to express in music, and this aria is a particularly protracted example of arrested time. Still, there are details in the instrumental writing that can suggest transience, such as the frequent up-turned phrase endings. Usually, the highest notes of the phrase would be emphasized, but here it would be more in keeping with the sentiment if they dissolved into thin air "just as the days of our life run by."

Further Reading

The concept of mimesis in Western culture is treated in a number of important works, including Auerbach, *Mimesis: The Representation of Reality in Western Literature*, Gebauer and Wulf, *Mimesis: Culture–Art–Society*, and Juslin, "From Mimesis to Catharsis." Montagu's *Expression of the Passions* provides a useful précis and interpretation of Le Brun's theories of the visual representation of the passions. Several essays in the recent volume *Representing the Passions* edited by Richard Meyer give pertinent critical evaluations of seventeenth- and eighteenth-century *Affektenlehre*.

The first version of Schweitzer's work on Bach appeared in French in 1905. This discussion is based on Ernest Newman's English translation of the expanded German version (Leipzig: Breitkopf und Härtel, 1911).

The Cantatas of J. S. Bach by Alfred Dürr is an indispensible guide. Unless otherwise indicated, all texts and translations are based on the revised English translation of 2005. Raymond Erickson's *The Worlds of Johann Sebastian Bach* is an excellent anthology on various aspects of Bach's life and work, including essays on religious, social, and musical contexts. John Eliot Gardiner's recent book *Bach: Music in the Castle of Heaven* is a personal interpretation written from the perspective of a prominent performer of Bach. The distribution of vocal parts in Bach's Passions is discussed by John Butt in *Bach's Dialogue with Modernity*.

4

Bach's Inner World

GEOFFREY BURGESS

> Speak! Bach, Graupner, Handel, Heinichen, Hurlebusch, Keiser, Stöltzel, Telemann and everyone else in today's world who knows how to move hearts through the art of music.
> —Mattheson, 1728[1]

> We must first feel [emotions] ourselves, for there is no attaining a proper sense of them from any system or body of Rules.
> —Batteux, 1747[2]

General and Particular Expression

In most of the music discussed in this book, passions are treated as static as opposed to continuous and developing. Capturing the pure essence of each passion or affect was prioritized over showing the movement from one to another. Like a painting that arrests a single moment, an individual aria or instrumental movement in the Rhetorical style captures a particular passionate state in a specific situation. The drama of Baroque operas and cantatas is built up from the sequence of alternately raising and quelling contrasting passions. Like an actor, an opera singer had to be able to represent anger in one scene, jealousy in the next, and compassion in another. The idea of expressing affects in this way is almost anathema to our fast-paced modern lives where everything is about change, but learning to appreciate the arrested emotional states of Baroque music has rewards that can be surprising and reassuring.

The concept of a single affect should not be taken as a hard-and-fast rule for all Rhetorical music. Over the course of the eighteenth century as the concept of art evolved from imitating an idealized concept of nature to more realistic representations, the idea of portraying distinct and immutable passions in isolation gave way to a more fluid interplay between emotional states. This also impacted the single-affect theory.[3] Already in the middle of the eighteenth century Quantz noted that "in most pieces the passions are constantly changing,"[4] and later in 1795 C. G. Körner commented, that "if the composer . . . imitates [only] a single passion he will depart from realism, for the soul experiences nothing but variety and constant change."[5] By the nineteenth century the distinct passion theory was well on the way to breaking down. Bach stands somewhere midflow in the course of this evolution.

Instead of viewing artworks from the Rhetorical era as expressing a single passion, it is perhaps more meaningful to think of them being centered around a predominant passion, with others being introduced to provide support, clarification, or contrast. In the visual arts, the "principal passion" or "general passion" (what Le Brun called *l'expression générale et particulière*) is the initial impression one gains at the first glance of a picture or sculpture.[6] Take Gian Lorenzo Bernini's *Ecstasy of St. Teresa* (1645–52). Here the principal passion seems to be the pain of ecstasy, but the two figures are undergoing quite different individual experiences (see fig. 4.1). The seraph is as important as the saint herself and offers a different perspective on the principal passion. With a joyful expression the seraph's presence reassures the viewer that what the swooning Teresa is experiencing is indeed positive.

A number of writers applied the idea of basing a musical composition on a unifying principal passion. Andreas Werckmeister mentioned it in 1700, and in 1708 J. G. Walther advised authors to hold to the principal passion even if some words contradicted it.[7] Mauritius Vogt recommended that when there are no clear affective words, the performer should try to grasp the "sense of the text [as a whole]."[8] The same principle was probably behind Mattheson's observation

Figure 4.1 Bernini, *Ecstasy of St. Teresa* (photo by Sailko)

that an aria should be "nothing else but a clear, thought-provoking scriptural text and axiom with a certain affection," it should comprise at least two or three sentences making up a paragraph, and in that way combine different ideas around the principal subject.[9] This is not so different from Rousseau's definition of an aria (published 1768) in which he explained how the treatment of an overriding passion from different perspectives in visual art might operate in music:

> [Aria texts] do not constitute a sequential narration; they paint either a *tableau* that should be seen from differing points of view, or a passion [*sentiment*] in which the heart indulges, and from which it is unable to detach itself (so to speak); the different phrases of the aria being nothing more than various ways of visualizing one and the same image. It is for this reason that an aria must have but one single subject. Of course, it is these repetitions of an imitation that at first could not move you, these repeated onslaughts, that finally sway you, agitate you, and carry you out of yourself.[10]

Baroque composers used various techniques to integrate different points of view within a single musical movement. The most obvious is in the treatment of the middle section or *confutatio* of *da capo* arias. In a verbal discourse the *confutatio* is where the speaker considers possible opposing arguments, and systematically refutes each in turn ("Others may feel . . .," "It might be argued . . .," "But let us consider the exception . . ."). These perspectives qualify and bolster rather than overturn the central argument. In musical terms, the *confutatio* also signals contrast, usually of passion, often of key, and sometimes of meter and tempo. The aria "Komm, mein Jesu, und erquicke" (Come my Jesus and replenish me) from *Ich hatte viel Bekümmerniss*, BWV 21, demonstrates this. The duet takes the form of a dialogue between the Soul and Jesus (soprano and bass). In the first section the Soul beckons to Jesus but is soon full of doubt. When the Soul acknowledges "Ach, Jesu, durchsüße mir Seele und Herze!" (Ah, Jesus, thoroughly sweeten my soul and heart!), the music takes on a more joyful gait; the meter shifts to $\frac{3}{8}$, and the tonality gravitates to the subdominant. After this, any further doubts are brushed aside. The *da capo* moves back to common time and the walking bass to restate the opening musical subject and text.

Reading Bach's Passions

Mattheson remarked, "we rightly ought to seek the widest use of truly joyous music . . . in the praise of God and in ever-jubilant gratitude for his all-embracing and innumerable blessings."[11] So it is not surprising to discover that the exaltation of God constitutes the largest single category of movements (totaling between eighty and ninety) in Bach's church cantatas. Bach's annotations in his copy of the Calov

Bible also attest to the importance he placed on the praise of God in his musical practice.[12]

Joyful praise is most often characterized by major keys, moderately lively tempos, and euphoric melismas on the words like *loben* (to praise) and *singen* (to sing); the presence of trumpets and drums adds to the victorious jubilation. The examples of joyous laughter in BWV 110 (*Unser Mund sei voll Lachens*) and 31 (*Der Himmel lacht, die Erde jubilieret*) mentioned in the previous chapter are prime examples in this category. Others include the opening chorus of Part 1 of the Christmas Oratorio (BWV 248:I/1) "Jauchzet, frohlocket" (Shout for joy, exalt); the chorale "Sei Lob und Preis mit Ehren" (Blessing and praise with honor) in *Ihr Menschen rühmet Gottes Liebe* (BWV 167); and the opening chorus in the Ascension Oratorio (BWV 11) "Lobet Gott in seinen Reichen" (Praise God in his kingdoms). The first movement of cantata BWV 28 (*Gottlob! nun geht das Jahr zu Ende*) is also built around this constellation of passions. In addition to the emphasis of the first word *Gottlob!* (Praise God!) through repetition and prolongation of the second syllable *lob* (= praise), the second part of the aria emphasizes the words "*fro*hes Danklied" (joyful song of thanks) and "ge*danken*" (remember) with extended passagework on the italicized syllables. However, this differs from other examples as it is a solo aria in a minor key, both factors that give a more intimate sense to the tone of jubilation.

Other celebratory choruses inflect the primary passion of praise in different ways. Dotted rhythms in the continuo part to the bass aria BWV 31/4, "Fürst des Lebens! starker Streiter" (Prince of Life, strong fighter) add a martial undertone and sense of amazement. "Lobe, Zion, deinen Gott" (Zion, praise your God, BWV 190/3) is an aria for alto accompanied by strings and continuo. This scoring provides contrast from the opening chorus, also a joyous celebratory movement "Singet dem Herrn" (Sing to the Lord), and the string texture provides a suitable setting for the image of God as shepherd introduced later in the text.

Although there are fewer movements centered on negative passions in Bach's cantatas, being more complex, these often call for more elaborate musical techniques and require more careful scrutiny. In these movements the concept of passion constellations can be particularly helpful to explain Bach's musical elaboration of the text.

In the tenor aria in *Ich glaube, lieber Herr, hilf meinem Unglauben*, BWV 109 (Ex. 4.1), the keywords *zweifelhaftig* (doubtful) and *geängstigt* (anxious) represent negative emotions that occur regularly in religious homilies but are hard to capture in musical discourse, and accordingly do not appear in Mattheson's list (see Table 2.1 in ch. 2).

Wie zweifelhaftig ist mein Hoffen,	*How full of doubt is my hope,*
Wie wanket mein geängstigt Herz!	*How my anxious heart wavers!*

Example 4.1 BWV 109/3, from bar 5

Bach's setting of the tenor aria is in e minor, which Mattheson described as "pensive and grieved" (see Table 2.1, ch. 2). This approximates sadness, so can be grouped with the second negative passion constellation (see Table 2.2, ch. 2). The expanding melodic gestures in the first violin part search for resolution but are unfulfilled as they come to rest on unstable dissonant appoggiaturas. This, together with dotted rhythms and trills convey a sense of restlessness—another passion in the sad constellation—and add to the sense of anxious tension. Bach added to his portrait of doubt by writing a contemplative vocal line at odds with the motion of the accompaniment. The singer seems unable to decide how to respond to the instruments. Only at the cadences are voice and accompaniment synchronized. A performance that ignores these subtle indications of discomfort might not capture the music's message of anxiety and distress.

Pieces that involve similar musical ingredients are likely to express similar passions. There are strong parallels between BWV 109/3 and the tenor aria "Ach, mein Sinn" from the end of Part 1 of the St. John Passion (BWV 245/13) (Ex. 4.2). Here the key is f♯ minor. Mattheson, one of the only composers to define the characteristics of this rarely used key, felt it evoked "languid, and lovesick" emotions, so not too far removed from the emotive connotations of e minor, and perhaps closer to dejection—another emotion belonging to the second negative passion constellation. Dotted rhythms again give the music a halting, breathless quality, and the high degree of dissonance maintained right up to the grating ♯7-8 appoggiatura on the final chord adds to the sense of anxious restlessness. The active sixteenth notes, awkward melodic intervals, and dotted rhythms all seem to call for an intentionally lumbering, disjointed style of delivery. This reading of the gestural language of the music is right in line with the sentiments expressed in the text that relates Peter's anxiety as he realizes he has betrayed Jesus.

Ach, mein Sinn,	*Alas, my mind,*
Wo willt du endlich hin,	*Where will you flee at last,*
Wo soll ich mich erquicken?	*Where shall I find refreshment?*

Performers approaching this set of pieces might discover that there is a thin line dividing anxiety and agitated distress from heroic affirmation. When the rhythms are too active, and the singer is a little too comfortable with the melismas, the effect can become a heroic bravura display rather than a doubtful and soul-wrenching experience. Similar musical features and passionate representation occur in the alto aria in *Du Friedefürst, Herr Jesu Christ*, BWV 116.

Example 4.2 BWV 245/13, opening ritornello

Again the key is the trepidatious f♯ minor, but here the insecure chromatic passages and special vocal techniques, including a *tremolo* marked on the word *Angst* (anguish), create an even more intense representation of frustrated anxiety (Ex. 4.3).

Ach, unaussprechlich ist die Not	*Ah, unspeakable is the distress*
Und des erzürnten Richters Dräuen!	*And the increased judge's threats!*

Example 4.3 BWV 116/2, opening, and vocal entry

Perhaps the most remarkable effect in this aria is the way Bach set the idea of speechlessness (not an easy concept to convey in a vocal performance!). The alto seems only to be able to utter "Ach!" before losing his voice, and the oboe d'amore completes his phrase. This is not just a compositional nicety: the performance can make sense of the effect by making it really happen. The vocalist could subtly gesture to the oboist, or perhaps suddenly break off the "Ach!" rather than melting into the tone of the oboe.

Fear and *Tremolo*

One emotion that music can capture particularly well is fear. In the seventeenth and eighteenth centuries this was typically depicted with the *tremolo*. In BWV116/2 the technique appears on the word *Angst*, but the musical technique also had symbolic connections with trembling, shivering, fear, awe, death, grief, and weakness.[13] We can get an idea of how *tremolo* on string and woodwind instruments sounded from the tremulant mechanism on Baroque organs that produced a regular undulation in the tone in one of two ways. The first was the result of a fluctuation in the wind supply, the second by the beating of two ranks of pipes intentionally set slightly out of tune from each other. Ultimately, both organ and instrumental *tremolo* emulated the tremble that the human voice takes on in heightened emotional states. Eighteenth-century *tremolo* resembles a breath- or bow-vibrato, but it was used as a figurative technique with distinctive expressive connotations. Vibrato on the other hand, can provide an effective veneer of beauty and semblance of expressivity, but it loses its ability to evoke specific emotions when applied indiscriminately as is often the case in modern performance (see chapter 6).

A defining characteristic of the *tremolo* was that it was rhythmically regular. To have the appropriate effect, *tremolo* requires the music to be at a tempo where the separate pulses are audible, but not so slow that they take on their own individuality rather than serve as oscillations coloring a single sustained note. In string and wind music, Bach notated the separate beats of *tremolo* as eighth- or sixteenth-notes, and frequently (but not always) under a slur. Audio Example 4.1 is a particularly moving rendering of *tremolo* in the final aria from the St. John Passion, "Zerfließe mein Herz in Fluten der Zähren" (Dissolve, my heart, in floods of tears), where it functions as a vivid imitation of sobbing. Bach notated the *tremolo* rhythmically in the instrumental parts, but in the soprano part book he marked a wavy line on the word *Tod* (death).

🔊 AUDIO EX. 4.1. "Zerfließe mein Herz," from the St. John Passion, Julianne Baird, Smithsonian Players, dir. K. Slowik (Smithsonian, 1989)

As the singer describes the horrors of the Day of Judgment in the dramatic recitative in mvt. 9 of *Wachtet! betet!* BWV 70, a subterranean rumble of pulsating repeated bass notes announces the world in collapse. The *tremolo* ceases once the text turns to the more positive images—"Jedoch, es gehet meiner Seelen / Ein Freudenschein ein Licht des Trostes auf" (Ah, yes, already to my spirit a light appears to comfort my fears). The meaning of the repeated notes in the bass is now clear. As heard in Audio Example 4.2, they paint not only the trembling earth but the sense of underlying fear.

🔊 AUDIO EX. 4.2. BWV 70/9 English Baroque Soloists, dir. Gardiner (Soli Deo Gloria, 2009)

Recognizing the *tremolo* as a musical figure with specific affective associations is important, when (as often happens) it is not notated or notated in abbreviated form. Bach was not inclined to write out something if he knew that performers already knew what to do. There are passages, such as in BWV 70/9, where it looks like Bach intended *tremolo* but the repeated notes lack slurs. This also happens in

BWV 46/3, 60/1, 114/1, and 124/3. Since all of these instances relate to fearful situations, it would have been easy for Bach to neglect to mark the slurs, knowing that his musicians would recognize the affect and perform the repeated notes as a *tremolo*.

Antithesis: At Odds with Oneself

In chapter 2 we touched briefly on the symbolism of the Cross. Conceptually, this is an example of the figure of speech known as *antithesis*. The masters of antithesis were the metaphysical poets of Elizabethan England. Shakespeare's sonnets often begin with negative passions, only to resolve the tension in the final lines by an about-face and a contradictory counterposition.

German Baroque art also nurtured an intense involvement in this rhetorical ploy. The paradoxical contradiction that through death comes life encapsulates one of the Christian church's central mysteries, and was a concept rehearsed countless times in Lutheran poetry. As Tisch-Wackernagel has explained, "underneath massed conceits and stylistic disintegration there glows a desire to announce truths transcending human utterance and therefore straining the language to breaking-point."[14] Rooted in a Cartesian worldview with its split between materiality and human psyche, the German Baroque "embraced dichotomy and tensions as well as reconciliation of polar opposites."[15] These issues surface in sacred poetry concerned with the peculiarly Lutheran paradox that has been called the "enthusiasm for the immediacy of eternity in each finite moment."[16] This reconciliation to face death "with heroic calm" is exemplified in "Gedanken über der Zeit" by Paul Fleming (1609–40). Probing the boundary between life and death, Fleming's influential poem impacted later writings that also address mortality and the acceptance of the afterlife. That poem is a beautiful example of playing with close homonyms (*Zeit, seit*) and rhyming antitheses (*geboren, verloren*) to reinforce the paradoxical nature of mortal temporality.

> *Gedanken über der Zeit*
> Ihr lebet in der Zeit und kennt doch keine Zeit;
> so wißt, ihr Menschen, nicht von und in was ihr seid.
> Diß wißt ihr, daß ihr seid in einer Zeit geboren
> und daß ihr werdet auch in einer Zeit verloren.
> Was aber war die Zeit, die euch in sich gebracht?
> Und was wird diese sein, die euch zu nichts mehr macht?
> Die Zeit ist was und nichts, der Mensch in gleichem Falle,
> doch was dasselbe was und nichts sei, zweifeln alle.
> Die Zeit, die stirbt in sich und zeugt sich auch aus sich.
> Diß kömmt aus mir und dir, von dem du bist und ich.
> Der Mensch ist in der Zeit; sie ist in ihm ingleichen,
> doch aber muß der Mensch, wenn sie noch bleibet, weichen.

Die Zeit ist, was ihr seid, und ihr seid, was die Zeit,
nur daß ihr Wenger noch, als was die Zeit ist, seid.
Ach daß doch jene Zeit, die ohne Zeit ist, käme
und uns aus dieser Zeit in ihre Zeiten nähme,
und aus uns selbsten uns, daß wir gleich könten sein, wie
der itzt jener Zeit, die keine Zeit geht ein![17]

Thoughts on Time
You live within Time and yet know not Time,
Therefore, you people, you know not from and of what you are.
This you know: that you are born in a particular Time
and that you will be lost in a particular Time.
What, however, was the Time that bore you?
And what is this thing that will make you into nothing?
Time is what is and is not; Man the same.
However, what likewise is and is not, all doubt.
Time, which dies in itself and manifests itself in itself
comes out of me and you, out of that which is you and I.
Man is within Time: Time is within man,
but Man, when Time stays, must advance.
Time is what you are, and what you are is Time,
but you are less than that which is Time.
Ah, if only that Time which is without Time would come
And draw us out of this Time into its Time,
and out of ourselves, that we could instantly be
in that Time into which no Time can enter.

If Bach did not know this poem, he was certainly familiar with other examples of Fleming's work, such as the famous hymn "In allen meinen Taten" (In all that I do) which he used in three of his cantatas (BWV 13, 44, and the eponymous BWV 97). The expression of joyful anticipation of death, of the rewards for suffering, likewise permeates the Lutheran texts from which Bach took inspiration. As an example, let us consider the opening chorus of BWV 103.

Ihr werdet weinen und heulen, aber die Welt wird sich freuen.	You shall weep and lament, but the world shall rejoice.
Arioso [bass]: Ihr aber werdet traurig sein.	Now you shall be sorrowful.
Doch eure Traurigkeit soll in Freude verkehret werden.	Yet your sorrow shall be turned into joy.
	—John 16:20

Two musical figures predominate (see example 4.4a and b). The first, the *corta*, is a rhythmic figure comprising three notes in which one note's duration equals the sum of the other two (here an eighth and two sixteenths). There are literally hundreds of motives based on the *corta*. Schweitzer called it "the most extravagant of all the motives of joy."[18] The second figure, the *passus duriusculus*, is a chromatic line closely connected to the *pianto* and, like it, is associated with grief. The *corta* predominates throughout the introduction, but when the singers enter, the instruments switch to the grief figure—more often descending, but sometimes rising. The two gestures continue in antithesis, following the shifts in the text.

Example 4.4 Two figures in BWV 103/1 a) *corta* b) *passus duriusculus*

Another instance of antithesis is seen in the opening chorus in BWV 50, which takes its text from Revelation 12:10:

Nun ist das Heil und die Kraft und das Reich und die Macht unsers Gottes seines Christus worden, weil der verworfen ist, der sie verklagete Tag und Nacht vor Gott.	Now the salvation and the power and the kingdom and the might of our God and his Christ have come, for he who accused them day and night before God is cast down.

This is a stand-alone chorus written for the feast of Michaelmas. The eight-part setting draws on a clamor of jubilant instruments that fill the music with majesty, power, and celebration. "Like a voice shouting across the heavens" (the way the quoted passage is introduced in the Bible), the vocal bass in the first chorus bellow forth the text to a rising subject—what rhetoricians termed *anabasis*. The second chorus enters singing an inversion of the subject, a descending figure, or *catabasis* (Ex. 4.5). These two antithetical figures stand out and highlight the central message of the text: "We can *raise* our voices in celebration because our accuser is sent *down*."

Example 4.5 *Anabasis* and *catabasis* in BWV 50/1

The full text has already been heard, but just in case the congregation missed the message, Bach added additional clues to the meaning of the antithesis. There is a marked distinction in his treatment of the words *Gott* (God) and *verworfen* (to cast down). *Gott* is given dependable long notes; *verworfen* is sung to active melismas that seem to gleefully jeer at the fallen angel.

Occasionally, rather than inventing different musical figures, Bach chose to create antithesis by specifying contrasting styles of performance. The "Et in unum Dominum" (And in one Lord) in the B-minor Mass (BWV 232) begins with two antithetical styles of elocution. The text affirms the doctrine of the dual nature of divinity in spirit and flesh. Appropriately, Bach sets it as a duet. It is equally fitting that the two instrumental treble lines in the ritornello play the same figure in close canon. But instead of being an exact imitation, they are distinguished in the details of *elocutio*: the upper part is marked with staccato dots, the lower part echoes but with the last notes slurred. This distinction is maintained clearly in the autograph score (see extracts in Ex. 4.6) for all of the reiterations of this figure up to the last part of the duet where the setting turns to the second portion of the text describing the Incarnation. At this point the canon is modified. In bar 58 the imitation is now between the paired voices and treble instruments, each pair performing the slurred version of the opening figure in parallel sixths. Twelve bars from the end of the movement the figure is heard for the last time in the instruments, reconfigured in harmonious contrary motion. The way the antithesis expressed in the opening canon gradually coalesces into a unified articulation acts as a metaphor for the dual nature of divinity fused in the person of Jesus. This progression toward resolution is effective only when the antithesis at the beginning of the duet is brought out in performance.

Example 4.6 "Et in unum Dominum" from the B-minor Mass, BWV 232

(a) opening

Example 4.6 (Continued)

(b) from bar 70

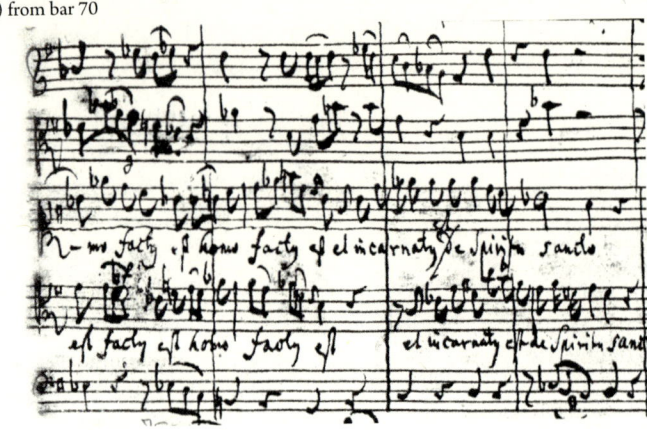

Bach frequently crafted contrast in his musical settings even where the text gives little indication of antithesis. The text of the first aria in BWV 199 *Mein Herz schwimmt in Blut* (My heart swims in blood) comprises three strophes of three lines. Each strophe lingers on images of weeping. Bach builds a *confutatio* by intensifying the gestures heard in the *exordium* with chromatic alteration and modulation. The music then breaks off, and the third strophe is set as a *secco* recitative. Even though the text focuses almost obsessively on one passion, the music of this mini-*scena* provides strong and dramatic antithesis.

On the page, many Baroque aria texts make dramatic reversals and end, like a Shakespearean sonnet, with a passion that is antithetical to the opening. But the *da capo* convention imposed a return to the initial passion after the *confutatio*. The repetition of the opening music reinforces the original point and draws the argumentation to a conclusion with any differences reconciled. But the *da capo* convention occasionally produced non sequiturs. In the opening Adagio section of the first aria in the wedding cantata BWV 202, *Weichet nur*, Bach focuses on the slow awakening of the brooding shadows, frosts, and tempests of winter ("betrübte Schatten, Frost und Winde"). With the entry of Flora's mirth in the second part of the aria ("Florens Lust will der Brust nichts als frohes Glück verstatten," Flora's joys will grant the breast naught but sheer delight), the setting amplifies the antithesis with a tempo change to Andante, three-part texture, and lighter skipping gestures. The full *da capo* is restated, but the next recitative confirms that the winter has yielded to Flora's mirth, so logically, the *da capo* takes a step backwards. The real story is told by just *exordium* and *confutatio*.

There is a higher percentage of through-composed and modified *da capo* arias in Bach's output than in contemporary opera where exact repeats are more frequent. The result is that in place of sectionalized contrasts, antithesis in Bach's works often permeates the entire aria, and reconciliation is a more continuous process. In *Meine Säufzer, meine Tränen* (BWV 13), the text of the fifth movement contrasts "Ächzen und erbärmlich Weinen" (Moaning and pitiful weeping) with the joy of those who seek comfort by looking to heaven. Bach already built antithesis into the instrumental *exordium* where the downcast sighs contrast with uplifting gestures (Ex. 4.7a and b). Other composers might have taken the line "Aber wer gen Himmel siehet" (Yet he who looks toward heaven) as a cue for an antithetical *confutatio*, but Bach does not interrupt the even flow of the walking bass, although he adjusted its contour to a diatonic line rather than the chromaticism of the opening bars. He also maintains continuity by using the same motivic material as in the *exordium*, but he evokes optimism by isolating and extending the heavenward thirty-second-note gestures, giving them flight from the sighing motif.

Example 4.7 BWV 13/5 a) opening b) B section, beginning in bar 38

Polyphonies of Passions: Passions in Polyphony

In some arias Bach composed abrupt changes of tone to set sequences of contrasting passions. In BWV 139, *Wohl dem, der sich auf seinen Gott*, the text of the bass aria presents three disparate passions:

[A] Das Unglück schlägt auf allen
    Seiten
  Um miche in zentnerschweres Band.
[B] Doch plötzlich erscheinet die
    helfende Hand.
[C] Mir scheint des Trostes Licht von
    weiten.
Da lern ich erst, daß Gott allein
Der Menschen bester Freund muß sein.

[A] *Misfortune throws around me*
    on all sides
  A hundred-weight bond;
[B] *Yet suddenly the helping hand*
    appears.
[C] *Comfort's Light shines for me*
    from afar
Then I first learn that God alone
Must be man's best friend.

To express each of these ideas, Bach composed sections in three disparate styles, each in a different meter, tempo, and key, and characterized by a distinctive gestural profile (see Ex. 4.8). **(A)** Misfortune is painted in f♯ minor with sharp dotted rhythms against the violin's relentless sixteenth notes. **(B)** The helping hand appears out of the turmoil in a vivacious ⁶⁄₈ in A major. **(C)** At the reference to comfort and light, the texture is reduced to voice and continuo with consoling figures over a walking bass. These sections have very little in common, and the overriding passion is built through juxtaposition rather than integration. The text is used in the standard *da capo* format (**ABCAB**) but as well as jumping between the corresponding musical sections in response to the text, Bach interjected parts of **A** as a ritornello between the other sections. This resulted in the musical form **ABACACABABA**. As this movement entails contrasting affects in the same musical form, it is as important for performers to find the appropriate balance between the sections as it is to capture the individual mood of each.

In addition to juxtaposing passions and characters in sequential presentation, music offers the opportunity to represent more than one affect simultaneously. Both horizontally and vertically, Sebastian Bach developed particularly complex means of imitating specific emotions. This provided opportunities for musical contrast and produced a wealth of richness in the expression of both complementary and antithetical passions. Polyphonies of passions are natural

Example 4.8 The three disparate passions in BWV 139/4 A) *Unglück* (Misfortune) B) *Helfende Hand* (The Helping Hand) C) *Trostes Licht* (Consoling Light)

Example 4.8 (Continued)

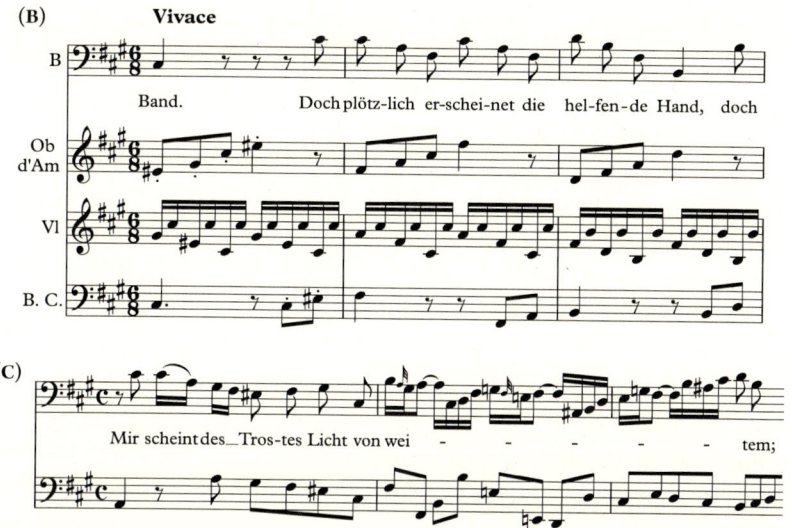

to contrapuntal textures, but they can also occur where we least expect them. Bach even layered meanings in recitative. Along with the depiction of fear at the vision of the Day of Judgment in BWV 70/9, as befitting the dramatic context and the reference to the last trumpet ("Und der Posaunen Schall, / Der unerhörte letzte Schlag," And the ring of the trumpet, the unheard-of last stroke) he added a trumpet part. But instead of playing fanfares as we might expect, he gave it a reassuring chorale tune "Es ist gewißlich an der Zeit" (Indeed the time is here). This both binds the recitative together and spells unease. Bach did not set the final notes of the chorale phrases to consonant harmonies, thus triggering harmonic unrest and a sense of disconnect between the recitative and chorale.

Here, as in some of the examples cited, Bach placed frequent and particular importance on chorale tunes. The heritage of Lutheran hymns was an important stock of musical references, and Bach could count on his listeners being familiar with them and responding to the allusions embedded in their melodies and associated texts. Johannes Mattheson referred to the significance of chorales in organ music and figural music such as cantatas as a way to move the congregation and instill in them a meditative attitude:

> Whoever has learned the common hymns of the church accurately and thoroughly in his youthful years and has also become accustomed to singing along and meditating on the first verse during the organ chorale prelude is able, whenever he hears the alternation of the diligent organist's apt inventions of toccatas, fugues, variations, etc., with the simple melody following—he is able, I say, not only to be sensibly moved or animated in

his heart but also at the same time to meditate on the words of the hymn in an edifying way and thus to carry out his devotions.... During figural music a two-part chorale verse is intermixed and can be heard, devotion is powerfully sustained and increased by such edifying variations.[19]

The juxtaposition of passions in the opening chorus of *Nimm von uns, Herr, du treuer Gott*, BWV 101 involves not only more extreme contrasts than in the previous examples but also simultaneity of opposing passions. The extraordinary confusion as the orchestra and voices follow their own paths, seemingly oblivious of each other, reflects the text that takes the form of a plea to God for protection from "die schwere Straf" (severe punishment), "große Not" (great distress), and "Krieg und teurer Zeit ... Seuchen, Feur und großem Leid" (war and the times of famine, from epidemics, fire and great harm). Bach responded to each of these images: the chromaticism, frequent dissonances, and cross-relations create nothing short of musical pandemonium. The resulting clash of two worlds often sounds like polytonality (if not cacophony) within the framework of a conventional choral fantasy, and the outrageous modernity of this writing must have perplexed Bach's listeners.

The orchestra begins in seven-part texture with an exchange between two motifs: one a drawn-out yearning suspension (**A**), the other involves repeated notes, and is more active and combative (**B**). These are heard over a tonic pedal, but already in measure 3 there is a direct clash of harmonies. A third motif (**C**) is introduced later in the extended instrumental ritornello (see Ex. 4.9). This gesture, comprising three quarter-notes and a downwards leap onto a dissonance followed by a quick release, is subjected to continuous chromatic alteration and results in further tonal strife.

Example 4.9 Passions in polyphony in BWV 101/1

Example 4.9 (Continued)

The harmonies finally calm down before the first vocal entries. A choir of trombones doubling the voices adds a sense of brooding to the fore-imitations of the chorale. The dissonance intensifies again as the orchestra carries on with the third motif, still apparently oblivious of the discord around them. Only with the entry of the actual chorale in the soprano part does the prayer take effect, and there is some harmonic clarity. The melody would have been well known to Bach's congregation as the tune Luther chose for the German Lord's Prayer, "Vater unser im Himmelreich" (Our father in heaven, Ex. 4.10).

Example 4.10 Vater unser im Himmelreich

The movement progresses in this fashion up to the episode before the third line of the chorale where images of mortal persecution proliferate. Now the third motif is developed more independently to sound like fateful strikes.

This is about the most violent and aggressive of any movement that Bach wrote; at the same time it stands as a powerful musical representation of redemption from worldly catastrophe through divine grace. The score has elicited divergent approaches from leading Bach exponents (refer to Audio Ex. 4.3). Nikolaus Harnoncourt's version is strikingly dramatic. As well as hammering out the strike motif with particular virulence, his recording is full of extreme tonal contrasts and generous timings that emphasize the music's incongruities. There are far fewer sharp edges to Masaaki Suzuki's interpretation. Hammered articulations are replaced with smooth articulation, and his slower tempo produces an overriding brooding quality. The trade-off is that the appeasing nature of the chorale is less apparent. John Eliot Gardiner's tempo is brisk, and while the broader outlines of the harmony are clean, the distressing foreground dissonances are less troubling. Explaining his interpretation, Gardiner reasoned that the wrenching harmonies should be treated as passing events, and that they only make sense "in contrapuntal terms at a specific tempo."[20] Pieter Jan Leusink's reading with the Netherlands Bach Collegium is the most disengaged of the four performances. Here the disturbing nature of the disjuncture between worldly strife and the redeeming chorale is all but lost.

🔊 AUDIO EX. 4.3. Bach BWV 101/1
 a) Concentus Musicus, dir. Harnoncourt (Telefunken, 1980)
 b) Bach Collegium Japan, dir. Suzuki (BIS, 2006)
 c) Monteverdi Choir and English Baroque Soloists, dir. Gardiner (Soli Deo Gloria, 2008)
 d) Netherlands Bach Collegium, dir. Leusink (Brilliant, 2013)

Bach's antithesis was not always so obvious as in BWV 101. In BWV 73, for instance, the opening chorus "Herr, wie du willt, so schicks mit mir" (Lord, as you will, so dispose things for me) is interrupted by the tenor with a recitative: "Ach! Aber ach! Wieviel/Läßt mich dein Wille leiden!" (Ah, but alas, how your will makes me suffer!). The movement is built as a sequence of choral and recitative sections, held together with motivic material derived from a chorale tune. Again, this chorale tune holds the music together in more than one sense. It serves as *inventio* and catalyst for the movement's compositional elements. The first three notes inspire the opening gestures of the vocal parts, and the tune's seven phrases dictate the movement's overall length and structure. The tune's historical allusions also reinforce the movement's general meaning. The text that Bach combined with the chorale in this instance was written in the late sixteenth century by Kasper Bienemann, but the melody had been associated with Justus Jonas's translation of Psalm 124 "Wo Gott der Herr nicht bei uns hält / Wenn unsre Feinde toben" (If God the Lord does not remain on our side when our enemies rage). Leipzig congregations would have been familiar with this allusion, particularly as Bach had used the melody and psalm text together in cantatas he wrote for the same year (1724).

By combining the chorale tune with Bienemann's text in BWV 73, Bach provided a more complex message. With its connection to "Wo Gott der Herr," the melody directly addresses the sufferings mentioned in the recitative, while Bienemann's more reassuring text reinforces the consoling message of God's protection. The recitative sections are symbolically defended (as it were) by the protective shield of faith expressed in the chorale. This is an example of where the full effect of Bach's music requires both a visceral response to its inherent emotional qualities and an understanding of its historical allusions. Similar textures are found throughout Bach's St. Matthew Passion where he layered contrasting and sometimes conflicting passions with chorales in an effort to express the paradoxical nature of suffering and redemption.

Bach integrated antithetical passions further in the bass aria "Herr, so du willt" from the same cantata BWV 73. This is about the closest that he came to writing a through-composed aria. The aria, which follows on from the preceding recitative, also sung by bass, passes through a series of closely related passionate states. There is no introductory ritornello; instead the singer begins by intoning the prayer "Herr, so du willt" (Lord, as you will), and so at first the aria seems to be an arioso epilogue to the recitative (not an infrequent practice in Bach's cantatas). Only as the movement progresses does it become apparent that it is an independent movement with a unique formal design.

The opening phrase (see Ex. 4.11) recurs as a refrain framing the aria's three sections. The first section is a supplication for forgiveness; the second an entreaty to be returned to dust and ashes; the third a plea for reconciliation with God

Example 4.11 BWV 73/4, opening

in death. Each refrain is recognizably the same, but although the text is identical, the musical setting mutates progressively to reflect the increasing despair expressed in the text. The integrated compositional process balances continuity with change: continuity through the progression of closely related passions;

change as Bach takes us from the opening c minor to the darkness of e♭ minor, and then as despair brings the hope of transcendence from earthly woes to E♭ major. The passions are relatively finely graded, so it is important for performers to guide listeners through the subtle yet meaningful metamorphosis. The structure can be clarified by pointing out similarities and coloring the differences in dynamics and tone color.

It is rare to find this type of progression in an aria without a restatement of the original premise. Open-ended antithesis like this is far more common in recitatives, which often function as emotional conduits from one aria or chorus to the next. The recitative "Mein Kummer nimmet zu" in *Meine Säufzer, meine Tränen* (BWV 13) traverses the lowest despair to optimistic hope in the space of fifteen measures with great economy of resources. Each signal of distress in the text is set to troubled musical effects: *Jammerkrug* (goblet of trouble) and *Kummernacht* (night of sorrow) receive diminished harmonies; a D♭ in the bass on the word *Not* (sorrow) takes the harmony into still darker realms. But from the singer's lowest note at "Drückt mein beklemmtes Herz darnieder" (oppresses my heavy heart), the vocal part climbs through a tortured line on *Wermutsaft* (wormwood draft), and an optimistic upwards scale through *Freudenwein* (wine of joy) to B♭ major.

Because there is no real way to express negation in music, antithesis can pose distinct problems for composers. This is all the more so in cases where, rather than concrete physical or emotional states, the antithesis is applied to abstract concepts. The way Bach negotiates the problem of expressing negation in *Aus tiefer Not schrei ich zu dir*, BWV 38 is worth mentioning. In the second part of the third movement, he could be accused of relying on madrigalisms when he sets the phrase "Sein Wort besteht und fehlet nicht" (His word prevails and does not fail) with *besteht* on a steadfast sustained tone, and *fehlet* to a descending line (Ex. 4.12), but the sly twist in the vocal part that places *nicht* (not) on an emphatic high note and jarring diminished harmony shows true ingenuity.

Example 4.12 Word painting in BWV 38/3

Laughing at Death: The Proximity of Opposites

There is more deliberate drollery and wit in the music of Bach than we hear in performances these days when Modernism imposes a false sobriety on "art music," particularly in works with a religious intent. Humor can be both positive and negative (even simultaneously) and can also be wittily suggestive. It can also be satiric, and could at times be subversive in intent. This is not unlikely for a composer like Bach, who is known to have been outspoken at times in his criticisms of his colleagues and employers. Predictably, explicit musical jokes are more common in Bach's secular cantatas than in his sacred works. Still, it can be disturbing how little difference there was between the secular and sacred versions.

Bach often used similar musical treatments to express antithetical concepts. This can produce another level of meaning. In *Wer mich liebet, der wird mein Wort halten*, BWV 74, we don't understand the victorious swaggering in the alto aria mvt. 7, "Nichts kann mich erretten / Von höllischen Ketten" (Nothing can deliver me from hellish chains) until we hear the entire text and realize that the singer is jubilant because, through Jesus's suffering, he can laugh at hell's rage ("Ich lache der Wut"). The jagged melismas on *Ketten* then pay double service: they provide a graphic image of struggling against the chains of hell, as well as laughter against hell's rage (Ex. 4.13). This poses a challenge to performers who must strike the right balance between struggle and jarring laughter. In the *da capo*, where the ambiguity is explicit, the singer can modify the performance style to sound more like laughter so that even if the notes are identical, they are inflected with new meaning. Tempo plays a crucial part here, as is demonstrated in the three recordings excerpted in Audio Example 4.4. Harnoncourt's interpretation is on the slow side, but this allows him to bring out the sense of struggle with hammered repeated notes, and to take time to emphasize the dissonant suspensions (another musical figure for "hellish chains"). Koopman's reading is more competent from a technical point of view, but the melismas on *lache* are a little too "correct" to be credible as laughter. In Gardiner's version, Robin Blaze has an unmistakably mischievous snarl in his voice, but rather than participating in the struggle, the instruments seem too playful in their antics.

🔊 AUDIO EX. 4.4. BWV 74/7 (*confutatio*)
 a) Paul Esswood, Concentus Musicus, dir. Harnoncourt (Telefunken, 1977)
 b) Amsterdam Baroque Orchestra, dir. Koopman (Challenge, 2003)
 c) Robin Blaze, Monteverdi Choir and English Baroque Soloists, dir. Gardiner (Soli Deo Gloria, 2006)

Example 4.13 Melismas on "Ketten" and "lachen" in BWV 74/7

The same comic staccato used to represent *wackelt* in the aria "Zu Tanze, zu Sprunge, / So wackelt das Herz" (In dancing and prancing my heart shakes) in the secular cantata *Die Streit zwischen Phoebus und Pan* (The Dispute between Phoebus and Pan, BWV 201) resurfaces as jubilant laughter in the opening chorus of the *Easter Oratorio* (BWV 249). Did Bach intend a discernible difference between Pan's boisterous guffawing and pious rejoicing in a sacred work? As always, the musical score is only a starting point. What *looks* the same on the page might have *sounded* very different in performance. Quantz reminded his readers that "a good and appropriate execution must also be extended to comical music," and specified that comic effects "must be accompanied ... in a low and very common manner by the attendant instruments, and not as in a serious opera."[21] From this we can infer that performers could intentionally inject comedy into the music by bringing into play special (unwritten, even undocumented) effects.

There are instances where Bach creates what seem to be humorous juxtapositions. In the opening chorus of the Epiphany cantata BWV 248:VI/1 the same melisma serves for *schnauben* (to snarl or snort) and *Glauben* (faith or belief). With these examples in mind, what was Bach really trying to say when he crafted a French overture for *Preise, Jerusalem, den Herrn*, BWV 119, the opening chorus of his first cantata for the investiture of the Leipzig town council in August 1723? Was there a hint of irony in making the stalwart elders of a staunchly Lutheran town process to music associated with the king of Catholic France? We know that over time tensions heightened between Bach and the Leipzig councilors, but was he already taking a jibe at his would-be noble employers in 1723 with *le style majestueux*? Bach did not leave any clues in the music to betray his motivations, and no contemporary commentaries mention any undercurrent implications, so we can only speculate on whether anyone got the joke—if there was a joke to get.

It is suprising that none of the surviving works Bach composed in honor of the closest there was to a Saxon monarch, Elector Augustus II, includes French overtures. Augustus had converted to Catholicism in order to claim the Polish crown, and Bach would certainly have wanted to flatter him with majestic music in the hope of recognition with a court appointment. The circumstances leading to the composition of the Four Orchestral Overture-Suites (BWV 1066–69) are not known, but Bach incorporated French overtures into sacred cantatas where there is no parodic intent. In the opening chorus of BWV 61 the overture form is used to support the hymn tune "Nun komm, der Heiden Heiland" (Now come, savior of the gentiles) and to herald the arrival of the savior on Advent Sunday; and BWV 110 is another joyous chorus composed for the celebration of the birth of Jesus on Christmas Day; but in BWV 20, *O Ewigkeit du Donnerwort* (O Eternity, you word of thunder), the French overture form is co-opted in a painting of the opposite to glorious majesty: the horrors of eternal judgment.

We might be disappointed with much Baroque music if we relied solely on the score for what it is trying to say. We can't always "see" the images in the notes on the page. We may struggle to get the jokes in Bach's secular cantatas; the ebb and flow in Telemann's *Wassermusik* might seem tame; and even Vivaldi's barking dogs and ice skating require an imaginative performer if they are to be audible. Published poetic parodies show that after-hours French overtures doubled as bawdy drinking songs. In French operas, demons dance to music that share the same dotted rhythms and musical gestures as the royal *entrée*. Does it make sense to perform the music the same way in such different contexts? What tips the scales from majestic and grandiose to malevolent and threatening, or lewd and subversive? Stressing dissonances, using a grating or unpleasant tone, snapping long notes off suddenly, and exaggerating the sharpness of the dotted rhythms and rapid *tirades* are all ways to inject a performance with creative authenticity.[22] Audio Example 4.5 is an effective performance of an anti-overture from an opera by Marin Marais, and a similar treatment may be appropriate for Bach's French overture in BWV 20 to express the terrified trembling heart as the "Schwert, das durch die Seele bohrt" (The sword that bores through the soul).

🔊 AUDIO EX. 4.5. Marin Marais, "Premier Air des Magiciens," from *Alcyone*, Les Musiciens du Louvre, dir. Minkowski (Erato, 1990)

Tempo, tone color, and the shaping of gestures have a decisive effect in resetting affect and character, and can even result in quite opposite meanings. Performance alone can transform a sequence of scales and fast repeated notes into a raging storm scene, or a learned fugue into the picture of straying sheep. The remaining chapters deal in more detail with the performer's responsibility to draw out the potential of the score by seizing the music's meaning (its *inventio*) and thereby bringing to life the passions that the composer may have only hinted at in the musical notation.

Further Reading

Acting manuals illustrate a vast vocabulary of affective gestures. See Barnett's comprehensive survey of the literature in *The Art of Gesture*. Tisch-Wackernagel's article "Baroque" provides a valuable synopsis of German Baroque poetry.

The Calov Bible was a seventeenth-century edition of Luther's translation with additional commentary by Abraham Calovius (1612–86). Bach's annotated copy has been studied extensively by Leaver in *J. S. Bach and Scripture*, and Cox's edition provides facsimiles of all the pages with marginalia in Bach's hand. For more on overlaps between the sacred and secular in Bach's thinking, see Michael Marissens's *Social and Religious Designs*.

A thorough catalogue, classification, and description of the *tremolo* can be found in Moens-Haenen *Das Vibrato in der Musik des Barock*.

PART TWO

PERFORMING ELOQUENCE

5

Enhancing Eloquence in Performance (*Elocutio*)

GEOFFREY BURGESS

Nature does not bestow the polish upon the diamond she forms, it is only labour and art that makes it shine.

—Luigi Riccoboni, 1738[1]

I have no hesitation in saying that even a mediocre speech, made attractive by the power of expression, will carry more weight than the best speech deprived of this help.

—Quintilian, *De Oratoria*[2]

The "Intentional Fallacy" Fallacy: Whose Intention?

The modern work-based understanding of art encourages us to think of the expressive qualities of art as decided by the composer and contained in the score—"sealed in the bag" as it were. But the concept was very different in the Rhetorical period. In line with Quintilian (see epigram above), Quantz wrote that the performer was just as important to the impact of the musical product as the composer:

> Attempts to perfect the expression of the passions in the art of composition would scarcely be useful, however, if at the same time similar efforts were not made in the art of performance.[3]

The performer personifies *actio*, the fifth Office of rhetoric. It is the performer's interpretation of the composer's *inventio* and *dispositio* that the audience will hear, and the audience is moved, not by recognizing the potential in the composer's notes but by depending on the performer's sensitivity and competence. As Mattheson commented:

> Ten good composers are often not capable of creating a single good singer; but a single good singer, . . . is easily capable of inspiring ten good composers, so that the latter sometimes do not know whence the magnificent ideas come to them.[4]

At the present time, all that is left from composers of the Baroque period are notes—"notes" in more than one sense. Their manuscripts are often no more than approximate jottings, what Barthold Kuijken has called road maps or *aide-mémoires*.[5] Quantz recognized that the performer had a multitude of choices available that could make or break any piece, regardless who had crafted it:

> Every musical gesture can be expressed in different ways: badly, passably, or well. A good, distinct, and appropriate expression can save a mediocre piece; but bad and indistinct expression can spoil the best of pieces.[6]

Since the eighteenth century, composers have progressively increased the precision of their notation as a means of imposing greater control over performers. Bach assumed that his string players could work out the most effective fingering for a given passage, but Gustav Mahler, reputed to have declared "steht alles in der Partitur" (everything's in the score), rarely left such details to chance and even indicated the string to use in particular passages. Handel did not specify which voice of a fugue should dominate; Arnold Schoenberg came up with signs to show this so that performers would not be in doubt. Few eighteenth-century composers found it necessary to notate dynamic nuances beyond basic distinctions of *forte* and *piano*; Pierre Boulez quantified dynamics and applied them along with pitch, register, duration, and attack to a serial technique. By the mid-twentieth century then, composers were demanding performers adhere to the letter of their score. Some carried this so far that the only way to perform their music is by machine. Now, with the availability of computer music–writing software and MIDI technology, it is all too easy to bypass performers altogether. Some have insisted on machine-like precision from "mere mortals" and criticize composers for not playing their own compositions "correctly." Gunther Schuller, for instance, unwaveringly stuck to what was on the page as the only valid way of realizing a composer's work; he discredited some composers' attempts to capture their actual intentions in performance when this differed from what their written notes seem to prescribe.[7] This type of text-fetishism is a product of our modern literalist culture that suppresses the live, communicative aspect of musical performance in favor of a "correct" execution of the score.

In reality, any musical notation is inherently imprecise and open to multiple meanings.[8] Notation gives only a vague idea of speed and the placement of notes; even the pitches are not indicated with absolute accuracy, particularly when we consider the array of tuning and pitch standards that have been used over the course of the past centuries. (Tuning is not an insignificant factor, as it often has a critical impact on the way the music is perceived. This is discussed in chapter 2.) Because of what notation leaves out and the range of possible interpretations, no musical score can never have the force of unalterable law.[9] On the superficial level, Claudio Monteverdi's and Domenico Scarlatti's notation may resemble Igor Stravinsky's or Elliott Carter's, but looking deeper, Rhetorical music notation carries very different intentions. It is no exaggeration to say that the level of decoding required when performing musical scores from previous centuries is akin to reading a literary text in a dead language.

We cannot assume that if certain effects do not appear in the notation that they were not part of the musical language. For instance, there is very little in the way of dynamic or tempo markings in seventeenth-century music, but that does not mean that performances contained no nuances of volume and speed. When we read a toccata by Frescobaldi with modern eyes, we might assume, as there is no indication to the contrary, that each section should be played in strict tempo. But when we read the composer's preface and other sources beyond the notes on the page, it becomes clear that strict rhythmic interpretation actually misrepresents the composer's intention. Ultimately, it can be said that for much of the history of Western music, more often than not, "literal" readings will misrepresent the spirit of the work.

All creative artists in the Rhetorical period recognized that once in the hands of performers, their work would become something beyond what they conceived. Quantz used an analogy with oratory to explain how this worked:

> Everyone knows that when the same discourse is delivered word for word by different people, the effect will be quite different. It is the same for expression in music; if the same piece is sung or played by different people, it will always produce different effects.[10]

C. P. E. Bach admitted that "it is possible, through different kinds of expression, to make passages sound so different that they are scarcely recognizable," but there is no reason to believe that this was always a source of displeasure.[11] Diderot reported Voltaire's astonishment at seeing the famous actress Claire Josèphe Hippolyte Léris de La Tude (known as La Clairon) play a role in one of his plays, to which the author asked "am I really the one who wrote that?" La Clairon had succeeded in creating dimensions beyond those that even Voltaire had envisaged.¹² That gives the sense that the "work" was a very flexible entity. Clearly it is not contained in the notation, and even what philosophers call the "Platonic ideal"—the form or essence that lies behind real-life manifestations and experiences of the notation, performance, listening, and analysis—is subject to "reworking" though these same processes.

Where does this leave us with regard to authenticity and the composer's intention? At base, as Leech-Wilkinson reminds us, the performers' responsibility was

> to move the audience as profoundly as they could: the composer's text was just one element that contributed to the result.... If we understand music as what it feels like then there can be no watertight objection to the means used to generate good feeling, provided that they do no serious harm.¹³

The distance between notation and performance is greatest in repertoires where the notation is most vague, and where it was intended for the performer to take a substantial share of responsibility in the *dispositio*. This is the case, for example, with most medieval music where the performer has little more than a sequence of notes that has to be given rhythmic organization, form, and (where appropriate) accompaniment. In this repertoire, the same text can result in very different "works" according to who is performing. This is also true in later music, where we imagine the text is relatively stable. The point of contention revolves around differences of opinion on what constitutes "serious harm" and different perceptions of what the music should feel like. Audio Example 5.1 presents three different versions of the aria from *Mein Gott, wie lang, ach lange*, BWV 155. On paper they all look the same. What makes them sound so different is that they are performed by three different groups:

🔊 AUDIO EX. 5.1. BWV 155/4
a) English Baroque Soloists, dir. Gardiner (Soli Deo Gloria, 2006)
b) Amsterdam Baroque Orchestra, dir. Koopman (Erato, 1996)
c) Concentus Musicus Wien, dir. Harnoncourt (Telefunken, 1985)

Wirf, mein Herze, wirf dich noch	*Cast yourself, my heart*
In des Höchsten Liebesarme,	*Into the loving heart of the Highest,*
Daß er deiner sich erbarme.	*That He may have mercy on you.*
Lege deiner Sorgen Joch,	*Lay your yoke of cares,*
Und was dich bisher beladen,	*And whatever has burdened you till now*
Auf die Achseln seiner Gnaden.	*Upon the shoulders of His grace.*

Here, tempo is a primary element, but the interpretation of the rhythm is also critical, and each performance produces decidedly different affects. Gardiner's ensemble plays the dotted rhythms with vigor and a sense of victory. Harnoncourt's tempo is overall slower and evokes a rollocking peasant dance, the rhythms sounding more like triplets. Koopman achieves a balance where the skipping quality of the dotted gestures is coupled with a quieter, reassured joy. Putting aside for the moment which is a more accurate rendering of the text or closer to Bach's intention, these three recordings clearly demonstrate that even among specialists, the field is still wide open for viable interpretations that affect the essential feeling of the music.

One way to evaluate what a performance can do to a work is to consider how closely the performers come to capturing the passions implied in the notation. To demonstrate how easy it is to alter or deflect a passion, let us compare two recordings of the opening movement of *Mein liebster Jesus ist verloren*, BWV 154 (Audio Ex. 5.2). Here is the text.

Mein liebster Jesus ist verloren:	*My beloved Jesus is lost:*
O Wort, das mir Verzweiflung bringt,	*O word that brings me despair,*
O Schwert, das durch die Seele dringt,	*O sword that pierces my soul,*
O Donnerwort in meinen Ohren.	*O thunderous word in my ears!*

🔊 AUDIO EX. 5.2. BWV 154/1
a) Gerd Türk with Bach Collegium Japan, dir. Suzuki (BIS, 2001)
b) Paul Agnew with Amsterdam Baroque Orchestra, dir. Koopman (Erato, 1995)

At the tempo Suzuki takes the aria, the short pickups and wide intervals convincingly express *Verzweiflung* as distress. But that word can also mean despair, and reading the whole text, that seems to better encapsulate the passion of the piece. Listen how that meaning is captured in Ton Koopman's version.

As opposed to our current artificial classical music culture that draws primarily on dead art, when the Rhetorical tradition was a living musical tradition, it was quite normal for composers and performers to change the text of a work and create multiple versions where no one is necessarily more the "work" than any other. There are many examples of composers themselves altering their works to accommodate changing circumstances. Handel was always revising his operas and oratorios to suit his singers, Bach reorchestrated his works according to the available players, and Rameau rewrote his *tragédies lyriques* to suit changing musical fashion and political circumstances. Practical considerations were paramount, and composers respected the performers' need to do their jobs of creating an affective performance and thus lent them what help they could. It can be immensely liberating to recognize that a work of art has such a mutable identity. It can also be a source of uneasiness. Which version should be privileged, and just how much liberty can a piece of music sustain?

In their 1946 essay "The Intentional Fallacy," William K. Wimsatt and Monroe Beardsley made the radical proposition that "the design or intention of the author is neither available nor desirable as a standard for judging the success of a work of literary art."[14] Pursuing that line of reasoning, twenty years later Roland Barthe announced "The Death of the Author" and argued for a neutral approach to literary criticism based on a transhistorical (actually ahistorical) technical analysis of texts.[15] These new Positivist and Postmodern approaches challenged the Romantic notion of the omniscient creative artist, and while they may have aimed to bring elitist art to a wider audience by effectively displacing authors, composers, and playwrights from their pedestals, they also opened the potential for general misunderstanding. If the author's intention is irrelevant, then the age in which it was created is equally redundant to the work's meaning. This in turn opened the way for any art to be made to conform to modern taste and practice. The Positivists' position was that works of art should be treated as autonomous objects that can resist "interpretation," and that they will remain intact in a Platonic ideal regardless overlayered interpretations.

Wimsatt, Beardsley, and Barthes formulated their propositions primarily for literature where there is a binary relationship between author and reader, but in performance arts the path from artistic creation to audience is more complex. Music, for instance, cannot exist without the mediation of an interpreter. The performer is (in differing degrees depending on the style) every bit as essential to the musical experience as the composer. This is no more the case than with Rhetorical period when music had no existence outside of the intentional interplay between creator and re-creator. Baroque and Classical music was "programmed" that way. The intention was for the performer to be involved in the creative process. We could call this "the composer's intention," but it was just as strongly "the culture's intention." By disregarding this intention, a performer may end up producing a different work: one that does not participate in the cultural milieu in which it was created. So, a "transparent" performance that follows the urtext to the letter can be just as far off the mark as one that (unwittingly or otherwise) distorts the work's meaning through "over interpretation." Real authenticity takes on vitality when it draws on the tension between composer and performer, intention and actualization, text and act, freedom and constraint. In short, when it comes to Rhetorical music, the composer's intention was always that the performer should participate. The performer must also set the intention to seize the work's potential, amplify it, explicate it, and elaborate it through the performance.

As well as the performer, the line of command in the interpretative chain from work to audience is mediated by the editor. Early music relies more than other repertoires on editors to produce practical publications and reproduce close copies of composer's scores. Editorial interpretation involves transcription and transliteration while the performer's task is to translate the text into a living event. The editor's terrain is relatively stable ground; the performer's is often much more unsure.

Elocutio: The Essence of Performance Practice

Elocutio, the "nuts-and-bolts" of stylistic attributes that we think of nowadays as "performance practice," was the professional lore of a musician in the Baroque period—the performer's toolbox, so to speak—the devices and contrivances that the audience didn't need to know about but were essential to an eloquent performance. The art that dissembles art. Gustav Leonhardt liked to call performance practice "the musician's kitchen" because, like the place in a restaurant where the food is prepared out of view of the diners, it is the behind-the-scenes preparation for the musical event. On this subject, Fénelon writes admiringly of Cicero:

> You do not *see* him use Points of Wit and quaint Antitheses: He's *then* truly eloquent. Every thing seems artless, as it ought to be when one is vehement. With a negligent Air he delivers the most natural and affecting Sentiments; and says everything that can move and animate the Passions.[16]

Much of the material found in treatises and instruction books from the seventeenth and eighteenth centuries falls under the category of *elocutio*: careful instructions on techniques, strategies, insider information, and tricks of the trade that produce effective and convincing expression of the passions. Books on *elocutio* serve as guides, or handbooks on a set of tried and tested procedures, written by master craftsmen and addressed to apprentices and other craftsmen.[17] We rely on performance-practice manuals for guidance on a wide range of topics, including: tempo, meter, rhythm, articulation and bowing, the delineation of musical gestures, phrasing, ensemble, balance, contrasts in volume and tone color, awareness of harmony and dissonance, and the like. But all of these are meaningless if they are not integrated into an eloquent reading of the music.

Because of the break in tradition and the essential differences between the Rhetorical and modern approaches, the HIP movement has been concerned to create a performing style for early music that differs from the modern one. It has grouped the information found in historical treatises and organized into a set of specific, more or less consistent instructions on how to play early music stylistically. Performance practice, as we are constantly learning, is something that applies to music of all styles and periods. But the authors of treatises were only concerned with the music of their own time. They were not written for the instruction of a distant future and uninformed audience like us, nor were they written to help us to unlearn a style or re-create a lost tradition. These sources do not promulgate rules for "correctness" written by infallible prophets. It is only too easy to get bogged down in the details of execution, and ignore intention and expression. It is useful to bear in mind that the information they contain is insider advice on effective ways of expressing the passions and moving the hearts of listeners, and how to be effective musical rhetoricians.

Michael Praetorius provided an example in his *Syntagma musicum* where he described the "swelling of the voice" known as *exclamatio* not simply as a musical device but as "the actual means whereby the passions are moved":

> It can be applied to all descending dotted minims and semiminims. The following note especially will have a greater affect and is also more pleasing if it moves somewhat more quickly than the semibreve, which is more frequently found with vocal crescendos and decrescendos [*messe di voce*], without *exclamatio*.[18]

In the 1970s many performers took these descriptions and others like them as a mandate that in order to be pleasing, every note should have a swell. The routine application of the *messa di voce* became ubiquitous—a technical habit. Known as the "Dutch bulge," it served not only as a defining feature of the Netherlands' early music style, but a badge of membership worn by eager initiates in the early music clique. But like vibrato in modern performances, it became overused, and its expressive capabilities all but lost.

"Humouring" the Score

The tasteful use of the *messa di voce* is just one of a multitude of tricks in a performer's toolkit to give the music character, or, to borrow an expression from Thomas Mace, to "Humour" the music. Referring to the Theory of Humours or Temperaments, the constituents of human character that was the basis of ancient medicine and particularly the Hippocratic system, "humour" as used by Mace could also become a verb. When he spoke in his treatise of "Humouring a Lesson," he meant giving it personality, imbuing it with affect, and therefore meaning.[19] Humouring, then, can be likened to how an actor portrays differences of character. Rémond de Saint-Albine called it *sentiment*, and put it this way:

> the facility among actors of being able to produce different passions in succession. Like a modelling wax that becomes, in the hands of a skilled craftsman, first a Médée, then a Sapho, the spirit and heart of a person of the theatre must be capable of receiving every mutation that a playwright wishes to proffer them.[20]

Like actors who create a voice to suit each character they play, singers can humour vocal music by tailoring a unique vocal personality to the roles they sing. In Audio Example 5.3, Dominique Visse brings out the evil and conniving character of the sorceress in Purcell's *Dido and Aeneas* through nasal tone, and a dose of "wayward" pitch bending. In 1922 the Austrian actor Alexander Moissi (1879–1935) made a compelling recording that demonstrates a remarkable command over four distinctive voices for each of the characters—narrator, father, son, and the Erlkönig—in Goethe's poem *Erlkönig*. Schubert's musical setting guides singers on how to humour the characters, but Jessye Norman's virtuoso performance, one of the most effective on record, goes well beyond the means provided by the composer (Audio Ex. 5.4 and 5.5).

🎵 AUDIO EX. 5.3. Purcell, *Dido and Aeneas*, Dominique Visse (sorceress), Les Arts Florissants, dir. William Christie (Harmonia Mundi, 1986)

🎵 AUDIO EX. 5.4. Schubert, *Erlkönig,* Jessye Norman, Geoffrey Parsons, piano (Philips, 1989)

🎵 AUDIO EX. 5.5. Goethe, *Erlkönig*, Alexander Moissi (, 1927)

This type of performance is usually not applied to Bach out of (misdirected) veneration for his music and the sense that it deserves more restrained treatment. There may not be as many chances to produce comic or grotesque effects, but there are certainly instances where the drama of Bach's music calls for other types of humouring. Take for instance, the depiction of desperation and horror in the tenor aria in *Lobet den Herrn, meine Seele* BWV 143. Gerd Türk conveys the sense of distress when he sings the declamatory vocal part "Tausendfaches Unglück, Schrecken" (Thousandfold misfortune, terror) almost sotto voce (Audio Ex. 5.6a). By contrast, Kurt Equiluz's inimitable stentorian control seems unmoved and, in this instance, less convincing at expressing the meaning of the text (Audio Ex. 5.6b).

🎵 AUDIO EX. 5.6. BWV 143/4
a) Gerd Türk with Bach Collegium Japan, Masashi Suzuki (BIS, 2000)
b) Kurt Equiluz with Leonhardt Consort (Telefunken, 1984)

> To Mace, humouring meant
>
> Playing some *Sentences Loud,* and others again *Soft,* according as they best please your own *Fancy,* some very *Briskly,* and *Couragiously,* and some again *Gently, Lovingly, Tenderly,* and *Smoothly.*[21]

This touches on several categories—dynamics, tempo, and articulation—and in technical terms we can probably be somewhat more specific. In order of their effect on the expressive result, we can name tempo, dynamics, timbre, articulation, pronunciation, phrasing, and ornamentation. The first of these will be treated in the later sections of this chapter. Articulation, ornamentation and timing are discussed in separate chapters.

Humouring in music was practiced across a broad chronological span and was described in one of the last treatises to refer to rhetorical interpretation: the *Nouvelle Méthode théorique et pratique pour le violon* (1803) by Giuseppe Maria Cambini (1746–ca.1825), an Italian violinist and composer who worked most of his life in Paris. The interest in the extensive passage quoted here is the way he expressed ideas derived unmistakably from traditional rhetoric in flamboyant Romantic prose. Cambini describes musical humouring through the gesture of playing, where the physical aspect of playing the violin becomes the means to eloquence: as he put it where "the bow can express the affections of the soul." To demonstrate his points, Cambini quotes two melodies. The first is from Luigi Boccherini's Quartet in c minor, op.2/1 (1761); the second the theme from the second movement of Symphony 53 (1778–79) by Joseph Haydn.

OF EXPRESSION AND ACCENTS

I shall choose only two phrases for the moment, one taken from the elegant and tender Boccherini, the other, from an Andante of the celebrated Haydn. Here is the first phrase.

I suppose that in executing this phrase one could dream of nothing save the mechanism of the fingers and of the bow, which one would pull and push for every note with equal weight, always producing a uniform and uniformly loud sound. This would create a meaningless [*insignifiant*] and raucous noise, which would invite no one to listen to the rest. In short, the intention of the author would be missing. If one executes the same phrase in the following manner, and with the fingerings I have indicated, one will make only half the volume of sound issue from the instrument, although always equal throughout.

position naturelle

One will hear that there is already an intention to reach us, albeit vaguely, and without creating in us any great interest in hearing what follows. The author would be able to say, All right, I have your attention; but I have not persuaded you: while my intention was both to persuade you and to move you. Then execute the phrase in the following manner, increase and diminish the sound as much as the sign shows you. Above all, think that you wish to move me. . . electrify your arm with the fire of this thought. . . so that your bow becomes your tongue and your countenance . . . then, strongly moved by the energy of this expressive interpellation, declaim the phrase as I have written it for you.

You will then have the pleasure of seeing the spectator moved, immobile, and ready to forget everything in order to hear you.

Let us turn now to the other example taken from the phrase of Haydn. Its expression is the naivety, candor, and innocence of a shepherdess who reproaches her lover for having betrayed her.

Let us believe for a moment that the musician sees there only the notes which he must make resonate with the mechanism of his fingers, pulling and pushing on the gut strings. The horsehair which he holds up with his arm, is all to the better if he can, in this way, excite a group of idle rustics who have already satisfied their uncouth appetites to dance. The goal of the author is again missing.

Now execute this phrase in the following manner. Do not seek to produce a big volume of sound, sustain the bow well, give to your arm only a very light weight, observe well the slurs and staccati, while ordinary fingering will serve.

You will already sense that the beginning of this air has acquired some nobility from this other manner of execution. It makes young women smile, inspiring in them the desire to hear what follows; but the intention of the author is still not yet realized. Do you wish to achieve it? Then learn from the following manner.

Enter, then, into the naive and tender sentiment that a pretty still virginal village girl feels when she reproaches her lover for the infidelity which she has so little merited. Give her a character even more naive than that of Colette in *Le Devin du Village*; she knows nothing of spite, she listens to nothing but her affection, and says nothing but the following words.

Quoi! Tu peux m'être infidel!	*What? You could be unfaithful to me!*
Qui t'aimera plus que moi!	*Who will love you more than I?*
Si je te parois moins elle,	*You may find me less beautiful,*
Mon cœur n'est il rien pour toi!	*But is my heart nothing to you?*

Here I am sure that this is what the author wanted: to engage, move, and affect the spectator. Alas! that those who view instrumental music as no more than meaningless noise could not have heard, as I did, quartets by Boccherini, Haydn and other celebrated masters played by Manfredi, Boccherini, Nardini, and myself, only too happy to play the viola! I am quite sure that they would speak in another way; they would avow that the dramatic art has always inspired these great masters, even in works which are not presented upon the stage [*les ouvrages ou elle ne peut se montrer aux yeux*].

I have always thought that he who said, Sonata, what do you want of me? [*Sonate, que me veux–tu?*] was right only because the musician who produced and executed the sonata was at fault.... had it been otherwise, that man of wit would not have had the time to have said this; he would instead have cried out, Sonata, you touch me . . . you move me! . . . Surely Apollo and Orpheus played sonatas![22]

Cambini's discussion reminds us that instrumental techniques like bowing and articulation are inseparable from dynamics and how all of these work toward projecting the character of the music. In order to touch the listener, each gesture is given its own dynamic shape requiring a specific technique that results in a physical gesture while playing. The motion from dissonance to consonance at the end of phrases suggests—or rather requires—legato and diminuendo. Pickups and downbeats are delineated, and the character of each musical gesture is expressed by variations in articulation. Still, some of the details are not quite what we might expect from a violinist at the turn of the nineteenth century.[23] Cambini slurs across bar lines, alters the rhythm of anacruses, and favors stopped notes over open strings. His bowing and dynamics not only transgress advice provided by eighteenth-century performance manuals: they go against Haydn's original markings (see Ex. 5.1). How can this be what the composer intended?

Example 5.1 J. Haydn, Andante from Symphony 53 (1774)

Evidently, for Cambini it was more important to satisfy the author's intention by creating music that was characterful and moved the listener, rather than a performance that adhered to the letter of the score. A translation rather than a literal reading. This is the type of "intention" that I have been speaking about. The effect that these types of adjustments have on the identity of the work is still an important consideration. Is Cambini's interpretation appropriate for Haydn, or do his changes disfigure the identity of the work by reinterpreting it with the tastes of early Romanticism?

The image of the rejected shepherdess (whether Colette in Rousseau's popular *intermède* or the unnamed character in Cambini's poem) may never have entered Haydn's mind when he composed the tune for his symphony, but over time his Andante accrued associations of this sort. Cambini's poetic response to Haydn's tune, even though it originated some twenty years after the music was composed and was expressed in unmistakably Romantic imagery, is not exaggerated for eighteenth-century taste.[24] The same melody was texted by numerous poets and presented in different scenarios. One was a dialogue and duet for the lovers Jenny and Jemmy in the musical play *Auld Robin Gray* by Samuel Arnold (first produced at the Theatre Royal, Haymarket, in 1794). Jenny is an innocent peasant girl, and Jemmy insists on leaving to seek his fortune before marrying her. This is not the frustrated jealousy that came to mind for Cambini, but their parting is equally full of regrets. The first verse begins: "Farewell, farewell, that sigh forbids me to depart."[25]

Another parody that Cambini may have known appeared in a French play by Jean Monnet, *Le Fat dupé ou l'Inconséquent* (1787–88). This version featured a coy expostulation on how love sees no class distinctions.

Je ne vous dirai pas j'aime	*I will not say that I love you;*
Votre rang me le defend;	*Your rank prevents me;*
. . .	. . .
Si la bouche ne dit j'aime,	*If one's lips do not utter "I love,"*
Le mot est dit par le cœur.	*The heart still says the word.*[26]

Poetic parodies like these provide creative impetus to imbue instrumental music with humour and character—often with comic innuendos. We return to the topic of parodies of instrumental music in chapter 7.

Tempo and Affect

Altering the speed of a piece is one of the most basic ways of humouring. A vestige of the passions remains in the tempo markings used at the head of each piece. These markings have always had the dual function of indicating pace and passion, and demonstrate the close connection between speed and affect. English speakers can easily forget that in Italian *Allegro* means happy and cheerful as much as fast, or that *Adagio* suggests gentle, soft, and cautious as well as slow. Some other character traits that correspond directly to humours include the following (beginning with positive moving to negative):

Spiritoso	wit, spiritedness
Gay, gayment	jollity
Légèrement	lightness
Dolce	kindliness
Soave	agreeableness, pleasing
Affetuoso	affective, that is, a more than usual passionate delivery
Pomposo	magnificence
Maestoso	majesty, stateliness
Gravement	seriousness
Mesto	melancholy
Pesante	ponderousness

It was no accident that markings like these were first applied to musical notation in the Rhetorical era. In the early seventeenth century Michael Praetorius wrote that even terms that indicate speeds like *Presto* and *Lento* "serve to imitate the passion and stir the listener,"[27] and Andreas Werckmeister (1645–1706) spoke of the tempo indications like *Presto* or *Adagio* primarily as "indications of the passion."[28] Gradually, certain tempo names took on specific affective associations. By 1739 Mattheson linked tempo terms with specific passions, which may not be as immediately obvious, but which he felt had been established by convention and use:

Adagio	distress
Lamento	lamentation
Lento	relief
Andante	hope
Affetuoso	love
Allegro	comfort
Presto	eagerness[29]

Around the same time, composers began to recognize the ambiguity of the standard tempo names and started to use qualifiers—not only *moderato, ma non troppo*, and *assai*, but affective terms like *con brio, spirituoso*, and *grazioso*—that could more effectively capture the unique character of a piece of music. This continued into the Romantic era when the affective element of tempo was often qualified with an absolute speed expressed as a metronomic value in recognition that the connection between tempo and affect was beginning to break down, and that the time signature was not always an accurate representation of the beat. (Does an Adagio in $\frac{3}{4}$ time imply three slow quarter-note beats, or six eighth-notes?)

The dual nature of tempo in Rhetorical performance is conveyed through the distinction that numerous French writers made between *mesure* and *mouvement*. *Mesure* is the mathematical and precise measure of rhythm (Couperin marked pieces *mesuré* when the performer needed to observe the rhythm more strictly than usual). *Mouvement* is less exacting and pertains to the mood conveyed by the speed and rhythmic shape of the music, and is open to supple stretching and compression. In the words of Bacilly, *mouvement* is what gives "soul" to a song:

> I have not doubt that the variety of metres [*mesure*] either quick or slow doesn't contribute greatly to the expression of the song; but without doubt there is another more refined and spiritual quality—*mouvement*—that always keeps the listener breathlessly enthralled and makes the song less boring and endows value in a mediocre voice more than a beautiful voice that lacks expression.[30]

Citing Bacilly, Etienne Loulié (*Elements ou principes de musique*), Jean-Jacques Rousseau (*Dictionnaire de Musique*), and others, Jed Wentz has drawn attention to the widespread opinion that a fluid sense of *mouvement* communicated emotion more effectively than *musique mesuré*.[31] Grimarest's bold assertion that, "in a word, passion cannot be measured [*ne saurait être mesuré*]" applied primarily to recitative, the subject of his treatise, but it still substantiates the premise that emotional performance was not held to a metric straitjacket.³² These opinions do not undermine the connection between tempo and affect; rather they indicate that speed was only one factor that went toward the end result. The concept of movement within the measure was not confined to French music. Italian writers also expressed the difficulty of expressing the character and rhythmic "feel" of a piece when adhering to a strict interpretation of the notated rhythms.³³

Mouvement is naturally linked to dance, and most dance titles also specify tempo and character. We know, for instance, that (choosing three triple-time dances) most minuets were faster than courantes, and that both were faster than sarabandes. Qualifying tempo markings were also used, such as *Courante gaye*, *Sarabande grave*. These were used both to distinguish different variants of dances with the same name, and to provide a more accurate reflection of the character of specific dances. In the theater, where choreographies were tailor-made to different characters, dances had an even closer association with specific humours.

Baroque dance characters are defined by meter, tempo, melodic style, phrase organization, and formal design, and are found in a wide range of musical genres in most European traditions. Just as today's ballroom dance enthusiasts know the tempos that work for waltz, tango, and foxtrot, in the Rhetorical period, it was as much part of every courtier's training as it was essential to every musician's education to be familiar with the tempo and character of the menuet, bourée, and passepied. Each dance had its own affective associations, and these served much like the text of a song to establish the character of the dance. Mattheson was one of the many writers to provide encapsulated descriptions of the common characteristics of each dance type. The following list comes from his *Vollkommene Capellmeister*.

Passacaglia	sublime and stately
Courante	tender longing
Sarabande	nothing but dogged seriousness
Entrée	pomp and conceit
Rigaudon	agreeable joking
Bourrée	contentment and pleasantness
Rondeau	cheerfulness
Passepied	vacillation and instability
Gigue	ardor and passion
Gavotte	exulting or unrestrained joy
Menuet	temperate diversion³⁴

In a similar vein Quantz provided some clues to dance interpretation, but he is less helpful to modern musicians. Trusting his readers' experience and instincts, he described the character of dances in relation to one another. *Entrées*, loures, courantes, chaconnes, and passacailles were majestic; the sarabande was similar but had a more agreeable character.³⁵ Quantz did not discuss the siciliana with the other dances, but elsewhere he indicated that it should retain its origins as a simple shepherd's dance, not unlike French bergeries and musettes.[36] We will have more to say about timing and articulation in dance music in chapter 8.

Light and Shadow

A key element of *elocutio* was contrast and variety. Quintilian recommended varied pronunciation to lend grace to an oration and refresh the ear of the listener.[37] Seventeenth-century authorities reiterated this advice. In his treatise on gesture for orators, Michel Le Faucheur inverted the metaphor, and advised speakers take note of musicians:

> Diversify your voice in accordance with the diversity of the subjects of which you speak, the passions you wish either to express or arouse, the parts of your oration, and the stronger or weaker and more or less striking words you use. For just as an instrumentalist who played on only one string would be ridiculous and unbearable, so there is nothing that is more boring and distasteful to listeners than a constantly uniform voice.[38]

A similar theme is found in many musical performance manuals. In *Musick's Monument*, Thomas Mace repeatedly emphasized the importance of contrasts (soft–loud, brisk–smooth, courageous–tender).[39] Of the three ways to achieve contrast he mentioned more than once—variation in dynamics, tempo, and the use of pauses—he saw dynamics as the most effective means of bringing out the passion of a piece. His advice is directed not only to the performance of pieces with obvious contrasts but to those where there is more uniformity, such as this lute piece (Ex. 5.2).

Example 5.2 T. Mace, Lesson 7, Suite 1, from *Musick's Monument*, transcr. André Souris

This is how he described the mixture of humours in this piece:

> *Toyish, Joccond, Harmless* and *Pleasant* and, as if it were, one *Playing with*, or *Tossing a Ball, up and down*; yet It seems to have a very *Solemn Countenance*, and like unto one of a *Sober*, and *Innocent Condition*, or *Disposition*; not *Antick, Apish*, or *Wild*, etc.[40]

Mace then indicated that if each passion is correctly observed, the performer's imagination will be directed to an effective humouring of the piece. In his words:

> As to the *Performance of It*, you will do well to *Remember*, (as in all the rest, so in This) to Play *Loud*, and *Soft*, sometimes *Briskly*, and sometimes *Gently*, and *Smoothly*, here and there, as your *Fancy* will (no doubt) *Prompt you unto*, if you make a *Right Observation* of what I have already told you [about its character].[41]

We might be surprised that Mace could find so much variety in such a simple piece, but his example can serve as a model for humouring larger-scale musical forms. The contrasting episodes in rondos, or the *confutatio* sections in *da capo* arias, or the different variations of a ground-bass dance are all candidates for this type of treatment.

Further Reading

Wimsatt's "Intentional Fallacy" is an oft-visited theme in performance practice writings. One of the most recent, Andrew Parrott's *Composers' Intentions?*, an anthology of previously published articles on the topic, is an excellent synthesis of problematic case studies closely pertinent to the interpretation of Rhetorical music.

Barthold Kuijken's book, *The Notation is not the Music*, is full of insightful observations based on the premise that the music's message is only partially transmitted by the composer's score. *Rethinking Music*, edited by Cook and Everest, is a series of provocative essays examining of the relationship between music theory and performance; Leech-Wilkinson's *Changing Sound of Music* discusses some of the same issues with reference to early twentieth-century sound recordings.

On dance tempi and characters, see Bang Mather, *Dance Rhythms*, and Harris-Warrick, "Pendulum Markings."

Boccherini's Body by Elisabeth Le Guin presents a pioneering study of the relationship between musical and physical gesture in late eighteenth-century music.

6

Figures: Spinning Straw into Gold

GEOFFREY BURGESS

Wie hetzelfde anders zegt, zegt iets anders. [To say something differently is to say something different.]

—Dutch saying[1]

She had no idea how straw could be spun into gold, and she grew more and more frightened, until at last she began to weep.

— Grimm Brothers, *Rumplestiltskin*

It is a matter of channelling the flood of tears in order not to drown the sublime.

—Darbellay, 1988[2]

Public Speaking, Public Musicking

"Unaccustomed as I am to public speaking..."

How often have we heard these words uttered by distraught next-of-kin at a wedding or funeral as they clumsily unravel the tightly folded pages of a prepared speech and proceed to read, their attention glued to the text, while everyone diverts their eyes in embarrassment? These are not orations. Amateur rhetoricians thrust into circumstances like these are rarely able to muster their own emotions, let alone master those of others. Fearing that they will lose control as their emotions well up and interfere with the task at hand, they hide behind the well-chosen words of a quieter moment. They are absent, as it were, incapable of seizing the moment (*kairos*), and their determination to remain in control often results in a deadpan recitation. Inhibited by their nervousness, the core of the matter remains unaddressed.

These are, of course, some of the most challenging moments in anyone's life, and it is not surprising that traditional cultures around the world employ professionals to lead communal celebration and mourning. In Karelia, a region presently divided between Finland and Russia, female specialists facilitate the mourning process. These women are specialists at eliciting appropriate emotions from those mourning a loss. Their singing and ritualistic practices are based on traditional formulas, but each occasion is improvised and elaborated to suit the circumstances. It is precisely because they are not related to the bereaved and therefore not themselves bound up with emotion that these professionals can evoke the emotions of sorrow and loss in others.[3]

The performer of Rhetorical music occupies a place somewhere between these two approaches. We are professionals whose task is to evoke the passions through spontaneous improvisations, but we also work from prepared texts. Western music culture is often treated as an exclusively literate, text-centered culture.[4] This may accurately describe musicking as it has developed over the past two centuries, but in the Rhetorical period, musical performance was treated more as a hybrid textual-aural practice. Baroque notation does not attempt to prescribe the work to the same extent as, say, a Mahler Symphony. A Baroque score served as cue sheet. To elaborate it, to give it life, and put a personal stamp on it, the performer drew from a catalogue of figures and ornaments. The score, then, serves as a prop for us to get on with the job and keep us focused instead of succumbing to nervousness or distraction. But how often does our text, like the unaccustomed speaker's script, serve as a barrier for communicating the soul of the matter: personally engaged eloquence?

In the Grimm Brothers' *Rumplestiltskin*, the miller was all talk and his daughter was forced to live up to his rhetoric. The king commanded her to spin straw into gold: an impossible task, akin to fashioning a silk purse from a sow's ear—if not for a touch of fairy-tale magic. The Rhetorical musician is likewise entrusted with the task of magically breathing life into a musical husk (the composer's jottings) by applying figuration and ornamentation, and other necessary finishing touches and embellishments. As C. P. E. Bach explained, "it is principally in improvisations or fantasias that the keyboardist can best master the feelings of his audience."[5] This means that, "in short, both composition and performance are to be taken as the two sides of a common process which is measured according to affect."[6] The performer's improvised response to the composer's text not only brings immediacy to the music, it injects it with a personal perspective, and reintegrates performance into the meaning of the "work." The practice of rhetoric in Western culture is not unlike the formulaic procedures that the Karelian women mourners draw from. The rules of rhetoric are there to facilitate expression, and as Peter Seymour reminds us, they provide a theoretical framework that "surely allows the performer greater freedom for his or her own inspiration and imagination because these can be based on discipline, not on anarchy."[7]

Declamation as Figurative Speech

It is hard for us to grasp what rhetoric might have meant to people in the sixteenth, seventeenth, and eighteenth centuries. What is sure is that there was a significant difference between everyday talk and the heightened speech of orators. According to Bacilly, the on-stage speech of orators and singers was entirely different from the familiar language heard in the streets.[8] Decorum demanded more dignified and refined language when addressing persons of higher birth, and religious observance also prescribed a reverential tone in worship. Today the art of public speaking may not be as widely practiced as it was in earlier centuries, and the distinction between erudite and vernacular discourse may be less apparent, but there is still a noticeable difference between how an ambassador addresses the United Nations or a mayor gives the inaugural speech at a music festival, and how the same people would go about ordering their morning coffee. The general tone of modern oratory may be "low brow" and include more colloquialisms compared with earlier traditions, and politicians' harangues, attorney's summaries, and preachers' sermons may not always adhere to the time-honored principles of Classical rhetoric, but they are all examples of heightened declamation calculated to influence the listener.

To declaim is to use language in an emphatic way. In speech, declamation is exaggerated in clarity, pronunciation, and the rising and falling cadence of the voice. It is also timed for maximum impact. The definition of "declamation" in the *Oxford English Dictionary* stresses the emotional force of heightened speech:

> Declamation: public speaking, singing, or playing in an exaggerated manner expressing strong feeling (as, for instance, vehemently, emphatically, or passionately); addressed to the passions of the audience rather than to reason.[9]

Declamation that grabs a listener by the scruff of the neck lives on. Among politicians and trial lawyers it may have become a pale shadow of former practices, but it can still be heard in a powerful form among evangelical preachers in the United States. A well-known example is the Reverend Martin Luther King Jr.'s speech "I Have a Dream" from 1963, which, with its sense of timing, tremors in the voice, and energy, illustrates how declamation can lift simple words to powerful oration (Audio Ex. 6.1). King's speech is not likely to bear much resemblance to the practices of eighteenth-century politicians, actors, and preachers, but it is a striking demonstration of the musical qualities of heightened speech and just how compelling a public speech in an emphatic tone can be.

🔊 AUDIO EX. 6.1. "I Have a Dream," Martin Luther King Jr., 28 Aug. 1963

Declamatory styles are in constant flux. Recordings of Shakespearean actors can give us a sense of how theatrical declamation has shifted over the course of the past century (Audio Ex. 6.2). For a good part of the twentieth century actors were expected to conform to an allegedly neutral "received pronunciation." Reserved for international communication (so-called BBC English, or Queen's English) and theatrical declamation, this heightened form of pronunciation strove for universal comprehensibility but was the everyday speech of nobody. Added to this artificial enunciation, actors developed distinctive ways of distinguishing their acting voice from their everyday talk. Around the middle of the twentieth-century, actors like Richard Burton dropped the pretense and started to "normalize" Shakespeare. Their modernized readings had the effect of turning Shakespeare's poetry into prose. More recently there has been a conscientious effort to substitute received pronunciation with actual regional accents or reconstructions of "authentic" Elizabethan pronunciation. The Globe Theatre Company currently offers performances of Shakespeare's plays in both original pronunciation and contemporary English. Both are markedly different from early twentieth-century traditions, but the Globe's performances are equally rich in emotive communication.

🔊 AUDIO EX. 6.2. W. Shakespeare, Hamlet's soliloquy, Hamlet act 3, sc.1
a) Herbert Beerbohm Tree (HMV, 1906)
b) Richard Burton (Electrovision, 1964)
c) Matthew Mellalieu, *Shakespeare's Original Pronunciation*
   (British Library, 2012)

What distinguishes actors and professional orators from the occasional public speakers at a funeral is their ability to control their own engagement with the subject without reducing the force of the message. Politicians like Margaret Thatcher and Adolf Hitler were effective communicators not only for what they said but for the conviction with which they expressed it. Their rhetoric could spread a contagion of respect or frenzied action that could alter their audience's sense of judgment. These orators never revealed personal weakness, and regardless of what we think of what they stood for, they were undeniably able to command the emotions of their listeners. Gifted orators must show some degree of personal engagement; they will occasionally get caught up in the emotions being expressed, but they are trained to maintain their cool. As the seventeenth-century French acting authority François Hédelin, abbé d'Aubignac wrote, "the disorder in the words of a man who mourns is a fault that enfeebles the external signs of mourning, and it must be corrected on the stage, which admits of nothing imperfect."[10] Julia Gillard, the former prime minister of Australia, demonstrated the self-control required of an orator in a formal report she presented to Parliament on the series of natural disasters that swept through parts the country in 2011 (Audio Ex. 6.3). With trembling voice she struggled to hold back tears as she described the courage of those who fought to save the lives of others. The way she pulled through and managed to stay in control of her emotions performed the endurance that she lauded in her compatriots. President Obama used a different tactic to maintain control during a public statement after a similarly painful tragedy—the shooting at an elementary school in December 2012. He never allowed his voice to falter; instead he took deliberate breaks of up to twelve seconds to still his emotions and wipe tears from his eyes.

🔊 AUDIO EX. 6.3. Julia Gillard, Speech to Australian Parliament, 8.ii.2011 (https://www.youtube.com/watch?v=27lNVExOC4c, accessed 25 June 2015).

Heightened speech served as the primary model for musicians in the Rhetorical age. In 1749 Geminiani commented that all good music has the sound of someone discoursing passionately. Singers were an important point of contact and were normally thought of as actors. They had to make sure their listeners heard and understood the text—not just the individual words, but what those words implied and their underlying passion. The necessity to make every word understandable in what amounts to "musical declamation" affects many aspects of a singer's delivery, not least their diction. Dubos spoke of the "elevated" voice characteristic of theatrical declamation:

> The French do not depend upon dress alone for giving the actors of tragedy a suitable dignity and grandeur. We insist likewise, upon their speaking with a tone of voice more elevated, graver, and more sustained than that which is used in common conversation. . . . 'Tis true this manner of reciting is more troublesome . . . but, besides being more majestic, it is also more advantageous for the spectators, who are better enabled thereby to understand the verses.[11]

To distinguish heightened declamation from so-called normal speech, Dubos drew attention to the use of the decorative elements that an orator would use but were not normally found in everyday speech. Being an ornamental form of communication, poetry is an important marker of heightened speech. "Poetic style," Dubos explained, consisted in "expressing by figures and images capable of moving us, that which would have no effect upon us, were it related in the simplicity of a prose style."[12] Poetry then, represents exceptional, heightened speech full of "elevated words and figurative uses," and is reserved for when quotidian talk is inadequate.

There is an intentional musical quality to poetry that requires a more nuanced delivery than prose. A novelist might effectively express the thoughts of his protagonist like this:

"Soon I will die in Fontanay, the village where I was born."

A poet, on the other hand, might embellish this with figures and cast it in a versified form to create something more like the famous verses of Guillaume Amfrye de Chaulieu (1639–1720):

Fontenay, lieu délicieux,	*Fontenay! forever dear!*
Où je vis d'abord la lumière;	*Where first I saw the light of day,*
Bientôt au bout de ma carrière,	*I soon from life shall steal away*
Chez toi je joindrai mes aïeux.	*To sleep with my forefathers here.*

—(trans. Longfellow[13])

We don't normally address places, but Chaulieu's narrator finds himself doing this, and in his heightened state of nostalgic reverie, expresses himself in verse. A recitation of his words demands heightened declamation. Prose can be read as ordinary speech, but it would be less than satisfying to hear Chaulieu's poem read that way. The rise and fall of the voice is important as much in the French as the English version: savoring the sonorous quality of the individual words (*délicieux, carrière*) adds meaning, and the timing of the rhyme is just as crucial to conveying the sense as correct diction. Longfellow's English rendering is not a literal translation, and the choice and order of the words lend it a specific rhythm that is unlike everyday speech. (Inversions like "Where first I saw" in place of "Where I first saw" is a common poetic figure.)

In music, we generally think of prose "talk" in recitatives and poetic declamation in arias. The distinction is relative, and both are on a sliding scale between everyday speech and heightened, extraordinary declamation. Characters in opera rarely have the need to order coffee or to engage in small talk, so at least in pre-Mozart opera even recitative is hardly ever simply talk, and the text is more often poetry and not prose. Whether they are divine beings, tragic heroes, or comic stereotypes, the characters in Baroque opera are constantly in a charged emotional state, and their speech is likewise in the realm of the extraordinary. This is true also of recitative in sacred cantatas. René Jacobs provides a beautiful example of heightened delivery and emotional expression in the recitative in Bach's cantata *Ach Herr, mich armen Sünder*, BWV 135, by convincingly introducing a tremor in the voice (Audio Ex. 6.4). After the first verse "Ich bin von Seufzen müde" (I am weary from sighing) he is able to gather enough self control to describe the circumstances that have led to his state of despair.

🔊 AUDIO EX. 6.4. BWV 135/4 René Jacobs with Leonhardt Consort, dir. Leonhardt (Telefunken, 1983)

Just as there are different levels of speech and oratory, including the art of debate and dialogue, Rhetorical music calls for different levels of declamation. There is place for humble or intimate communication, such as the polite musical discourse that the Besozzi brothers brought with them from Turin to Paris in the Spring of 1735. One contemporary described their playing as follows:

> The two Bezzuzzi, the one oboist and the other bassoonist, who held little musical conversations together, which almost make one swoon with enjoyment; I cannot express the raptures into which one is thrown. I have never in my life experienced anything more enchanting.[14]

Only one of Alessandro Besozzi's "little conversations" for hautboy and bassoon is known to survive (and that, of course, only in note form on paper).[15] Over the next couple of decades this style of musical discourse was very much in vogue in Paris. Chamber music in which the instruments take equal roles advertised this quality in titles such as *Conversations en manière de sonates* (Alexandre de Villeneuve, 1733), and *Sonates en quatuors, ou Conversations galantes et amusantes* (Louis-Gabriel Guillemain, 1743).

The concept of musical conversation implies that the dialogue could be appreciated by the players without the presence of an audience, and listening to this music can be a little like eavesdropping. Its charm is in the dynamic of the performance and the exchange of wit, even more than the art of convincing a listener who is not an active participant in the musical dialogue. This type of colloquial conversation is appropriate to many other pieces, for example C. P. E. Bach's remarkable study in dueling characters, the trio sonata *Sanguineus & Melancholicus* Wq 161/4. Program music like this calls for some level of theatrical engagement, perhaps reflecting the way Cambini identified musical humouring with the technical gestures of performance. Throughout the first movement the two characters are virtually incapable of engaging in civil conversation as they hold to their own humours. But by the third movement, they have reconciled their differences and are able to share the same thematic material. Bach fashioned a musical subject that blends the two humours. The two characters are clearly audible in the recording by violinists Rachel Podger and Lucy Russell (Audio Ex. 6.5). More than simply playing the notes, their interpretation responds to the two character-humours as eager Sanguineus interrupts Melancholicus's lethargy.

🔊 AUDIO EX. 6.5. C. P. E. Bach, Trio Sonata *Sanguineus & Melancholicus*, Wq 161/4 Ensemble Florilegium (Channel Classics, 1997)
a) Allegretto–Presto
b) Allegro

Other pieces in Rhetorical style require a single player to engage in dialogue by finding different characters within a single melodic line in much the same way that a recitalist has to find different voices to set off the characters in a Lied (listen to Audio Ex. 5.4). In Corrette's *Délices de la solitude* (op. 20, ca. 1738; Audio Ex. 6.6) there are no actual characters, nor is the piece programmatic: the music's appeal lies instead in discovering an agreeable musical discourse in the interchange of gestures in the simple melodic line.

🔊 AUDIO EX. 6.6. Michel Corrette, *Les délices de la solitude*, Sonata 2, Allegro, Napper, Les Voix humaines (ATMA, 2006)

Figures as Ornamental Glosses

Elocutio, then, can be thought of as a set of techniques that transform prose text into poetic declamation. In music this involves glosses or elaborations of simpler ideas to create more eloquent forms. Fénelon argued that to transform "a plain narrative [that] does not move People" into a stirring oration that "strikes the senses" required "a lively moving representation of the manner and circumstances of the facts we relate."[16] So, too, elaboration is one of the principal ways in which recreative artists can put their personal stamp on a work. There is no essential difference between the figures used by the composer to flesh out a compositional skeleton and the improvised embellishments added by a performer. Both are aspects of the *elaboratio*, the layering of paraphrases and glosses that gives life and eloquence to the *inventio*. Quantz developed the essential point played by ornamentation in expressing the passionate qualities of the music:

> Liveliness and sadness exist in several different degrees, so that for example a furious passion demands expression [Ger. *Vortrag*/ Fr. *expression*] more full of fire than a playful one, even though both involve liveliness. This applies also to graces that may be added in order to embellish and characterize a simple song or melody. Ornaments, whether simple essential graces or free *passaggi*, should never be contrary to the dominant passion of the principal melody, so the sustained and drawn-out melody shouldn't be confused with movements that must be playful,

whimsical, sprightly, or astonishing movements; nor the bold with the flattering, and so on.[17]

Ornament is usually contrasted with structure, but thinking of them as opposites can be misleading. The relationship is one of mutual dependence. Ornamentation was a way to soften lines and offset predictable structures. It was also responsible for the uniqueness of each new design. This applies as much to Baroque architecture and garden design, which like the music of same period, were highly symmetrical in structure garnished with ornamental variety.

The structure–ornament relationship does not equate with the division of labor between composer and performer. Mattheson, for instance, listed many figures that are identical to graces, and other writers stressed the need for performers to have grounding in composition in order to invent suitable embellishments.[18] The process of *elaboratio* was shared by both creative artists. The composer began with a basic idea, fleshed it out by elaborating it with figures to produce the score, which then became the performer's blueprint to further gloss with improvised embellishments.

By scrutinizing eighteenth-century composition manuals, figured bass treatises, *solfigetti*, and *partimenti*, Robert Gjerdingen has identified a series of compositional prototypes—what he calls *schemata*—that permeate all types and genres that fall within the span of High Baroque and Early Classical music.[19] These schemata are the stock harmonic progressions and voice-leading procedures (such as the "rule of the octave," and ground-bass patterns) used to generate musical structures. They unfold over time and take the music to specific destinations, but they are themselves without meaning or passionate implications and can therefore be pressed into service in virtually any context. They are elements of structure to hang an *inventio* on, and to then elaborate with figures. As such these formulas constitute the most basic level of *dispositio*.

The Romanesca was a favorite schema, found in music from the sixteenth to the end of the eighteenth century (Ex. 6.1).

Example 6.1 Giacomo Tritto, *partimento*, ca. 1810 (from Gjerdingen, *Music in the Galant Style*, 26)

Clothed with added dissonances, varied or inverted harmonies, and different melodic gestures, the Romanesca can serve as the basis for a multitude of compositions in contrasting guises. Examples 6.2a, b, and c show how it can be

Example 6.2 Figural variations of the Romanesca a) Stanislao Mattei, *partimento*, ca. 1780 (from Gjerdingen, *Music in the Galant Style*, 26) b) G. F. Handel, Exercises for Queen Anne, 1724–34 (from Gjerdingen, 28) c) G. F. Handel, Adagio from Sonata HWV 366

elaborated to create pieces with divergent details and affects. The two excerpts from Handel use the Romanesca bass in contrasting movements. The lively figuration and interplay between the hands in the exercise for Queen Anne paint a very different affect from the lugubrious opening melody and walking bass in the oboe sonata.

Filling out the harmonies is the first step toward transforming these schemata into pieces of music. Musical training in the seventeenth and eighteenth centuries involved the practice of elaborating harmonic formulas such the Romanesca at the keyboard as accompaniment exercises or autonomous keyboard pieces (*partimenti*). The elaboration of the harmonic structure in performance—the realization of the basso continuo—was the most essential type of *elocutio* in the Baroque period. It is just as common to find an unfigured bassline as one provided with accurate and useful figuring. With or without figures, a continuo player had to be adept at realizing the composer's intentions by entering into the compositional process. Like melodic ornamentation, continuo playing should be spontaneous in order to be able to adapt to the circumstances, provide support for the other players, complement the melodic parts, and balance the other instruments and voices. Most basso continuo treatises and written-out examples demonstrate the importance of correct harmonic treatment and good voice-leading. The nature of the continuo player's collaboration in the process of musical elaboration is primarily harmonic. Engaging in creative melodic interplay is a further refinement but if not handled judiciously, can interfere with the other written parts.

Essential Graces

Just as any well-bred member of society would never have appeared in public without the adornments of fashion, so Rhetorical music was never aired without embellishments. An unornamented melody was an uncut diamond, a lifeless skeleton, with only potential significance, that would never be heard (unless it was the product of bad taste or poor training).[20] Bacilly was not alone in believing that music could be beautiful, but that without ornaments it failed to please.[21] Here I do not intend to add to the already extensive literature on the technical aspects of ornamentation. Tables of ornaments are very useful for building a ready vocabulary of ornaments, but they do not address the questions of *why* ornaments are used and *how* they contribute to eloquent performance.

In much the same way that performers were expected to fill out continuo parts in full harmonic realizations, composers habitually notated vocal parts and melodic lines in shorthand, anticipating that they would be elaborated in performance. Some ornaments are indispensable to the musical grammar—whence their common name "essential graces." A cadence implies the graceful gesturing of a trill as a necessary finishing touch. A falling third implies filling in with the intervening passing note. Dissonances imply emphasis and release on the resolution.

These ornaments were so obvious that adding them was virtually instinctual. Leopold Mozart wrote about this in reference to the appoggiatura, one of the most common and versatile ornaments:

> [Appoggiaturas] are demanded by Nature herself to bind the notes together, thereby making a melody more song-like. I say by Nature herself, for it is undeniable that even a peasant closes his peasant-song with grace-notes... Nature herself forces him to do this. In the same way the simplest peasant often uses figures of speech and metaphors without knowing it.[22]

On the next level of less-than-essential graces, appoggiaturas and other dissonant tones add spice to a plain melody, and repetitions (either exact or in sequence) imply more ornamental elaboration on each reiteration, because saying something differently is to say something different. These were all part of a context in which (as Roger North wrote in the 1720s) "a master can tell by the plaine notes, and the course of the air, how to Grace with advantage, as well as he that made the composition."[23] The addition of essential graces was not only obligatory according to the principles of musical grammar and style, their performance had to comply with a certain range of grammatically correct versions. Appoggiaturas should be slurred to their resolution, trills need to start on the upper note in recognition of their function as ornamented appoggiaturas, and so forth.

Rules like these notwithstanding, the notation of ornaments was deliberately approximate to allow for subtle variations. Mattheson commented that graces were subject to modification, according to fashion, innovation, and local style.[24] That is in part why symbols (+ or *tr* for trill, ⁎ for mordents, ∞ turns, etc.) were favored for the essential graces. They are like punctuation in prose: grammatically necessary, but in performance take on multifarious forms.[25] Roger North spoke of the inadequacy of notation to capture the art of ornamentation:

> It is the hardest task that Can be to pen the Manner of artificial Gracing an upper part; It hath bin accepted, and in print, but with Woefull Effect ... the Spirit of that art is Incommunicable by writing, therefore it is almost Inexcusable to attempt it.[26]

Trills, for instance, are by definition indeterminate and ambiguous and can take on an almost infinite number of variations: longer or shorter appoggiatura, two beats or four, faster or slower, as well as variant terminations. These niceties of execution often defy accurate notation and for that reason even though François Couperin used equal note values when he wrote out his trills, his prose explanation calls for a slight, almost imperceptible acceleration in the alternation.[27] Alexander Pope may well have been thinking of the finer art of musical gracing when he wrote in his *Essay on Criticism* (1711) of the "nameless Graces" that are learned from experience alone:

> Some Beauties, yet, no Precepts can declare,
> For there's a *Happiness* as well as *Care*.
> *Musick* resembles *Poetry*, in each
> Are *nameless Graces* which no Methods teach,
> And which a *Master-Hand* alone can reach.

In the early twentieth century when the original significance of graces was not generally known, most musicians performed them out of a sense of historical responsibility and with an air of polite tolerance. Most trills heard on early recordings are short, fast, and often with the main note rather than the upper note receiving the attention. Graces were so little understood that editors felt the need to instruct players by writing them out in full. This is an oxymoron, a conceptual contradiction, because what is essential about all ornaments is their spontaneous, ephemeral nature that defies accurate transcription. It is in the detail of how the speed of a trill increases, or the exact degree of stress applied to an appoggiatura that performers can convey affect and express individuality.

In the end, there is no definitive code to be cracked, no one way to realize ornaments. In Paris where the same symbols appeared in music by different composers, we know on the authority of Michel Pignolet de Montéclair that there was still disagreement as to how ornaments were played.[28] Recognizing the coexistence of different conventions, François Couperin used ⁕ in his keyboard music, and + in vocal works. Joseph Bodin de Boismortier even occasionally used two systems of notation in the same piece. His *Sonates pour un Clavecin et une flûte traversière,* op. 91, contain multiple instances where a + is notated in the flute part, while a ⁕ appears in the keyboard part. The fact that instrumental treatises provide more detailed information on gracing than vocal tutors may reflect the tendency that instrumentalists learned from printed material, and singers from the example of their masters.

There are rare instances where an unadorned version of the "naked text" is called for as a special effect. Nonfigured music could paint certain ideas very effectively. In the Frost Scene from *King Arthur* and Winter from the *Four Seasons,* Purcell and Vivaldi wrote frozen, lifeless music in the form of unadorned chordal progressions. These are examples of *dispositio* with no figural *elaboratio;* nascent music awaiting to be given life as spring melts the ice of winter. Adding ornaments to these progressions would make no sense: their effect is palpable precisely because of the way they arrest the listener's attention. Unadorned harmonic progressions are sometimes used to elicit awe and to conjure up the transcendent state of the sublime. *Zadok the Priest,* one of the anthems Handel composed in 1727 for the coronation of King George II, begins with a bare series of chords where the only figural elaboration consists in pulsing repeated notes and arpeggios (Audio Ex. 6.7). The breathtaking effect of these ravishing chords originates from their simplicity. As the harmony unfolds over the course of more than a minute, there is a mounting expectation for the music to break into melodic figuration. Handel calculated this strategy to coincide with the most solemn moment of the coronation: the anointing of the king.

🔊 AUDIO EX. 6.7. G. F. Handel, opening of *Zadok the Priest* (abbreviated) Choir of King's College, Cambridge, Academy of Ancient Music, dir. Stephen Cleobury (Warner Classics, 2001)

Graces as Glosses

It is enlightening to consider musical figures and graces as a close analogy to figures in rhetoric.[29] Treatises on rhetoric devote considerable attention to figures of speech. They are what make arguments more immediate and compelling by giving them relevance and personability. Figures often take the form of cleverly put statements that not only communicate a thought or feeling, but do so in an elegant or amusing way. Take this example by Fielding from *Tom Jones*:

> Having left Mr. Miller a little while *to chew the cud* (if I may use that expression)...[30]

Repeated over time, certain expressions got to be known well—then only too well, eventually to become commonplaces, sayings, banalities, and platitudes. Whatever their degree of familiarity, figures of speech are, by nature and use, formulaic. They are stock phrases that a speaker has up his sleeve (if *I* may use that expression) and can draw from in a diversity of contexts. They make up a veritable toolbox of rhetorical tricks to embellish an argument. Some will be planned out, like a choice anecdote to illustrate an argument; others may be more spontaneous, taking inspiration from unique circumstances at the time of delivery.

The spontaneous patterns improvised by singers and players in the polyphonic music of the sixteenth century began to take form as they were passed on to the monodists of the seventeenth century, and eventually became the set formulas for the gracings of the eighteenth century which were essentially stereotyped musical clichés.[31] Following rhetorical treatises that demonstrate the versatility of figures of speech, musical texts from Diego Ortiz's *Trattado de Glosas* of 1553 to Johann Georg Tromlitz's *Ausführlicher und gründlicher Unterricht die Flöte zu spielen* (1791) supplied catalogues of ornaments, figures, gestures, and ways of negotiating melodic intervals or harmonic sequences that could be inserted wherever appropriate.[32] Example 6.3 shows the table of sample ornaments to grace the rising figure of 3-#4-5 from Quantz's *Versuch*. From a grammatical standpoint, any one of the twenty-three variations is as good as any other, but there will be only one that will match the desired passion. Quantz's ornaments comply with Robert Marshall's observations on effective diminutions. They

- avoid fundamental changes in the structure of the musical material;
- embellish and elaborate the original ideas, leaving them essentially unaltered in basic character and contour.
- consist of the addition of tones, and the subdivision of long notes into a number of shorter notes of various pitches.[33]

Variations with more notes and wider leaps are suited to more lively affects. Flamboyant, melodically wide-ranging, and rhythmically striking ornaments draw attention to themselves and are hence more appropriate to structural points in the movement. Written-out embellishments for whole movements by

Quantz and other composers often show the gradual accumulation of detail over the course of the piece and particularly toward cadences. Quantz's variants (a), (c), and (i) are the simplest and could be used to elaborate the repetition of a phrase; (b), (d), and (e) show different ways of introducing harmony notes; (g) and (t) use virtually the same contour, with the intervening passing notes filled in as triplets in (g). The triplets give a more flowing sense than the animated, even frisky, feel of (t). Some of the ornaments are suitable for passing gestures; others, like (n), (o), (q), and (w), for cadences.

Example 6.3 Quantz, *Versuch*, ch. 13 §17, Table 11

The Salt of Music, the Spice of Dissonance

In 1738 Johann Abraham Birnbaum, professor of rhetoric at Leipzig University and a friend of J. S. Bach, wrote the following, probably inspired by Bach's music:

> The true amenity of music consists in the connection and alternation of consonances and dissonances without hurt to the harmony. The nature of music demands this. The various passions, especially the dark ones, cannot be expressed with fidelity to nature without this alternation.[34]

Rhetorical music relies on the counterplay of consonance and dissonance, and as we saw with the Romanesca, a simple musical *dispositio* can be given musical expression with the addition of ornamental figures and carefully placed dissonances. There was a coincidence between the decorative function of dissonance and the elaborative role of figures. Prior to about 1660, German sources describe the figure as "an artful and irregular manner of musical text expression" that introduces dissonance.[35] Christoph Bernhard, for example, defined a figure as "a certain way of employing dissonances that renders them not only inoffensive but rather quite agreeable."[36] Using a culinary metaphor, in 1678 Wolfgang Printz described musical figures as the salt of melodies because, just as with an unsalted dish, a melody without figures had little appeal.[37] Another way of looking at this is that enhancing a schema of harmonic consonances with dissonance is equivalent to figures of speech that are licenses to the rules of everyday communication.[38]

Dissonance was subjected to its own special rules—not just the rules of counterpoint passed down from the Renaissance but specific rules for how they were to be treated in performance. These rules do not restrict the expressive potential of dissonance; on the contrary they actually provide the means for performers to take particular delight in the dissonant effect. As Quantz explained, dissonance was as much the domain of the composer as the performer who had to be constantly aware of how to bring it forth to the listener.

> In order to express the different passions eloquently, the dissonances are played more strongly than the consonances. . . . The more a dissonance is distinguished from the other notes, then, the more it is noticed, and the more it touches the ear. And vice-versa, the more something that interrupts our pleasure is disagreeable, the more pleasurable is that which follows. Thus logically, the more painful the dissonances are, the more pleasure we will feel when they are resolved. Without this alternation of agreeable and disagreeable notes, music would be unable to instantly excite the different Passions, nor to calm them again.[39]

Quantz gave precise instructions for the dynamic intensity implied by specific dissonances, and again compared dissonance to seasoning in cooking: "For (as I said before) not all dissonances are of equal importance; they can be regarded like salt and spices in dishes, some of which have more effect on the palette than others."[40]

Graces as Passionate Expression

One should play from the soul, and not like a trained bird [*abgerichteter Vogel*].[41]

This remark from C. P. E. Bach on performance in general may have been intended as a commentary on a passage in his colleague Quantz's treatise that encouraged singers to use their "own fantasy in applying ornaments, not learning them by ear from others, like many do, using only words like a bird-brained parrot [*Papageh/simple perroquet*] who knows only what he has learned from his master."⁴² Both reinforce the importance of ornament as personalized and impassioned expression. Still, as Étienne Darbellay has remarked, C. P. E. Bach's admonition for the performer to launch into free flight is tethered to a profusion of restrictive rules.⁴³ Improvising ornaments requires walking a fine line between being oneself and complying with the work's prescribed structure.

To match music and expression, it is useful to look at how different writers described standard ornaments. Certain graces were associated with specific passions and affections. Bacilly's *Remarques curieuses* of 1668 is one of the earliest sources to give a prose description of graces. In addition to the general observation that ornaments "should never be contrary to the dominant passion of the principal melody" by upsetting a sustained melody with "playful, whimsical, sprightly, or astonishing" elements or mixing bold music with flattering ornaments, Bacilly provided a succinct guide to identifying the affective characteristics of specific essential graces. He noted that delicate *tremblements étouffés* (or half trills), slow trills, certain types of *ports de voix* (appoggiaturas), and *accents* (short ornamental notes slurred to the end of the main note) are appropriate for the expression of sadness, sorrow, and for laments. The *doublement de gosier* (a vocal *pincé* or mordent used in conjunction with the *port de voix*) on the other hand added joyous gaiety.⁴⁴

We might hope for more precision on the affective connotation of ornaments from Quantz's detailed treatise. Concerning specific ornaments, he states that

> appoggiaturas bind together the different voices and enhance the harmony. The trills and other little Graces like the half-trills, mordents, turns, and battements add vivacity to the expression. The alternation of *piano* and *forte* brings notes into relief, or suggest tenderness.⁴⁵

However, apart from giving examples of ornaments suited to Adagio movements, Quantz's comments are confined to the harmonic function of different ornaments. From what he said elsewhere we can extrapolate that he thought they should be chosen according to their suitability to the principal passion of the movement, the humour of the specific passage, their place in the overall shape of the movement, and how the performer wished to characterize each gesture.

Significantly, Quantz attributed dynamics with a similar ornamental function to added grace notes. Other sources give more guidance on the subject. Published immediately prior to Quantz's treatise, Francesco Geminiani's *Art of Playing on the Violin* (1751) provides more specific directions for fourteen "Ornaments of Expression, necessary to the playing in a good Taste." Geminiani explained that the *plain shake* (trill) is used in quick movements, and that the *turned shake* expresses gaiety, but when extended, it is more suited to tender passions.

The appoggiatura "is supposed to express Love, Affection, Pleasure, &c.," and should be lengthened for maximum effect. Like Quantz he treated *swelling and diminishing the sound* as ways of adding more beauty and variety to melodies in any tempo, and described *piano* and *forte* as an imitation of the raising and lowering of the orator's voice, and consequently necessary for expressing "the intention of the melody." The *separation* (an escape note, similar to the French *accent*) between rising or falling intervals can be used to add tenderness. As for the *beat* (or mordent), Geminiani explained how to combine it with other graces to produce specific emotions. When performed "with strength, and continued long," it "expresses fury, anger, resolution, &c., but if you play it quite soft, and swell the note, it may then denote horror, fear, grief, lamentation, etc. By making it short and swelling the note gently, it may express affection and pleasure."[46]

Geminiani's fourteenth ornament, the *close shake* "cannot possibly be described by notes" (i.e., cannot be notated), but from his detailed description of the technique of rocking the left-hand finger stopping the violin string, it is clear that he was referring to what we now call vibrato.[47] Like the other thirteen, this ornament of expression also evoked various passions depending on how it was used:

> When it is continued swelling the sound by degrees, drawing the bow nearer the bridge, and ending it strong it may express majesty, dignity, etc. But making it shorter lower and softer, it may denote affliction, fear, etc. *and when it is made on short notes, it only contributes to make their sound more agreable and for this reason it should be made use of as often as possible.*[48]

Modern performers have struggled to reconcile what seems to be a recommendation for the continuous use of vibrato with other (admittedly scant) eighteenth-century sources that imply it was used selectively as an expressive ornament. Even Geminiani's pupil Robert Bremner, while conceding that vibrato was considered a virtue among singers, felt that when it came to orchestral violin playing, his teacher's opinion was suspect, and consequently removed this passage from the posthumous editions of the treatise that he supervised.[49] Still, it seems significant that Geminiani categorized the *close shake* as an ornament, and it is possibly because of its versatility in expressing a range of affects that he recommended its use "as often as possible" and not "as continuously as possible."

Like the *close shake* on string instruments, woodwind *flattement* (a finger vibrato, or a microtonal trill produced by alternately partially covering and opening a hole), and clavichord *Bebung* were often used to give shape to the movement from dissonance to resolution, and to enhance the *messa di voce*.[50]

By adding a slight tremor to the sound, these techniques imitate the human voice in an impassioned state and thus bring out the music's expressive component. (For an example of the emotional charge conveyed by a tremulous speaking voice, listen to Audio Ex. 7.1a.) Considered the very soul of a musician's tone, vibrato remains a hotly debated topic because of its loaded emotional associations. In the 1960s and '70s, vibrato was mistakenly viewed as a Romantic indulgence that period performers were eager to suppress (we now know that it had more to do with the twentieth- rather than the nineteenth-century practices). Although it is fairly clear that the exaggerated, wide vibrato (or wobble) we tolerate in *verismo* opera from singers such as Luciano Pavarotti and Dame Joan Sutherland would have been scorned in the eighteenth century, it remains unclear whether a less obtrusive oscillation (of pitch or intensity) was considered natural or a desirable attribute. Nor is it clear whether this was a regular feature of vocal production. Only a small variation in pitch (less than a semitone) is practicable; otherwise the vibrato interferes with the production of other ornaments. In particular, it can be confused with ornaments that involve pitch oscillation such as trills. Early recordings give a strong indication that vibrato (often called *tremolo* at the time) started to become a standard adjunct to vocal tone production only in the early twentieth century.[51]

With the rise of HIP, the absence of explicit references to vibrato in eighteenth-century treatises was taken at face value, and vibrato was for a time "outlawed." "White," vibrato-less singing became an admired quality. But even Emma Kirkby, who established a career on her pure boy soprano–like tone, never totally eliminated vibrato from her technique and was not averse to using it as an ornament for expressive purposes. In "Sit nomen Domini" (Let the name of the Lord) from Handel's *Laudate Pueri*, HWV 237 for instance, her tone is generally straight, but she enhances the first dissonance (on *Do-* in "Domini") with vibrato (Audio Ex. 6.8). As well as reinforcing the focal word in the text, adding vibrato here helps to give the first vocal phrase direction as the repeated pitches give way to melodic motion.

⏺ AUDIO EX. 6.8. Handel, "Sit nomen Domini" from *Laudate Pueri* HWV237, Emma Kirkby with The Orchestra of the Antipodes, dir. Walker, G. Burgess, oboe (ABC Classics, 2006).

As vibrato became an integral part of tone production in modern performance, it has been robbed of much of its passionate significance. Many well-known HIP singers use vibrato in a way that is closer to modern practice than as an ornament. David Daniels, schooled in the Metropolitan Opera style, hardly ever drops his vibrato. His performance is engaging because of how he constantly modulates the speed, intensity, and amplitude of his vibrato. The sustained opening note in "Ombra mai fù" from Handel's *Serse* in Audio Example 6.9 is an ideal opportunity to demonstrate his *messa di voce* and control of vibrato.

🔊 AUDIO EX. 6.9. Handel, "Ombrai mai fiù" from *Serse*, David Daniels, *Handel Operatic Arias*, Orchestra of the Age of Enlightenment, dir. Norrington (Virgin, 1998)

A singer's ability to draw out long notes such as this was a much-admired trick in the eighteenth century, particularly among castrati. The famous story of Farinelli outdoing a trumpet player in a competition of breath control and thrilling the audience by expanding the tone on a sustained note with a *messa di voce* formed the basis of a scene in the 1994 film *Farinelli* where the protagonist holds a note for a staggering length of time (Audio Ex. 6.10).[52] The audience grows silent in amazement. Heads turn, and women swoon. While a vivid replay of the *primo uomo*'s power over his audience, the cinematic performance is the result of technological trickery. The castrato's voice on the soundtrack is spliced together from two singers, and the note is prolonged artificially with no variation in the tone for a full twenty-four seconds, which would have seemed disturbingly unnatural to eighteenth-century audiences.

🔊 AUDIO EX. 6.10. Riccardo Broschi, "Ombra fedel anch'io" from *Idaspe* (1730) from *Farinelli*, dir. Gérard Corbiau, 1994, Derek Lee Ragin, countertenor, and Ewa Malas-Gollewska, soprano, Les Talents Lyriques, dir. Christoph Rousset.

When vibrato is the norm, nonvibrato becomes a special effect. Recently some singers have experimented with reversing the application of vibrato in Rhetorical music. Admired for her performances of Handel's operas, Cecilia Bartoli treats vibrato as a part of normal vocal production, and nonvibrato as exceptional (Audio Ex. 6.11). Although the reverse of what we know of historical practices, her instincts direct her performance in intelligent and effective ways.

🔊 AUDIO EX. 6.11. Handel, "Lascia la spina," *Il Trionfo del Tiempo e del Disinganno*, Cecilia Bartoli (Live from Teatro Olimpico, Venezia, 1998, https://www.youtube.com/watch?v=VhNRWduBPmY, accessed 25 June 2015)

This use of vibrato resembles the practice of contemporary jazz and Broadway singers. Audio Example 6.12 is a touching demonstration from one of the great contemporary exponents of affective singing. Notice how the white breathy quality of Barbra Streisand's "the" dissolves into a resonant tone on the final word "world."

🔊 AUDIO EX. 6.12. Barbra Streisand, *People* (CBS, 1964)

Essential graces and *passaggi* demand fundamentally different abilities and levels of engagement. While graces can be added in an almost formulaic and superficial way, *passaggi* (divisions, or Italian-style ornaments) demand a deeper understanding of the harmonic structure (*dispositio*) of the composition. Here are Quantz's comments on passaggi:

> Virtually no one who applies themselves to music (at least music outside of France) is content with only the essential graces, but wishes to study the performance of passaggi, or improvised variations. Such an ambition is not misguided in itself, although it is responsible for many inappropriate and awkward gestures, due to the fact that passaggi are impossible to produce in a tasteful and pertinent way without understanding composition, or at least the rules of basso continuo. Most musicians lack this ability, however, which takes time to acquire; so that it would be better to play the melody just as the composer wrote it, than to spoil it with bad variations.[53]

Many HIP performers have taken Quantz's advice to heart, and the result is that the art of ornamentation is currently disparaged and underdeveloped. There are two main factors are responsible for this: (1) our reverential attitude to canonical works, and (2) the influence of the recording industry. The higher the regard for a composition, the less willing we are to tamper with even the smallest of details in the score, or to offer an interpretation that might be considered in any way "intrusive." Like placing a fine painting in a decorative frame, embellishment is an act of respect. Instead of contaminating a masterpiece, it is a way of enhancing it and bringing out its essence. Our training may make us no better than the musicians Quantz criticized, but in many cases total abstinence is a flagrant contradiction of the composer's intention and of historical practices.

The recording industry has had an equally profound impact on current ornamentation practices. The notion of recording a single performance suitable for on-demand listening by unknown audiences at some future time is, of course, anathema to the spirit of eloquent performance. In the heyday of recording in the 1980s and '90s, when companies sought to market "definitive" performances and "authentic" versions that could bear multiple hearings, their editing techniques required all takes to be as close to identical as possible. In the interests of recording-studio efficiency, performers had to be note perfect, and in turn they became reluctant to add any form of elaboration, or to characterize their performances in any distinctive way. Through international distribution, these interpretations became benchmarks and undercut fresh efforts of spontaneous ornamentation. Instead of inspiring new paths for further elaboration, they spawned multiple recorded versions of the same select repertoire, most of which are equally indistinguishable in their lack of personality.

Structuring Ornaments: *Passaggi* and Paraphrase

The issue of ornamentation opens up the question of defining what constitutes a musical "work." Speaking of C. P. E. Bach, Étienne Darbellay explains:

> The paradox is plain: the composition exists, so to speak, entirely in its written code, which must be as exhaustive as possible in order to programme the performer all but unequivocally in its course; but this same performer must be free to recognize in that course another possible course that will maintain the identity of something (the composition) which, for its part, is not notated. That other, further thing, which is the music, the idea, and is not the notes that are its setting—what exactly is it like? In what way can one musical object be extended into another which is reducible to the first?[54]

When he uses the term "composition," Darbellay is really talking about the *inventio* and *dispositio*: the original inspiration, and the basic modes chosen by the composer to express the underlying premise. Discerning the *inventio*, as we have already discussed, is the player's first priority in studying a piece. The *inventio* cannot be changed without losing the piece's identity, but practically everything else is fair game for alteration and variation.

As much as the performer should give the impression of creating the music *ex tempore*, there also needs to be a way of distinguishing the performer's contributions from the composer's. Embellishment provides a framework for dialogue between the two creative artists. That is why most authorities recommended leaving the initial statement unadorned and begin ornamenting on repeats in a sonata movement, or the *da capo* of an aria so that the listener can distinguish the composer's "plaine notes" from the performer's take on them. One of the most effective ways that the roles of composer and performer were clarified in the Rhetorical era was through the principle of varied reprise. This is founded on the general principle that to repeat something is to say it differently. In the late seventeenth century Wolfgang Caspar Printz remarked:

> Why should not also the musician [*Musikant*] who is concerned with delighting the ear, apply as much as a cook or painter in discovering

every variation [*Varietaet und Abwechselung*] in order to do justice to his calling? After all, music itself consists only of variations in sound, and everything which is repeated without change is an annoyance rather than a pleasure to the ear."[55]

C. P. E. Bach wrote at length about the procedure of varied reprises in his own keyboard solos. To him, the principal task of the performer was to paraphrase or gloss. At the same time that he assumed total compliance with his notational code as the surest way of communicating his intended meaning, he believed that it was also indispensible for the performer to vary the repeats.[56] This means the performer was responsible for transmitting the original idea of the piece in a somewhat different form—but without falsifying its meaning. The performer's job was to "get the composer's drift," as it were, and elaborate on it, or to show that drift in a new light. The contributions of both composer and performer create a work that is no longer simply sectionalized with repeats. The ornaments overwrite the redundancy of repetition with a developing narrative. This is even truer in the case of *da capo* arias where the singer's ornaments restate the same ideas from a new perspective. The performer's gloss transforms the *da capo* from a static formula to a dynamic form. One of the best illustrations of where ornamentation reinforces the message of the text is "The Trumpet Shall Sound" in *Messiah*. Handel placed the cadenza—the point where the performer is given free rein to implement change—on the phrase "And we shall be changed," that way enabling the ornamentation to literally perform change.

An ornamented repeat in music of this kind acts as a paraphrase—a rewording or a reworking (in the case of nonverbal arts) of someone else's idea. But C. P. E. Bach's conditions also demand that the variations "correspond and agree with the passion of the piece. And they must always be—if not better—at least equal in quality to the original."[57] This sounds much like what jazz musicians do, except—because the standards they work with are so familiar—they can start varying the tune even before laying down the "straight" version.

In C. P. E. Bach's *Sonatas with Varied Reprises*, performers have to choose between playing the composer's ornaments, or using them as a model to improvise their own. Either way they must commit to the graces and make them their own. Many early musicians are still resistant to the quantity of embellishments that Bach provided, and the degree to which they transform the score (Ex. 6.4).

Are these and other models of written-out embellishments such as the printed ornamentation of Corelli's violin sonatas, Telemann's *Methodische Sonaten*, William Babell's sonatas, and elaborated repeats in Mozart's slow movements extreme demonstrations of just how far ornamentation can be taken?[58] Or are they concentrated models from which performers can extract their own discreet or tasteful version? Whatever the implication, they demand

Example 6.4 C. P. E. Bach, Sonata 1 from *Sechs Sonaten für Clavier mit veränderten Reprisen* (Berlin, 1760), opening two phrases (ms 1–5) with varied repeat (ms 12–16)

a high level of commitment, and our resistance to fully embrace them may be a reflection of our reticence to fully immerse ourselves in the Rhetorical style.

Ornaments in History

The boundary between what are considered essential and nonessential interpretative details can shift over the course of the work's performance history. The second movement from the concerto for oboe and strings by Alessandro Marcello is a case in point (Exx. 6.5 and 6.6).

We are lucky to have a master musician's ornamentation of this piece. When J. S. Bach transcribed the work for harpsichord (BWV 974), he provided ornamentation for all three movements and a particularly elaborate embellishment of the Adagio. As this work has taken on canonic status in the oboist's repertoire, Bach's ornaments are so deeply embedded in the work's identity that it is difficult to recover Marcello's original text. The situation is further complicated by additional levels of intervention. Richard Lauschmann's 1923 edition, used as the standard version by many twentieth-century oboists, was long considered an accurate transcription of Bach's ornaments. In reality, Lauschmann made small but distinctive changes to Bach's embellishments.[59] The British oboist Léon Goossens, who

Example 6.5 Marcello, Adagio from Concerto for Oboe (*Concerti a cinque*, Amsterdam: Roger, 1716)

Example 6.6 Opening phrases of Marcello's Adagio with ornamentation by J. S. Bach

famously refused to add his own ornaments and took pride in playing Handel concertos exactly as they were written, was willing however to play the ornamented version of Marcello's Adagio as written out by Bach. Lauschmann's edition gave no clues as to what Marcello's original might have been like, and Goossens and his contemporaries never stopped to consider. They played Bach's ornamented version as if *it* was the original text. Their performances plod along slow enough for the ornaments to be heard as the structure. At their hands the work became an endurance test—not only for the oboist but also for the listener who was asked to admire a featureless landscape where the emphasis on sublime simplicity robbed the chance of savoring Marcello's occasionally startling harmonies and turns of phrase.

Bach's version begins virtually unadorned, and each repetition of the rising arpeggic figure accumulates more detail. This performs the process of the soloist easing into creative paraphrase at the same time revealing Marcello's text behind the elaboration. The temptation to treat Bach's ornaments as the primary melody is strong because they are notated with metric precision. Most modern oboists take Bach's notation at face value, down to the distinction between sixteenth and thirty-second notes. But, if they are written-out ornaments, wouldn't it be appropriate to treat them with more flexibility? It would seem more appropriate to interpret them more in line with the suggestive notation of a French unmeasured prelude, or Corellian-style ornamentation, such as notated in William Babell's Sonatas (see Ex. 6.7) where it is up to the performer to fit the ornaments into the

Example 6.7 William Babell, Sonata 1 (London: Walsh, c.1725)

available time. This approach is much easier to do when there are three quarter-note beats in the measure rather than six slow eighths. Treating ornaments with rhythmic freedom within the regular metric framework can also give them an improvisatory flavor, and distinguish ornament from structure.

Undeniably, Goossens's performance is compellingly beautiful, but it leaves the simple structure of the original far behind (Audio Ex. 6.13). HIP performers have endeavored to reassert Marcello's *urtext* as the essential and stable form of the work: not by presenting unadorned performances of Marcello's original but through an array of unique interpretations. Haynes played Bach's ornaments (with some simplifications to adapt keyboard figuration to the Baroque oboe) in a chiaroscuro that highlights the contrast of structure and ornament. In Audio Example 13.6b I take the profile of Bach's ornaments as a starting point to conceive an original elaboration.

🔊 AUDIO EX. 6.13. A. Marcello, Adagio from Oboe Concerto,
a) Léon Goossens, Philharmonia String Orchestra, dir. Susskin (Columbia, 1947)
b) Bruce Haynes, Orchestra of the 18th century, dir. Brüggen (Seon, 1979)
c) Geoffrey Burgess, Old City Music (private release, 2011)

In this example, it is relatively easy to distinguish between what Marcello wrote and Bach's gloss, but Bach also left hundreds of examples of more fully elaborated melodies where the degree of ornamental detail even confused some of his contemporaries. In 1737 Johann Adolph Scheibe faulted Bach for obliterating his melodies with ornamentation that was, at any rate, not the composer's business but the performer's.[60] Bach's notation also caused confusion for later performers. Behind the decorative foreground of countless Bach aria obbligati and instrumental Adagios lie simple melodies much like Marcello's. In order to appreciate Bach's graces—to see the forest for the trees, as it were—and realize what to bring out as structural and what to leave in the shadow, it can be useful to deduce a "plain," unornamented version. The simple exercise of making a reduction and listening to Bach's graces can be a positive step forward in the process of learning to improvise ornamentation in the Bachian style.

Let us take the cantata *Ich habe genung*, BWV 82. This cantata is a meditation on the words of Simeon who, having seen the savior, is resolved to joyfully embrace his own mortality. The opening aria couples reconciliation with ecstatic rapture. Bach achieves this counterpoint of passions by elaborating the settled, melancholic underlying musical structure (Ex. 6.8) with uplifting activity in foreground ornaments (Audio Ex. 6.14).

🔊 AUDIO EX. 6.14. BWV 82/1 Bruce Haynes with ensemble dir. Frans Brüggen (RCA Seon, 1980)

Example 6.8 BWV 82/1, hypothetical unadorned basic melody

Today we may marvel at the accounts of legendary performers who were able to improvise ornaments *ex tempore*. As much as this ability enhanced the vitality of the musical experience, how much of it was real on-the-spot creativity, how much planned procedures or formulaic patterns? Quantz and C. P. E. Bach implied that there was no shortage of parroting song birds, but most players and singers had a broad enough vocabulary of embellishments to trick listeners (even those who heard them on multiple occasions) into believing that they drew from a seemingly bottomless reservoir of inspiration. The best ornamentation is the fruit of contemplation, practice, and memory. From the reminders he sketched in small notes in some of his violin parts we can tell that Johann Georg Pisendel (1687–1755), the leader of the Dresden court orchestra, planned his ornaments in advance. Many other performers likely prepared their improvisations. The art of spinning straw into gold lies in knowing how to give a prepared routine the semblance of spontaneity. (This is an aspect of the art of feigning, to be discussed in chapter 9.)

The process of performing Rhetorical music is not unlike simultaneous interpretation, where the task is to convert a thought or expression in real time from a source language into an expression with identical meaning in a target language. The interpreter aims to convey every semantic element (tone and register) and every intention and feeling of the message. There are, of course, different ways of translating from one language to another. In order to effectively communicate a speaker's message and match the spirit of the original, an interpreter may need to deviate from a literal word-for-word translation, and substitute idioms and figures of speech. At what point does the original lose its identity and the work become the interpreter's?

In the case of early music, translating across the cultural and historic divide that separates us from the Rhetorical period presents its own set of problems. What *is* different between the linguistic and musical practices in this comparison is that, generally, the musical performer is expected to maintain an awareness of the composer's idiomatic usage and not to lose sight of the style and context of the original work. At the end of the day, good taste and awareness of style must come into play to maintain the balance between the underlying musical structure and the level of ornamental incursion. The "free" translation of the passionate implications of Baroque music into modern idiom, such as we hear in Romantic interpretations of Rhetorical music, is what the HIP movement assiduously set out to avoid. But in its eagerness to wipe out past mistakes, it has unwittingly created its own brand of anachronism in the form of literal, unadorned readings.

At the other end of the spectrum there are groups like Red Priest that have gone farther than many to uncover—even exploit—the possibility of a radically postmodern cultural translation. Although they use historical equipment and cannot be criticized for ignoring the music's passionate message, Piers Adams and his accompanying musicians push the envelope of taste to the extreme. Their performance (as exemplified in the excerpt, Audio Ex. 6.15) is recognizably of Vivaldi's music, and they indisputably "own" their performances and embellishments. So what is the problem? Is it a question of degree? Drawing on performance techniques and an aesthetic more in keeping with the twentieth-century avant-garde than eighteenth-century practices, their performances are highly planned and consequently suppress much of the spontaneity called for by the Rhetorical style.

🔊 AUDIO EX. 6.15. Vivaldi, *La Notte*, Red Priest, *Nightmare in Venice* (DOR, 2002)

Ornamentation does not only take the form of essential graces, passaggi, and divisions. There is a range of ornaments, like the close shake and *messa di voce* that defy notation and even categorization. This type of ornament is often overlooked but can be extremely effective. In her performance of Barbara Strozzi's *Lamento* (Audio Ex. 6.16), Isabelle Poulenard gives a poignant example of just how far ornamentation can be taken by responding to the passions of the text rather than following prescribed musical rules.

Lagrime mie, à che vi trattenete,	*Tears of mine, why do you hold back,*
Perchè non isfogate il fier' dolore,	*why don't you wash away the pain*
Chi mi toglie'l respiro e opprime il core?	*which takes my breath and crushes my heart?*

🔊 AUDIO EX. 6.16. Strozzi, *Lamento*, Isabelle Poulenard, Marianne Müller, gamba, Emer Buckley, harpsichord (Adda, 1989) opening, and closing section.

Each time the opening text and music return, Poulenard gives them a different inflection. The differences enact a transformation in the character and impact the song's dramatic progression. Most of her ornamental figures defy notation. She performs the seventeenth-century one-note *trillo* as an outpouring of raw emotion. Her embellishment relates not just to the notes but also the underlying ideas (tears, loss of breath, heartbreak) and the result is that composed text and performer are barely separable. Like a fine orator, she balances heartfelt emotion with artistry, and just when we sense that she has lost control towards the end of the song, she regains decorum at the final cadence. These are no trained bird's warblings; the threads of gold are spun from an emotional response to Strozzi's text. Even if carefully planned, the result sounds both genuine and spontaneous.

Further Reading

Ornamentation has occupied a central place in secondary literature since the inception of the discipline of performance practice. Early studies include Edward Dannreuther's *Musical Ornamentation* (1893–95), Arnold Dolmetsch's *Interpretation of the Music of the 17th and 18th centuries* (1915). In his introduction to *Ornamentation in Baroque and Post-Baroque Music* (1978), Frederick Neumann took care to discuss the basic principles of rhythmic flexibility, and the use of ornaments as expressive devices, but this is largely overshadowed by the ensuing 500-page treatment of ornaments (mostly essential graces) organized systematically according to the number of notes they contain.

Robert Gjerdingen's recent study *Music in the Galant Style* is an invaluable survey of intersections between musical training, improvisation, composition, and performance in the eighteenth century, and includes copious examples of various types and levels of figuration. For examples of figured-bass realizations from the Rhetorical period, see Arnold's *Art of Accompaniment*. Williams's *Figured Bass Accompaniment* and Heinichen's *General-Bass in der Composition* also provide copious material on figured bass practice.

For discussions of vibrato, see Neumann, "Authenticity and Vocal Vibrato," Moens-Haenen, "Holzbläservibrato," Gable, "Some Observations," Wistreich, "Reconstructing pre-Romantic singing technique," 184–85, and Burgess, "Vibrato Awareness." On Geminiani's controversial position regarding vibrato, see Hickman, "Censored Publications of *The Art of Playing on the Violin*" and Walls, " 'Ill-compliments and Arbitrary Taste'?"

Great Shakespeareans (Pearl, GEMM 9465, 1993) includes numerous recordings of several important twentieth-century Shakespearean actors.

7

The Expressive Gesture

GEOFFREY BURGESS

The structure of the work is in fact its sense.
—Paul Ricœur, 1977[1]

There is nothing so beautifully necessary, as this Knowledge, of *pausing, significantly*.
—Aaron Hill, 1735[2]

And forget not especially, in such *Humours*, to make your *Pauses*, at *Proper Places*.
—Thomas Mace, 1676[3]

Audible Architecture

To understand a piece of music, listeners need to be able to perceive how it is put together. They need to be able to distinguish its large and small sections, and how they relate to each other. Hearing the structural pattern, whether it is in a folk song or in a five-part fugue, is just as vital in music as it is in language. From the time of the masters of rhetoric in ancient Greece and Rome developed the science of *diastolica*, punctuation has been recognized as essential to good grammar and crucial to effective oratory. After discussing the importance of giving every word its full phonetic value, Quintilian outlined the second essential to clear delivery: proper punctuation, which he said

> may be seen to be but a trivial merit, but without it all the other merits are worth nothing . . . We must also note where our speech should be held up and *as it were left in the air*, and where it should be brought to rest.[4]

Writers like Hill and Mace in the epigrams quoted above attest to the continued importance placed on punctuation in seventeenth- and eighteenth-century rhetoric and music. Their prose may seem quaintly halting to our modern ears, but it speaks to the essential differences in pacing and organization that separate our speech from theirs. Indeed, punctuation and articulation constitute perhaps the most marked difference between modern and Rhetorical approaches to both verbal and musical performance. Just as oratory calls for clear pronunciation and the correct observation of punctuation, musical eloquence depends on the delineation of gestures as well as the timing between them. The concept of parsing music along the same lines as the patterns of language was common in the Baroque and Classical periods, and the idea is behind the way musicians still speak of musical phrasing and articulation.

Affective speech depends on the appropriate weight and accent afforded to individual syllables. Although not meaningful on their own, syllables constitute the essential building blocks of words, phrases, and sentences. The musical analogy to the enunciation of syllables is the articulation of individual notes by means of bowing and tonguing patterns, and combinations of slurred and nonslurred notes. As singers work with both words and music, the combination of consonants and vowels and the like are part of this level of articulation. In music the basic signifying units are what we refer to in this book as "gestures." This chapter discusses the way musicians build a type of audible architecture out of gestures, and how they are given character through different forms of "humouring."

In 1765 John Rice, whose primer on the art of reading strongly influenced Thomas Jefferson's rhetorical sensibility, stressed the need to distinguish the components of a discourse to avoid confusion, and to support his point of view quoted from Batteux:

> [The objects of a discourse] should be all represented distinct and without Confusion; and consequently require to be separated by some Kind of Interval. Let us consider them as they are found in Nature, or in a Picture; not one but has its Line of Circumscription, which bounds it and separates it from every other Object. And is it to be imagined, that in a [rhetorical] Discourse . . . they ought not be drawn separately, and distinguished from each other in the same Manner?[5]

Grimarest was more succinct when he wrote in 1707 that punctuation "is the art of marking, with the use of small symbols, the places in a discourse where pauses should be made, [thereby] giving meaning to one's Delivery." He also noted that the correct placement of pauses was essential to imbue expressions with their intended spirit or energy (*l'esprit ou l'action*).[6]

The job of punctuation, then, is not only to make distinct the constituent parts of an oration (whether verbal or musical) but also to forge relations between those parts and thereby create meaning. For example, the presence or absence of commas in the following sentences radically alters their meaning:

> A woman without her man is nothing.
> A woman: without her, man is nothing.
>
> Let's eat, Mommy.
> Let's eat Mommy.
>
> All we like sheepe haue gone astray: we haue turned euery one to his owne way.
> —*Isaiah* 53:6 (King James Version, 1611)
>
> We all, like sheep, have gone astray, each of us has turned to our own way.
> —(New International Version, 2011)
>
> All of us, like sheep, have strayed away. We have left God's paths to follow our own.
> —(New Living Translation, 2007)

These are relatively straightforward examples of where punctuation affects meaning. The ambiguity of the word order in the verse from Isaiah is a recurring source of humor at annual *Messiah* performances. As these different translations show, there have been numerous attempts to rectify the ambiguity with punctuation.

Even with the same punctuation, a great deal of nuance is possible simply by changing the emphasis. Consider this selection of possibilities:

> A woman: with*out* her, man is *nothing*.
> A woman: without *her*, man is nothing.
> A *wom*an: without *her*, *man* is nothing.

The timing of punctuation breaks and emphases like this also have a significant impact on rhythm and pacing. Much of the actor's craft is concerned with the inflection of meaning and nuance through subtle adjustments like these.

Attitudes to punctuation have changed radically over the past four centuries. One decisive factor is the evolution of reading practices. Today we skim and speed-read, but in the early modern era, texts were designed to be read aloud or, if silently, at the same pace and with the same attention to detail as if the reader were reciting aloud. The highly punctuated extracts quoted here from writers such as Thomas Mace preserve some of the performative nature of early modern prose. Recorded examples of Shakespearean actors illustrate changing practices in pace and punctuation. Beerbohm Tree's grandiloquent Romantic sing-song delivery of Hamlet's soliloquy is a vestige of bygone age (refer to Audio Ex. 6.2a). His pace is slow, and he takes more space between phrases than we are likely to hear from actors today. The Austrian actor Alexander Moissi (1879–1935, Audio Ex. 7.1a) also made much use of punctuation breaks in a recitation style characterized by pitch variation—a style that must have been close to what Schoenberg had in mind for *Sprechstimme*.[7] Most mainstream actors from the second half of the twentieth century tended to pass over punctuation and iron out tonal differences (Audio Ex. 7.1b and c). Following that tendency, modern performances of Baroque recitative also tend to run gestures together. This has the effect of eliding smaller units into longer "phrases," often in a breathless rush through the tedium of recitative to get to the next aria.[8]

🔊 AUDIO EX. 7.1. Shakespeare, Hamlet's soliloquy, *Hamlet* act 3, sc. 1.
a) Alexander Moissi (Electrola, ca.1910)
b) Sir John Gielgud (Naxos, 1948)
c) Kenneth Branagh (Sony Pictures, 1996)

Articulating the Musical Gesture

Structural punctuation was a key element of musical performance over much of the Rhetorical period. Details varied according to national preference (language exercising the most obvious influence), style, and musical genre. In the preface to his first volume of toccatas of 1615, Frescobaldi spoke of taking time between phrases in solo keyboard music so as to bring out the distinctive character of each section:

> On the last note of the shakes, or passages by skips or degrees, you must pause, even if [for only] a quaver or a semiquaver [eighth- or sixteenth-note], or unlike the following note, for such a stop avoids confusion between one phrase and another.[9]

Decades later Thomas Mace wrote that the length of articulation depended on context and affect.

> Although it be not a *Grace*, nor likewise *Numbered* amongst the *Graces*, by others, yet the performance of It, (in proper Places) adds much *Grace*: And the thing to be done, is but only to make a kind of *Cessation, or standing still*, sometimes *Longer*, and sometimes *Shorter*, according to the *Nature*, or *Requiring* of the *Humour* of the *Musick*; which if in Its *due Place* be made, is a very *Excellent Grace*.[10]

Just as in Mace's aphoristic and highly punctuated prose style (the italics are his), punctuation is used in Rhetorical music to separate short, distinctive musical segments or gestures. The term "phrase" appears only rarely in musical writings up to the later eighteenth century, and when it does occur, it usually refers to longer musical units built from smaller segments. Again, the concept of building meaning from small units upward, rather than taking in a broader overview of musical structure reflected the way literary texts were read. From what we learn from manuals, readers were taught to start from the small units of syllable and word, and then string them together to form phrases and sentences.[11] In music, a number of alternate names were given to the smallest signifying units. Quantz spoke of *Gedanke* or *Sinn* in German and *pensée* or *sens* in the French version (a thought or the sense of an idea), and *Einschnitt* and *membre d'une periode* (literally incise or clause); C. P. E. Bach favored *Gedanke* or *Ausdruck* (thought, or expression).[12] These are all grammatical terms and designate units of structure as much as units of meaning. Quantz provided a clear illustration of what he meant by an *Einschnitt* in a short segment of (textless) recitative (Ex. 7.1). The *Einschnitte* are separated by rests; the shortest is three notes, the longest eight.

> In a recitative that is sung from memory, the accompanist can be of great help to the singer by anticipating the first notes of each gesture [*Einschnitt / chaque membre des periodes*], pointing to them, as it were.[13]

Example 7.1 J. J. Quantz, *Versuch*, ch. 17, 6 §33 Fig. 23/5

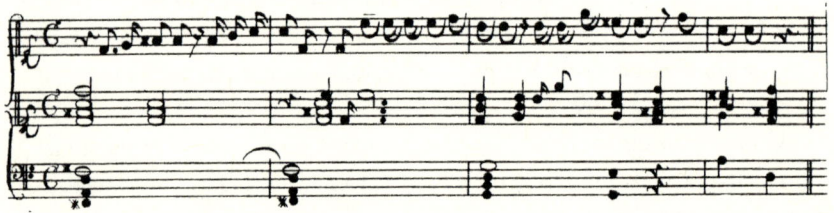

"Gesture" is a convenient English equivalent for *Einschnitte, Gendanken,* and the like. Gestures are musical statements that convey a sense of some kind, as an exclamation, a passion, a character, an idea, or a physical condition, an action, or an object. They have integrity but are inconsistent in length and unpredictable in form, and are not always complete in a musical sense (e.g., they do not always terminate with a cadence). They can take on motific significance, but they are not always repeated and developed like motifs.[14] When gestures have conventional or metaphoric associations they are termed "figures." So even though every figure is a gesture, not every gesture is a figure. In the same way that a speech is made up of more than "figures of speech," so a piece of music is made up of more than figures. Quantz pointed out that gestures succeed each other in a continuous sequence throughout a movement and need to be distinguished by means of breaths or breaks:[15]

> Breath must be taken before the repetition of the principal subject [*Hauptsaßes*] or the beginning of a new gesture [*Gedanken*], so that the end of the preceding gesture and the beginning of the following one are clearly separated from each other.[16]

With its shorter expressive units, the gestural makeup of Rhetorical music had close affinities to the style of acting and public speaking during the same period. Dean Barnett has written this about gestures used in eighteenth-century acting technique:

> Because each of the basic gestures had an individual meaning and is of short duration, the action tended to be matched to the short phrase rather than to whole passages. . . . One acted by the word rather than by the paragraph or by the pervading emotion. Like the text which it complemented, the art of gesture was detailed; its basic gestures were distinct and discrete, but elegantly linked together.[17]

Musicians were routinely instructed to imitate orators, but occasionally the analogy was reversed, and the musicians' art of separating gestures held up as a model for orators. For instance, De Richesource wrote that in order for their sermons to be pleasing and agreeable, preachers must scrupulously observe

> pauses and silences from the shortest commas, [followed by] semicolon, colon, stops, and paragraphs [*articles*] . . . in imitation of musicians who use them to enliven their melodies, just like painters who enhance their painting and give it color with them.[18]

Likewise, Monsieur de Saint-Lambert indicated that

> A piece of music is not unlike a piece of rhetoric; or rather, it is the rhetoric that resembles the music, since harmony, number, measure, and the like, which a skilful orator uses in composing his work, belong more naturally to music than to rhetoric.[19]

Just how much the space taken to articulate the gestures and sections of a piece influences meaning can be heard in the sampling of recordings of the slow movement Bach's Brandenburg Concerto 2, BWV 1047 (Audio Ex. 7.2). The shape of the individual gestures is clear in Pinnock's recording, and the most characteristic articulation of the individual gestures comes from Ensemble Caprice. Stokowski encouraged his players to relax the tone on the final notes of gestures, but in his interpretation subtle adjustments in tempo are more meaningful as markers between gestures than punctuation breaks.

🔊 AUDIO EX. 7.2. J. S. Bach, Brandenburg Concerto II, Andante
a) Philadelphia Orchestra, dir. Leopold Stokowski (Victor, 1928)
b) Vienna Philharmonic, dir. Felix Prohaska (NIXA, 1956)
c) English Consort, dir. Trevor Pinnock (Archiv, 1980)
d) Ensemble Caprice (Analekta, 2012)

Punctuation was graded according to grammatical importance. In 1731 Telemann instructed singers to make a clear and sensitive distinction between commas, colons, semicolons and periods.[20] Four decades later John Mason still felt the need to remind singers to insert perceptible punctuation breaks in the music as follows: "a Comma stops the Voice while we may privately tell [= count] one, a Semi-colon two; a Colon three: and a Period four."[21]

Of all the musical genres in currency during the Rhetorical period, recitative came closest to emulating speech rhythms. Naturally, here where the text rules, and music exercises less impact on the timing of the delivery, punctuation was of vital importance. With the music out of the way, as it were, the punctuation of the text can be given due worth. Tempo flexibility was an important element in Baroque recitative. Time was also routinely taken at the end of the grammatic units of recitative. The cadences in the continuo, usually notated synchronous with the singer's last notes, were frequently delayed, thereby providing a musical equivalent to the time taken for textual punctuation. In practice this is not always possible, and the appropriate time depended on musical style and taste. The cadences can be overlapped (as written) with the last notes of the singer's gestures or extended according to the circumstances of the drama.[22] The notation of Italian recitative left room for the singer to manipulate the rhythm and timing of gestures to the punctuation. French *récitatif* on the other hand tended to be more lyrical than Italian recitative, and the fluid rhythm of the verses was conveyed more accurately with changing meters. Because French recitative did not always allow singers the freedom to take time may have been why the critic Grimarest found musical declamation restrictive, and only a pale imitation of what an actor could communicate through verbal declamation.[23] Not everyone agreed. Later in the century, the German commentator Friedrich Wilhelm Marpurg felt that the diversity of cadences and melodic gestures available to musicians meant that the notation of recitative (he was referring to Italian recitative) could be far more nuanced in distinguishing the different types of punctuation than written language.[24]

The broad implication here is that the affective performance of late-eighteenth-century recitative depended as much on the singer's pacing than on the composer's ability to create varied and eloquent punctuation.

The Breath of Life

There was general agreement that recitative was adaptable to speech rhythms, but how much time is admissible when articulating music with a regular metric organization and rhythm? In some instances composers wrote breaks into the music. Vivaldi, a master of punctuation, left no doubt where to articulate the gestures in the opening ritornello of his concerto *La Notte* RV 439 (Ex. 7.2).

Example 7.2 A. Vivaldi, *La Notte*, RV 439, opening ritornello

Breaks like these can be extended, as C. P. E. Bach suggests:

> In slow or moderate tempos, the rests are generally held longer than they should be, especially when the rests and notes in the bass are the same as in the other parts (or the same as the principal part, if one is playing a solo). In those cases, [the players] should make a special effort to be together; no one earlier or later than the others.[25]

Prolonging the rests in *La Notte* can be very effective and adds an element of surprise and suspense, especially when the exact length of each rest is treated freely and slightly different from the others.

The points of articulation are not always obvious in the music of J. S. Bach. It is worth considering an example in detail. In Example 7.3 the length and punctuation of the text underlay in the singer's part can be used as a guide for how the oboes articulate the opening ritornello. The first two words of the text "Ich sehe" define the first gesture. After it is repeated, a new gesture begins with the ascending scale in bar 3. The punctuation occurs on the tied notes, so in this case there is good reason to shorten the ties to conform to how Bach breaks the instrumental lines with rests when the voice enters. Playing the second note of the pair lighter with a diminuendo into the tie will also prepare the emphasis and shape of the notes "Ich *sehe*" for when the gesture is given over to the singer. A sequence of short repeated gestures can sound predictable and tedious if not inflected with some difference. Here the opening gestures can be thought of as two propositions: "on the one hand," "on the other"; and after a short pause for reflection, the response draws them together toward resolution.

How should the continuo part be coordinated with the gestural patterns in the upper parts? At first glance, the bassline suggests an articulation after the first note of each measure, creating a series of long pickups settling on the downbeat (Ex. 7.3 version a). This, however, creates overlaps between treble and bass. Articulating after the third eighth of the first bar (version b) is also possible and is more supportive for the other parts. The appearance of the four-note gesture in isolation later in the aria validates this interpretation.

In language, punctuation breaks not only help to make sense out of a sequence of thoughts, they also give the speaker the chance to breathe. Singers and wind players are closest to the orator when it comes to articulation because they share the need to take breath. But Bach often seems to place superhuman demands on singers' and windplayers' lungs, and string players' bows, but the principles of gesture and articulation can teach us how to literally breathe life into what might otherwise become a meaningless sequence of uniform notes. Articulation provides both welcome respite for players to replenish their breath supply and relief for the listener's ear. Admonishing

Example 7.3 BWV 43/9 opening ritornello and vocal entry from bar 13

players who join everything together like a hurdy-gurdy (an instrument where it is impossible to break the sound), Quantz emphasized the expressive potential of articulation:

> One should make an effort to gain full insight and understanding of the nature of a musical gesture [*Sinn/sens*],[26] and as a function of that, which notes should be kept together. Take equal care to avoid separating that which belongs together as connecting passages that consist of

more than one independent meaning [*Sinn/sens*] and ought not, therefore, to be connected. For on that [understanding] depends a significant part of true expression in performance.²⁷

Quantz provided guidelines for recognizing natural breathing points in the music based on musical grammar. He noted that breaths can be taken between long and short notes, and where the melody leaps, but never over bar lines where a breath would interrupt the rhythm.²⁸

Other composers used special punctuation markings. From 1722 François Couperin began the habit of marking articulation points between gestures with comma-like symbols. He explained his notation in the preface to his *Troisième Livre de Pièces de clavecin*:

> [In this third book] a new sign appears that is marked thus ≖; its purpose is to mark the ends of a melody [*chants*] or our harmonic phrases [*phrases harmoniques*], and to indicate that it is necessary to slightly separate the end of a melody before proceeding to the next one. This separation should be scarcely noticable; but if it is missing, persons of taste will sense that the performance lacks something. In a word, it is the difference between those who read aloud without stopping, and those who pause at the points and commas. These silences should be perceptible without changing the beat [*sans alterer la mesure*].

Couperin was not asking for anything out of the ordinary. His commas should be taken as rare indicators of a widespread practice that was otherwise generally assumed. Signs like Couperin's commas are also found in music by other eighteenth-century French composers. Pierre Philidor used a similar symbol in his *Suittes* for treble instrument and bass (1717/18) to clarify punctuation that would otherwise be ambiguous, or point out short gestural units. In his op. 3 flute sonatas (1740) Michel Blavet indicated breathing and/or articulation points (with an "h" for *haleine* = breath). Like Philidor's commas, Blavet's breath marks clarify ambiguous gestural groupings and simplify scanning the music on a first reading. The practice was still alive two generations later when C. R. Brijon used similar wording in his violin method of 1763 to describe the short space between musical phrases and, like Couperin, warned that the breaks should not disrupt the beat:

> You must observe a short space [*un petit intervalle*] between the note that finishes a phrase and that which begins the next, without it compromising [*préjudicie*] the beat [*la mesure*].²⁹

The prelude from Septième Concert from *Les Goûts Réunis* (1724) provides a clear demonstration of Couperin's notation (Ex. 7.4). In this piece, the gestures make up units comparable to poetic verses; each unit terminates with a cadence emulating a poetic rhyme punctuated by articulation breaks.

Example 7.4 F. Couperin, Prelude from Septième Concert from *Les Goûts Réunis* (Paris, 1724)

Let us consider two interpretations of this Prélude that give different senses of its meaning and structure through the way the sections are punctuated (Audio Ex. 7.3a and b).

🔊 AUDIO EX. 7.3. François Couperin, Gravement from Septième Concert
a) Bruce Haynes, hautboy, Susie Napper, gamba, and Arthur Haas, harpsichord (ATMA, 1999)
b) Barthold Kuijken, traverso, Wieland Kuijken, gamba, and Robert Kohen, harpsichord (Accent, 2003)

Haynes takes a moderate tempo but allows a generous amount of time at each of Couperin's commas. Kuijken, on the other hand, is generally slower and articulates without disturbing the pulse or interrupting the easy flow of musical ideas. His breaks are rhythmic: the articulation silences "robbed" from the preceding note without delaying the next gesture. The result is a less distinct structure with fewer clear divisions, but with the major sections still clearly defined (the reduced texture at these points already makes them more audible). Haynes's performance is more punctuated, the gestures are clearer, and the breaks add time outside the measured pulse of the music. By dwelling on those moments where, as Quintilian might say, the music is "held up and left in the air," he gives the listener time to reflect as the music unfolds. In keeping with the improvisatory nature of the French *prélude*, he gives the impression that he is creating the music *ex tempore*. Taken in this vein, punctuation gives him time to set the intention of each subsequent gesture.

These contrasting approaches highlight an inherent contradiction in Couperin's directions. How is it possible to make a separation at the commas without altering the beat (*sans alterer la mesure*)? Did Couperin mean that the break should be made while maintaining an uninterrupted beat, or was his intention that the break should be interpolated in an *otherwise* unaltered pulse—that is, that the beat should be taken up again with the next gesture? It seems that there is more than one solution to these questions, and this points to a flexible concept of beat and rhythm. (This is explored further in chapter 8.)

Another important consideration is the medium of performance. Woodwind players have the advantage that they can draw on dynamics, note length, and accentuation, among other techniques to articulate gestural units. In Audio Example 7.3b, Kuijken demonstrates this in bar 2 where he terminates the first gesture softly, and marks the beginning of the next gesture with a stronger tongue-stroke and *flattement*. But Couperin's directions preface a collection of music for harpsichord. As dynamics and variety of attack are virtually irrelevant on that instrument, harpsichordists rely on note length and breaks to create articulation, and that is why Couperin confined his comments to separation and silence. The low G in bar 2 can be shortened to articulate the new gesture beginning on the upper G. This note occurs on an unaccented beat and, as the terminal note of a *tierce coulée* (the ornamented falling third), it needs to be weak to effectively emulate the mute *-e* of French poetry (the so-called feminine ending). Shortening it on the harpsichord where it will be the same volume as other notes would have the effect of giving it inappropriate emphasis. The solution is to hold the low G close to its full value, and inserting a *silence d'articulation* before the next beat. Couperin marked a comma only in the upper part, so in this instance the bass can maintain the beat while the treble is delayed. The music can then return to the same measure after a slight hiatus at the comma. Taking time like this within the structure of a regular meter is an example of what is called "note-placing," or agogics.

Agogics

Agogics (from the Greek ἀγωγός agogos = leading) is a term as widely used as it is little understood. It was first introduced into music discourse in the late-nineteenth century by the German music theorist Hugo Riemann (1849–1919) who used it to describe accentuation by duration rather than volume or attack.[30] This, however, tells only part of the story, and does not reflect the full range of practices developed in the Rhetorical period to produce emphasis and articulation. Here we will use "agogic" to refer to:

(1) articulation silences,
(2) the prolongation of notes beyond their written value,
(3) expressive hesitations, and
(4) the "placing" of notes in order to clarify metric structure or to draw attention to special events such as a dissonant harmony or the focal point of a gesture.

An agogic accent always involves some degree of adjustment to the rhythm. An accent is agogic when the accented note is delayed or prolonged, thus creating some "disturbance to normality" (Haynes's Couperin). If an articulation occurs *within* the regular pulse it is not agogic: it is "in time" (Kuijken's Couperin). Agogic techniques are particularly useful on instruments with limited dynamic capacity like the harpsichord, organ, and (to a lesser degree) the recorder.[31] They provide the means to create the illusion of dynamic difference and gradations of emphasis and articulation. Harpsichordists can do this by parsimonious and sensitive use of note lengths and timing in attacks, releases, and silences. Here we are concerned with the structural use of agogics to define articulation. (More exceptional cases involving the expressive use of agogics are discussed in the following chapter.) Agogic devices include:

The Agogic Accent (prolonged beat)

The prolongation of notes to give extra emphasis for expressive reasons such as important words in the text, or interesting harmonies. In Audio Example 7.4 Gustav Leonhardt shapes an uninterrupted series of triplet sixteenth notes with a subtle gradation of note lengths and rhythmic shifts. These clarify the harmony and provide the music with structure to enhance the music's comprehensibility.

🔊 AUDIO EX. 7.4. J.S. Bach *Chromatic Fantasy* BWV 903, Gustav Leonhardt, harpsichord (Telefunken, 1970)

The Agogic Pickup

Lifted upbeats (softer and shorter), and emphasized and placed downbeats. This is essential to the musical grammar in the Rhetorical style and refers to gestural punctuation or articulation at the foreground level. Audio Example 7.5 is a good example of lifted upbeats, coupled with agogic delay of the downbeat on the repeat.

🔊 AUDIO EX. 7.5. Jean-Baptiste Forqueray, *La Morangis ou La Plissay*, Lars Ulrik Mortensen, harpsichord (Chandos, 1992)

The Agogic Placement

A slight delay to draw attention to a note, often a downbeat, or the first note of a gesture. William Cockin described a parallel technique used by public speakers to produce emphasis "effected by a manifest delay in the pronunciation, and a tone something fuller and louder than is used in ordinary."[32] In Audio Example 7.6 Arthur Haas allows the dominant harmony to settle before drawing breath and resuming the flow of the music with a repetition of the opening gesture on the second eighth note of bar 3 (Ex. 7.5). Even though the piece is marked *mesuré* (i.e., in strict time), making an agogic placement here seems justified as a natural parsing of the musical versification, and it does not cause undue disruption of the beat.

Example 7.5 Couperin, Troisième Prélude from *L'Art de toucher le clavecin* (Paris, 1717)

🔊 AUDIO EX. 7.6. Couperin: Prélude 3, *L'Art de toucher le clavecin*, Arthur Haas, harpsichord (ATMA, 1999)

The Hesitation

A pause is effective as a means of expression. In the 1670s, Fénelon remarked that

> There are some Occasions where an Orator might best express his Thoughts by Silence. For, if, being full of some great Sentiment, he continued immoveable for a Moment; this surprizing Pause wou'd keep the Minds of the Audience in suspence, and express an Emotion too big for Words to utter.[33]

When a speaker or musician pauses on a note as if searching for an appropriate word or phrase, it gives the impression of hesitation, or suspension (of meaning). Hesitations work in many situations to lend dramatic interest, by lingering on a syllable before moving on to the close of a sentence or clause (Audio Ex. 7.7). They can also give the impression of spontaneity by giving the impression that the musician is "thinking" of what to play next, as if improvising and unsure what should come next.

🔊 AUDIO EX. 7.7. Buxtehude, Praeludium BuxWV 163, Leon Schelhase, harpsichord (private release, 2014)

Finding the Poetry in the Notes

In his *Vollkommene Capellmeister,* Mattheson provided a detailed excursus on punctuation filled with advice to composers on how to match the punctuation of aria texts with musical caesuras.[34] Like Quantz, Mattheson believed that punctuation was essential to musical composition because it provided structure and, therefore, meaning. Some of his observations are based on inflections familiar from everyday speech—the semicolon indicated by a slight drop in pitch, a question mark signaled by raising the voice.[35] Mattheson believed that the same principles of articulation that governed song should also operate in instrumental music, and that the punctuation in a well-constructed melody should be as clearly discernible as if it were sung to a text.[36] As a demonstration, he provided a short minuet (Ex. 7.6).

Mattheson used literary punctuation marks to show different levels of division based on the relationship between the different parts of the melody (, ; : and a triangle of dots for a full stop or period). ˇ & – indicate rhythmic feet. The † indicates the division of four-bar sections of the dance form built on the two-bar step pattern common to most minuet choreographies. The first two four-bar clauses are related by rhythmic and melodic similarities; the second half is contrasted

Example 7.6 Mattheson's Minuet (*Vollkommene Capellmeister*, 2, ch. 13 §82)

with the short, short, long, long (*v v – –*) rhythmic profile and conjunct melodic motion. Mattheson was directing his comments primarily to composers, so he did not elaborate how the different types of punctuation should be rendered in performance. Presumably he would have subscribed to the standard procedure of allocating briefer breaks to commas, and longer ones to colons and periods. What is clear, however, is that he was thinking in gestural units of two or four bars.

Mattheson's musical units scan and rhyme like a poem. Indeed, it would be safe to say that the great majority of Baroque melodies is poetic in this sense.[37] The following passage from the *Principes* of Monsieur de Saint-Lambert (1702) develops a reversible analogy between rhetoric and music, showing that many of Mattheson's ideas are directly applicable to French music:

> Just as a piece of rhetoric is a whole unit that is usually made up of several parts [*parties*], each of which is composed of sentences [*périodes*] that each have a complete meaning, these sentences being composed of clauses [*membres*], the phrases of words [*mots*], and the words of letters, so a melody in a piece of music is a whole that is composed of several sections [*reprises*]. Each section is composed of phrases [*cadences*] that have a complete meaning and are the sentences of the melody. The phrases are often composed of clauses [*membres*], the clauses of measures [*mesures*], and the measures of notes. Thus the notes correspond to letters, the measures to words, the phrases to sentences, the sections to parts, and the whole to the whole.[38]

Returning to Couperin's *Septième Concert*, we can posit a similar grammatical reading based on the models provided by Mattheson and Saint-Lambert. The first two one-bar gestures contrast in rhythm and melodic shape: the first is somewhat closed, but while it cadences to the tonic, the melody settles on the weak second eighth of the bar; the second gesture comes to a stronger closure on the dominant. These two gestures could be likened to two poetic verses separated by a comma, and concluded by a semicolon (see Ex. 7.7). The next section is built up of shorter gestures, and the contrapuntal overlap between treble and bass resembles a list of propositions that takes the music to a new conclusion in the relative major. This terminates the first sentence. The music then returns to the opening idea. This time the response is twice as long and reaches a more decisive cadence to the dominant with a rising melodic line. The next two units continue the upward motion and have a more urgent quality. In rhetorical terms a musical sequence such as this is called a *climax*: that is, a restatement with emphasis. These gestures resemble questions or exclamations demanding a response. They arrive at a colon before the discourse is rounded out with a *peroratio* in the form of a repeated iteration of the opening gesture, now extended to settle on the tonic.

Following the advice of Telemann and Mason quoted earlier, none of these breaks should be exactly the same in length: the intermediary commas are the shortest, the stops at periods longer and more settled. The exclamation points in bars 8 and 9 can be played with a more "up in the air" feel. The performance thus builds an audible architecture with a logical flow.

Example 7.7 Couperin, Prélude from Septième Concert with detailed punctuation

Pause to Reflect

We often forget just how telling pauses can be. As musicians, we have an instinctive need to fill the vacuum of silence with sound. The result can be breathless—in both the positive and negative sense. We may *think* we are breaking sufficiently for it to be perceptible to listeners, but daring to take enough time for the appropriate punctuation is a lesson hard learned. Allowing sufficient pause for punctuation is a long-standing problem and even in the early nineteenth century, when more continuous unbroken phrases became more common, the famous singing teacher Domenico Corri complained that

> singers are too apt to neglect the rests in Music, which is no doubt a palpable error as being a part of the Composition, and frequently of great importance to relieve the ear from a monotony, and are always productive of effect.[39]

Judging the appropriate time depends on a number of factors that are not so different from those that concern actors: the acoustics of the performance space, the proximity of the audience, the sensitivity of the instrument, the size of the ensemble, and most importantly, the passion being expressed and the degree of emphasis required for eloquent delivery.

Articulation breaks will only seem like dead time if they are not treated as vital to musical expression. Breaks can be instilled with active intent. It is during the punctuation breaks where actors and orators often used the mute rhetoric of gesture to prepare the audience for the next idea. The eighteenth-century theater manager, opera impresario, and dramatist Aaron Hill left this eloquent explanation of how actors can use punctuation to set the intention of the next phrase:

> To pause, as some Actors do, at the End of Each Word or two, is to speak, like the Minute Hand of a clock, that measures TIME, not MEANING.—All the Pauses, in Utterance, shou'd, like the Pointings [i.e. commas, full stops, etc.] in Reading, serve to mark out the sense, and give Harmony and Force, to the Cadence: and, to do This effectually, the Pause, in the SOUND, must be accompanied with no Pause in the ACTION; but fill'd out, by such agitated Perturbation, in the Look, and the Gesture, as may (instead of interrupting the course of the Passion) seem but the Struggling, of its inward Emotion; preparing for the Utterance of what arises to the Conception.[40]

Articulating a musical piece is key to distinguishing and characterizing its different sections. At the same time that there was general agreement that a musical movement or aria was built around one principal affect, eighteenth-century writers acknowledged that the sequence of contrasting gestures in a musical composition should emulate the constant mutability of the passions. What Friedrich Wilhelm Marpurg wrote in 1749 about expressing constant shifts of passion in music represents an opinion that also holds for at least the previous half century:

> The rapidity with which the emotions change is common knowledge, for they are nothing but motion and restlessness. All musical expression has as its basis a Passion. . . . the orator, poet, and musician seek more to inflame than enlighten. . . . The musician must therefore play a thousand different roles; he must assume a thousand characters as dictated by the composer. . . . . A musician must therefore possess the greatest sensitivity and the happiest powers of divination to execute correctly every piece that is placed before him.[41]

It is up to the performer not only to understand what notes belonged together but how to "humour" each gesture or section. In order to bring out the most from a piece of music, the performer must be able to capture a succession of passions, like an actor who, chameleon-like, switches from one character to another. This seems to be what Mattheson meant when he wrote in connection with articulation: "the instrumental melody can indeed do without the words themselves, but not the affections."[42] This means that it was part of the performer's responsibility to discern the passionate content and choose an appropriate mode of delivery. Quantz noted that

> if, in an Allegro, there are more happy gestures than majestic or flattering ones, it should be played mostly happily and quickly. But if majesty is the character of the principal gestures, the piece should generally be played more seriously. If the principal sentiment is flattery, greater composure must prevail.[43]

For Quantz, the passions were constantly in flux and changed with mercurial speed. So, in addition to the general affect of each movement

> each piece may have in it a diverse mixture of pathetic, flattering, happy, sublime, and humorous ideas, so that one must be able to feel different passions in every bar and imagine oneself now grief-stricken, now elated, now serious, etc., and these transformations are vital in music.[44]

How did players acquire experience to judge which passion was implied by a given gesture and how to adjust their expression accordingly? Unfortunately, Quantz is less helpful than he could be on this matter. His advice amounts to "in order to express a passion, transport yourself to that state."[45] This is not only subjective but, given the historical distance that separates us from mid-eighteenth-century Germany, is open to misinterpretation. Quantz admits that acquiring the knowledge and taste to interpret is something that takes time and comes "only with the growth of feeling and judgement" that life's experiences teach us. But in more concrete terms, he outlines four main factors that influence affect:

- mode (major or minor),
- melodic style whether comprising mainly wide or narrow intervals, and in rapid, dotted or sustained note-values,
- the degree and amount of dissonance,
- the tempo marking.

In order to characterize or "humour" the music, Quantz mentioned dynamics and tone color as the most important means of distinguishing different affects. Although he is not forthcoming with exact details, we can assume that articulation and tempo can also be brought into play.[46]

Quantz's procedure is not so dissimilar from those promoted by Mace seventy-five years before (discussed in ch. 5). Mace drew attention to the process of delineating the structure of the piece by first deciding how the sections relate to each other.

> And forget not especially, in such *Humours*, to make your *Pauses*, at *Proper Places*, (which are commonly at the *End* of such *Sentences*, where there is a *Long Note*, as easily you will know how to do, if you give your mind to regard *such Things*, which give the *Greatest Lustre in Play*, as I have already told you.[47]

He also gave specific observations on the passions of each phrase (what he refers to as a "strain") in his fifth Lesson (see Ex. 7.8).

> The *Form* is *Uniform* (*each Strain* within *Itself*) though not All of the same *Number of Barrs*; and yet the *1st. Two Strains* are; which is *no Errour*, but sometimes, (for *Humor-sake*) more *Pleasant, and Delightful* as in this *3d. Strain*, which is *Humorous*, and *Conceited*, and seems to *Mock*, or *Mowe*, or *Jest*; to be *Blyth*, or *Merry*; as if it were telling some *Jiggish Story* and *Pointing* at *This*, or *That Body*, all along,

Example 7.8 T. Mace, 1st Set, 5th Lesson, *Musick's Monument*, transcr. André Souris

till it comes to the 4 *last Barrs*, where you see the *Letter* (f) [bar 27] upon the *2d. String*, with a *Full Stop*; and where you must *Pause*, and use the *Stinging Grace a Pritty while*; and then *Softly whirl away*, and Conclude.[48]

The first two strains share a similar opening gesture but progress to different cadences; the third strain takes up the harmony of the previous strain, the idea of "Pointing at This, or that Body" comes through in the interrupted melodic line. The most surprising thing about this strain is that it is a bar longer than the first two, ending on a unexpected pause, which the performer is instructed to draw out and emphasize by adding "the Stinging Grace" (a form of vibrato) before gracefully concluding with the final short strain. For Mace then, pauses added grace by allowing the full intention of the different affects of the separate sentences of a piece to be brought out.

Gesture and Character

We have seen how to transform a piece of music into a "mute" poem that only lacks words to give it concrete meaning. With little effort we could take this structure and compose verses to fit the music. In fact, in the seventeenth and eighteenth centuries there was a flourishing industry of crafting poems to existing melodies. These poetic parodies (also called contrafacta, or *vaudevilles*) took the form of drinking songs, love ditties, or even personal devotional texts, and were used by a wide cross-section of society. As well as instrumental music, popular tunes and opera hits were supplied with substitute texts, usually with an undercurrent satirical or subversive tone. Music like François Couperin's *pieces de clavecin,* composed for the rarefied *salons* of the French aristocracy became known to plebeians through these parodies. Couperin looked at this somewhat askance but was flattered all the same by the free publicity that his music got from this clandestine circulation.[49]

One of the most frequently parodied of Couperin's pieces "Les Calotins ou pièce à tretous" from the Dix-neuvième Ordre (1722) can be found in a continuous stream of publications from the 1730s. It was doubtless the satiric nature of the original harpsichord piece that piqued the parodists' interest. The title refers to the Régiment de la Calotte, a bogus organization invented by disillusioned courtiers as an excuse for ribald fun. It was the subject of a comic play staged at the Paris fairground theatres the year before Couperin's piece appeared in print. The music, a foppish *marche en rondeau,* features short repetitive gestures separated with commas (Ex. 7.9). Couperin didn't always bother to add commas where breaks were otherwise obvious, such as where a large leap made punctuation technically necessary, or at a structural point where there were other indications. In bar 4, for instance, the reprise sign substitutes for an articulation mark. The poets of two of the earliest published parodies (1730 and 1731) closely follow the composer's punctuation. The parodists picked up on the missing punctuation in measure 4 and inserted a colon. There are only two discrepancies between Couperin's punctuation and the parodies: (1) In bars 10–11 the musical gestures are elided in both parodies; and (2) in the second half of the third *couplet* commas appear in the 1730 text where there are none in the music. These commas separate terms in a list, and thus would have been performed as "almost imperceptible breaks."[50]

The parodies demonstrate how Couperin's instrumental music is already song. They also provide words that replicate the phraseology of the music as well as specific images and passions that give us an indication of what contemporary listeners found appropriate poetic reflections of the musical sense. As we would expect in a rondo form (ABACCDA), the texts introduce contrast in the episodic *couplets* (B, C, and D). Both poems begin by exalting the libertine life. The 1730 text satirizes the benefits that come from membership in the Calotte; the *Critique du genre humain* from the next year exhorts all to celebrate in the folly of life. In both parodies the first *couplet* (B) introduces antithesis by referring to what libertinage evades—boredom, sorrow, and

Example 7.9 F. Couperin, "Les Calotins" from the Dix-neuvième Ordre *Pièces de clavecin,* livre 3 (Paris, 1722)

responsibility. The second *couplet* (C) introduces different imagery—wolves and owls on the earlier text, lovers in the later. The most active portion of both poems is the third *couplet* (D). They call for the expulsion of skeptics to assure uninterrupted festivities. Looking at Couperin's music, it is not difficult to see how the poets translated the humours of the music into poetry. The first *couplet* begins in the major and inverts the melody in rising gestures. The next *couplet* is less fragmented and repetitive, is lower in tessitura, and melodically more flowing. The third *couplet*, with its octave leaps, serves as a call to combat against dissenters.

Calottinne
Marche de M. Couperin

A Fine Calotte,   Little beret,[51]
    Folle Marotte,   Crazed obsession,
    Seule vous reglez nôtre charmant destin: You alone rule our charming destiny:
    Aimer & boire   Loving and drinking
    Fait nôtre gloire;   Brings us glory;
    Vous accordez l'amour & le vin.   You give us love and wine.

B Dans nôtre allegresse,   In our jubilation
    Nous fuyons sans cesse   We constantly flee from
    Les ennuys & la tristesse;   Boredom and sorrow;
    Les bons mots s'y disent à propos;   Wisdom confirms it;
    Souvent l'on y pique,   Often one prides oneself,
    L'on critique   And criticizes
    Les Nigauts   Giant antilopes
    Et les Sots;   And fools;

A Fine Calotte...   Little beret...

C Loin de vous,   Far from you,
    Tous les jaloux,   All those who are jealous,
    Ce sont les plus tristes foux,   Are the saddest of fools,
    Ce sont de vrais Loups garoux,   The truly wild wolves,
    Pleins de couroux,   Full of rage,
    De francs-Hybous,   The sad owls,
    Portant les dégouts   Carrying aversion for
    Dans les plaisirs les plus doux: The sweetest of pleasures:

D Chassons de ces lieux   Dispel from here
    Tous Mortels facheux;   All annoying mortals;
    Que les Ris & les Jeux,   May laughter and games,
    Venus & les Graces,   Venus, and the Graces,
    Avec Comus s'emparent de leurs places.   With Comus take their places.

A Fine Calotte...   Little Beret...

Parodies nouvelles et vaudevilles inconnus (Paris, 1730): 5–8.

Critique du genre humain
Rondeau: Marche du Regiment de la Calotte

A Toute la vie,
    N'est que folie,
    Badinons, dansons, chantons,
        rions des fous:
    Boire sans cesse,
    C'est la sagesse,
    Les autres biens ne sont rien pour nous.

All life
Is but folly,
Let's banter, dance, sing and laugh
    like fools:
To drink endlessly
Is only wise,
Nothing else does anything for us.

B Le pédant fatigue,
    Le moine s'intrigue,
    Le grand seigneur est prodigue,
    Le guerrier qui cherche les combats,
    A pour recompense
    L'indigence
    Au défaut du trépas:

The pedant tires,
The monk schemes,
The grand seigneur is lavish,
The soldier in search of battles,
As recompense
Has only poverty
If he cheats death.

A Toute la vie …

All life …

C Moquons-nous des amoureux
    Avec leur ton douloureux,
    Leur air triste & langoureux;
    Il depend d'eux de vivre
        heureux,
    Et eignant leur feux
    Dans ce jus délicieux:

We make fun of lovers
With their sorrowful tone
Their sad and languishing air;
Which they depend on for
    their happiness,
Extinguish their fire
With this delicious juice:

D Chassons les bigots,
    Ce sont des magots,
    Sans esprit sans bons mots,
    Préchant vie austere,
    Mal à propos,
    Et faisant le contraire:

Dispel bigots,
They are hoarders,
With neither wit nor sound advice,
Preaching an austere life,
Against all odds,
And doing the opposite:

A Toute la vie …

All life …

Parodies nouvelles et vaudevilles inconnus (Paris: 1731): 81–85.

Couperin's music doesn't "mean" either of these poems, but the parodies propose hypothetical interpretations, and examples for the type of creative exploration that could be applied to any untexted music from the same period. We can approach the "meaning" of the music by examining the common features of these poems. They have virtually identical rhyme schemes. The *rondeau* (A) features feminine endings on the first short phrases (*calotte/marotte; la vie/la folie*) to complement Couperin's falling gestures, and the colon and period coincide with masculine rhymes and perfect cadences. Both B sections feature contrasting rhymes and end with absurdities. One can imagine a performance of these texts where the irony is accompanied by an impish wink. Couperin's *traits de liaison* (lines joining the notes, indicating legato) can serve as cues to draw out the cadence in a humorous way. The second *couplets* complement the smoother contour of the melody with a single terminal sound—in both cases sonorous and rounded sounds: *vous, jaloux, foux* . . . (1730), and the liquid *amoureux, douloureux* . . . (1731). At the same time these passages are mocking in tone. An instrumental performance could bring this out with an exaggerated "slur." The D sections of the parodies characterize the fanfare-like gestures in the music with more strongly rhythmic verses, a clue to use more incisive articulation at the gestural level. The poems also return to the same principal idea at each recurrence of the *rondeau*, suggesting that it would also be appropriate to maintain the *gay* affect on each return in a musical performance. In such a witty bagatelle, there is plenty of room to play with timing before the return of the *rondeau* and allow a moment's reflection on the new significance introduced by each episode.

The technique of parody was not restricted to France. Few Baroque opera composers were spared their music being adapted to different dramatic situations with substitute texts. Bach and Handel were also experienced parodists of their own music. Shifts from secular to sacred were not unusual. Handel routinely reworked music to accommodate a new text in a different language. Some of the most famous settings of English texts such as "His Yoke is easy," "And he shall purify," in *Messiah* began life as Italian love duets. Bach was in the habit of recycling music that had been written for a one-off event in religious contexts where they would be assured of a more extended life. This meant finding a parody text that would fit the music, and a poetic theme that was compatible with the affect of the music. We know that the Leipzig poet Christian Friedrich Henrici (known as Picander, 1700–64) was responsible for some of the parody texts, but for others it is not clear how much of the poetic adaptations are Bach's own work. The interchangeability of the original and parody texts show that whoever was involved was skilled at the task.

Examining the passions expressed by alternate versions of the same music can help to clarify the range of humours that a piece of music can encompass. The practice of using words to make sense of the musical logic of instrumental works did not die out with the waning of the Rhetorical era. It is recommended as late as 1905 in Joachim and Moser's *Violinschule*. Much can be learned from inventing parody texts for instrumental music, and it can be highly instructive as a creative way of approaching the rhetorical quality of any music.

Gesturing toward the Phrase

The modern term for dividing music into units is "phrasing"—a concept that gained widespread acceptance in the nineteenth century. Since then, "phrasing" has become a one-size-fits-all approach to all musical styles, but as this chapter demonstrates, it does not fully capture the nuanced gestures characteristic of Rhetorical music. The stability and coherence natural to the longer phrases of Romantic music are not appropriate to the Rhetorical style in which each gesture, however brief and temporary, captures a fixed passionate state just long enough to be perceived and appreciated. The effect is rather like a musical kaleidoscope.

The gesture doesn't necessarily have harmonic integrity, but as the prime structural unit it usually forms part of longer units—phrases, periods, and sections—demarked with cadences. The hierarchic combination of gestures into larger unit phrases is what projects a melodic line forward. At the same time the larger structures tie the smaller units together. This technique of building upwards from smaller to larger units helps avoid the tendency to atomize into disjointed statements. Finding the appropriate balance between separating by gesture and maintaining a continuous thread can be challenging, especially for instrumentalists who lack the coherence that comes with a song text.

As the eighteenth century progressed, greater emphasis was placed on the larger units of musical organization. As noted, up to the 1750s the concept of the phrase is conspicuously absent from musical sources. The prototypical Galant and Classical musical unit is the symmetrical *Periode*, consisting of two eight-bar phrases in four-bar units bound in logical sequence by their cadences. This model served as the starting point for modern musical analysis and was first fully articulated in H. C. Koch's *Versuch einer Anleitung zur Composition* (1782–93), which was in turn built on the work of Joseph Riepel and Johann Philipp Kirnberger from the previous decades.[52] The distinction between the *Periode* and the gesture is one of the most important defining features of Classical and Baroque styles. Like other fundamental shifts, the transition from gesturing to phrasing happened gradually over the second half of the eighteenth and into the nineteenth century. As the phrase emerged as the basic unit of musical expression, there was a tendency to treat it as an indivisible unit, thereby losing sight of the distinctness of musical gestures in the more highly articulated Baroque style.

Evidence suggests that by 1770 longer structural groupings were gaining ground over the isolation of local, gestural events. When Charles Burney heard Quantz in Berlin, he found that instead of following the "modern manner," which he was familiar with from players in London, of "gradually enforcing and diminishing whole passages," Quantz reserved this effect for *messa di voce* on individual notes, a practice more in keeping with the style from forty years before.⁵³ Quantz's style is illustrated in his famous Adagio, where twenty-two dynamic changes are indicated in the first two bars alone (Ex. 7.10). Such highly nuanced playing was appropriate to slow movements, particularly those marked *Cantabile* or *Arioso* where Quantz recommended all notes "of a suitable length" to be performed "in a simple and flattering way with the alternation of *forte* and *piano*."⁵⁴

Example 7.10 Quantz, Adagio, *Versuch*, ch. 14 §23–43, Tab. xvii, xviii, and xix. (A full transcription of Quantz's instructions is given in Haynes's *End of Early Music*, 198–99)

Quantz's Adagio captures the concept of an expressive gesture as the brief embodiment of a passion. In movements like this where the emphasis is on legato and continuity of tone, dynamics take on greater importance than simply adding variety to the gestures: here they also serve as punctuation. Mozart thought of *cantabile* as essentially legato, so in 1781, when he heard the pianist Josepha Auernhammer, he criticized the way she clipped [*verzupt*] everything instead of playing in "the real delicate singing style."⁵⁵ We get a glimpse of what he had in mind when we read what his father wrote in 1756 about the special use of dynamics in *cantabile* movements and the importance of the voice as a model for instrumental performance:

> A singer who, during every short phrase stopped, took a breath, and specially stressed first this note, then that note, would unfailingly move everyone to laughter. The human voice glides quite easily from one note to another, and a sensitive singer will never make a break unless some special kind of expression of the division of rests in the phrase demands one. . . . One must therefore take pains where the cantilena of a piece demands no break, not only to leave the bow on the violin when changing the stroke, in order to connect with another, but also to play many notes in one stroke, and in such fashion that the notes which belong together shall run into each other, and be differentiated in some degree by means of forte and piano.⁵⁶

This quotation shows Leopold Mozart focusing on singing not so much as a model of eloquent declamation, but for the materiality of the human voice itself. So instead of referring to the rhetorical elements of singing and punctuation, he stresses the voice's ability to move seamlessly between pitches while maintaining continuity of sound, a context in which gestures were differentiated "by means of *forte* and *piano*"—that is, where gestures were demarked by dynamic contrasts rather than articulation silences.

Composers rarely bothered to indicate the minutia of nuance like Quantz's Adagio, but vocal performance manuals such as the *Vocalises* of the famous castrato Girolamo Crescentini (1762–1846) show that the tradition continued into the nineteenth century. Just as Quantz had maintained a conservative style of performance to the end of his career, Crescentini also held to an antiquated performance style. The castrato's sensitivity earned him high praise from the novelist Stendhal, who believed that even the most ingenious composer would fail to capture with precision all the "infinitely minute nuances of emotional suggestion [that] form the secret of Crescentini's unique perfection in his interpretation."[57] Apparently no one took up the challenge of notating Crescentini's practices, but the singer himself provided some valuable details in his widely disseminated vocal exercises. In his *Discours préliminaire* he outlined basic rules for the use of dynamics: (1) Rising melodies are to be performed with crescendo, descending passages with decrescendo; (2) Appoggiaturas receive more strength; (3) All notes of a reasonable length [*une certaine durée*] are sung with a *messa di voce* [*enflé et diminué*]; and (4) The pattern of grace notes preceding eighth and two sixteenths is performed with a diminuendo. In addition to these guidelines, there are copious dynamic markings on the *vocalises* themselves. A survey of various editions and manuscript copies from the nineteenth century reveals a gradual move to replace Crescentini's small-scale dynamics with longer arch-like phrases that rise toward a climax and away again (Burney's modern manner of "gradually enforcing and diminishing whole passages"). Examples 7.11a and b compare two passages from Crescentini's original with a transcription for oboe made by the Paris Conservatoire professor, Gustave Vogt (1781–1870). Notice how Vogt effectively obliterated Crescentini's internal subdivisions and distinctive gestures. Vogt's transcription was published in 1860, but in the 1820s nuancing by gesture was already out of fashion in Paris, and was dismissed by Vogt's pupil Henri Brod as "papillotage" ("flickering" or "fluttering").[58]

Not surprisingly, the shift from a gestural, highly nuanced approach to less articulated phrasing coincided with the dissolution of the connection between music and rhetoric. Meaning was still an element of a Romantic phrase, but its primary characteristic was physical. In the long-line phrase, each note cannot "have its own piano and forte," because it is a segment of a larger dynamic unit with a more integral shape. Like the slur, which in Rhetorical music was connected with enunciation and later

Example 7.11 Dynamics in Crescentini's Vocalises taken from G. Crescentini, *Raccolta di Esercizj per il canto all'uso del Vocalizzo*, nos. 8, 2 (ca. 1810), and G. Vogt, *Vocalises de Crescentini, transcrites pour le hautbois* (ca. 1860)

became a structural imperative, the Romantic phrase is defined by its physical rise and fall. To adapt the analogy in *The End of Early Music*, it resembles more closely an arching rainbow than an ever-changing kaleidoscope of gestural articulation.[59] The long-line phrase promotes a legato ambiance and broad movement, and is suited to the expansive scale of Romantic lyricism—although it should not be taken as the only dimension of Romantic expressivity.[60] There are no real stops or silences in the long-line phrase. The heavier bows used by string players, and the larger Romantic brass, reed instruments, and organs required more even wind pressure. All this equipment was designed to make it easier to produce a continuous, sustained tone at the expense of the finely etched gestures of the Rhetorical style.

Long-line phrasing became even more the norm after World War II when the younger generation of musicians reacted against the rapid mood swings and idiosyncratic interpretations of their immediate predecessors by imposing a structuralist approach on all music from old to avant-garde. A full, sonorous, and even tone color became the goal of every instrumentalist, and singers downplayed the declamatory aspects of inflected, punctuated singing. Leech-Wilkinson sees this as endemic of a broader cultural reassessment of the function of music:

The more austere analytical view of post-War performance (and commentary, of course) increasingly downplayed music's entertainment value and insisted instead on its music-structural integrity.[61]

Since 1800, vocal technique has moved toward a fixed, flattened larynx position—effective for producing greater volume but detrimental to diction and articulation. As well as complicating the quick stops, starts, and nuances appropriate to Baroque music, it is likewise less than ideal to handle the bravura technique demanded in Romantic opera up to Wagner and Puccini.[62] The pervasive presence of vibrato has been another factor in modern performance that reflects the more structural, less rhetorical approach to shaping music in performance.[63] By further ironing out unevennesses of expression, vibrato focuses on the medium (the physicality of the voice or instrument) rather than the eloquent articulation of the message.

Further Reading

This chapter amplifies and elaborates Haynes's discussion of punctuation and gesturing in *The End of Early Music*, (190–96).

Important writings on the development of phraseology in the eighteenth century include Marpurg *Kritische Briefe* (1759), the *Allgemeine Theorie der schönen Künste* by Schulz in Sulzer (1774), Kirnberger's *Kunst des reinen Satzes* (1776), Forkel, *Allgemeine Geschichte der Musik* (1788), and Türk's *Klavierschule* (1789). Useful secondary writings include Bonds, *Wordless Rhetoric*, McClure's "Making the Music Speak," and Thurmond, *Note Grouping*. Vial's *Art of Musical Phrasing* provides detailed readings of key sources and sound guidance on the changing aesthetic of articulation from Baroque and Classical styles. *Bach Interpretation: Articulation Marks in Primary Sources of J. S. Bach* by John Butt catalogues gestures and articulation patterns in Bach's notation, but does not address the vexing lack of clarity in many autograph sources. The theoretical basis of gesturing as a means of constructing meaning in both composition and performance is explored in Cumming, *The Sonic Self*, ch. 5.

In *The Harmonic Orator*, Ranum presents an alternative approach to the rhetorical analysis of song based on the principles of French prosody. In "The Expressive Pause," Toft presents evidence to demonstrate continuity in the theory of punctuation and articulation in rhetorical and singing traditions from the eighteenth up to the middle of the nineteenth century.

For examples of using parody texts for the analysis of instrumental music by C. P. E. Bach, see Plebuch, "Dark Fantasies." In "Die Sprache in der Musiktheorie," Göner examines Jérôme-Joseph de Momigny's application of Dido's lament to a Mozart string quartet.

8

Kairos:
Expressive Timing

GEOFFREY BURGESS

In a word, passion should never be measured.
—Grimarest, 1707[1]

To every thing there is a season, and a time to every purpose under heaven.
—*Ecclesiastes* 3:1

Dum loquimur, fugerit invida aetas:
Carpe diem, quam minime credula postero.

[Even as we speak, envious time flies further:
Seize the day, do not count on the future.]
—Horace, *Odes*, 1.11

Chronos and *Kairos*: Two Kinds of Time

The theme of time appears in numerous Bach cantatas. In *Christus, der ist mein Leben*, BWV 95, clocks are given play in pizzicato string figures. When their ticking suddenly stops, the oboes d'amore break from the precision of the worldly chronometer in syncopated figures—a graphic depiction of the desire, expressed in the text, to escape time in long-awaited death (Ex. 8.1).

This piece is an ingenious illustration of the two types of time that the Greeks called *chronos* (Χρόνος)—chronological or sequential time, and *kairos* (καιρός)—meaning the appropriate or opportune moment and also the idea of "taking time." *Chronos* was thought of as quantitative and measurable, while *kairos* had a qualitative nature. *Kairos* represented the fullness of time, the propitious moment, and was thus a key element in eloquent rhetoric. The concept of *kairos* folds into Horace's aphorism *carpe diem* (to seize the day, or moment), while the religious allusion in BWV 95 and other cantatas of Bach stems from the Old Testament book of Ecclesiastes 3:1, and the reference to the Second

Example 8.1 BWV 95/5, opening measures

Coming in Mark 1:15. This tradition was developed extensively in the writings of Augustine of Hippo (354–430 AD).

This ancient heritage is reflected in the way that musicians still speak of timing, which refers to the interplay of these two types of time: the seizing of *kairos* within the inexorable flow of *chronos*. Timing is an expressive device that allows musicians to convey elaborate concepts of structure and organization, as well as subtle and intimate feelings and thoughts. The validity and force of any message depends on when it happens. Knowing the right moment, and seizing it, is crucial to how any message is transmitted. There is a perfect moment for every gesture, a time when it will have its optimum effect. A gesture that might be compelling at the right moment can be incomprehensible an instant earlier or later. Related to timing is the concept of agogics (already introduced in chapter 7), which as a playing with time in order to highlight time, constitutes an array of musical techniques of working with *kairos*.

Musical time can unfold only in space; *kairos* must take into consideration the performance environment. Just as orators need to enunciate clearly and pace their speech to the size of the space so that each word can be distinctly heard, musicians need to accommodate their timing to the acoustics of the concert venues so that their musical gestures will not blur into one another and lose intelligibility. This means, for example, that what sounds well-paced in a small room might require more time in a larger, more reverberant hall.

The themes of the passing of time and the end of time coalesced and pervaded Bach's world. The pizzicato clock ticking in BWV 95 and bell tolling in others of his compositions allude to a commonplace in the cultural world of early modern Europe. Other composers occasionally alluded to clocks and passing bells with more realistic means. Bach was probably familiar with *Schlage doch, gewünschte Stunde*, a one-movement cantata famous for being the first musical composition to specify bells by Melchior Hoffmann (1679–1715, organist at the Neukirche in Leipzig). (So close is this work to the Bachian ethos that the work was erroneously attributed to Bach, catalogued as by Bach as BWV 53.)[2]

The Metronome and the Modern Tendency toward *Chronos*

The use of timing as an expressive device is one of the most obvious differences between the Rhetorical and Modernist approaches to performance. Jazz, and certain vernacular forms such as R&B, cultivate an expressive fluctuation of the beat or uneven pulses, but in the current classical tradition the general tendency is toward strict uniformity. This has instilled in us a resolute aversion to histrionics ("schmaltz" as it is known in the classical music trade). In 1990, Paul O'Dette commented that "Fifteen years ago, it was fashionable [in HIP, especially Renaissance music] not to bend any rhythms at any time. Bending rhythms was felt to be something unhistorical."[3] This is still true in the present Modernist climate, where musicians—and none more than HIP specialists—studiously avoid taking time for fear of being accused of holding "Romantic" sympathies. Fluctuations of the beat are regarded as self-indulgent, unprofessional lapses of control. Our reluctance to step outside the dominant paradigm of mechanical, metronomic timekeeping may not be conscious, but that doesn't make it any less widespread or systemic. These comments apply to the full spectrum of classical music, and today it is even hard to encounter a performance of Romantic music that isn't subject to a metronomic straitjacket.

Without question, the development of mechanical music reproduction has been an important contributing factor. More often than not the recording industry has forced musicians to obsess over technical perfection and consistency, including a strict adherence to chronometic accuracy. From a detailed study of early twentieth-century recordings, Daniel Leech-Wilkinson has concluded that recording has pushed for the more literal performance of scores. Along with the abolition of standard practices like *portamento, rubato,* spontaneous ornamentation, and nonsynchronization of left and right hand in piano performance, recorded musicians over the course of the twentieth century have increasingly adhered to an unwavering beat. This pursuit of perfection led to performances that Leech-Wilkinson has called "increasingly regular in all their dimensions" and from which have been expunged

> all the things that musicians used to do as a matter of course in order to intensify the expressivity of a performance. As in so many other respects, the post-War generation marks a watershed in these habits too.[4]

This "chronomania" has been imposed through the use of click tracks to regiment pop music and to coordinate movie soundtracks where music arguably plays one of its most emotive functions in contemporary society.

The use or nonuse of timing as an expressive device is clear when we listen to recordings made before and after World War II. Audio Example 8.1 presents two performances of "Buß und Reu" from Bach's St. Matthew Passion: Willem Mengelberg's remarkable live performance from 1939, and Paul McCreesh's studio version from sixty years later.

🔊 AUDIO EX. 8.1. J. S. Bach, "Buss und Reu," St. Matthew Passion, BWV 244/6
(a) Concertgebouw Orchestra, dir. Mengelberg (1939)
(b) Gabrieli Consort, dir. McCreesh (Archiv, 2002)

To our "chronomanic" ears, Mengelberg's interpretation seems like a ship adrift on the sea of time, but it still manages to convey a sense of taking time *within* time. In other words, there is a "beat" against which the *rubato* is perceived as a fluctuation. Mengelberg's timings might seem exaggerated to us, but they are proportioned to his monumental tempos, and dynamic palette. His reading is directed by the expressive potential of the text and Bach's writing as viewed from a Romantic performance aesthetic. He prioritized melodic considerations over harmonic, and his tempo fluctuations often disturb the momentum of ostinato patterns. Likewise, the way the appoggiaturas are lengthened conforms to Romantic aesthetics, and implements advice given by Hugo Riemann in the 1880s.[5] So while his performance may have little to do with how Bach performed his own music, its *kairos* has its own logic, and results in a remarkable piece of musical architecture. The vocal soloists are allowed *verismo*-style indulgences, but the tempo is just as fluid in the large choruses. The first aria, "Buss und Reu" demonstrates a keen sense of collaboration among all the musicians. The flutes prolong their suspensions and drag the beat with them, but the tempo is then artfully brought back to the original speed. Each cadence is marked with a structural *ritardando* and there is hardly one bar that is in "strict" time. All this is executed with a conductor whose function is more than a time keeper. In this style of performance, every player needs to be acutely aware of the fluidity of musical time, and that requires a very different sense of orchestral discipline than currently taught in most modern conservatories.

Keeping strict time might seem an easy "fix" to Mengelberg's excesses and bring them in line with a more historically informed interpretation. Life would indeed be simpler if beats and tempos were as regular and consistent as the machines we use for measuring them (the click track is after all a way of saving time in the recording studio—literally and economically). But, as Robert Hill has pointed out,

> One of the advantages of choosing to adhere to an objectively regular beat is that the player is not obliged to make significant and perceptible but very delicate time-organizing decisions.[6]

Simplifying the job of interpretation in this way would also lead to a hollowing-out of the performer's role in shaping a performance, and therefore curb the opportunity for eloquence. Such is the effect, whether consciously intended or not, in McCreesh's recording when we listen to it along side Mengelberg's. It demonstrates a clean, Modernist, nonsentimental interpretation built on a different rapport between director and players. There is still much expressivity here—just not in matters of timing.

Neither of these recordings is ideal. Rather, they represent opposites and together they illustrate the breadth of approaches that have been taken with Bach's music over the past century. As we proceed, it should become apparent that the musicians in Bach's day would have practiced a sense of timing somewhere between these two performances. A regular beat was an essential basis of much Rhetorical music: but it was a basis that was set up in order to be broken.

The Beat, or Pulse in Baroque Music

Music often involves setting up expectations by repeating a pattern which is then broken just as the listener is lulled into presuming its recurrence. This is the musical counterpart of the visual artist's trompe l'œil—a "trompe l'oreille" if you will. Haydn was a master of wittily playing with time. He set expectations for balancing phrase lengths, and then shifted the pattern to put the listener off guard to give the design a new perspective. Whether the result is amusing or frustrating, this type of "setting up" always elicits a subjective reaction.

The concepts of "beat" and "tempo" operate in the same way. Like the musical trompe l'oreille, the beat is based on expectation—a repeated pulse falling precisely on the place it is *expected* to fall—based on what has been set up. It is "strict" in the sense that the performer and listener agree about where it should fall. But the musical beat is always (at least where live performance is involved) a human rather than a mechanical construct so, although it is predictable, the beat can only be known subjectively. This means that even in the seeming inexorability of an absolutely precise musical beat, *kairos* already operates in collusion with *chronos*.

Every musician has experienced how unnatural it can seem to play strictly in time with a metronome. That has a lot to do with trying to make musical *kairos*—the timing that "feels right" for the music—conform to the abstract and humanly unobtainable ideal of chronometric precision. Our modern sense of tempo is influenced, whether we wish it or not (and often, whether we are aware of it or not) by the existence of *chronos* in the form of the metronome. Even those who don't like or use a metronome know in the back of their minds that it is the reference of last resort. Consider this phrase from the definition of tempo in the *New Grove Dictionary*:

> Even within passages that seem to be in stable tempo, the beat rate is not mechanically constant. . . . In normal performances tempo systematically fluctuates within the bar and the phrase.

We may well ask how this can be applied to musical performance *before* musicians had any mechanical means of regulating their playing. In a world where the precise division of time into units small enough to be meaningful to musicians presented real problems, tempo and pulse could not be objectively measured. Prior to the availability of portable timepieces in the seventeenth century, for many the only means of telling the time was the church clock tower. But even with the development of pendulums and portable timepieces, strict time and tempo remained relative concepts, and most authorities riled against the mechanical regulation of musical time.

How could tempo fluctuation be defined when not only tempo was based on a subjective sense of the "right feel," but also that the very beat itself was based on human expectation? The concept of a regular unwavering beat was encapsulated in the sixteenth-century concept of the *tactus*.[7] Related to the unchanging, divinely regulated cosmos, the tactus was a theoretical constant within which musical rhythm operated as mathematical subdivision. Most writers described using their pulse or a regular bodily movement such as an arm motion (today many prefer to tap their feet) to maintain the tactus, but in practice the absolute speed of the tactus varied from person to person and, without the means of rigorous control, was subject to fluctuation. In the eighteenth century, musicians advocated a default "normal tempo." Called variously *tempo ordinario* by Handel and *tempo giusto* by Bach, the means to objectively measure its rate were still lacking. The musical chronometers that appeared from the middle of the seventeenth century, were useful to record a tempo, but of limited application for the strict regulation of the beat in performance (more about this later). Quantz was aware of their existence, but as he had never seen one in use, he based tempo on the heart beat. Because this varies from person to person, he specified the pulse of a "high-spirited, jovial yet rather fiery and volatile person" (is that how he thought of himself?), which he set at ca. 80 beats per minute.[8] But what happens when this person gets even more excited with the adrenalin of performance? His sense of tempo will doubtless be affected.

Both Quantz and C. P. E. Bach emphasized the need to maintain the same tempo throughout a movement. This was not always an easy enterprise as it meant finding a speed appropriate to all the figuration and passions contained in the movement. Quantz decried that "daily experience shows that one very often sins in this way."[9] And C. P. E. Bach also recognized how difficult it was to meet this ideal. From what he says in his *Versuch*, the problem often arose from tempo adjustments taken to accommodate difficult passages.[10] Ornamentation could be another cause of tempo loss. At the turn of the eighteenth century, Roger North complained that gracing lacked competence when it caused a change of speed. "Musicians," he wrote,

> may assume as slow a measure as they please, but then they must keep to it, and the gentlemen of such libertys shew rather their want of justice, then overmuch skill; for if they do not in all their movement, even gracing of the hand or voice, use the measure of the gross strokes, and fall in exactly with them, they pretend what they doe not perform.[11]

In his inimitable prose, North is criticizing those who want to show off, and instead of exercising good judgment ("shew rather their want of justice, then overmuch skill"), set a tempo that they fail to stick to ("pretend what they doe not perform"). North was not advocating that players had to be precisely together throughout. What he did insist on, however, was that all the parts come together on the main beats ("the gross strokes"), meaning that for the rest of the time the graces could be rhythmically free.

If you've ever tried to match a metronome to a recording made by live musicians (rather than synthesized music such as techno), you will have noticed that the tempo constantly varies slightly. And this is even with performances produced in the mechanical age. Such a means of analyzing or controlling rhythm and tempo in performance was unavailable to North, Quantz, or Bach. Chronometers had been around from the 1630s (Mersenne proposed a pendulum chronometer in 1636 that proved impractical), but musicians did not use them in the same way that we use metronomes as absolute musical time keepers. The following comment, published in a collection of essays on mathematical subjects by Denis Diderot (ca. 1748), voices an opinion that numerous other eighteenth-century musicians must have held:

> Those who are connoisseurs of music would object against all chronometers in general, that there are perhaps not even four bars in an air which have exactly the same duration.[12]

Later, the introduction of metronomes like those we know today met with similar reactions. In 1804 J. F. Reichardt reported that even the finest musicians were unable to play more than a few bars against the clockwork timekeeper devised by J.-A.-C. Charles. And even after the release of Johann Nepomuk Maetzel's device, few musicians were willing to subject to its rigor, and even fewer knew how to use it accurately. It is thus not suprising that Beethoven's metronome markings have led to more confusion than clarification of his intentions regarding tempo.[13]

While chronometers may serve a valuable function by offering an abstract external standard, they have never represented musical tempo; they can only show speed—*chronos*, not *kairos*. They do not describe on-going tempo because that is always being gradually and subtly mutated by the musicians. Accurately speaking, tempo doesn't "systematically fluctuate within the bar and the phrase"; it just "does its thing," slowing down and speeding up ever so slightly, often for the purpose of bringing out the sense and meaning of the music.

"The true motion of the Bass"

Timing in Rhetorical music still requires a point of reference. C. P. E. Bach spoke of a "precisely maintained tempo"[14] and many eighteenth-century writers confirmed that it was the "true motion of the Bass" that was the arbiter of tempo.[15] To many modern musicians, the terms "strict" and "precise" may conjure up the image of machine-like accuracy and metronomic objectivity, so let us consider what the "true motion of the Bass" would have meant to a musician in the eighteenth century. When Quantz called for the bass to be "secure in rhythm" (*recht sicher im Zeitmaaße/ferme dans la mesure*), he still left room for inflection in the bassline as much as flexibility in the upper parts.[16] This is clear from the advice he gave to continuo players:

> After all, it isn't as if there is only one player who performs a piece with the real passion while the others acquit themselves of their duties inattentively and with indifference (which would be like a situation where some destroy what others create).[17]

The attributes of the Rhetorical style—phrasing by gesture, dynamic inflection (individual note-shaping), beat hierarchy, agogic accents, emphasis of dissonance, contrasts in volume and tone color, the placement of up-bows and down-bows corresponding with the desired emphasis and articulation—would all add variety to the bassline. Even if the player does only these basic things, the music will not lack life and variety. It will also not be rigorously strict.

In addition to laying down the beat, the continuo players' function was to provide harmonic support to the melodic parts. It is thus follows that in the same way, harmony should be the continuo player's primary point of reference for expressive tempo fluctuation. Denis Diderot made these observations on tempo:

> Two things make it necessary to slow some down and to speed up: good taste as dictated by the harmony in ensemble music, and good taste implied by harmony in solos. A musician who understands his art seizes the character of an air after playing only four bars and abandons himself to it. The pleasure of the harmony alone enthrals him: here he wants to accentuate the chords, there he wants to obscure them, which means that he sings or plays more or less slowly from one measure to another, and from one beat—even from one quarter of a beat—to the next.[18]

Thorough-bass manuals provide further instructions on how to vary the texture of the part according to the level of consonance and dissonance in the harmony. Quantz gave detailed instructions on the different dynamic strengths that should be applied to harmonies, and further explained how the harpsichordist achieved this by varying the number of notes and the manner of rolling the chords. Although he did not mention agogics, given what he said regarding the continuo players participating in the eloquent expression of the music, it is logical that they were also expected to bring out special features—such as chromatic shifts or deceptive cadences—with momentary fluctuations, agogic delays, prolongations, and the like. In that way the continuo player "can contribute much by way of perfecting good music, if he is not lacking in feeling, and if he is listening to everything that's happening and not merely his own part."[19]

It was also the duty of the continuo players to keep the other musicians "in order." Audio Example 8.2 demonstrates some of the maneuvers required of the cellist:

🔊 AUDIO EX. 8.2. BWV 171/4, Helmut Wittek, soprano with Concentus Musicus, dir. Harnoncourt (Telefunken, 1987)

In this recording the cellist is faced with several bouts of "rushing" in the upper parts: the singer's first entrance and the violin a little later. You hear him supervise and, like any good player, resolve the problem by performing two contradictory services at the same time. He does his best to regain the original, slower tempo, while playing close enough to the other musicians so that they sound superficially together. By the violin's second solo entrance, he has managed to reinstate the first tempo. This is not an example of the expressive use of timing, but how the continuo players can drive the tempo by reacting to the inevitable accidents that occur when players take untoward liberties. It was just as relevant in the eighteenth century as it is now, as is seen in this description from Corrette's cello method of 1741:

> In a solo concerto or a violin sonata, if the upper part rushes, the cellist, being a good musician, must play strongly and hold forcefully to the beat of the start of the piece for a bar or so: this will bring the treble instruments back to the correct speed [*mesure*] and prevent them from rushing even more.[20]

Corrette also explains how musicians normally dealt with a situation that appears to have been fairly common in the absence of a conductor:

> Although good violinists play Adagios and Largos without respecting the time, that doesn't keep everyone else from playing in time, which is what the cellist should also do. This is something the Italians put into practice very well, as they [unlike the French] only beat the time [at times audibly with a stick] in music for large ensembles.[21]

Diderot's remarks about chronometers quoted earlier refer specifically to the performance of French music, and it is often assumed that other styles did not admit the same degree of tempo flexibility. This quotation from Corrette would suggest that in certain contexts Italian musicians were just as free with the beat. Contrary evidence comes from another music commentator equally well versed in French and Italian styles. When he came to write the entry on "Chronomètre" for the *Encyclopèdie*, Jean-Jacques Rousseau relied heavily on Diderot's article but added the following comment, suggesting that Italian musicians were even more strictly wedded to the beat than French:

> Nothing better illustrates the total opposition of [French and Italian] music. If the energy of Italian music is drawn from the rigorous submission to the beat [*la mesure*], French music puts all its energy into mastering the same beat [*à maîtriser à son gré cette même mesure*], to rush and retard it according to the taste of the melody [*le chant*] or the flexibility of the singer's voice.[22]

This, however, may reveal more about Rousseau's entrenched bias against the fickleness of French musical taste in favor of more solidly conceived Italian music than presenting an accurate picture of national tendencies relating to tempo in the mid-eighteenth century. It is also possible that he was not comparing like genres. From the broader context of the article, he seems to be pitting the fluid nature of French recitative against Italian measured arias: music in which there is tempo fluctuation compared with music where a strict beat is maintained, but can in practice be broken. This is an important distinction that we will turn to in the following sections. In the absence of more concrete documentation from outside France, it is hard to pin down how national tendencies in tempo compared with the French, but it is still a strange irony that France, the nation that was reputed to have the most flexible sense of tempo, was also at the forefront of inventing mechanical devices to measure musical time.

Kairos takes on many different forms; certain strategies have been favored at different times and have come to be associated with different styles. Mengelberg's *kairos* reflected early twentieth-century practices and the remnants of the Romantic tradition, but in 1727 when Bach first performed his St. Matthew Passion, *kairos* would have operated within the "true motion of the bass," which was consistent with practices established at least a generation or two earlier. In 1676 Thomas Mace formulated the difference between *kairos* and *chronos* as follows:

> You must know, That, although in our *First Undertakings*, we ought to *strive*, for the *most Exact Habit*, of *Time-keeping*, that possibly we can attain *unto*, (and for severall *good Reasons*) yet, when we come to be *Masters*, so that we can *command all manner of Time*, at our *own Pleasures*; we Then *take Liberty*, (and very often, for *Humour, and good Adornment-sake*, in certain Places) to *Break Time*; sometimes *Faster*, and sometimes *Slower*, as we perceive, the *Nature of the Thing Requires*, which often adds, much *Grace*, and *Luster*, to the *Performance*.[23]

For Mace, then, learning to play *in* time was only a means to understand how to *break* time. As he explained, "breaking time" was a musical refinement; it was how practiced musicians played. This is what subsequent generations of musicians called *tempo rubato* (robbed time): the artful shifting of the music around a strictly regulated beat.

Inconsistent terminology has created confusion, so for the sake of clarity, we will adopt the following usage:

Strict tempo: keeping a steady beat (N.B., this is not necessarily metronomic time!).
Tempo Fluctuation: temporary changes to the beat involving all parts ("tempo rubato" in modern usage).
Borrowed time: rhythmic displacement in some parts (usually the melodic line) while the beat (usually in the bass) remains steady. Called "breaking the time," or "tempo rubato" in the eighteenth century.

Having already established the role of the bass in laying down the tempo in Baroque music, the purpose of the next sections is to survey historical material that substantiates the presence of tempo fluctuation and borrowed time in the Rhetorical style.

Before going any further, it is important to emphasize that I am not advocating freedom for the sake of freedom. Playing Rhetorical music is about understanding and projecting the *inventio*. Once the subject of the music is clear, the musician exercises the appropriate liberties to make it eloquent. Rhetorical performance is not boundaryless play. Rather it provides freedom within a well-considered structure. This means that in place of arbitrarily imposed liberties that can lead to a wayward and misdirected sense of timing, rhythmic freedom should always be grounded in a sound understanding of the musical structure and figuration—its *inventio* and *dispositio*.

Tempo Fluctuation

Today musicians use the term "tempo rubato" to mean a deliberate, but temporary, alteration of tempo for expressive purposes, but in the Baroque period there was no single word for tempo fluctuation because it was, so to speak, music's middle name. More of a state of mind than an external, added effect (like a *flattement* or a slur), tempo fluctuation was much more prevalent than our Modernist sensibilities might imagine. We have already considered how continuo players introduced expressive timing in the theoretically strict metric progress of the music, and Diderot's observations make it clear that eighteenth-century musicians were unaccustomed to adhering to a rigid beat for more than a few notes.

Like gracing and improvisation, rubato in the seventeenth and eighteenth centuries was the territory of the performer. Tempo directions were not usually written into the score: that was not part of the composer's job. How and where to apply tempo fluctuations was decided in the here and now of performance. As a consequence, we are left with very few written traces of the practice and those that have survived often contradict what would have come instinctively to musicians: the exceptions to rules and expectations learned through experience. We might look with derision at those early twentieth-century editions that attempted to notate rubato in Baroque music, but in concept they are not entirely at odds with the Baroque spirit. What is anathema is the idea that tempo fluctuations can become part of the written text or *dispositio*, rather than the prerogative of the performer's *elocutio*.

Whether the words at the beginnings of Baroque movements are tempo indications or advice on a piece's principal character is moot, but this ambiguity shows the importance of tempo as an expressive device. What interests us here is the way tempo heightens and transmits emotional states to clarify the communication of meaning. In Audio Example 8.3 the performance of an intensely passionate slow movement by C. P. E. Bach directed by Geoffrey Lancaster moves with the music's changing moods. The average speed is 88 beats per minute, but this is hardly meaningful: the pulse shifts gently but perceptibly to the harmonies and the changing nature of the gestures. As well as the time taken between phrase endings, at harmonic surprises, the subtle ebb and flow to the foreground rhythm in this performance—faster on optimistic rising phrases, retarded on sighing appoggiaturas—lends greater impact to the composer's carefully notated dynamics by emphasizing the angularity of the lines and the surprising harmonic twists that contribute to the music's pathos.

🔊 AUDIO EX. 8.3. C. P. E. Bach: Poco Adagio, Symphony in B♭, Wq 182/2 Tasmanian Symphony Chamber Players, dir. Lancaster (ABC Classics, 1990)

We normally think of tempo fluctuation as the prerogative of soloists, but this was not true in the Rhetorical period. The new understanding of rhetorical performance, and particularly the eloquent delivery of texted music associated with Baroque art, was a prime justification for tempo fluctuation. The following quotation from Marin Mersenne, who proposed the first musical chronometer, indicates how widespread the practice of tempo fluctuation had become:

> It is difficult to generalise because [musicians] change the beat many times, in performing the same piece of music, rushing and slowing the down- and upbeat, according to the letters and the words, or the different affects of the passages they perform. They would have to use as many different lengths of pendulum string as the different beats they wish to make.[24]

This tradition did not originate with the creation of monody, as we might assume, but had its roots in polyphonic music. Already in 1555 Nicola Vicentino compared the effect of "changing the measure" to an orator's technique, which "has a powerful effect on the soul" through speaking "now loud and now soft, now slow and now fast, thus greatly moving his listeners. . . . What effect," he asked,

> would an orator have if he were to recite a fine oration without organizing accents, pronunciations, fast and slow rates of motion, and soft or loud levels of speaking? He would not move the audience. The same is true of music. If the orator moves listeners with the devices described above, how much greater and more powerful will be the effect of a well-coordinated music recited with the same devices, but now accompanied by harmony?[25]

Vincentino seems to be talking about tempo fluctuation and shifting beats through the course of the piece, because he says the method "cannot be written down," so he cannot be referring to proportional changes as they are fairly straightforward to notate. From this it is reasonable to assume that Mannerist and *seconda-prattica* polyphony of the turn of the sixteenth century was performed with nuance and tempo fluidity.[26] In 1619 Praetorius concurred with Vicentino, but suggested that there may have been more restrictions in the performance of sacred music:

> Often the composition itself, as well as the text and the meaning of the words, necessitates that the beat now and then, accelerates and slows down, but not too frequently, and also that the choir resonates softly and gently at times and firmly and lively at other times, no doubt, greater restraint will be necessary in the church than at table with such alternations [of instruments and voices].[27]

This style of performance where timing and tempo were dictated by the eloquent declamation of the text still seems to have been relatively new in 1615. Frescobaldi referred to it in the preface to his first volume of toccatas where he indicated that he based his written-out improvisational solo keyboard style on vocal practice:

> We see the same thing done in modern madrigals, which, notwithstanding their difficulties, are rendered easier to sing, thanks to the variations of the time, which is beaten now slowly, now quickly, and even held in the air, according to the expression of the music, or the sense of the words.[28]

With the blossoming of monody, the tempo fluctuation inherited from the madrigal became part of the elusive concept of *sprezzatura*. The same rhetorical intent is evident in Giulio Caccini's description of tempo fluidity in the introduction to his *Nuove Musiche* from just a decade earlier:

> I have endeavour'd in those my late Compositions to bring in a kind of Musick, by which Men might, as it were, Talk in Harmony, using in that kind of Singing a certain noble neglect of the Song [*una certa nobile sprezzatura di canto*] (as I have often heard at *Florence* by the Actors in their Singing *Opera's*).[29]

Caccini provided many expressive markings above the staff in his musical examples. Some are indications of the affect of the passage. The following direction is particularly telling: "exclamation, without measure, as it were Talking in Harmony, and neglecting the Musick." Commenting further, Caccini wrote:

> I call that the *Noble manner of Singing*, which is used without tying a man's self to the ordinary measure of Time, making many times the Value of the Notes less by half [i.e., often decreasing their duration by half], and sometimes more, according to the conceit of the words; whence proceeds that excellent kind of Singing with a graceful Neglect [*sprezzatura*], whereof I have spoken before.[30]

A more generalized concept than tempo fluctuation, *sprezzatura*, which Caccini elucidated as "that elegant casualness that feels no constraint to follow literally that which is written on the page," encompasses all aspects of free-spirited improvisation and affect-based performance.

With the emergence of new musical forms, certain genres evolved where a more liberal use of tempo fluctuation was practiced than in others. The most important of these are recitative, improvised preludes, and cadenzas, but these are merely the "official" documentation of this spirit—the places when composers took the trouble to indicate them in their scores.

As recitative originated in the *seconda pratica* and was modeled on speech patterns, it is natural that here the singer should follow the passions of the text and pace the performance to imitate the timing of a skilled orator. From what C. P. E. Bach says, this applied equally to both *secco* and accompanied recitative:

> It's clear to see in accompanied recitatives that the tempo and the beat have often to be changed, in order to excite and calm the many passions that follow quickly on one another. In recits, the beat is written for the sake of form, with the understanding that it is not obligatory. As with the fantasy, it's a clear advantage that, in complete freedom from the limitations of the beat, we are able to realize such music on our instrument.[31]

Bach's opinion is corroborated by other writers including Quantz, who explained that in Italian recitative the singer adjusts the beat according to the affect.[32] French recitative operated somewhat differently. Notated in shifting meters, tempo fluctuation was written into the score. Still, Etienne Loulié described a special *mesure de recitatif* in which first beats of bars were coordinated, but where otherwise the singer exercised rhythmic freedom.[33] The free interpretation of accompanied recitative may surprise us today where the need to coordinate multiple parts is often taken as an indication to hold to an unwavering beat. This applies less to Arioso style, which is structured within a meter and tempo.

Handel used both of these styles of declamation in Part 2 of *Messiah*. "Thy rebuke hath broken His heart" is accompanied recitative, followed by the arioso "Behold, and see" with more measured gait, followed by another accompanied recitative dominated by the rhythm of the text leading to the air "But Thou didst not leave his soul in hell" where again the balance shifts to more regular meter. Bach often gave tempo markings for arioso passages. In Part 1 of the *Christmas Oratorio* BWV 248, mvt. 7 ("Er ist auf Erden kommen arm") alternates between "Arioso Andante" and "Recitativo." In instances where the distinction between rhythmically free recitative and strict arioso was less clear, he used terms like "a tempo giusto" or "a battuta" to specify that the performers should observe the rhythm with a fair degree of precision.[34]

Measured and unmeasured preludes and *tombeaux*, toccatas, fantasies, and the like were frequently invented on the spot, and those that have been preserved in notation imitate the effects of improvizational practice. Particularly in seventeenth-century works belonging to the aptly named *stylus fantasticus*, where contrasting or disparate musical ideas are bound together with flashy (fantastic) gestures, it rarely makes sense to hold to a single tempo through an entire piece. French unmeasured preludes, with their graceful, sweeping lines, are beautiful to look at. They are usually associated with seventeenth-century harpsichord repertoire written without indications of rhythm and the beat by such composers as Louis Couperin, Nicholas Lebègue, and Jean-Henri d'Anglebert. Even here rhythm is not completely free. The horizontal positioning of notes on the page, special notational signs, and the sequence of harmonies compels certain decisions. The logic of these pieces is also defined by the conventions of punctuation and hesitation. Unmeasured music also survives for viola da gamba by De Machy (1685) and Monsieur de Sainte-Colombe. Music by the latter composer includes remarks like "because it is unmeasured, one plays it as one wishes," and "because it is unmeasured, it should be played only by ear."[35] In the early eighteenth century unmeasured notations were largely abandoned, but the improvisatory spirit lived on in metrically notated preludes. François Couperin's remarks in the preface to his *L'Art de toucher le clavecin* of

1717 suggest that rhythmic freedom was still the norm in this genre, unless the composer requested performance in strict rhythm:

> Those who avail themselves of these written-out preludes [*préludes réglés*] should play them in a relaxed way [*une mainère aisé*] without worrying too much about the rhythm [*des mouvements*] unless I have deliberately added the word "mesuré" [measured].[36]

Couperin is referring to the set of metrically notated preludes that accompany his method. Half of these preludes are marked *mesuré*; the others should be performed according to the taste in practice: that is, in freer rhythm. This tradition continued for some time, and in the 1750s C. P. E. Bach was still able to write that

> a keyboard player can practice the declamatory style when playing fantasies ... Bar lines are always omitted in this kind of piece. ... Common time is indicated but not prescribed, and for this reason bar lines are always omitted. The unmeasured fantasy seems especially appropriate for expressing the passions, since any time-signature carries with it a kind of constraint.[37]

Later still, Mozart left musical fragments from which he presumably improvised fantasies, and for those of his acquaintances and students with more limited experience improvising in that style, he composed fully realized fantasies.[38]

Given this context, the literal reading of preludes with continuous notated rhythm, like the C-major Prelude in Book 1 of Bach's *Das wohltemperierte Clavier* and the preludes to Bach's cello suites was, more than anything, responsible for the mid-twentieth-century mislabeling of Baroque music as "sewing machine music." This style of interpretation not only distorts the improvisatory quality of these works but misrepresents the Baroque spirit.

More than anywhere else, cadenzas are where the performer takes charge, and are consequently not subject to strict meter. Baroque cadenzas often resemble little preludes. In fact, some authors equated preludes with *points d'orgues* or cadenzas and provided examples of the type of passages and showy gestures that players might have had on hand to elaborate cadences.[39] Example 8.2 gives the first two from Wragg's *Oboe Preceptor*. Notice the absence of meters signs and bar lines.

As the name implies, cadenzas are elaborated cadence points, and as well as the standard $^6_4$ chords that grind the recapitulation to a halt in late eighteenth-century concerto movements, the cadential tags at the end of Baroque sonata movements call for improvised flourishes and should also be treated as cadenzas and opportunities to break from strict meter. Many of these movements conclude with open

Example 8.2 Three cadenza–preludes from Wragg, *Oboe Preceptor* (London: 1792)

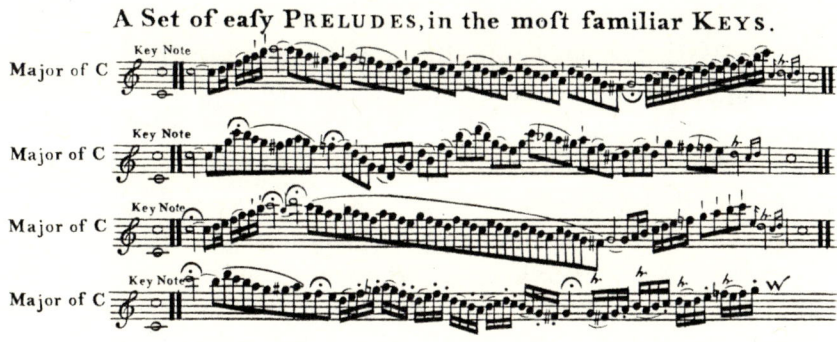

cadences on non-tonic harmonies. C. P. E. Bach indicated that "when a composer ends a movement in a foreign key, he usually wanted the players to proceed directly to the next movement."[40] But the frequency of page turns between movements in original part books suggests that performers were at liberty to take some time, and let the harmony "hang in the air" like a musical question mark before resolving it with the opening of the next movement. Either way, the customary cadenza and time taken call attention to the special nature of these moments.

When Quantz wrote his flute treatise in the 1750s, the cadenza had developed into a more extended opportunity for the soloist to escape from the tyranny of the tactus.

> Only rarely is the meter [*Tactart/la mesure*] observed in cadenzas; it would even be a mistake to make an effort to constrain one's self in that regard. Because cadenzas should not have a single consistent melody, but consist rather of detached gestures [*Gedanken/pensées*], though appropriate to the dominant passions of the movement.[41]

Mozart operated in the same tradition. He had to mark the cadenza in his Quintet for Piano and Winds, K. 452 (1784) "in tempo" because the idea of continuing in strict time would have been an unexpected novelty to his performers.

A fermata sign was a way of indicating that time should be taken, or a cadenza added in a less expected place. This occurs in numerous arias by Bach. Looking back at this use of the fermata H. C. Koch quite aptly described it as where "the spirit [*Geist*] itself comes to a brief standstill, or where the actual feeling [*Empfindung*] appears to have exhausted itself through its full effusion [*völlige Ergießung*]."[42] A wonderful example of this occurs in the opening chorus of BWV 95. *Christus, der is mein Leben* (Christ is my life). The second strophe of the chorale "Sterben ist mein Gewinn" (Death is my reward) is an antithesis to the first, and to highlight the contrast Bach set the word *Sterben* to a prolonged harmonic progression terminating with a fermata on a diminished seventh on ♭V: the harmonic antipode to the G-major opening. The sense of emotional exhaustion is equally evident in "Zerfließe mein Herz" in the St. John Passion where the fermatas coincide with the word *tot* (dead). The two examples from "Aus Liebe" in the St. Matthew Passion given in Example 8.3, are also associated with death, but are slightly different. In bar 11, the pause sign can be taken as an indication to break from the beat that effectively turns the second part of the measure into a written-out lead-in in free time. Measure 53 provides the opportunity for the singer to add a simple embellishment that would enhance the sense of despair in the face of death. In both cases the fermatas appear on dissonances so that as well as a warning to the performers that the music halts on unresolved harmony, they imply additional time to allow the special harmonies to take their effect.

Even when not interpreted as an opportunity to add an improvised cadenza, fermatas signal special treatment with the timing.[43] Bach followed the custom of indicating the ends of phrases in chorales with fermatas. The fermatas are a convenient guide to the phrasing of the hymn and usually correspond to the punctuation in the text. Even in simple congregational singing, a range of different treatments of chorales was practiced. In some cities breaks were made between the strophes, with or without a pause on the last note (fermata as punctuation; Audio Ex. 8.5b); in other towns organists improvised connecting passages between each strophe (fermata as cadenza; Audio Ex. 8.4). Bach provided examples of improvisations in early chorale settings BWV 715, 722, and 732, and the chorale prelude genre grew out of the tradition of interstrophic improvisations.[44] Where a break is observed, how much time was taken probably depended to some extent on the context, the performance space, and whether the chorales were being sung by the choir or by the congregation.

Example 8.3 Fermatas in J. S. Bach, "Aus Liebe," St. Matthew Passion BWV 244/49

🔊 AUDIO EX. 8.4. Fermatas as cadenzas: J. S. Bach, *Von Himmel Hoch* with interstrophic organ elaborations by James Johnstone; J. S. Bach, *Epiphany Mass;* Gabrieli Consort, dir. McCreesh (Archiv, 1997).

Various approaches to interpreting fermatas in chorales continue to be practiced. There are those who believe the fermata convention overrides the punctuation of the text, and others who privilege punctuation over the fermatas and elide verses that are not separated with punctuation even when a fermata is marked. Consideration should also be given to the chorale's function in its liturgical and/or musical context. Some of the four-part chorale settings that appear in Bach's Passions are meditative reflections on the drama of the narrative; here more generous timing can be effective. Others are dramatic interjections, and so their rhetorical function may be better served with less spacious delivery. Audio Example 8.5 gives three interpretations of the concluding chorale in Bach's St. John Passion. Here is the chorale text.

Ach Herr, laß dein lieb Engelein	*Ah Lord, let your dear little angel*
Am letzten End die Seele mein	*At my final end, take my soul*
In Abrahams Schoß tragen,	*To Abraham's bosom.*
Den Leib in seim Schlafkämmerlein	*Let my body in its little sleeping-chamber*
Gar sanft ohn einge Qual und Pein	*Softly and without anguish or pain*
Ruhn bis am jüngsten Tage!	*Rest until the last day!*
Alsdenn vom Tod erwecke mich,	*At that day wake me from death*
Daß meine Augen sehen dich	*So that my eyes may see you*
In aller Freud, o Gottes Sohn,	*in all joy, son of God,*
Mein Heiland und Genadenthron!	*My Savior and Throne of grace!*
Herr Jesu Christ,	*Lord Jesus Christ,*
Erhöre mich, erhöre mich,	*Hear me, hear me,*
Ich will dich preisen ewiglich!	*I will praise you eternally.*

(The last syllable of each line coincides with a fermata in Bach's setting.)

🔊 AUDIO EX. 8.5. J. S. Bach, St. John Passion, final chorale "Ach Herr, laß dein lieb Engelein."
(a) Fermatas as pauses: Concentus Musicus Wien, dir. Nikolaus Harnoncourt (Telefunken, 1978)
(b) Fermatas as punctuation: Taverner Consort and Players, dir. Andrew Parrott (Virgin, 2005)
(c) Textual punctuation prioritized over fermatas: Monteverdi Choir and English Baroque Soloists, dir. Gardiner (Soli Deo Gloria, 2011)

The pervasiveness of metric flexibility in Rhetorical music is one reason why, in most contexts, a time-beating conductor was not necessary in performances until after the period we are addressing. Where the musicians could hear (and see) each other, they could usually self-regulate tempo without too much difficulty. But where the ensemble was too large and required centralized coordination, or the acoustics and size of the performance space presented difficulties, a "conductor" (whether officially designated so or not) was often used.[45] The incessant banging of the conductor's staff at the Paris Opéra was a constant source of irritation tolerated up to the Revolution as a necessity to coordinate stage and pit. Other large ensembles were directed by time keepers wielding a scroll of music (see Fig. 8.1). Still, this did not mean that the beat was unyielding in its regularity or that there was no flexibility within the structure of the beat.

Figure 8.1 "Conductor" shown on frontispiece from Johann Walther, *Musikalisches Lexikon* (Leipzig, 1732)

In his *Vollkommene Capellmeister*, Mattheson advised that indicating the beat was the music director's basic function, but that

> the beat must not only be attentively maintained, but as circumstances demand (as for instance when a skilled singer makes a fine ornament) the director can and should make a small exception in the movement, giving way and delaying the beat, or also, in accommodating the passion or for other reasons, make the beat faster or stronger than before.[46]

It seems difficult to understand this as anything other than an indication that tempo was expected to fluctuate. How much the tempo changed is, of course, hard to say, and Mattheson was appropriately vague. We can surmise that it would not be as extreme as would become common with the larger performing forces and more grandiose attitudes of the nineteenth and twentieth centuries, such as illustrated in Mengelberg's performance of the St. Matthew Passion, but it is equally clear that the slavish precision insisted on by so many early music conductors is just as antithetical to the Baroque style. Indeed, the presence of the conductor is more of an imposition than is immediately apparent. The authority they wield more than often overrides individual interpretative decisions, making for a radically different distribution of musical responsibility from that of Bach's day.

From the information I have presented it should be clear that rhythmic flexibility in Rhetorical music is not an excuse for "freedom for freedom's sake." The sources may give a picture of much greater liberties than we currently take, but apart from the exceptional genres—preludes, fantasies, and recitative, most Baroque music is highly structured, and timing in performance operates *within* the structure and serves to eloquently *articulate* the structure. The hierarchic organization of the beats is a predictable pattern that should be broken only by exceptional events. As well as overriding considerations of genre and the ideas expressed in the text (where there is one), Baroque musicians took their cues for agogics first from harmonic events, then melodic gestures, phrasing, and the like. The equilibrium between the characteristic *sprezzatura* of Baroque musical elocution, and the structured metric profile of the music takes time to acquire and experience to regulate. That equilibrium is no better illustrated than in the practice of Borrowed Time.

Borrowed Time

In 1723 the eminent singer Pier Francesco Tosi wrote, "whoever does not know how to steal the Time [*rubare il Tempo*] in Singing, knows not how to Compose, nor to Accompany himself, and is destitute of the best Taste and greatest Knowledge."[47] From his assertive tone, Tosi clearly considered stealing time a skill essential for all musicians: composers and performers alike. When Tosi was on tour in London in 1693/94, Roger North heard him demonstrate the normal approach of Italian musicians to the practice of "borrowing time" (or "broken time" as some British writers called it). North wrote about this experience and commented that "it would be vanity to attempt a description of this manner, but it is easily shewed and made understood by the demonstration of example" and indicated that "most persons that performe well doe the same thing . . . by habit rather than designe."[48] If to North borrowed time defied verbal description and was a musical instinct that could be learned only by example, in the 1740s Johann Ernst Galliard, himself a composer and accomplished instrumentalist, still attempted to provide an explanation in this footnote to Tosi's text:

> It regards particularly the Vocal, or the Performance on a single Instrument in the *Pathetick* and *Tender*; when the Bass goes an exactly regular Pace, the other Part retards or anticipates in a singular Manner, for the Sake of Expression, but after That returns to its Exactness, to be guided by the Bass. Experience and Taste must teach it. A mechanical Method of going on with the Bass will easily distinguish the Merit of the other Manner.[49]

Other sources attest to the practice of treble instrument players routinely responding to "pathetick and tender" passages by adhering less strictly to the written rhythms.[50] In such moments, the accompanying parts acted as a foil by playing in "strict" rhythm. Their "normalcy" set into relief the "singular manner" of performing the solo part and "distinguished its merit." Roger North was particularly fond of this style of playing, which he identified with Andante movements. This description provides a delightful image of performance from the pre-mechanized age:

> That species of consort musick that proceeds with an easy familiar air, and a *basso andante* [lit. walking bass] is my option. The chief reason is that it expresseth steddyness of mind, not affected or altered by the *cantabile* of the upper parts. And it humours a voice most exquisitely; for that is always melodious, and moves with a self-regard, as if unconcerned with what waits upon it. And the stepps of the base make out the time, which is not in the voice distinguishable, and that is a constant vertue of it; for it keeps the time of the whole consort and all fall into just measures with it; as one may fancy a rider singing finely while his horse trotts in time.[51]

Borrowed time was practiced across the Rhetorical period, and well into the following century it is equally familiar from accounts of Chopin's playing.[52] It was considered a technique of high refinement, particularly in keyboard performance where the same player has to keep the strict tempo in one hand against a free-spirited melody in the other. C. P. E. Bach wrote in his *True Art of Keyboard Playing* that "when the execution is such that one hand seems to play against the bar and the other strictly with it, it may be said that the performer is doing everything that can be required of him."[53] For that reason, in 1777, Wolfgang Mozart complained of those who cannot grasp "that in *tempo rubato* in an Adagio, the left hand should go on playing in strict time. With them, the left hand always follows suit [i.e., coordinates with the right]."[54]

Above all, borrowed time seems to have been associated with Italian vocal style. Quantz recalled hearing the "so-called tempo rubato" for the first time when Santa Stella Lotti visited Dresden in 1719, but there is evidence that it was already around much earlier.[55] Monteverdi noted that in the central part of his *Lamento della ninfa* (Eighth Book of Madrigals, 1638) the role of the nymph should be performed in "the tempo of the passion of the soul, and not that of the normal beating of the hand [*tempo dell'affetto del animo e non quello de la mano*]."[56] The composer's instructions seem straightforward until we realize that the nymph is accompanied by the inexorable cycle of a ground bass. How can the soprano follow the passions of her soul if she is held to the strict timing of the other parts? What Monteverdi asked for was an astute playing with time where the bass provides an uninterrupted metric framework against which the soprano can freely move—North's "breaking yet keeping the time." When performed effectively this creates a type of sonic perspective where the nymph is placed in emotional relief against the background of the pitying male onlookers.

As it turns out, Monteverdi set a challenge that few modern performers have been able to meet. The four recordings surveyed in Audio Example 8.6 span the sixty-year period from 1937 to 1997, but only one is faithful to Monteverdi's directive. The soprano on Nadia Boulanger's recording from 1937 sounds like she would have been more comfortable singing Puccini, but she performs with very little of the *rubato* associated with *verismo* style. The male trio in Harnoncourt's recording is very free with the rhythm of the opening phrases; Ann Murray who sings the nymph, however, is barely able to resist holding to the regular beat of the ground bass. The effect is similar in the reading from The Consort of Musicke, except here Emma Kirkby as the nymph takes liberties that oblige a stretching of the beat in all parts. This is tempo fluctuation rather than borrowed time. In the recording from Alessandrini and Concerto Italiano the regularity of the bass is respected, while soprano

Rossana Bertini follows the emotional contours of her part. The faster tempo taken by the Italians facilitates timing between the major pulses in the music. As often as dragging the tempo and singing later than the other parts, Bertini anticipates the beat. This is a feature Monteverdi notated in other contexts (such as in *Orfeo* where Orfeo laments the loss of Euridice). Bertini's dynamic contrasts add to the poignancy of this performance, and her emphasis of particularly emotive words offsets the effect of the faster overall tempo.

🔊 AUDIO EX. 8.6. Monteverdi, Lamento della Ninfa
(a) Vocal and Instrumental Ensemble, dir. Nadia Boulanger (HMV, 1937)
(b) Concentus Musicus, dir. Nikolaus Harnoncourt (Telefunken, 1984)
(c) Consort of Music, dir. Anthony Rooley (Virgin Classics, 1991)
(d) Concerto Italiano, dir. Rinaldo Alessandrini (Opus 111, 1997)

Concerto Italiano's recording is unsettling; it sounds "untidy," almost "dirty" in comparison to the "correct" in-time interpretations of the earlier three recordings. Other performances bring out the almost sublime beauty and chaste purity of Monteverdi's music, but that is not what is called for. Instead of being awestruck by the beauty of the nymph's voice, the male singers should express pity for her as they register her distracted emotional state. The effect achieved by Alessandrini's group resonates with the way North described his encounter with the great Italian singer Tosi:

> And there is no greater grace than breaking the time in the minutes [i.e., the smaller subdivisions of the measure], and still holding it punctually upon the maine, to preserve the grand beat or measure. . . . For this sprinkling of discord or error is like damask, . . . or any unaccountable variegation of colours that renders a thing agreeable.[57]

In the music of J. S. Bach there is no shortage of opportunities for this treatment, but it takes great conviction to apply it to music where the notion of textual sanctity remains hard to dislodge. In his performance of the second movement of the Italian Concerto BWV 971, Bradley Lehmann captures the spirit of spontaneous melodic invention over the patient walking bass (Audio Ex. 8.7a). As well as tempo rubato, tempo fluctuations draw attention to structural cadences. By contrast, in his 1960 recording (Audio Ex. 8.7b), Glenn Gould achieves contrast between the treble and bass parts more with articulation (notice the chopped repeated notes in the left hand) than with rhythmic interpretation. Tonally beautiful and taken at a much slower overall tempo, Gould's reading sounds static and mechanical. His accurate note-by-note approach treats Bach's right-hand part as structural melody rather than elaborate ornamentation—a misunderstanding of Bach's notation.

🔊 AUDIO EX. 8.7. J. S. Bach, Andante, Italian Concerto, BWV971
(a) Bradley Lehmann (private recording https://www.youtube.com/watch?v=OhdwhDsuy2Y, accessed 25 June, 2015)
(b) Glenn Gould (Columbia Masterworks, 1960)

Related to borrowed time is what Mattheson called playing a little behind the beat (*"eine kurtze Zeit nach dem Tact"*).[58] This will work only when, instead of reacting to the soloist's dragging, the accompanying parts maintain a forward-moving pulse. Quantz explained:

> Because the best way to play an Adagio requires that the soloist lets himself drag a little in order to be carried forward by the accompanying parts, rather than being ahead of them, and because this makes it seem as if he wants a slower tempo, the accompanying parts must not allow themselves to be influenced by this, but must firmly maintain the tempo and not indulge the soloist, unless he gives them a sign. Otherwise, one will end up in a kind of stupor.[59]

🔊 AUDIO EX. 8.8. J. S. Bach: Siciliano, Concerto in D major BWV1053a, Haynes, oboe d'amore (Atma, 1999)

This type of playing heard in Audio Example 8.8 requires a different discipline from what most players are used to today. The accompanists must resist their instinct to follow the soloist; if they do not, the music can easily grind to a halt as both soloist and accompanists follow each other like a dog chasing its tail. Eighteenth-century musicians were not immune to this problem, as we read in Quantz:

> If the accompanist does not have a steady beat, or if he lets himself be influenced to slow down in the *tempo rubato*, ... he not only surprises the soloist, but inspires his mistrust.[60]

Kairos: Isolating Musical Events

Timing is essential in oratory, and its importance was emphasized by countless writers. After pointing out how effective an actor's eyes can be in the expression of passions, Luigi Riccoboni (1738) made the following observations on the timing of gestures and speech:

> If a Speaker is deeply skilled in his Art he will not be satisfied with barely making the Expression of his Eyes attend that of his Tongue, but

take care that the former shall have a Moment's Start of the latter. For Instance, in a period, which ought to set out with a burst of Anger, if the Speaker, in a little Pause which he artfully makes before he speaks, shall by a single Look express his Anger, he can so effectually prepossess the Spectator with what he is to say, that he will all of a sudden mould him into that Temper which most easily admits of the Impressions that he designs to convey in the rest of his Discourse. The same Observation holds of all the other Passions.[61]

Delays, silences, and pauses are all powerful rhetorical devices. Agogics can be used to produce emphasis by preceding a musical event with an articulation silence, or by delaying it, or lengthening it. In 1717 François Couperin described the affective qualities of two agogic ornaments. The *aspiration* was a shortening of a note, and the *suspension* indicated a hesitation or delay:[62]

> The emotional response [*l'impression sensible*] to which I refer is the result of the deliberate cutting short [*cèssation*] or delaying [*suspension*] of notes in a manner appropriate to the character of each particular *prélude* or piece. By opposite means [*par leur opposition*] these two ornaments [*agréments*] disorient the ear. In the same way that string instruments swell the tone [*enflent leurs sons*], delaying notes [*suspension*] on the harpsichord gives the ear the impression of a similar effect (though achieved by different means).[63]

Both Couperin and Rameau described the *aspiration* (Rameau called it *son coupé*) as a truncation of the note within its "correct" rhythmic value. Couperin instructed that the degree of shortening depended on the tempo and style of the piece, and that less shortening should be applied in tender and slow pieces. However, there seems to be no indication that the *aspiration* invited the performer to take time beyond the value of the note, that is, to break with time. By creating an articulation silence, the *aspiration* drew attention to the *following* note; strictly speaking, it works with articulation rather than with timing. The *suspension*, on the other hand, is when an isolated note is delayed against the regular beat, and from Couperin's explanation, it was a way of giving the impression of delaying the bloom in the sound of a melodic note, and stood in for the *messa di voce* on other instruments. The *suspensions* in the Premier Menuet of the Deuxième Concert of Rameau's *Pièces de clavecin en concert* indicate the right hand of the harpsichord along with the flute or violin, and gamba to play slightly after the bass (see Ex. 8.4).

Example 8.4 J. P. Rameau, Premier Menuet from *Pièces de clavecin en concert*, Deuxième Concert (Paris, 1741)

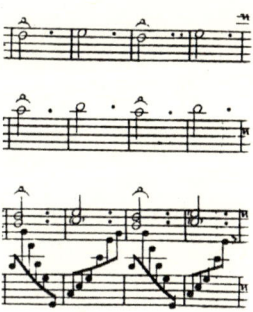

Because there is little detailed discussion of the *suspension* by authors from outside France, it is often assumed to be uniquely French. But, like other practices such as *notes inégales*, it was likely part of a more widespread and persistent convention. The syncopated displacement of isolated notes in the treble line somewhat before or after a strictly beaten bass is also described by Roger North,[64] and in the early nineteenth century, Pierre Baillot referred to a device used to emphasize notes that involved starting them with a rest, similar to the *suspension*.[65]

In his article on rests C. P. E. Bach discusses places where it is appropriate to take time for expressive purposes. Some of these involve pausing between phrases, or taking liberties with time to reinforce expressive chromatic notes and harmonic surprises. Example 8.5 shows the relevant passage.

> [The figure] shows several examples where, for expressive reasons, either the notes or the rests should be played longer than they are notated. I have clearly marked some of these pauses, and indicated others with small crosses. The last example shows how a gesture [*Gedanke*] with two different accompaniments offers the possibility of an expressive pause. Generally, this device is more appropriate in slow and moderate tempos than in very quick ones.[66]

Example 8.5 C. P. E. Bach, *Versuch* 1, ch. 3 § 28, Fig. 13.

Articulation and lengthening can happen within the beat, or they may produce an irregularity in the metric pattern. The default style of articulation has a bearing on this. In the eighteenth-century the norm was nonlegato, so agogic lengthening could be achieved by holding notes their full rhythmic value without disturbing the beat, but in the following century, when legato became more common, agogics took the form of stretching the beat. The effect of the overall sense of articulation and degree of sustain can be heard in two recordings of the Bach Cello Suites. Even though Pablo Casals recorded his Bach suites at the height of the Modernist era in 1936, his performance is rhythmically flexible, but other aspects of his playing give it a sense of rigidity (Audio Ex. 8.9a). His tempo fluctuations are based more often on melodic than on harmonic considerations; his tone is generally strong, often reinforced across the bar line and on structurally insignificant notes. These factors have the effect of distorting the beat hierarchy and making the performance sound less articulate. Anner Bylsma, using gut strings and Baroque bow, draws on a wider range of inflection and articulation (Audio Ex. 8.9b). There is also more "air" in his sound, so in addition to agogic emphasis there is a good deal of variation in the shaping and duration of individual notes. Bylsma's more nuanced approach goes towards an overall effect of greater fluidity, which affects the sense of tempo fluctuation.

🔊 AUDIO EX. 8.9. J. S. Bach, Prelude, Cello Suite No. 3, BWV1009
(a) Pablo Casals (HMV, 1936)
(b) Anner Bylsma (Sony, 1992)

Timing in Dance Music

There is a time-honored assumption that dance music must adhere more closely to a strict beat than other types of music. This is a crucial issue because so much Baroque music is dance inspired. In the beginning of the seventeenth century Caccini wrote that "*Airy* Musicks or *Corants*" should be characterized by "only a lively, cheerful kind of Singing, which is carried and ruled by the *Air* itself."[67] This suggests that dances like courants did not admit a wide range of passions and consequently would not have been suited to the type of tempo fluctuations we have been discussing, particularly those identified with the pathetick style. But from the second half of the century, a closer affinity was cultivated between dance and vocal music. In French opera, dances were often repeated as songs, and so the music acted as a synesthetic bridge between the words of the song and the gesture of the dance. There is no mistaking that for the Frenchman François Fénelon writing in the 1670s, dance participated in passionate expression:

> All those Arts that consisted either in melodious Sounds, regular Motions of the Body, or the Use of Words; Musick, Dancing, Eloquence, and Poetry, were invented to express the Passions; and by that means to communicate these Passions to others.[68]

Charles Batteux likewise felt that a gesture in dance was beautiful "only as it expresses the most lively passions of the soul, in short the soul itself."[69] Here it makes good sense for dances and their sung parodies to share the same *mouvement* and for both to be open to flexible timing.

It is fair to say that in dance music, setting the right tempo requires taste and judgment, and that this is often more important than the timing within the course of the dance. From the second half of the seventeenth century up to the French Revolution, dance fashions across Europe were set by the French court. French dance had been brought to the residents of Leipzig from the early eighteenth century through publications like Samuel Rudolph Behrens's *Maître de danse* (Leipzig, 1703), and Gottfried Taubert's *Rechtschaffener Tanzmeister, oder gründliche Erklärung der Französischen Tanz-Kunst* (Leipzig, 1717). Taubert included choreographies in the notation system devised by Pierre Beauchamp in the 1680s and disseminated through the publications of Raoul-Auger Feuillet from around 1700, and so the French *belle danse* was likely known to Bach and would have informed his dance movements.

Quantifying the speed of dances became a pressing concern, and the use of musical chronometers was closely aligned with the codification of dance notation. Even though the primary purpose of the *chronomètre* was to preserve the basic pulse of the French dances, they were not used to control the rhythm of the entire dance.[70] As we have seen, around the middle of the eighteenth century, Diderot indicated that chronometers were of limited use and concluded that "the only good chronometer possible is a skilful musician who has taste, who understands thoroughly the piece he is to perform and who knows how to beat time accordingly."[71] From this it would seem the musicians in Diderot's day did not feel obliged to play in strict time, whether accompanying vocal music or dance.

Today, performing dance movements with original choreographies can be instructive for (re)gaining an understanding of their timing. Certain movements and step combinations help delineate the musical gestures and points of articulation. The French tradition cultivated a close marriage of music to bodily movements, and writers talked about the dancer's gestures mirroring the music. Like singers, dancers also need to breathe, and it is rare for dancers to be uncomfortable with some flexibility to articulate the divisions of the form. Dance steps require a certain time to execute and often need a specific energetic musical "trigger." It is hard to perform lively dance steps to plodding music; jumps depend on gravity and cannot be slowed down in midair. Notated choreographies can give vital clues on how to time phrase endings and sectional transitions. When the dance comes to repose, the musicians can likewise "place" the cadence; but when continuous movement implies a liaison between the phrases, the musician may need to maintain a constant beat.

Not all dance movements were composed for dancing. They were often sung and played as "topics"; that is, the music referenced dance even if no one was dancing. Bacilly mentioned this in 1668, and from his comments it is clear that there was no general agreement as to whether singers should perform dance airs in a tempo appropriate for dance or accommodate them to vocal performance "in which the dance beat is abandoned for the sake of a more brilliant effect." He proposed that dance tunes were greatly enriched by "showing them off in a hundred different ways, each more charming than the last, and using the best art and technique of good singing, even expressing certain exclamations better and more gracefully." He also condoned singers taking a slower tempo than in the danced version for the sake of the intelligibility of the text, especially when the words are not "simple doggerel, but are made with wit." He did, however, caution that not all dance types were adaptable to vocal performance. Some were suited to "prolongations or expressive pauses" and "even displacements of the beat in order to provide enough time to add gracing," but he felt that when singers perform a minuet or a sarabande in a slower tempo than the danced version and did not respect the metric proportions of the music, it lost its character as dance and become indistinguishable from sung airs in free time.[72]

In the eighteenth century the adaptation of dance idioms became increasingly complex, and often composer and performer walked a tightrope between the affect of the dance and the details of the musical composition (this is the case, more than anywhere, with J. S. Bach's instrumental dances). Issues to consider are the changes to tempo and character that dances underwent over time, and the features of the dance that are required for the allusion to work.

The following observations on the sarabande illustrate some of the issues relating to timing in dances. Like many other Baroque dances, the sarabande started out as a fast dance (in the 1660s it was described as *gay*), but by the eighteenth century it had taken on a slower tempo. One source from 1737 gives ♩ = 63, the slowest recorded.[73] In 1741 Rémond de Sainte-Mard characterized the sarabande as "always melancholy and exuding a delicate yet serious tenderness," which aptly summarizes the affect found in many texted sarabandes, particularly of the later, slower type.[74] The special treatment of second beats in sarabandes has led to the erroneous notion that they must always be accented. When the second beat is emphasized, it is usually by virtue of a longer note value. French sarabandes (which served as models for German composers including J. S. Bach) are characterized by rhythmic variety. The short-long rhythm ♩ ♩ or ♩ ♩ ♪ is common, but never appears systematically in every measure. (In some sarabandes, like Bach's Fifth Cello Suite, it never appears at all). More often it forms one-half of the two-bar units typical of many sarabandes. None of the bowing patterns for string players associated with sarabandes found in pedagogic works suggest that the long second beat was routinely accented or separated from the downbeat with a retake of the bow.[75] And in sung sarabandes the long second beat is very frequently set with an unimportant syllable. This has the effect of directing the sense of text and music forward to the next downbeat (see underlined words in Ex. 8.6).

Special harmonies are often placed on the second beat and can be enhanced with an agogic delay (*aspiration*). But, especially when the dance is taken in a slow tempo, it is important not to lose momentum. Delaying the second beat of the first measure, for instance, might initiate the tempo on the wrong footing (as it were). Taking time between the first and second beat is often prevented by the motion of the bass, as in the second and fifth measures of the Sarabande from Couperin's *Troisième Concert Royal* shown in Example 8.7. Where the short-long

Example 8.6 F. Couperin, Sarabande, *Huitième Concert dans le Goût Théâtrale*, from *Les Goûts Réünis* (Paris, 1724) with text from *Recueil d'Airs sérieux* (Paris: Ballard, March, 1699): 48–49. (Nonaccented syllables on prolonged second beats are underlined)

Example 8.7 F. Couperin, Sarabande from *Concerts Royaux*, Troisième Concert (Paris, 1722)

rhythm occurs in the final bar of a phrase, it is usually a re-striking of the harmony and thus inappropriate for rhythmic adjustment as the dancer does not stop until the musical cadence comes to a close (see Ex. 8.7, bar 12).

Further Reading

For a survey of the use of kairos through history, see *Rhetoric and Kairos*, ed. Sipiora and Baumlin. John Eliot Gardiner contrasts *chronos* and *kairos* as the passing of time as opposed to distinct moments *in* time (*Bach*, 292).

Rosamond Harding's pioneering study "The Metronome and its Predecessors" (chapter 1 of *Origins of Musical Time and Expression*) contains much useful information. For more on timing in Romantic style, see the discussion of Beethoven's and Liszt's experiments with expressive timing in John Rink, "Translating Musical Meaning." The controversy over Beethoven's metronome marks is considered in Taruskin's essay "Resisting the Ninth" (reprinted in his *Text and Act: Essays on Music and Performance*) and Clive Brown's "Historical Performance, Metronome Marks, and Tempo in Beethoven's Symphonies." Ido Abravaya's book *On Bach's Rhythm and Tempo* provides a thorough survey of Bach's markings and a practical guide to the topic.

In his carefully researched and user-friendly book, *Stolen Time*, Richard Hudson misleadingly calls borrowed time "the earlier rubato." This implies that it was the only kind of rhythmic flexibility used in music up to the nineteenth century and that tempo fluctuation did not exist up to that time. In fact, Hudson advocated neither of these ideas. His book presents evidence for the existence of tempo fluctuation as far back as Gregorian chant. Sandra Rosenblum uses different terms: her "agogic rubato" is the equivalent of Hudson's "modern tempo rubato" and our "tempo fluctuation." Her "contrametre"—the "redistribution of rhythmic values in a solo melody against an accompaniment that maintains a steady beat in a constant tempo"—is what we call "borrowed time" (*Performance Practices in Classic Piano Music*, 382, 373).

Jed Wentz's dissertation "Gesture, Affect, and Rhythmic Freedom" is a provocative re-examination of tempo in Baroque music and incorporates perspectives from oratory, vocal music, and dance and contains much valuable information.

For more on the concept of *sprezzatura*, see Anthony Rooley, "Renaissance Attitudes to Performance." Most of Caccini's preface was translated and published by Playford in later editions of his *Introduction to the Skill of Music*.

Colin Tilney's three-volume study *The Art of the Unmeasured Prelude* is the most complete survey of this genre. For more information on fermatas in the performance of chorales, see Konrad Ameln, "Die Fermate im evangelischen Kirchenlied"; Christopher Hampson, "Pausing for Reflection"; and Don Franklin, "The Fermata as Notational Convention." Important background to note lengths can be found in Babitz, "Concerning the Length of Time that Every Note Must be Held," and Peres da Costa, *Off the Record*, 64–66.

Harris-Warrick's article "Interpreting Pendulum Markings" is an indispensible guide to dance tempi. A brief account of the history of the sarabande is given by Ranum in "Audible Rhetoric and Mute Rhetoric."

9

To Kindle the Heart: Engagement in Performance

GEOFFREY BURGESS

A skilful experience'd Orator adapts Things to the Capacity of his Hearers.
—Fénelon after Plato

It takes little to read music exactly to the letter; you must also enter into the composer's thoughts, to sense and render the fire of expression.
—Rousseau, 1768[1]

The audience's reception of a musical performance closes the circuit and completes the rhetorical process. Performance is not possible without audience reaction. It is always a two-way street. Interaction between artist and audience is vital to any performance art, and it goes without saying that it is essential to oratory and music alike. This chapter revisits many of the topics already introduced in previous sections as they pertain to delivery, or *actio*.

Today's performers of Rhetorical music face the challenge of making music conceived within the social traditions and expectations of a different era speak to modern audiences. Regardless the distance that exists between modern listening practices and "authentic ears," all performers need to induce sympathy in their listeners, that is, to put them in a receptive state, in order for their eloquence to work its magic. Our modern training has encouraged us to ignore, and even suppress, vital performance survival instincts. Often caught up in technical details, we forget that eloquence demands more than getting the notes right or playing "in style." Other ingredients like deportment, body language, and facial expressions can all communicate just as much and, in many cases, even more of the message than the notes we play. At the end of the day, to arrive at an eloquent musical performance—even when we don't feel capable, or it seems beyond the reach of our sincerest efforts—our listeners, too, must be engrossed in the story we spin.

The Sovereign Audience

Baroque music was not "Art" (with a capital *A*) in the modern sense, created in the abstract, to be performed at some unspecified future time, and possibly incomprehensible on first hearing. It took place in the here and now (or the "there and then"), created for a specific event and a known audience, tailor-made, so to speak, rather than off the rack. That applied not only to the composition but to the way the performer interacted with the audience. Fénelon wrote in 1674:

> A skilful experience'd Orator adapts Things to the Capacity of his Hearers; and varies his Discourse according to the Impression he sees it makes upon their Minds. For, he easily perceives whether they understand him, or not; and whether he gains their Attention, and moves their Hearts.[2]

Quantz also addressed this topic:

> He who has the intention of being heard in public would do well to inform himself in detail about his audiences; especially those he has an interest in pleasing. He should know whether they are knowledgeable about music. For connoisseurs it is possible to play somewhat more complex pieces, and to display one's skill in Allegros as well as Adagios. But if one plays before simple amateurs who understand nothing, he would be wise to stick to pieces with brilliant and agreeable melodies. He might also play the Adagios a little faster than otherwise, in order not to bore listeners of this kind.[3]

Quantz was no doubt familiar with how lawyers pleading a case would put themselves in the place of the judge to better formulate their arguments and pace their rhetoric. This type of advice is common in treatises on rhetoric, going as far back as Quintilian, for example, who thought that an orator should "consider in the first place, what he is to say, who are to be his Judges, and who are to be his hearers."[4] Mattheson recommended musicians to consider how they need to adapt their performance to the setting and audiences, and found from experience that an informed audience made for a sympathetic performance environment:

> It is much easier to perform something pleasing at the homes and courts of great nobles than at large gatherings: for one has only to examine the temperament of the nobles and to probe their sensitive side, then everything else is ordered according to the tastes of the most noble.[5]

Keeping the audience's response in mind is a useful check for all performers. It allows us to make sure we are not deceiving ourselves about the effect we are creating.[6]

Those who attended concerts or the theater in the seventeenth and eighteenth centuries were usually better heeled than the musicians or, for that matter, even the theater owner. There was an element of "audience sovereignty" that is unknown today. Until about the first third of the nineteenth century, audiences considered themselves in charge of the event. They paid attention and listened as they pleased. Opera theaters were lit throughout performances and audiences could indulge in a variety of activities. The situation at other musical entertainments was not so different. Performers had to win their audience's attention before they could win them over. Few of the "auditors" in Rowlandson's painting of the Vauxhall Gardens seem to feel obliged to give the music their entire attention (see fig. 9.1).

The musicians are even less prominent in a side gallery in Canaletto's depiction of another famous London pleasure garden of the time, the Rotunda of Ranelagh (fig. 9.2). Christopher Small's description of the relationship between performers and audience in this picture emphasizes how different it was from the social interaction expected at a modern classical music concert:

Figure 9.1 Francis Jukes, *Garden Concert in the Rotunda at Vauxhall Gardens*, 1785. Aquatint after the painting by Thomas Rowlandson (ca. 1784) (A detail from the original is reproduced in color on the dust jacket)

Figure 9.2 Giovanni Antonio Canal (Canaletto), *The Interior of the Rotunda, Ranelagh*, 1754 (detail). Compton Verney, Warwickshire, UK/Bridgeman Images (a color version of the entire painting can be found at the companion website)

> The people in this picture . . . are standing or walking about, talking in pairs and in groups, or just coming and going, in much the same way as people do in the foyer of a modern concert hall. It appears that the building has not caused socializing and enjoying music to be divided into two separate activities as does a modern concert hall, and the members of the audience seem to be perfectly capable of doing both things at the same time.[7]

These audiences were not in the habit of waiting passively and humbly for favors granted by benevolent masters. Masters the musicians may have been, but of a craft rather than an art, and their mastery over their audiences had to be earned *ex tempore*, rather than through hype and advance publicity. Those musicians we would now call professionals because they rely on music as their primary source of income were usually servants, and on a lower social level than the audience. There was none of this nonsense about *artistes* in those days. Roger North, who was himself an accomplished amateur player, referred to professional musicians as "mercenaries" and considered them "a morose, ungentile and unsatisfyed nation."[8] As servants to their aristocratic audiences, musicians, dancers, and actors were there to divert and entertain. They could as easily be ignored. With a snap of his fingers, patrons could stop a piece, or have it repeated. Like CDs and iTunes now, concerts existed for the convenience of the users, and musicians often found themselves playing in banquet halls, in gardens amid fountains and fireworks, or even in the boudoir.

Also in those days, many more amateurs had time to cultivate and become proficient in music. The leisured class could afford to pay good teachers for lessons, and they had time to practice and to play with other amateurs. It is entirely possible that some of them were better performers than the professionals. As a result, audiences could be knowledgeable and critical in ways that are encountered only rarely today.

Behavior at a modern classical concert is highly proscribed. For audiences, it can hardly be thought of as natural or comfortable, but it is worse for the performers. Modern concert etiquette makes them keenly aware that they have only one chance to get it right, and that the people listening have paid good money and are not prepared to hear wrong notes. We rarely perform at our best in a situation where undue attention is directed at the product. It is much more comfortable, and therefore propitious to perform, when the audience has a choice whether to pay close attention or wander off to look for refreshment or company. In less formal situations like parties, there can be several kinds of listeners and quite often people from diverse social backgrounds.

What are we to make of the seemingly inattentive and even unruly audiences that we see in these images and written accounts of premodern concerts? Referring to eighteenth-century audiences, William Weber expressed confidence that in most cases a balance was struck between art and socializing:

> People whose musical needs differed sharply coexisted successfully enough. Some people listened and some socialized, but no one objected to their being together in one audience—as would not be the case today.[9]

The Rhetorical period was the age of patronage. The quantity of fine music attests to the support of sovereign audience members interested in cultivating their musical tastes. Musicians today require special tolerance to play at social events where they know their efforts will be inaudible above the din of a party crowd. There were undoubtedly similar events in the seventeenth and eighteenth centuries, but there were also plenty of patrons for whom music mattered and who listened attentively. Patrons who spent wealth on music made sure their guests attended to the products they sponsored. If the music was routinely ignored, why was such a vast quantity produced? If no one paid attention, it would have been easier to recycle works rather than constantly write new ones. A composer with highly developed business acumen like Telemann was no doubt primarily concerned that his music publications would sell, and would be less inclined to go to the trouble of composing sophisticated Tafelmusik (banquet music) if he knew it would not be heard and appreciated. Haydn spent years of his life providing new music for the regular entertainment of his patrons, the Esterházy family. His composing could easily have slipped into routine drudgery, but instead he continuously experimented with form and texture, resulting in countless surprises and varied permutations for his patron, who clearly took notice and were musically educated enough to appreciate his servant's abilities. When works were recycled, they were rarely revived without revisions. These could be superficial but significant enough to rekindle the audience's attention. Rameau was an exception and went far beyond merely freshening up his operas for revivals; his revision process often resulted in virtually new works. Bach's reuse was generally of a practical nature, and his revisions chronicle the availability of specific performers. Still, after three years at his post in Leipzig he came to realize that, given the limited attention the congregants paid to his music, the corpus of music he had accumulated would be substantial enough for years to come.[10]

There are other issues when considering artist's depictions of concert life in the Rhetorical period. Paintings differ from photographs in a number of essential ways. It is quite possible, as some art historians have argued, that eighteenth-century paintings of social gatherings do not depict a single moment but a succession of episodes that made up an event. So if an artist showed some of the audience members engaging in small talk, promenading, or taking refreshment, while others listened to the music, the various activities may actually have happened in sequence rather than simultaneously. Still, the fact that the artist considered it appropriate to conflate them in one image shows that all of the activities were considered part of a single event, and that music was likely present throughout—the main focus at some moments, peripheral or accompanimental at others.[11]

Conditions also varied according to the locale. The inattention of audiences in opera houses is legendary. James Johnson has assembled proof of the near chaos at the Paris Opéra, and it appears that Leipzig congregations were not always devoted listeners to Bach's music. But a higher level of connoisseurship and dedicated listening were cultivated among those who attended concerts in Leipzig than in other centers.[12] In 1743 Johann Andreas Cramer praised the members of the Großes Concert for their attentive listening habits. Cramer craved silence while listening to music and recounted the annoyance of being distracted from enraptured listening when a member of the audience asked him an unrelated question.[13]

Inattentive as they sometimes were, audiences also gave signs of their understanding of the finer points of the music. In general, performances were far more interactive than the hushed reverence called for by modern concert-hall protocol. Audiences made their opinions known when the performer succeeded with a particularly fine performance or a novel effect. Mozart described the impact his Paris Symphony K. 297 had on the audience at the première in 1778 in a letter to his father:

> Right in the middle of the first Allegro was a passage that I knew they would like; the whole audience was thrilled by it and there was a tremendous burst of applause.

The response he described is more like how spectators behave at a baseball game, or the way fans react when the fat lady hits her high note at the opera, or a pop star introduces a hit. In the last movement of the same work Mozart recounted just how enthusiastic and attentive the audience was to the details of the music:

> The audience, as I expected, said "Shh!" at the soft beginning, and then, as soon as they heard the *forte* that followed, immediately began to clap their hands.[14]

Mozart knew that he had to elicit attention from his listeners, but that they would react, and he was particularly skillful at orchestrating specific responses.

It is one thing to appreciate the historic novelty of this passage, but it is something else to produce the same effect in a modern audience. Nikolaus Harnoncourt had this to say about Mozart's surprise tactics in the Paris Symphony:

> Most performances gloss over this passage. Today's listener is aware of nothing unusual in this place. Yet earlier composers could expect an attentive and informed audience, which noticed each new idea, each effect in instrumentation, each unusual harmonic or melodic feature, and which passionately expressed its approval or disapproval.[15]

Even if the novelty of Mozart's musical effect is lost today, we need to find a way of giving it freshness as if we are performing it for the first time. This does not have to involve chicanery, or cheap effects, nor is it something inherently inappropriate to pre-Romantic music. There are plenty of instances of ecstatic audience reaction in eighteenth-century accounts.

William Thomas Parke (1762–1847) elicited a similar reaction in a performance in the 1790s. Never shy of praising his own accomplishments, Parke described how he performed a concerto in which he "introduced some of my newly discovered high notes, (up to G in alto [g3]), particularly a shake on the upper D, which was greatly applauded."[16] In fact, Parke was repeating a similar success of his predecessor, Johann Christian Fischer (ca.1733–1800), but with a different technique. During a concert in London in 1785, Fischer introduced an "octave shake" in a cadenza of his concerto. According to the eyewitness account of the courtier Mrs. Papendiek, "the effect drew down applause scarcely ever equalled, and Fischer was extremely gay to have succeeded in this new trickery."[17]

This is an instance of where the performance is crucial to the music's effectiveness. Virtuosos have facility to bring off any technical feat with apparent ease, but when the audience is not aware (or made aware) of the technical difficulties involved, the effect can be lost and the result nil. If the performer plays impeccably, a technical feat may go unnoticed ("So what if he played a high G?"). Musical virtuosity also involves alternately dissembling and revealing art. Oboists can appreciate the technical feats of Parkes and Fischers, but other listeners need "schooling." This may take the form of a simple gesture from the performer. Like a skilled trapeze artist who builds suspense by intentionally slipping up the first time, only to show off when she executes the feat perfectly the next time, a clever musician can show listeners just how hard a certain feat is while doing it. Gesturing of this type might involve a singer slowing down before reaching for a high note, or a wind player adding a slight quiver to the tone at the end of a long note to give the listener a sense of the effort involved in sustaining the breath, or a string player who intentionally plays double-stopped notes slightly out of tune so that the audience will not miss the point.

Authentic Ears

Certain modern writers have expressed misgivings at the idea of having their hearts seized and their souls excited by some stranger—and in public at that. The philosopher Peter Kivy feels that "no sensible person would want to feel many of the emotions music is said to express."[18] But, as we have shown in chapter 2, music was once considered appropriate for expressing a wider range of passions than what current audiences expect.

With the highly proscriptive format of modern concerts comes a limited range of expectations for what the performance of classical music can bring about. The concert hall provides genteel comfort and social reassurance, and today's performers ignore (largely unconsciously) much of the music's intended effect in order to conform to the limited gamut of acceptable expression. This often results in a pale echo of the music's full power. What if we reinstated music's ability to go beyond the known? Film soundtracks demonstrate how palpable music can be to transport us to foreign places and even uncomfortable emotional states. Divorced from images, the same music can still shock us as much as soothe us. When we embrace our role as oratorical musicians, we open a range of expression well beyond playing "correctly," or producing "beautiful" effects and can approach the ideals expressed by Athanasius Kircher in 1650:

> Just as rhetoric through various arguments and reasons as through the complex of various figures and tropes now delights, now saddens, now provokes anger, pity, indignation, revenge, vehement passion and other affections, and, in sum, inclines the consenting listener completely to whatever commotion the orator intends, so music through the construction of a variety of musical periods excites the soul to diverse states.[19]

The concept of the "consenting listener" is key to the equation. Performers must not only know who they are playing for and thus evaluate how best to present their music, they must also win the consent of listeners by putting them in a sympathetic state receptive to their eloquence. Dubos wrote "the painter and poet afflict us only inasmuch as we desire it ourselves; they make us fall in love with their heroes and heroins [sic], only because it is thus agreable [sic] to us."[20] Every audience needs to be won over in a slightly different way, and performers will lose their audience if they do not adapt to the capacity of their listeners. A masterful performance requires sensitivity to respond to audience reaction. Performing a musical work, then, is not a single, set enterprise but a moving target.

Rhetoric nowadays is often seen as calculated and coercive, and the relationship between the speaker and audience viewed as antagonistic and unidirectional. But orator, audience, and subject form a dynamic and interconnected relationship. Pathetick expression is not *done to* an audience; it happens with the consent of all parties and is impossible without that understanding. The original concept of an orator was less that of a puppeteer who manipulates his audience through his persuasive skill than that of "a mid-wife who focuses and directs energies already inherent in the listener."[21] In other words, eloquent performance depends on the predisposition of the audience. Because the artistic imitation should have the semblance of reality, the audience has to be convinced, persuaded, or better yet, to be moved by it. Considering that most listeners had gone to a certain amount of effort to be present at the performance, they came with a willingness to be moved; they were expecting it and might even have been displeased if it did not happen.

The audience's receptive state was generally referred to as *sympathy*, the condition of being open to suggestion. The term is discussed at length by the eighteenth-century English philosopher David Hume. In simplified terms, Hume proposed that sympathy consists of feeling the passions we suppose others feel; it is triggered by observing in someone else the outward signs of a passion—facial expressions, talk, general bearing, behavior, or hand gestures. Sympathy used in this sense is

> the quality or state of being affected by the condition of another with a feeling similar or corresponding to that of the other; the fact or capacity of entering into or sharing the feelings of another or others.[22]

It is well known that we are naturally open—sympathetic—to persuasion, as Dubos explained:

> We are moved by the tears of a stranger, even before we are apprized of the subject of his weeping. The cries of a man, to whom we have no other

relation than the common one of humanity, make us fly instantly to his assistance, by a mechanical movement previous to all deliberation. A person that accosts us with joy painted on his countenance, excites in us a like sentiment of joy, even before we know the subject of his contentment.[23]

Sympathy is closely related to the stronger passion of empathy. A more modern term, empathy entails projecting one's feelings into someone else's position, rather than the sympathetic compassion for that position.[24] Both are basic, almost primal instincts in humans. A recent study of involuntary facial matching in primates indicates that orangutans have "a sense of empathy and mimicry which forms an essential part of laughter. Facial expressions, such as the open, gaping mouth resembling laughter, were picked up and copied.... The speed with which they were mimicked suggests these expressions were involuntary.... In other words, the 'laughter' was contagious." The study concluded that "the building blocks of positive emotional contagion and empathy that refer to rapid involuntary facial mimicry in humans evolved prior to humankind."[25]

The term "contagion" was already used in 1725 by the influential Scottish philosopher Francis Hutcheson in connection with responses to music:

> There is also another Charm in *Musick* to various Persons, which is distinct from the *Harmony*, and is occasion'd by its raising agreeable Passions. The *human Voice* is obviously vary'd by all the stronger Passions; now when our *Ear* discerns any resemblance between the *Air* of a *Tune*, whether sung or play'd upon an Instrument, either in its *Time* or *Key*, or any other Circumstance, to the sound of the *human Voice* in any Passion, we shall be touch'd by it in a very sensible manner, and have *Melancholy, Joy, Gravity, Thoughtfulness* excited in us by a sort of *Sympathy* or *Contagion*.[26]

As it is such a basic part of human behavior, one of the most effective ways to elicit sympathetic contagion is through body language.

Music in the Body

> Words have only the tongue as a tool; gestures however can make use of all parts of the body.
> —Mattheson, 1739[27]

Anyone who has studied music in film and video will know how easy it is for us to confuse what we *see* with what we *hear*. Today's musicians often need to be reminded of the essential role played by bodily deportment in performance. Acting is not part of the musician's conservatory training, but we need only observe the most successful popular classical music performers to realize the important impact it can have on listeners' reaction. Audiences read Lang Lang's playing through his histrionics. They are compelled by Pavarotti's handkerchief. They take Nigel Kennedy's furrowed concentration to heart. None of these are musical ingredients per se, but they are undeniably part of affective music making. By contrast, an awkward, self conscious stage presence will communicate anxiety and fail to elicit consent or the right sort of sympathy from the audience. The statuesque poses and aloof facial expressions that so many HIP performers strike out of a false sense of reverence to history can be just as off-putting, and are actually aligned closer to a Romantic sensibility than the spirit of the Baroque.

First impressions count, and even before an orator utters a word or a musician plays a note, their deportment speaks and sets the tone of the performance. Aristotle commented that an orator is better able to "persuade" his audience if his general bearing (what he called *ethos* or character) is pleasant and easy to relate to.[28] Eighteenth-century writers considered communication by means of visual signs and body language more direct than spoken or written language. Batteux explained this as follows:

> Words may express the passions by simply naming them; as when I say, *I love you*, or *I hate you*; but if I do not accompany these words, either by some tone of voice or gesture, I rather express an idea than a sentiment. Whereas a single motion, a look, speaks the passion immediately. . . . Speech indeed is the organ of reason, it instructs and convinces us; but the tone and gesture are those of the heart: they move, win, and persuade.[29]

His comments reflect the advice of Quintilian:

> The great Consequence of a proper Gesture in a Speaker appears from this, that it generally has more Meaning than the Voice itself. For, not only our Hand, but our very Nod is expressive of our Sentiments; nay Mutes themselves converse by their Gestures. A common Salute, even before the Party speaks a single Word, gives an Intimation of his Disposition and we know by the Face and the Walk, the workings of the Mind.[30]

By adopting a simple, naturalistic pose as their starting point, orators encouraged their listeners to be well disposed to what they had to say. Quintilian directed that an orator's body

> ought to be erect, his Feet at a little Distance, but upon the same Line, or the Left a very little advanced, and his Knees in a straight, but not in a stiff Posture. His Shoulders ought to have an easy Fall; his Look should be serious.[31]

(a)

(b)

Figure 9.3 Examples of musicians' and dancers' postures a) Hautboist, Johann Christoph Weigel, *Musicalisches Theatrum* (Nuremberg, ca. 1720) b) Pierre Rameau, *Maître à danser* (Paris, 1725)

Opera singers were normally seen as specialized actors, so this advice on gesture is most useful to them. They would no doubt have carried some of these techniques over into chamber and church music, as appropriate. Mattheson recommended that church musicians use gesture just as much as the preachers:

> Now it really seems as if clergymen have reserved the commodity of gesture [*de gestibus*] strictly for themselves in church; but would it be so terrible if the singing or playing choral and concert orator also gave force to his words with appropriate gestures?[32]

It is worth remarking that Mattheson mentions instrumentalists as well as singers here. The instrumental parts in Baroque vocal music are often much more than incidental to the vocal part. Instrumental obbligatos should be treated as equals to the vocal line, and musicians should be just as conscious of their bearing, movement, gestures, and facial expressions as the singers. Instrumental-vocal duets are a wonderful place for musicians to learn the art of eloquent gesture.

As instrumentalists took singers as their model, they too would use parts of this lore. The musician begins by making a good impression on his audience by his cultivated bearing and appropriate gestures; above all, he gives an appearance of sincerity and personal involvement with the passions of the music. To judge from Jacques Hotteterre's advice on traverso playing (1707), a similar stance to what Quintilian described was normal for instrumentalists: "If you play standing, stand firm, with ye left foot a little advanc'd, and rest the weight of your Body on the right leg, and all without any constraint."[33] Figure 9.3a, taken from a contemporaneous collection of engravings of instrumentalists by Johann Christoph Weigel, shows an oboist in just such a posture.

It is also useful to consider advice from dance instructors. In his detailed treatise from the 1730s, Kellom Tomlinson stressed the importance of adopting a graceful and unaffected stance before entering "upon the stage of life." Just as an orator's posture put their listeners in a receptive state of mind, Tomlinson advised that "we ought to set our Bodies in such a Disposition, when we stand in Conversation, that, were our Actions or Postures delineated, they might bear the strictest Examination of the most critical Judges." Rather than rely on natural instincts, he recommended imagining "ourselves, as so many living Pictures drawn by the most excellent Masters, exquisitely designed to afford the utmost Pleasure to the Beholders." Although not precisely the same, Hotteterre's recommendation resembles the posture adopted for the reverence or bow, the dancer's fourth position, which Tomlinson described as "most genteel and becoming" (see a depiction of the reverence in Fig. 9.3b).[34]

Bodily gestures were used more commonly in some contexts than in others. In *Der Vollkommene Capellmesiter* Mattheson reminded his readers that gestures should always be chosen judiciously in accordance with the setting:

> Often the most serious and sacred pieces are sung and played in such a shameless manner, chattering, smirking, trifling, so that devout listeners are very annoyed.
>
> If we go from the church to the concert room, one likewise encounters quite marvellous and diverse unseemly poses at *Concerten* which sometimes do not have anything in common with what is going on.[35]

The choice of appropriate stance and gestures related both to the prevailing passions and the tone and seriousness of different genres. In the theater and on the operatic stage, gestures could be showy and exaggerated: noble and refined gestures for tragedy; while less refined and out-of-balance postures were appropriate to comedy and grotesque characters. Church music demanded less ostentatious gestures than the theater, while more subtle and charming gestures were appropriate to the intimate setting of chamber music performance.

Sometimes the music itself depicts gestures. Mattheson cited some recent musical compositions in which

> movements, steps, glances, and counterglances, as purely natural actions and individual gestures, are so expressively and cleverly represented (sometimes in a diverting style, yet naturally and, for singing, fecundly; sometimes more seriously) that they are able to provide ever new occasion for musical expression.[36]

Baroque art did not shy away from redundant reiteration, and there was no sense that musical gestures render physical gesture superfluous. This is seen particularly in opera where stage movement, text, and music all add up to a composite representation of the same action: overlapping complementary representation was an accepted aspect of synonymy in the arts.

There is also a type of musical choreography that results from the practical aspects of performance. String players gesture with their bows; the attack and release of notes on keyboard instruments choreographs the player's fingers and arms; organists dance as they play the pedals; and the wind player's breathing creates bodily motion that is a by-product of the technique of playing. These gestures (what Elisabeth Le Guin calls "mechanical embodiments") are choreographed by the music and occur naturally and in time with it.[37] Gestures such as the conductor's cues, singer's breath, violinist's tapping foot, or flute player's cut-off—even a subtle smile acknowledging a fellow-musician—are tricks of the trade that likewise help musicians coordinate their performances. These visible cues also allow the audience to see the inner workings of the ensemble and "read" the performance and the group dynamic. All of these types of gesturing are part of a complete, eloquent musical performance.

Traditionally, stage gesture was subdivided into several parts, described by Anselm Bayly in 1771 as "the attitude of the body, and the motion or action of the hands and countenance." The countenance comprised the face and eyes, which Bayly called "the great index of the passions," since "by it the speaker may on many occasions prevail more upon his audience than by language . . . for a look oftentimes hath in it more force than words, or even blows."[38] The eyes were described as the gateway to the soul because they could reveal the full range of human emotion. Franciscus Lang, a rhetoric professor in Munich, commented in 1727:

> Concerning the face and eyes, as the primary seat of the feelings as I shall say again, it is to be understood in general, that in these the heart of the Actor is to be perceived, and what is contained within, or should be contained in accordance with the nature of the subject-matter on stage, the state of mind is to be revealed, so that in this way it may be provoked in the other Spectators.[39]

The face and eyes of a musician are no less exposed than those of an actor, though musicians rarely exploit their expressive potential. Several authors, including Quantz, warned against making faces or unpleasant expressions that may reveal the performer struggling with his craft rather than the passions that he wishes to communicate through the music:

> Expression should be easy and flowing. Regardless of the difficulty of the written notes, the player must give no hint of problems. In both singing and playing, great care must be taken to avoid anything that would suggest coarseness or presumption. One should be sure not to make any grimaces, and, as much as possible, give the impression of being relaxed and composed.[40]

Unlike the histrionics of Romantic performers calculated to draw the listener to a transcendent state of reverie, Rhetorical expression is able to transport listeners in a more concrete sense to known experiences, the here and now of passionate states. Along these lines, François Couperin recommended that, rather than giving the impression of being preoccupied with something beyond the immediate concerns of the music, keyboardists should remain engaged as they play and in that way command their audience's attention.[41]

The Meaning of *Vortrag*

In the mind-set of the 1960s, Reilly was frankly flummoxed by the idea of the passions on which Quantz based his *Versuch einer Anweisung die Flöte traversiere zu Spielen*.[42] When he chose to render *Vortrag* as "execution," his translation of the title of chapter 11 became "Of Good Execution in General in Singing and Playing." This carried the implication that Quantz was writing about the dispassionate science of "correct" historical playing (covering subjects like whether to begin trills with the upper "auxiliary," beat hierarchy, and where to use *ti ri* tonguing patterns etc.). Using the word "execution" in the translation gives this critical chapter—and indeed the entire book—an antiseptic cast and tends to dry up what is in reality (or at least seems now) a book devoted to the expression of emotions.[43]

Quantz's essay appeared in German and French versions simultaneously in 1752.[44] The French preface explains that Quantz translated the German version so that it would be useful to other nations. Actually, this version may also have been prepared for the benefit of his patron, King Frederick of Prussia, who had difficulty reading and speaking German.[45] Quantz must have taken a good deal of time with this French version; it is (as Reilly remarked) carefully done. In fact, some passages in French version are clearer and more complete than the German.[46]

The fact that this book exists in two languages is an advantage for us because it allows us to understand with greater precision what the author was trying to say. This is especially useful with a book as old as Quantz's, as his terminology may have since changed in meaning. (The etymology of *Vortrag* is comparable to that of the English terms like "gay" and "pathetick" that have changed in meaning and use since the Rhetorical period.) The term *Vortrag* appears countless times in Quantz's book as well as the *Versuch über die wahre Art das Clavier zu spielen* which C. P. E. Bach published the previous year. In fact, both these writers devoted entire chapters to it ("Vom guten Vortrage" and "Vom Vortrag," respectively). *Vortrag* has application in the art of rhetoric, and is used quite commonly in modern German to refer to a lecture, speech, discourse, recitation, delivery, or declamation. All of these types of oral presentations would be rendered in French as *conférence, présentation,* or *récitation,* but in his French *Essai,* Quantz consistently translated *Vortrag* as *expression*. As well as the rhetorical connotation implied by the German term, the French version clarifies that what Quantz was talking about was not so much technical execution but the expressive artistry of musical eloquence.[47]

We can get a clear sense of Quantz's idea of *Vortrag* from the last paragraph of chapter 11 of the *Versuch*. This passage outlines the characteristics of bad *Vortrag*—that is, the musical and technical aspects of a performance that will irritate listeners or send them to sleep rather than divert them and sustain their interest. From this negative description, we can extrapolate three general attributes of good *Vortrag*:

- Clarity and coherence of meaning, including: clear and logical articulation, correct tempo, stressing notes differently according to their functions, observing the beat, respecting the written values of notes.
- Control and mastery of the material: playing with an unforced tone and pure intonation; keeping ornamentation in a reasonable relation to the piece's pulse and in agreement with the harmonies, finishing with assurance and poise, preparing and resolving dissonances clearly and gracefully, playing quick passagework roundly and distinctly and with seeming ease and composure.
- Expressing the passions of the music: playing with warmth, dynamic contrasts, enhancing the passions intended by the piece's composer, and showing obvious personal commitment to them, with an agreeable physical bearing and facial expression.

The first and second of these attributes are practical devices that belong to the office of *elocutio*, or technique and style. The third clearly belongs to expression, or *actio*. From this we see that *Vortrag* straddles two offices that both relate directly to the performer's role in the creative process and that are, at any rate, often conflated in other sources. This understanding of *Vortrag* as expression gives a different sense to Quantz's directions when we return to the three attributes of good *Vortrag*. Instead of being just about getting the notes right, *Vortrag* is the nuts and bolts of expressive playing and therefore essential in the performer's task of producing an eloquent performance.

"The unutterable ravishing Soul's delight"

The performance of Baroque music should coax, entice, cajole, stimulate, seduce, sway, inspire, exhort, and convince listeners to surrender to the passion being expressed. Seventeenth- and eighteenth-century audiences could be quite uninhibited in their reactions. Here are some striking examples: Athanasius Kircher observed that in opera the emotion "is often so great and intense that the listeners begin to scream, groan, and weep loudly, especially in the tragedies."[48] Penned in 1650, this is thought to reflect practices in Rome where Kircher lived. A little later in 1676 Thomas Mace described his ecstatic response to sacred music:

> But when *That Vast-Conchording-Unity* of the whole *Congregational-Chorus,* came (as I may say) *Thundering in,* even so, as it made the very

> *Ground shake* under us; (*Oh the unutterable ravishing Soul's delight!*) In the which I was so *transported*, and *wrapt* up into *High Contemplations*, that there was no room left in my *whole Man*, viz. *Body, Soul* and *Spirit*, for any thing below *Divine* and *Heavenly Raptures*.[49]

Dubos wrote in 1719 how tragedies served as surrogates for real experiences and compared musical expression with the achievements of the greatest playwrights of his time:

> Do not we ourselves feel that these airs make such impressions on us as the musician desires? Do not we perceive that these symphonies inflame us, calm us, soften us, and, in short, operate upon us, as strongly as Corneille's or Racine's verses?[50]

Cristoforo Bronzini wrote that when Francesca Cavalli (1587–1641) accompanied her own singing, she would "work such stunning effects in the minds of her listeners that she made them pliant, agreeable, or many other things by turn, so that it was a wonder, to tell the truth something almost unbelievable," and how her singing could take

> the mantle of joy from hearts and faces, so that, wrapped only in the sadness of melancholy and the denseness of dark clouds, there was nothing to do but weep. . . . This same woman, whenever it suited her, . . . so ignited wonder and daring in the breasts of the people that they would have done anything, no matter how difficult.[51]

Another striking example of the potency of music is Giuseppe Tartini's account of an opera performance he witnessed in Ancona in 1714 which Jean-Jacques Rousseau reported in his *Dictionnaire de Musique*. In an unnamed opera, "a piece of recitative of one single line, and without any accompaniment but the bass," produced such "a prodigious effect" that the entire audience was compelled to leave whatever else occupied their attention to engage with stunned silence:

> At each representation, a profound silence amongst the whole audience announced the approach of this terrible piece. The faces grew pale; they felt themselves shiver; and they beheld each other with a kind of terror: It was neither tears nor groans; it was a certain sensation of rough and disdainful rigour, which troubled the soul, confined the heart, and froze the blood.[52]

Reichardt's description of the effect of the flute-playing of King Frederick of Prussia, who was a stickler for court etiquette, is also indicative:

> And that was perhaps an unusual character trait, that [Frederick] delivered Adagios with so much inner sensitivity, and such a noble, touching simplicity and truth, that one seldom heard them without tears.[53]

These quotations provide a sense of what has been lost ever since the Authenticity Movement set about to sanitize the performance of early music and make it satisfy modern demands in the mid-twentieth-century. The initial goal was to purge the music of anachronistic Romantic grandiloquence and suppress emotional excess, but no music can speak on its own. Mediation is necessary in any performance art. There is really no such thing as a "transparent" performance that presents the score without emotional engagement. A performance that tries to politely avoid any position and "leave it up to the composer" will inevitably fail to convince.[54] In the attempt to purge our performances of Romantic tendencies, we often do them an equal disservice by disfiguring them with neutrality. What we need to do is to realign our intentions with the music's affective content. This does not mean returning to a Romantic style of performance, but if our audiences are not moved by turns to tears, jollity, and melancholy, then we have to reevaluate our *Vortrag*, and reforge sympathetic connections with our audiences.

Dance: *Une poésie muette*

Just as our bodies respond to the pounding beat at the nightclub, and our feet tap in time with rock 'n' roll, an equally physical relation was recognized between dance music and the human body in the seventeenth and eighteenth centuries. In the French language the expression *faire danser quelqu'un* ("to make someone dance") refers to how music could set bodies in motion and *faire danser même les ombres* (make even the dead dance). Baroque stage works are full of scenes that display the power of music. Orpheus, a prized model for Baroque opera as he could entrance both mortals and immortals with his singing, embodied of the singer's aspirations to move the audience, but there are just as many demonstrations of how music acts as a contagion that takes over listeners' bodies by imposing movement. Naturally, this takes place more often in French opera where dance was an essential element of the form.

Dance, like music, was thought of as an expressive language and was frequently described as mute poetry. Michel de Pure defined ballet as "a mute representation where gestures and movements signify what could have been expressed in words"; in the following century Louis de Cahusac wrote in a similar vein of ballet as "a type of mute poetry [*poésie muëtte*] that speaks because, in the words of Plutarch, without saying anything, it communicates in gestures, movements and steps."[55] Like the bodily gestures used by orators and actors, dance was considered a more direct form of communciation than words because it could be absorbed directly by the body, whereas language was mediated by the intellect and so required time to be comprehended. This concept is encapsulated in the eighteenth-century poet Pierre Charles Roy's *Ode de la Danse*:

Tout ce que la langue exprime	*All that language expresses*
Saisit lentement l'esprit;	*The intellect catches only slowly;*
Par la danse tout s'anime,	*Through dance everything is animated,*
En un instant, tout est dit.[56]	*And in an instant everything said.*

Let us scrutinize in greater detail the metaphor connecting dance and poetry. If dance is a language, how can it be read? Seventeenth-century French theorists of dance saw dance as capable not only of reflecting but also of replicating and perpetuating cosmological harmony in the bodies of those who performed it—both the body of the individual dancer and the communal body of all who participated.[57] The choreography embodied the proportions and harmony of music, and dance was seen as a gestural counterpart, a bodily response to music. As dance was an essential part of the education of the core of most aristocratic and *bourgeois* audiences, it could "speak" to them through kinesthetic empathy—that is, spectators at the opera could relate to dance through a virtual physical appreciation of bodily motion, and "sense" the gestures of the music as if they were dancing themselves.

But if dance is poetry, it stands in a different relationship to the dance music than the text of a song does to its musical setting. In song, the poetry generates the music; in dance, it is the music that triggers bodily (re)action. Ménestrier affirmed this when he described the effect that instruments have over the body and how, by replicating the music's *cadence* (i.e., its meter and phrasing), the dancing body is brought under the subjugation of music. Ménestrier also hinted at the power of music to block resistance and impose movement:

> And certainly, if the sound of instruments moves the body by vibrations of the air and if, by impressing on the ear the measure [*cadence*] of its movements, the vibrations inspire us to follow their measure by the melody [*le chant*] that is naturally associated with the sound of instruments, regardless of how little musical disposition one might have, or even by the movement of the body which can scarcely prevent itself from dancing or become agitated when any instrumental

music [*symphonie*] is played... The body, thus finding itself in a disposition related to the tune being played, more readily accepts the impressions of the music and transmits them to the soul, which then—if I may so speak—finds itself in unison with the instrument being played.[58]

Dance music is most effective when it dances itself: that is, when the musical gestures, articulation groupings and phrases are given the type of impetus that will elicit bodily response. Dance was a crucial part of eighteenth-century cultivated European society. Some musicians, like Jean-Baptiste Lully and Pantaleon Hebenstreit were also dance masters, and were consequently attuned to the musical needs of the dancer: dance was literally in their bodies. But, our modern bodies are outside this "authentic" experiential frame, making it virtually impossible for us to fully decode the language of Baroque dance. Choreographies preserved in notation can help to give a sense of what the dances might have been like, but just as in musical notation, they transmit only a portion of the total experience. Feuillet notation, for instance, specifies only the dancer's foot- and leg-work, and movement across space, but gives no indication of arm movements and the carriage of the torso. Some initial steps have been taken to recapture the communicative potential of Baroque dance by plotting musical gestures and form alongside the step sequences and floor plans of surviving choreographies.[59] Ultimately, the only way to comprehend dance music is to learn the steps, and to integrate a bodily connection between musical and dance gestures, as well as the character of different dance forms.

Sincerity in Performance

> A passion is but poorly imitated, which appears only from the teeth outward. To express it well, it should have made at least some slight impression upon the heart.
> —Jean-Baptiste Dubos, *Réflexions critiques* (quoting Horace)

> *Man merkt die Absicht und man ist verstimmt.*
> [If intention is noticeable, one is annoyed.]
> —Goethe, *Torquato Tasso*, 1790.

To elicit sympathy and seem credible, a performer must convey a sense of commitment. No one believes a politician who is obviously insincere in his promises, or a car salesman who waxes lyrical over a wreck, but there is a long-standing division of opinion on the question of sincerity in theatrical and musical performance. On the one hand there are those who hold to the imperative of sincerity, as expressed by Joseph de Templeri in 1698:

> One can't move [others] if one is not moved [oneself], nor kindle the hearts of those who listen, if flames do not blaze from the eyes of the speaker.⁶⁰

On the other hand, there are those, following an equally venerable Classical tradition stemming from Cicero, who feel that it is necessary to give only the semblance of true passion:

> Eloquence ensures that what the orator is saying *seems* to come from his heart.⁶¹

Those in the first camp believe that "genuine" passions aid affective performance, the others argue quite the contrary: that it can hinder communication. The lines got blurred when some writers took it upon themselves to reinterpret or gloss their sources to make them say the opposite. Bernard Lamy, for instance, adjusted Horace's epigram *Si vis me flere dolendum est primum ipsi tibi* (literally: If you want me to weep, you must first grieve yourself) as "One cannot touch others, if one does not *appear* to be touched one's self."⁶²

The flames mentioned by de Templeri that seem to blaze from the eyes of the inspired performer, were taken as a mark of artistic sincerity. They symbolized the fabled state of fury of poets and prophets referred to in Classical writings as "enthusiasm," and thought of as an induced or unnatural condition, a state of inspired possession. In Classical mythology, enthusiasm resulted from drinking the waters of the Hippocrene source on Mount Helicon. (Allusions to this continued to appear in later musical works like François Couperin's *Parnasse, ou l'Apothéose de Corelli*.) In the Rhetorical age, the ultimate praise artists could win was to be recognized for kindling the fire of creative enthusiasm (in the sense of possessed frenzy), and it was also taken as a sign of how closely they approached the emotional power of the Ancients. This brings to mind descriptions of violinists like Nicola Matteis and Arcangelo Corelli,⁶³ or Charles Burney's famous account of C. P. E. Bach's improvisational skill:

> He grew so animated and possessed, that he not only played, but looked like one inspired. His eyes were fixed, his under lip fell, and drops of effervescence distilled from his countenance. He said, if he were to be set to work frequently, in this manner, he should grow young again.⁶⁴

C. P. E. Bach, himself in the sincerity camp, wrote that a musician "cannot move others without himself being moved," and had to "feel all the emotions he hopes to call up in his audience."⁶⁵ Mattheson said something not too dissimilar: "No one who is not acquainted with a passion as if he had experienced it himself or is experiencing it, will be skilled in exciting a similar passion in other people."⁶⁶

There was no denying that there is some sort of magic in the creative process, but as the eighteenth century progressed, Enlightenment philosophers sought to replace the putative divine or supernatural origins of inspiration with a more reasoned and scientific explanation. Charles Batteux believed that "the enthusiasm of artists is only a lively sentiment, produced by a lively idea with which the artist has himself affected his own mind."[67] The French dance scholar Louis de Cahusac redefined enthusiasm to mean the infectious spark of communal acceptance shared by performer and audience whenever a performance "got it right."[68] Other eighteenth-century writers took a more ambivalent view of sincerity. Quantz charms us with his pious sincerity when he says "that which comes not from the heart, will not enter the heart."[69] But after providing occasional and oblique warnings, further into his treatise he takes us aside, as it were, like a wise old teacher, to confide a professional secret:

> One must work hard at learning the art of feigning or dissembling whenever one has a piece of music to execute ... always to put one's self in the passion that the piece demands. It is only in this way that he will manage to play the pieces with the composer's conception, while *seeming* to play his own ideas.[70]

Quantz underscored that feigning or dissembling was not only permitted, but "in fact absolutely necessary, and commits in no way an offence to morals."[71]

Feigning had occupied a key place in the arts and acting for centuries. Presenting the outward signs of inner emotions without actually experiencing those emotions is the very heart of the actor's craft. Quintilian wrote of "false and fictitious or imitative affections" much as later writers do, and reasoned that

> some affections are real, others are false and fictitious. The real ones, however, naturally burst out thro' the Force of Grief, Anger, or Indignation; but they are all of them artless, and therefore not subject to any Rules; but fictitious or imitative Affections are.[72]

What Quintillian is saying here was that if an actor is not moved by the emotion that he needs to express, he can still induce it by means of artifice or study.

Feigning also entails disguising or denying one's true sentiments. Servants in European courts recognized how essential counterfeit passions could be for survival. According to Wolfgang Caspar Printz (1641–1717), cantor at the court of Count Balthasar Erdmann von Promnitz, dissembling was *die vornehmste Hof-Tugend*—"the foremost courtly virtue, and a fawning courtier's greatest art is surely to behave and appear completely different than he is."[73] Quantz, who could easily outshine his master the king of Prussia, would likewise have been familiar with the strictures of court etiquette and the need to feign obsequious admiration for his royal pupil. He was also writing at a time when Enlightenment thinkers were beginning to interrogate the imperative of sincerity. When discussing the theater in 1746, Charles Batteux put it bluntly: "Nothing here is truth."

> If it happens, that the musician or the dancer should really feel the sentiment they express; this is a circumstance quite accidental, as being without the least design on the side of art.... Art is formed but for deceit.[74]

One of the sharpest observers of feigning and dissembling was Denis Diderot who described the actor's talent in his controversial *Paradoxe sur le comédien* (1773) not as feeling emotions as we might suppose, but in "scrupulously producing the exterior signs of emotions that fool you. The cries of sorrow are imprinted on his ear; the gestures of despair memorised, prepared in front of a mirror."[75] The crux of Diderot's paradox then is that moving an audience to tears takes stoic calculation; just as being a hilarious comic is deadly serious.

Like actors, musicians need to take on different characters as appropriate to the music. Rameau clearly considered it the musician's responsibility to be personally involved:

> A good musician should surrender himself to all the characters he wishes to portray. Like a skilful actor he should take the place of the speaker, believe himself to be at the location where the different events he wishes to depict occur, and participate in these events as do those most involved in them.[76]

To continuously hold the audience's interest, performers must be able to capture a range of passions, and to shift with the changing humours of the music. As Quantz put it:

> Each piece ... can be comprised of a mixture of pathetic, flattering, happy, sublime, and humorous gestures; so that one must be able to feel one's self different passions in every bar, as it were: now grief-stricken, now elated, now serious, etc. This ability [to transform one's feelings] is vital in music. The musician who can master this art will not fail to win the approval of his auditors, and his expression will always be moving. [Such mastery] is not to be looked for in younger people, who are usually too speedy and impatient. It develops only along with deeper sensibilities and judgement.[77]

For it to elicit the appropriate response, each passion needs to be presented as genuine and expressed in terms that the audience can also relate to through a shared experience. This is part of the reason why artists in the Rhetorical age drew from the stock of generic passions rather than specific personal emotions. Passions can be remembered from past experiences, or experiences learned from other artistic expressions and—genuine or feigned—pressed into service on call. We all have some passions that we relate to easily, while others come less naturally to us and have to be "studied" to be conveyed convincingly. If we have not experienced a particular emotion ourselves, we can still imitate what we have observed in others. These "studied" passions require more diligence. This seems to be what Diderot meant when he wrote "that which passion itself cannot achieve, simulated or imitated passion [*la passion bien imité*] can bring off."[78] In this context, it is interesting to read these insightful observations from the actor François Riccoboni:

> I don't mean to say that the actor doesn't feel the emotions in a play with strongly passionate passages—that is, in fact, the most exhausting aspect of theatre acting. But the agitation comes from the effort required when painting a passion that the actor does not feel himself.[79]

An important part of developing skill as a musician involves coming to know one's own strengths and weaknesses. As Shakespeare's Polonius advised Hamlet: "To thine own self be true."[80] That is, performers must believe in their own performance. If they do not find their own performance convincing, then there is little chance that they will be able to move their audience. Quantz wrote about this:

> It is thus important that a student cultivate and excite this sentiment in himself, little by little. Because if he is not himself touched by what he plays, he need not expect profit from his cares and efforts, nor will he ever achieve the true purpose of music, which is to touch another through one's playing.[81]

There are days when we feel nervous, or angry toward the conductor, or perhaps sad that a friend couldn't make it to the concert, but these emotions are not appropriate to bring to our performance. We need to learn how to channel these real and immediate feelings through the passionate language of the music. And whether the emotions are real or induced, genuine or feigned, the way we convey them is the means by which we can touch others. Quantz described a type of role play where the musician takes on different characters, "trying on" various states or attitudes like masks that disguise our immediate emotions and at the same time allow us to more fully bring out the affections appropriate to the performance:

> On this subject of dissembling, each musician has also to take account of his own temperament and know how to accommodate it suitably to various situations. A lively person, full of fire, for instance, who finds himself drawn to great and serious issues, as well as excessive speed, should when playing an Adagio find a way to moderate his fire, as much as he is able. On the other hand, a melancholy and gloomy person would do well in order to play an Allegro in a brilliant way to try to catch some of the former person's excessive fire. . . . It is true, however, that our inherent attributes are always better than those we borrow.[82]

What those writers who talked about feigning in performance were proposing was a type of musical fiction. In the early seventeenth century, the word "fiction" was close in meaning to "deceit" and implied feigning, counterfeiting, dissembling, or pretense. Shortly after, it began to take on its present, morally neutral meaning and no longer meant deception, but instead suggested an imaginary situation or circumstance the artist explored in collusion with the audience.[83] This was also the period when the concept of imitation was the prevailing model for expression in the arts. As an invention of the imagination and a hypothetical construct, imitation can, in this sense, also be seen as a form of fiction.

In music, as with any imitative art, there is always an element of fiction—both in the sense that it is fabricated, as well as in that it serves as an artificial imitation or substitution for genuine objects or emotions. The audience in a theater, for instance, is well aware that they are witnessing a fiction, but they temporarily accept the product of the artist's imagination as real. They must suspend their disbelief and to do this, the fiction must *seem* to be real—or at least probable. Michael Kelly explains how the seeds of imitation-as-fiction were sown in Aristotle's *Poetics*:

> Works of art are encoded in such a way that humans are not duped into believing that they are "reality," but rather recognize features from their own experience of the world within the work of art that cause the representation to seem valid and acceptable.[84]

This notion of artistic plausibility or probability is what French theorists called *vraisemblance*. Dubos put it as follows: "As truth is the soul of history, so *vraisemblance* [probability] is the soul of poetry."[85] Even though theatrical oratory is highly artificial and musical composition requires a high level of technical skill, it is the task of both actor and musician to make the spectator believe that what they are witnessing is a spontaneous emotional expression rather than the result of studied practice—in other words, to demonstrate the credibility of the fiction.

Performance, then, is a test of how well an actor or musician can convince the audience that what they witness is indeed "from the heart," and a performance is judged on how well it renders art believable. As soon as it is clear that the artist is trying too hard, that (as Goethe put it) "the intention is noticeable," the artifice is broken. This brings us full circle back to eloquence, which, as the art of convincing is also the art of dissembling so that the passions being expressed seem genuine. As Jean Poisson, well-known actor at the Dresden court, wrote in 1717:

> All the rules of Cicero, of Quintilian, and of the illustrious moderns who might have written on declamation, are useless to the orator, if he does not follow the first, which is, to clearly understand what he is saying and feel it strongly himself, in order to make it perceptible to the listener.[86]

Mental Multitasking

There is also a practical side to feigning passion. Performers cannot allow themselves to be completely overtaken with passion because that would make them incapable of effective communication. Put succinctly by François Riccoboni: "It has always seemed obvious to me that if one had the misfortune to truly feel that which one is expressing, one would be in no state to act."[87] On the other hand, performers can permit a part of themselves—their musical instincts—to be consumed by an emotion while another part—their technical autopilot—keeps objective self-control and thinks ahead, calculating "how" and "when." Keeping enough control to function effectively while undergoing passions, as well as evoking them, is possible, at least some of the time.

A vital stage in a musician's development is learning to listen and react to all the parts in the ensemble. Musicians often begin by listening just to themselves. The next step, paying attention to other parts in an ensemble at the same time as playing, implies a high level of technical control as well as familiarity with ensemble routine. This is the mark of a socialized musician. It involves taking cues from other players, mimicking phrasing, catching tempo changes, coordinating parts, and adjusting intonation. Without these things, accurate ensemble playing and responsive musical dialogue are hardly possible.

There is another related skill that involves balancing one's own contribution relative to the other parts, and also assessing how the whole is perceived by the audience. By a type of teleporting or virtual role-switching, performers can put themselves in the listener's seat and assess the effect of the music in the acoustic and on the audience. Imagining that you are listening to yourself as you play also allows you to respond to your own feedback. This is what musicians and orators meant when they wrote about putting oneself in the place of those who are listening and judging.

These examples of multitasking in musical performance demonstrate the human brain's ability to divide attention into multiple activities happening at the same moment. It comes as no surprise, then, that we are also capable of experiencing profound emotions while at the same time remaining coldly logical and employing the so-called tricks of the trade in a practiced way. This is the essence of what Diderot described when he commented in awe and wonderment on the performances of the actress La Clairon:

> It is when, suspended between reality and their representation [*ébauche*], these artists with their experience pay the closest attention to all these things at the same time: the beauties of inspiration, the fortuitous attributes that they scatter through their works, which, appearing suddenly, astonish even themselves.... *Sang-froid* is needed to temper the delirium of ecstasy [*enthousiasme*].[88]

Such moments of inspiration do really happen. All involved (fellow musicians, attending technicians, and audience) become infected with and inspired by the same mysterious enthusiasm. They all revel in it and celebrate in it. That is, after all, the goal of any performance.

Further Reading

Johnson's *Listening in Paris* is a thought-provoking reassessment of audience engagement at the Paris Opéra and concert halls during the eighteenth and early nineteenth centuries. In *Opera and Sovereignty* Martha Feldman also takes a close look at the sociological aspects of *opera seria* and examines some of the ways by which eighteenth-century composers calculated audience response in their music. *Baroque Piety* by Tanya Kevorkian is an informative discussion of the habits of those who made up the audiences of Bach's church music.

Richard Leppert's studies on musical iconography, *Music and Image*, and *The Sight of Sound*, are full of valuable visual resources and insightful observations on listening practices in the Rhetorical and Romantic periods. For a summary of theories on simultaneity in eighteenth-century painting, and an interesting case study of Michel-Barthélémy Olliver's painting *Le Thé à l'anglaise* depicting Mozart performing in Paris, see Hanning "The Iconography of a Salon Concert." Tom Beghin presents a stimulating extension of the discussion of the musician's facial gesture in an analysis of the physiognomy studies of late eighteenth-century caricaturist Franz Xavier Messerschmidt in *The Virtual Haydn*, chapter 4.

Over the course of the book we have borrowed the term "musicking" from Christopher Small who coined the term as a convenient catchphrase for music making in the broadest sense, including all activities that are encompassed by the rhetorical process as applied to music. Small reminds us that rehearsing, tuning up, instrument making, editing, listening, and other peripheral activities such as performer's deportment are just as valid and meaningful to the total musical process as composing and performing.

Of all writings on sincerity in performance, Diderot's *Paradoxe* has stimulated the most controversy since it was first written in the 1770s. The dossier recently compiled by Jean Bardet in his edition is one of the best synopses of the work's reception history.

Schneider, "Die Funktion des Divertissement und des Ballet" quotes extensively from Baroque sources on dance. *Dance, Spectacle and the Body Politic*, a collection of essays edited by Jennifer Nevile contains important scholarship on the social significance of dance and the analysis of original choreographies. For a list of surviving choreographies in the French tradition, see Lancelot, *La Belle danse*, and Little and Marsh, *La Danse noble*.

10

Analyzing Expression in Period Recordings of Bach's Cantatas

BRUCE HAYNES

The following discussion is based on the five recordings of the complete Bach cycle using period instruments available in 2006:

- The joint Harnoncourt-Leonhardt project with Concentus Musicus Wien and the Leonhardt Consort of Amsterdam (Telefunken, 1971–89)
- Ton Koopman with the Amsterdam Baroque Orchestra (Erato, later Challenge Classics, recorded 1995–2006)
- Masaaki Suzuki and the Bach Collegium Japan (BIS, 1995–2013)
- John Eliot Gardiner with the English Baroque Soloists and Monteverdi Choir (Archiv and later Solo Dei Gloria, most recorded 1999–2000)
- Pieter Jan Leusink, Netherlands Bach Collegium (Brilliant Classics, recorded 1999, 2000)

For the purposes of this discussion it is important to hear the complete movement (or better still the entire cantata) to evaluate my commentary, but as most are too long to excerpt on the companion website, readers are directed to the recordings in CD or other digital format.

As recently as 1970, those who listened to Bach cantatas and studied them would have been impressed with the current situation: not only can we now hear all the cantatas next to each other, we can even compare the same cantata performed by (on average) five different groups promoting their endeavors as historically inspired. This has never occurred before in history. If, as Plato observed, eloquence is measured by its effect on the listener's soul, a corollary is that an eloquent representation must by definition be recognizable by the beholder or listener. If we make that our principle, then the ideal performance of a movement of a Bach cantata would be one that expressed its subject (in Schweitzer's words) "as clearly as running water."

Audio Example 10.1 offers five examples of clear and convincing presentation of the passion of the text in Cantata BWV 127/3.

Die Seele ruht in Jesu Händen,	My soul rests in Jesus's hands
Wenn Erde diesen Leib bedeckt.	When earth covers this body.
Ach ruft mich bald, ihr Sterbeglocken,	Ah, call me soon, you death-bells:
Ich bin zum Sterben unerschrocken,	I am not afraid of dying,
Weil mich mein Jesus wieder weckt.	For my Jesus shall rouse me again.

🎵 AUDIO EX. 10.1. BWV 127/3

(a) Amsterdam Baroque Orchestra, dir. Koopman (Challenge, 2005)
(b) Leonhardt Consort, dir. Leonhardt (Telefunken, 1982)
(c) Bach Collegium Japan, dir. Suzuki (BIS, 2006)
(d) English Baroque Soloists, dir. Gardiner (Soli Deo Gloria, 2006)
(e) Collegium Vocale Ghent, dir. Herreweghe (Harmonia Mundi, 2007)

Each of these performances remains unique and captures a subtly different view of the piece and its prevailing passion. This is an example of a complex emotion, and there is little concrete to latch onto from which we can evaluate the performance. Other situations present clearer cases. Among the existing recordings of BWV 110/1, *Unser Mund sei voll Lachens* (May our mouths be filled with laughter), the clearest laughing is in Harnoncourt's version (Audio Ex. 10.2). If eloquence is our criterion, this version by Concentus Musicus is the most successful.

🎵 AUDIO EX. 10.2. BWV 110/1, Concentus Musicus, dir. Harnoncourt (Telefunken, 1980)

Still, at the time of this writing, there are numerous movements in Bach's cantatas that have yet to get on to disk in entirely convincing performances. The subjects of these pieces—that is, their passions—have not yet been adequately addressed, even by specialists. I would like to examine the performances of some of these pieces, not with the purpose of criticizing the performers but rather of discussing ways that the music might be made more eloquent. The issue of evaluating others' interpretation of human emotions looks subjective, of course, but, as the rhetorical procedure teaches us, there is an objective aspect. What I propose is to comment on several specific cases using the concept of humouring: tempo, articulation, and dynamics. Naturally, reader-listeners can decide for themselves if they agree. Whether my opinions match up with yours or not, I hope these remarks will at least serve the purpose of drawing attention to the things Bach was trying to express, and the methods he and his contemporaries employed to bring them about.

BWV 102/3

In terms of expressing the passions, several movements of Cantata 102 have proven particularly challenging to realize in recording. Part of the problem is that the passions expressed by the text are extreme. In aria mvt. 3 in BWV 102, *Herr, deine Augen sehen nach dem Glauben!* they are frustration, agony, and a warning of God's wrath (Ex. 10.1). Bach used the same music in the Lutheran Mass BWV 233/4 where the text "Qui tollis peccata mundi" is a supplication for mercy (essentially, this is synonymous with "Erbarme dich" from the St. Matthew Passion).

Weh der Seele, die den Schaden	*Woe to the soul that no longer*
Nicht mehr kennt	*Recognizes its lostness*
Und, die Straf auf sich zu laden,	*And, to burden itself with punishment,*
Störrig rennt,	*Rushes willfully!*
Ja von ihres Gottes Gnaden	*Indeed, even from its God's grace*
Selbst sich trennt.	*Cuts itself off!*

Example 10.1 BWV 102/3, opening ritornello

This aria is known among hautboists because of its unusual key of f minor, which, because of the number of cross-fingerings and difficult trills, gives the hautboy a muted, deformed sound (cf. mm. 5 and 8). F minor is very rare in surviving solo repertoire for hautboy; there are only three solo concertos known in this key.[1] In BWV 233 the music is transposed up a tone to g minor, an easier key, but not without trepidation, and still appropriate to set the image of the sins of the world (*peccata mundi*).

In BWV 102, the dominant passion, I would say, is agony; the word *Weh* in German has the same root as the English "woe" and "wail"; it is an exclamation of grief or lamentation, a denunciation and a curse, and a warning of impending affliction and the pains of hell.[2] Alfred Dürr writes of this aria that its gestures "could hardly be surpassed for compelling effect. Entering with a long-held dissonant d♭2, the obbligato oboe seems to call out 'Woe!' over the impenitent soul."[3] This is one of Bach's most effective uses of the expressive qualities of the hautboy through the use of its technical properties. The d♭2 to which Dürr refers is one of the instrument's sensitive notes, tending to be too low in pitch even as a c♯2; Bach puts it against an e♮ in the bass. The line proceeds through a series of excruciating, sinuous gestures of different and irregular lengths, finally coming to rest on c2, but this is immediately disturbed by the alto entrance, again on a d♭2, creating the strongest possible dissonance of a semitone. Only one of the hautboists in the recordings takes advantage of this piquant event, the others apparently deeming it of less urgency than their supply of oxygen, even though a breath is quite possible three beats later.

Nor, I might add, do the singers seem very emotionally involved. This often happens because singers prepare separately and often have different agendas from the instrumentalists for how to fit their parts with the harmony. On this question, Quantz remarked on the importance of all members of the ensemble being engaged and working towards the same goal:

> [Bringing] out the character of the different passions that the composer wants to express in the piece ... is as much the responsibility of the accompanying parts as it is of the solo parts, and achieving it is the main thing that distinguishes a good accompaniment. After all, it isn't as if there is only one player who performs a piece with the real passion while the others acquit themselves of their duties inattentively and with indifference (which would be like a situation where some destroy what others create).[4]

Because the opening ritornello is normally given to the obbligato instrument, the instrumentalist is usually responsible for introducing the movement's dominant passion. By the time the voice enters, the *inventio* of the piece—its argument, and its passion—should be clear. Bach has certainly provided the necessary material. These pieces, then, are essentially duets in which the instrument and singer collaborate in expressing the same passion.

In the existing recordings of BWV 102/3 it is not always evident that all members of the team share a common understanding of the prevailing passion. Some recordings suffer from tempos that are fast and drain the music of its seriousness.

To repeat what Batteux wrote in 1746: "Every piece of music and dance should have its signification, or meaning;"[5] as well as Rousseau's advice to the musician: "Begin then by a complete knowledge of the character of the air which you are going to render."[6] In the case of this piece, I suggest that knowledge of the character means performing it with a sense of urgency, with an extreme, even panicky feel. This is not so difficult; the music supports this approach quite plausibly. What is needed is rhythmic unpredictability (localized rushing of beat 3 in bars 3 and 4) or holding back, quick and extreme changes of dynamics (something the hautboy does better than any other instrument, by the way), and placing phrase breaks as a function of the harmony. The ritornello can be effectively punctuated by releasing resolution notes. Many of the small musical gestures are just written-out graces, which can be more telling if not performed too squarely. To do only these few elocutionary tricks of the trade can already move listeners, even on a recording.

Assuming that the passion has been successfully communicated from the beginning of the piece, what normally remains throughout the rest of the piece is to confirm the potential of this musical idea by hearing its different facets, in much the same spirit as the consistency of a character in a Baroque opera is maintained through the turns of the plot. The passion is viewed and tested in various contexts, such as the interfacing between voice and instrument, the effects of different tonalities, etc.

Example 10.2 BWV126/4, opening

Cantata 126/4

The text is:

Stürze zu Boden schwülstige Stolze!	Cast to the ground bombastic pride!
Mache zunichte, was sie erdacht!	Bring to desolation what it has devised!
Laß sie den Abgrund plötzlich verschlingen,	Let the abyss suddenly devour it;
wehre dem Toben feindlicher Macht,	Curb the raving of hostile might,
laß ihr Verlangen nimmer gelingen!	Let its desires never succeed!

This represents the passion wrath. The existing recordings of this aria tend toward a general legato, which I would not associate with wrath; rather short and sharp articulation, especially on the two syllables of "Boden" (which is set to the interval of a major 7th), and should be charged with the tense energy of outrage, and sung loudly, almost shouting. All the performances achieve these effects some of the time, but in each of them at some point the singer lets up, relaxes, and begins to connect the notes; the result is that the passion is compromised, and none of the singers' performances is entirely convincing.

Cantata 171/2

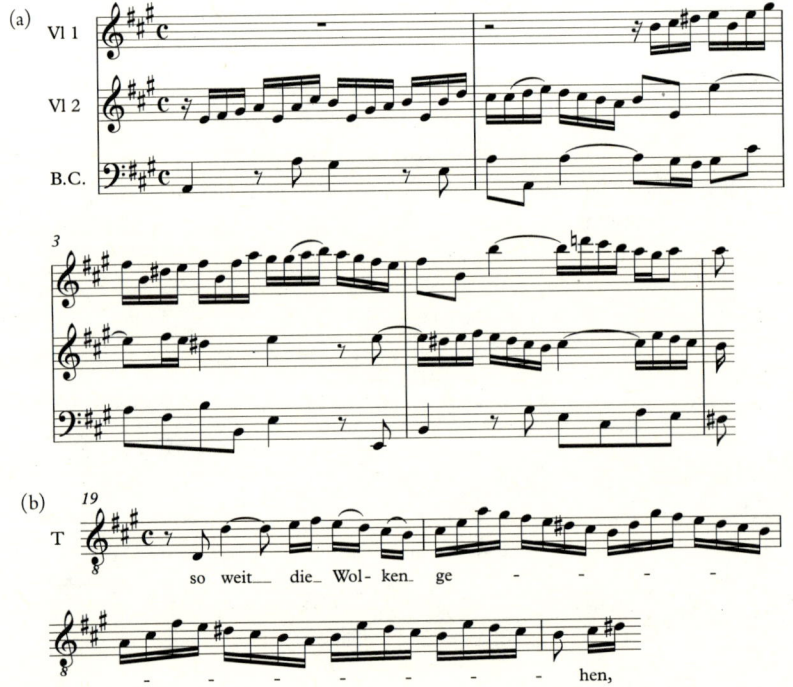

Example 10.3 BWV 171/2 (a) opening ritornello (b) melisma on "gehen"

The text is:

Herr, so weit die Wolken gehen,
Gehet deines Namens Ruhm.
Alles, was die Lippen rührt,
alles, was noch Odem führt,
wird dich in der Macht erhöhen.

Lord, as far as the clouds go
So goes Your Name's renown.
All that stirs the lips,
All that yet draws breath
Will exalt You in Your might.

This is the passion of praise, or more exactly, exaltation. Much of the effect of this passion is a product of tempo. If it is too slow, it will not give as positive an impression, and if it is too fast, the tenor will "crash and burn" as he joins the violins on the sixteenth-note melismas, or else he will draw undue attention to the technical difficulties of his part. He should project a positive, approving attitude (we should be able to hear his smile). In the existing recordings very little of any attitude is evident. They bring to mind Quantz's admonishing remarks. "The expression is poor," he wrote,

> when the player . . . executes everything in general without feeling, without passions, and without being moved himself, so it seems he is obliged to sing or play as an agent on commission for someone else.[7]

One of the tenors uses strong attacks on every word to give a powerful, vehement, and negative feel. The effect is that every word is given exaggerated emphasis, as if he is telling someone off. As a result, he expresses a passion that is almost exactly the reverse of exaltation.

Cantata 105/3

Example 10.4 BWV 105/3, opening ritornello

O wie zittern und wanken	How they tremble and waver,
der Sünder Gedanken,	The thoughts of sinners,
indem sie sich untereinander verklagen	As they accuse one another
und wiederum sich zu entschuldigen wagen.	And again dare to excuse themselves.
So wird ein geängstigt Gewissen	Thus a frightened conscience
durch eigene Folter zerrissen.	Is torn on its own rack.

Nothing comfortable or beautiful here. One would expect some frightening music to go with a torture scene, and Bach provides an almost melodramatic portrait of fear. *Tremolo* strings provide the classic signal of fear; the hautboy begins with a minor 7th, imitating repeated sobs. Yet none of the HIP recordings I've heard of this piece succeeds in calling to mind either fear or anguish. Some of them actually manage to express what sounds like sublime beauty, and none of the sopranos seems to have taken the meaning of the text seriously, or considered it worth passing on to us. This might be excused from a young boy treble, but even the mature women who sing on the majority of the recordings seem generally disengaged from the process. I suppose the musicians are trying to convey the sense of rising above mortal torture, but it is fairly easy to make this piece sound innocuous. To achieve the aria's real intention of terror takes effort. These recordings are good examples of the pointlessness of the idea of "letting the music speak for itself." In order to express their meaning, the sobbing exclamations at the beginning have to be full of energy and slightly out of control (that is, out of stable rhythm), with little space between them; relaxing is not what you do when you're fearful. All the hautboists on these recordings sound very comfortable; no cries of anguish audible. I hear what sounds like a reading of the scripture lesson for the day, or a folksong around the campfire. No one has come close to communicating the urgency and danger that both the text and the music could express.

The question of taste and degree often come up. Can we communicate a sense of discomfort while at the same time retaining an adequate degree of comfort to cope with the pressures of the concert hall or the recording studio? Decorum still reins, and like a tightrope walker, our path between what we represent and how we perform it can sometimes give us very little wriggle room.

BWV 136/2 and 3

As far as their passions are concerned these two movements create a continuous flow. The passion of the recitative is fury. The last two lines of the recitative lead to the following aria full of righteous indignation:

Der wird, ihr Heuchler, euch ein Schrecken,	You hypocrites! When a terror
Ja unerträglich sein.	Will indeed be unbearable for you!
Es kömmt ein Tag,	A day is coming
So das Verborgne richtet,	That will judge the secrets of men,
Vor dem die Heuchelei erzittern mag.	And before which hypocrisy will tremble!
Denn seines Eifers Grimm vernichtet,	For the wrath of his jealousy annihilates
Was Heuchelei und List erlichtet.	What hypocrisy and cunning contrive.

This is a good example of an unpleasant, anti-Beauty piece. None of the presently available recordings seems to even try to express the impatience, outrage, and threat in this text. The more recent ones seem to approach it like a light-hearted dance. One of the altos sings "A day is coming that will judge the secrets of men" as if it were "Some day, my Prince will come."

As I say above, it is the responsibility of the instrumentalist playing a piece's first ritornello to state the *inventio* clearly and unambiguously on its very first hearing. The rest of the piece will simply elaborate what has already been stated instrumentally. After the *expositio* a standard *da capo* aria has another three critical presentations of the *inventio*: the singer's first statement, the reprise of the first statement at the *da capo* (when it should have at least a little ornamentation), and the "last chance" at the final ritornello (likewise ornamented, ideally in a way that makes reference to and comments on the singer's graces). But none of these three is as important as the very first time the *inventio* is heard.

To express the passions in BWV 136/3 (see Ex. 10.3), each of the first three statements must be louder than the last, and the two eighth-notes at the end of the first two should be strong and violent; the long note of bar 5 should be energetic with a crescendo, and there should be an air of impatience, created by rushing slightly. The thirty-second note gestures that follow should be loud and violent like a boxer's jabs. After the half-cadence, which offers no repose, the next two musical gestures are each independent, with strong emphasis on the figure that follows the three-note pickups. Finally, the last phrase includes a surprise extension on the third beat. This adds vehemence to this angry outburst. The die is now cast. Having made a very explicit representation of vexation, one must maintain it right to the end of the aria (though hopefully with a couple of gentler passages that by their contrast will actually reinforce the dominant fiery passion).

Example 10.5 BWV 136/2, last 3 measures; 136/3 opening ritornello, and vocal entry from bar 11

From the above examples, it is clear that passions are not aroused automatically when a piece is performed. Bach did his best to provide his performers with material that would make it possible to evoke the intended passion, but the performer must carry on from there. The five complete recordings of the full cycle of Bach's sacred cantatas now available are still only the first five. They should not be taken as the final word. Often the most affective performances with the richest insights are unrecorded, lost in the ether. There is plenty of room to refine our understanding of this rich repertoire, and as our tastes change, our musical techniques develop, and Bach's music and his world continue to speak to future generations, the journey will continue.

Appendix

BRUCE HAYNES: LIST OF PUBLICATIONS

1968   "The Decline ... A Further Scrutiny," *Recorder and Music Magazine* 2, no. 8: 240–42. A response to Daniel Waitzman, "The Decline of the Recorder in the 18th Century," *American Recorder* 8, no. 2 (Spring 1967): 47–51; repr. in *Recorder and Music Magazine* 2, no. 7 (Nov. 1967): 222–25; response from Waitzman, *American Recorder* 9 (Fall 1968); and a further reaction from Haynes and Steven Silverstein in *American Recorder* 9 (Sept. 1968), 329–30.

1968   "The Baroque Recorder: A Comparison with its Modern Counterpart," with drawings by Friedrich von Huene, *Recorder and Music Magazine* 2, no. 11 (Dec.): 364–68; repr. in *American Recorder* 10, no. 1 (Winter 1969): 3–8.

1970   "The Baroque Oboe," *Woodwind World* 13:6–7.

1971   "Avant-garde Music on the 18th-Century Recorder: Frans Brueggen's Recordings on Original Recorders," *Recorder and Music Magazine* 3:377.

1976   "Interim Repertoire List for Baroque Oboe," typescript, 9pp.

1976   "Making Reeds for the Baroque Oboe," *Early Music* 4, no. 1:31–34, 173–79; repr. as "Baroque Oboe Reed-Making," *Double Reed* (hereafter *DR*) (1979).

1977   (With Hansjürg Lange) "The Importance of Original Double Reeds Today," *Galpin Society Journal* (hereafter *GSJ*) 30: 145–49.

1977   "A Register of Early Double Reeds," *GSJ* 30:150–51.

1978   "Oboe Fingering Charts, 1695–1816," *GSJ* 31:68–93.

1979   "Tonality and the Baroque Oboe," *Early Music* 7, no. 3:355–57.

1980   *Catalogue of Chamber Music for the Oboe, 1654–ca. 1825*, 4th ed. (Author).

1984   "Double Reeds, 1660–1830: A Survey of Surviving Written Evidence," *Journal of the International Double Reed Society* (hereafter *JIDRS*) 12:14–33.

1985 "Johann Sebastian Bach's Pitch Standards: The Woodwind Perspective," *Journal of the American Musical Instrument Society* (hereafter *JAMIS*) 11: 55–114; in French as: "Les diapasons à l'époque de Jean-Sebastien Bach: L'apport des instruments à vent," in *Le Tic-toc-choc: Journal du Studio de musique ancienne de Montréal* 6 (1985), repr. in *Flûte à bec & instruments anciens*, no. 22 (1987): 11–19; no. 23 (1987): 4–8; no. 24 (1988): 11–18; no. 26 (Nov. 1988): 11–17.

1986 *Music for Oboe 1650–1800: A Bibliography* (Berkeley: Fallen Leaf Press). Available online at www.haynes-catalog.net.

1986 "A Preliminary Checklist of Iconography for Oboe-type Instruments, Reeds, and Players, 1630–1830," *Fellowship of Makers and Researchers of Historical Instruments Quarterly* (hereafter *FoMRHIQ*), no. 45:58–73.

1986 "Questions of Tonality in Bach's Cantatas: The Woodwind Perspective," *JAMIS* 12:40–67.

1986 "Telemann's *Kleine Cammer-music* and the Four Oboists to Whom it Was Dedicated," *Musick* 7, no. 4 (March): 30–35; repr. in *JIDRS* 15 (1987): 27–32; and *DR* 19, no. 3 (1996): 75–80; in German as "Telemanns *Kleine Cammer-Musik* und die vier Oboisten, denen sie gewidmet ist," *Rohrblatt* 12, no. 3 (1997): 119–23. Revised repr. from preface to facsimile ed. of Telemann's publication (Basel: Musica Musica, 1983).

1986 "'Temperamento per comune opinione perfettisimo': 18th-Century Tuning for Singers and Orchestral Instruments," *FoMRHIQ*, no. 43:56–68.

1988 "Aufsteig und Fall der Solo-Oboe, 1650–1800," *Tibia* 13, no. 2 (2/88): 94–100.

1988 "Eighteenth-Century German and French Pitches?" *FoMRHIQ*, no. 53:32.

1988 "... In Death I Sing," *FoMRHIQ*, no. 53 (Oct.): 25–26; response by Jonathan Swayne, *FoMRHIQ*, no. 55 (April 1989): 22.

1988 "Lully and the Rise of the Oboe as Seen in Works of Art." *Early Music* 16, no. 3 (Aug.): 324–38.

1988 (with Marc Écochard) "Les diapasons à l'époque de Jean-Sébastien Bach. III: Description de diapasons anciens; sources, hauteurs relatives et absolues," *Flûte à bec et instruments anciens*, no. 24:11–18.

1989 "The Oboe Solo before 1800," *JIDRS* 17: 7–14 (revision of "Aufsteig und Fall"); reprinted in *DR* 19, no. 3 (1996): 147–54; Italian version: "L'oboe solista prima del 1800. Un'indagine," *Aulos (Bollettino semestrale dell'Accademia Italiana dei Legni)* 4, no. 2 (1991): 63–71.

1989 (with Ardal Powell) "Urgent Communication on Ivory," *FoMRHIQ*, no. 54 (Jan.): 64–65.

1990 "Bressan, Talbot and the 'Galpin' Oboe," *GSJ* 43: 112–23.

1990 "Generic 415," *Traverso: Baroque Flute Newsletter* 2, no. 4: 1.

1991 "Beyond Temperament: Non-Keyboard Intonation in the 17th and 18th Centuries," *Early Music* 19, no. 3 (Aug.): 357–81.

1991 "Appeal for Pitches of Original Traversos and Recorders," *FoMRHIQ*, no. 63: 56.

1991 "Mozart's Oboe Solos," *Musick* 13:12–14.

1992 "Johann Sebastian Bachs Oboenkonzerte," *Bach Jahrbuch* 1992:23–43.

1992 "Mozart and the Oboe," *Early Music* 20, no. 1 (Feb.): 43–62; trans. Marc Ecochard as "Le hautbois de Mozart," in *La Lettre du hautboïste* 1 (1999): 44–51.

1992 *Music for Oboe: A Bibliography*, 2nd ed., rev. ed. (Berkeley: Fallen Leaf Press). Available online at www.haynes-catalog.net

1992 "Willkommene Bereicherung des Oboen-Repertoires," *Tibia* 17, no. 2 (2/92): 158–60.

1993 "Von Mozart zu Beethovens Neunter: Die technische Entwicklung der Oboe zwischen 1790 und 1830," *Tibia* 18, no. 4 (4/93): 15–18.

1994 "The Addition of Keys to the Oboe, 1790–1830," *JIDRS* 22:31–46. (A modified version of previous entry).

1994 "Cornetts and Historical Pitch Standards," *Historic Brass Society Journal* 6:84–109.

1994 "Pitch in Northern Italy in the 16th and 17th Centuries," *Recercare* 6:41–60.

1995 "Pitch Standards in the Baroque and Classical Periods," PhD diss., Université de Montréal.

1996 "Hautboy Taxonomy," *FoMRHIQ*, no. 83:29

1997 "Changing Images of the Hautboy in the Seventeenth, Eighteenth, and Early Nineteenth Centuries," in *A Time of Questioning: Proceedings of the International Early Double-reed Symposium, Utrecht 1994*, ed. David Lasocki (Utrecht: STIMU): 67–88.

1997 Comments on Matthew Cron's article "In Defense of Altenburg: The Pitch and Form of Foreign Trumpets," *Historic Brass Society Journal* 8 (1996), in *HBSJ* 9:206–10.

1997 "Das Fingervibrato (*Flattement*) auf Holzblasinstrumenten im 17., 18. und 19. Jahrhundert," *Tibia* 22, no. 2 (2/97): 401–7; 22, no. 3 (3/97): 481–87.

1997 "Der Hautboy (1630–1800)," in "Oboe," in *Die Musik in Geschichte und Gegenwart*, vol. 7: cols. 510–24, 2nd ed. (Kassel: Bärenreiter).

1997 "New Light on Some French Relatives of the Hautboy in the 17th and Early 18th Centuries: the Cromorne, *hautbois de Poitou*, and *chalumeau simple*," in *Sine musica nulla vita: Festschrift Hermann Moeck zum 75. Geburtstag am 16. September 1997*, ed. Nikolaus Delius (Celle: Moeck): 257–70.

1997   "Playing 'Short' High Notes on the Hautboy," *JIDRS* 25: 115–18.

1997   "Tu ru or not Tu ru: Paired Syllables and Unequal Tonguing Patterns on Woodwinds in the Seventeenth and Eighteenth Centuries," *Performance Practice Review* 10, no. 1:41–60.

1998   "Stimmton," in *Die Musik in Geschichte und Gegenwart*, vol. 8: cols. 1814–31, 2nd ed. (Kassel: Bärenreiter).

1998   'Versuch der Rekonstruktion eines spielbaren Oboenrohres nach dem Maßangaben von James Talbot," *Tibia* 23, no. 3 (1998): 191–96.

1999   "Pitch" and other related articles, *J. S. Bach*, Oxford Composer Companions, ed. Malcolm Boyd (Oxford University Press).

2000   "Oboe," "Oboe d'amore," and "Stimmtonhöhe" in *Bachs Orchestermusik*, ed. Siegbert Rampe & Dominik Sackmann (Kassel: Bärenreiter).

2000   "A Reconstruction of Talbot's Hautboy Reed," *GSJ* 53: 78–86 (revised version of "Versuch der Rekonstruktion," 1998).

2000   "'Sweeter than Hautbois': Towards a Conception of the Schalmey of the Baroque Period," *JAMIS* 26: 57–82.

2001   *The Eloquent Oboe: A History of the Hautboy, 1640 to 1760* (Oxford University Press; paperback ed., 2007), German trans. as *Die gleichsam redende Hoboe*, by Carin van Heerden (Weikersheim: Margraf, forthcoming 2015).

2001   "Die Entwicklung des Hautboys im Wandel der Stile," *Tibia* 26, no. 4 (4/2001): 629–35.

2001   "Flattement," "Hautboy," "Historical pitch standards," "Intonation," and "Schwartzenberg dit Le Noble," in *The New Grove Dictionary of Music and Musical Instruments*, ed. Stanley Sadie, 2nd ed. (London: Macmillan).

2002   "Die Anciuti-Hülse," *Tibia* 27, no. 3 (3/2002): 188–90.

2002   *A History of Performing Pitch: The Story of "A."* (Lanham, MD: Scarecrow Press).

2002   "Die Kunst des Präludierens auf Holzblasinstrumenten im 18. Jahrhundert," *Tibia* 27, no. 2 (2/2002): 91–93; letter to the editor, 27, no. 4 (4/2002): 317.

2003   "The King's Chamber Pitch," *Early Music Performer*, no. 12 (Aug.): 13–25; in French as "Le ton de la Chambre du Roy," *Recherches sur la musique française classique* 31 (2004–7): 93–125.

2003   "Oboe," in *The Harvard Dictionary of Music*, ed. Don M. Randel, 4th ed. (Cambridge, MA: Harvard University Press): 575–76.

2004   (with Geoffrey Burgess) *The Oboe* (New Haven: Yale University Press).

2005   "Baptiste's Hautbois: The Metamorphosis from Shawm to Hautboy in France, 1620–1670," in *From Renaissance to Baroque: Change* in *Instruments and Instrumental Music in the Seventeenth Century.* Proceedings of the National Early Music Association Conference Held, in Association with the Department of Music, University of York and the York Early Music Festival, at the University College of Ripon and York St. John, York, 2–4 July 1999, ed. Jonathan Wainwright and Peter Holman (Aldershot: Ashgate): 23–46.

2007 "The Accommodating Recorder," in *Recorders Based on Historical Models: Fred Morgan—Writings and Memories,* compiled by Gisela Rothe (Fulda: Mollenhauer), 119–27.

2007 *The End of Early Music: A Period Performer's History of Music for the Twenty-First Century* (Oxford University Press). Major reviews in more than twelve publications.

2008 "A Correctly-Attributed Fake," *Performance Practice Review* 13 (online: available from ccdl.libraries.claremont.edu/collection.php?alias=/ppr).

2009 "Un faux aussi vrai que son modèle," booklet article for CD *Musiques pour un musée: La Couture-Boussey* (Association des Amis du Musée La Couture-Boussey).

Posthumous

Althea of Tarsia, pastiche opera based on the music of J. S. Bach.

Works about Haynes

Published reviews of his books are too numerous to list.

1973 Lee McRae, "Bruce Haynes: Performer, Instrument Maker and Teacher," *American Recorder* 14, no. 2:46–50.

1995 Aaron Cohen, "Bruce Haynes: Oboe-ologist," *DR* 18, no. 3:77–82.

2005 Marc Ecochard, "Une conversation avec Bruce Haynes," *La Lettre du hautboïste* 16: 14–17.

2012 Geoffrey Burgess, "Piper at the Gates of Dawn; Bruce Haynes: Legendary Pioneer of the Hautboy," *DR* 35 no. 1:65–108.

Discography

1972 J. B. Lully: *Le bourgeois gentilhomme.* La Petite Bande, dir. Gustav Leonhardt. Deutsche Harmonia Mundi HM20320–21; re-released on DHM 7576312 (2010).

1972–88   J. S. Bach: *Das Kantatenwerk* (Complete cantatas). Leonhardt Consort, dir. Leonhardt. Teldec/Das Alte Werk. Haynes played on most volumes featuring the Leonhardt Consort (beginning with vol. 6). Notable solos include BWV 100/5 (oboe d'amore) and 187/3. Haynes and Ku Ebbinge made great oboe partners, whether on oboe or oboe d'amore, and often traded places; even where they did not, Bach's writing afforded them both almost equal opportunities. Listen to: BWV 88/3, 5; 113/3; 117; 133/3; 134/2; 135/3; 176/5; 187/3, 5.

1973   André Campra: *L'Europe galante* (suite). La Petite Bande, dir. Leonhardt. Deutsche Harmonia Mundi 25 21954–2 (1974); re-released on DHM 7576312 (2010)

1973   J. S. Bach: *Weihnachts Oratorium*. Collegium Aureum, dir. G. Schmidt-Gaden. DHM/BASF 59 21749.3; re-released on BMG 77046–2–RG (1989).

1973   F. Couperin: *Concerts royaux, Nouveaux concerts,* etc. Kuijken Ensemble. Seon/Philips AX–67045/2; *L'Apothéose de Lully* re-released on Sony SEON 62941 (1997).

1973   G. F. Handel: *Sämtliche Sonaten für ein Blasinstrument und Basso Continuo/Complete Sonatas for Wind Instruments*. With Frans Brüggen, Anner Bijlsma, Bob van Asperen, Hansjürg Lange. Seon/Philips ABCL–67005/3 (1974); re-released on Sony Classical SEON 60100 (1998).

1975   G. Muffat: *Concerti & Suiten*. La Petite Bande, dir. Sigiswald Kuijken. Deutsche Harmonia Mundi 25 22086–9; re-released on DHM 77074–2–RG (1991).

1975–76   F. Couperin: *Pièces de clavecin (pièces croisées)*. Alan Curtis (harpsichord), Frans Brüggen (traverso), Lucy van Dael (violin) EMI 1C 151–30750–51 (1977); re-released on Virgin Veritas 385 806 2 (2007).

1977   G. F. Handel: *Admeto*. Complesso Barocco, dir. Curtis, EMI 1C 163 30 808 (1978), re-released on Virgin Veritas 7243 661369 2 2 (1997).

1977   Jacques Hotteterre: *Première flutiste français* (2 discs). With Frans Brüggen (traverso), Gustav Leonhardt (harpsichord), Kuijken Ensemble et al. Seon RL 30425; re-released on Sony SEON 62942 (1997).

1977   J.-P. Rameau: *Zaïs*. La Petite Bande, dir. Leonhardt. STIL 1010577 (1979); re-released on STIL 1010SAN77 (1993).

1978   J. S. Bach: *Cantatas 82 and 56*. With Max van Egmond, Members of the Orchestra of the 18th Century, dir. Brüggen. Seon/RCA RL 30387AW; re-released on Sony SEON SBK60373.

1979   G. F. Handel: *Partenope*. La Petite Bande, dir. Kuijken. Deutsche Harmonia Mundi, 4PAL–4000; Pro-Arte; 1C 157–99 855—1C 157–99 858. re-released on Sony 7529972 (2009).

1979   Philidor, Dornel, Marais: *Concerts en symphonie*. Philidor Ensemble: Ku Ebbinge (oboe), Ricardo Kanji (recorder and traverso), Wilbert Hazelzet (traverso), Christopher Farr (harpsichord), Danny Bond (bassoon). Philips 9502 104.

1979   J.-P. Rameau. Suite from *Hippolyte et Aricie*. La Petite Bande, dir. Kuijken. Deutsche Harmonia Mundi 1 C 065–99 837; re-released on DHM 7709-2-RG (1990).

1979   Vivaldi, Marcello, Platti: *Concerti per oboe*. Baroque Orchestra, dir. Brüggen. Seon/RCA RL 30371; re-released on Sony SEON 62945 (1997).

1981   J. S. Bach: Orchestral Suites. La Petite Bande, dir. Kuijken. Deutsche Harmonia Mundi 1C 165–99 930; re-released on Pro Arte 2PAD–205 (1983), DHM 7708-2-RG (1990), & Musical Heritage Society 523889W (1995).

1984   G. F. Handel: *Theatre Music for Woodwinds*. Philidor Ensemble. Philips Living Baroque 412 048-1.

1985   G. F. Handel. Concerto for Oboe in G minor, *Apollo e Dafne*. Judith Nelson (soprano), David Thomas (bass), Philharmonia Baroque Orchestra, dir. Nicolas McGegan. Harmonia Mundi HMC 5157, *Apollo e Dafne* re-released on Harmonia Mundi 2907348 (2003).

1987   J.-P. Rameau. *Les surprises de l'amour*. Les Musiciens du Louvre, dir. Marc Minkowski, recorded in the Barbarini Palace, Rome, 1987. Musifrance 245 004-2.

1998   J. S. Bach. *Concerti for Oboe d'amore, Arias with Countertenor*. With Daniel Taylor (countertenor). Atma ACD 2 2158. Concerto in A for oboe d'amore BWV1055, Concerto in D for oboe d'amore BWV 1053 (both reconstructed by Haynes), arias from cantatas 116, 147, B-minor Mass, and Easter Oratorio; Concerti re-released on *Naturally Bach*, ATMA 3007 (2008).

1998   F. Couperin. *Concerts royaux* and *Les goûts-réünis*. With Arthur Haas (harpsichord) and Susie Napper (gamba). Recorded partially on original Naust hautboy, ATMA ACD 2 2168; memorial re-release, 2011.

2005   G. F. Handel, *Musick for the Royal Fireworks*. Festival Montréal Baroque, dir. Matthias Maute, ATMA Classique 2–2367.

2012   J. S. Bach, *Nouveaux "Brandenbourgeois"* reconstructed by Bruce Haynes, Bande Montréal Baroque, dir. Eric Milnes, ATMA 2526.

NOTES

Foreword: Aus der Tiefen

1. Interview, *American Recorder* 15/3 (1974): 72.
2. Letter, Bruce Haynes to Frans Brüggen, 15 July 1982.
3. Others voiced similar opinions. See Zaslaw's comments on "increased professionalism and commercialism" in his editorial, *Early Music*, 20 no. 2 (1992): 194.
4. See in particular Taruskin, "The Pastness of the Present and the Presence of the Past," in *Text & Act*, ch. 4.
5. This also applies to texts like Quantz's and C. P. E. Bach's *Versuche* where modern editions exist, but which we feel in many cases have specific shortcomings that misrepresent the authors' intended meaning.
6. Boyden, *History of Violin Playing*, 2.
7. *The Notation is not the Music*, 32.

Preface: Pipe Dreams

1. Haynes, *The Eloquent Oboe*, xi.
2. Wilson, *Roger North on Music*, xxiv.
3. Quantz, *Versuch einer Anleitung die Flöte traversiere zu Spielen*, Preface.
4. Vickers, "Rhetorical and Anti-Rhetorical Tropes," 109; emphasis added.
5. Rifkin, in *Inside Early Music*, 388.
6. Interview, *American Recorder* 15, no. 3 (1974): 72.

Introduction: The Eloquent Musician

1. Galilei, *Dialogo della musica antica et della moderna*, §90, trans. 225.
2. *English Literature in the Sixteenth Century*, 61.
3. Aristotle, *Rhetoric*, 1.2.
4. Fénelon, *Dialogues sur l'éloquence*, 63.
5. Ibid., citing Plato.
6. Ibid.
7. Ong, *Orality and Literacy*, 1, 3.
8. Jensen, *Signs and Meaning*, 18.
9. My discussion is indebted to Jensen, *Signs and Meaning*, 21–24.
10. See George Buelow, "Rhetoric and Music" in *NGD*.
11. Interview, *American Recorder*, 15/3 (1975): 73.
12. Batteaux, *Cours de belles lettres*, trans. 4:21.
13. Quantz, *Versuch*, ch.11 § 1.

14. Batteux, *Les Beaux-Arts*, 262; trans. 1:180.
15. *Fanny Hill*, 286.
16. *Oxford English Dictionary (OED)*, definition 1b of the adjective "pathetic" (obsolete).
17. Ibid.
18. s.v. "*Pathopoeia*."
19. Batteux, *Cours de belles lettres*, 4:43–44; trans. 4:42.
20. Quantz, *Versuch*, ch. 11 § 1.
21. Ibid., ch. 17, vii § 25. In this passage Quantz recommends using dynamic shading to constantly maintain the listener's attention.
22. Batteux, *Cours de belles lettres*, 4:41; trans. 4:39–40, quoting Cicero (*De Oratore*).
23. Marissen, "On the Musical Theology."
24. Dubos, *Réflexions critiques*, trans 1:656, citing Cicero "pro Archia."
25. Ibid., 1:634–3; trans. 1:360.
26. Its earliest occurrence is in Horace's *Ars Poetica*. 5. 361. Cf. Gay, *The Enlightenment*, 162–63.
27. Quoted by Rousseau in *Dictionnaire*, trans s.v. "Contrary Sense."
28. Wolfgang Mozart, in a letter of 1778, quoted in Marshall, *Mozart Speaks*, 201.
29. Mace, *Musick's Monument*, 147. Cf. Mace's meaning of "Humour" discussed in ch. 5.
30. Batteux, *Les Beaux-Arts*, 264; trans. 1:182n.
31. Mattheson, *Vollkommene Capellmeister*, 2, ch.5 § 74–78, trans. 109.
32. Rousseau, *Dictionnaire*, s.v. "Exécution."
33. Fénelon, *Dialogues sur l'éloquence*, 63, citing Plato.
34. Quantz, *Versuch*, ch.11 § 21.
35. Burney, *The Present State of Music*, 2:157.
36. *Weapons*, iii, 9ff.

Chapter 1: In the Realm of the Passions

1. *Der General-Bass*, trans., 310.
2. Preface to Claudio's *Scherzi musicali* (1607), see Ossi, *Divining the Oracle*, ch. 1.
3. Letter to his father, 13 October 1781, quoted in Marshall, *Mozart Speaks*, 239.
4. See Palisca, *Music and Ideas*, 180–81.
5. *Vita del facondo poeta volgare Serafino Aquilano*, quoted in Smith, *The Performance of 16th-century Music*, 131.
6. Quoted in Dunning, "Musica reservata (i)," *NGD*.
7. *Solitaire second*, quoted in Walker, "Musical Humanism," 112–13.
8. Timotheus's musical prowess features in writings from the first and second century AD by Lucian and Dio Chrysostom. This quotation is from Isherwood, *Music in the Service of the King*, 12.
9. See for instance, Mattheson, *Vollkommene Capellmeister*, 1, ch. 3 § 44–48.
10. Palisca, *The Florentine Camerata*, 50.
11. Ibid., 57.
12. See Hilse, "The Treatises of Christoph Bernhard," 35.
13. Walker, "Musical Humanism." 9.
14. Mattheson, *Vollkommene Capellmeister*, 2 ch. 14, §14–43.
15. See Dahlhaus, *Aesthetics of Music*, ch. 4, and Buelow, *History*, 50.
16. Mattick, *Eighteenth-Century Aesthetics*, 15.
17. Hummel, *A Complete Theoretical and Practical Course*, 54.
18. The analogy is borrowed from Winn, *Unsuspected Eloquence*, 239.
19. Baillot, *Méthode de violoncelle*, 1, 6, trans. based on Le Guin at http://epub.library.ucla.edu/leguin/boccherini./section17.htm, accessed 29 April 2014. See also Le Guin, *Boccherini's Body*, 78–79.
20. Quoted in Dahlhaus, *Absolute Music*, 69.
21. The *OED* dates the first use of the term in this sense to 1832.
22. Pepys, *Diary*, 27 February 1668. The play was *The Virgin Martyr* by Thomas Dekker and Philip Messinger. The music is apparently lost.

23. See annotations by Jacob Wilhelm Lustig to his 1773 Dutch translation of Burney's *Present State of Music in Germany . . .*, quoted in Zaslaw, "Ornaments for Corelli's Violin Sonatas," 111.
24. See, for instance, Kivy, *The Fine Art of Repetition*, 233.
25. Cited in translation in Montagu, *The Expression of the Passions*, 79.
26. *Poetics* ch. 4; as quoted in Dubos, *Critical Reflections*, 1:24.
27. Mattheson, *Vollkommene Capellmeister*, 1 ch. 3 § 79.
28. Wilson, *Roger North on Music*, 118 and Plate 5.
29. Ibid., 129n38.
30. Batteux, *Les Beaux-Arts*, 280; trans. 1:191. Italics added.
31. Mattheson, *Vollkommene Capellmeister*, 1, ch. 3 § 75; 3, ch. 9 § 38.
32. Avison, *Essay on Musical Expression*, 19. For other references to this idea, see Morley, *Plaine and Easie Introduction*, 177; Batteux, *Les Beaux-Arts*, 3, trans. 1:19; and Rousseau, *Dictionary*, 161.
33. W.A. Mozart, letter to his father, 26 September 1781, cited in Donington, *Interpretation*, 116.
34. Mace, *Musick's Monument*, 118.
35. Abrams, *Mirror and the Lamp*, 94.
36. Pater, "The School of Giorgione," *The Renaissance: Studies in Art and Poetry*, 135.
37. Letter to Marc-André Souchay, 15 October 1842, trans. G. Selden-Goth in Mendelssohn-Bartholdy, *Letters*, 313–14.
38. Stravinsky, *Autobiography*, 53.
39. Burkholder, "Rule Breaking," 378.
40. Baillot, *Méthode de violoncelle*, 6, trans. based on Le Guin at http://epub.library.ucla.edu/leguin/boccherini./section17.htm, accessed 29 April 2014.
41. Lévi-Strauss, *The Raw and the Cooked*, 18.
42. Jensen, *Signs and Meaning*, 32–33.
43. Fénelon, *Dialogues*, trans. 81.
44. Batteux, *Les Beaux-Arts*, 7; trans. 1:31.
45. *De Oratoria*, quoted by Mason, *An Essay on Elocution*, 31.
46. Harnoncourt, *Baroque Music Today*, 39 (original emphasis).

Chapter 2: The Principles of Rhetoric

1. *The Raw and the Cooked*, 18.
2. Mattheson, *Vollkommene Capellmeister* 2, ch. 4 § 3–5.
3. Marshall, *Compositional Process*, 1: 237–8, quoted in Gardiner, *Bach*, 205.
4. Mattheson, *Vollkommene Capellmeister*, 2, ch. 4 § 14.
5. Reynolds, *Discourse* no. 2 (1769).
6. Wilson, *Roger North on Music*, 141–42.
7. As quoted in Sherman, *Inside Early Music*, 383–86.
8. Mattheson, *Vollkommene Capelmeister*, 2, ch. 14, §14–24.
9. *Les Beaux-Arts*, trans. 1:179.
10. Avison, *An Essay on Musical Expression*, 67.
11. *The Garden of Eloquence*, s.v. "Figures."
12. From the Grimm Brothers' recounting of the story of Rumplestiltskin.
13. *Dictionnaire de l'Académie française*, s.v. "Figure."
14. Gottsched, *Ausführliche Redekunst*, 273.
15. Bartel, *Musica Poetica*, 72.
16. Ibid. Buelow, in "Figures, theory of musical" in *NGD* provides a somewhat different classification.
17. On the distinction between these terms, and particularly the use of *hypotyposis* in both verbal and musical rhetoric to describe "an image rather than express an affection," see Bartel, *Musica Poetica*, 196–98, 307–8.
18. Quoted in Gardiner, *Bach*, 131.
19. Dubos, *Réflexions critiques*, 1:33, trans. 1:234.
20. Fénelon, *Dialogues sur l'éloquence*, trans. 80, 74. Rameau also used the verb *peindre* in this sense. See his *Observations sur notre instinct*, 99, and *Erreurs sur la musique*, 49–51.

21. Vogt, *Concluave thesari magnae artis musicae*, 1719, trans. from Gardiner, *Bach*, 131.
22. Montagu, *Expression of the Passions*, 1.
23. The core of the important art collection, the Gemäldegalerie Alte Meister in Dresden, was assembled in the eighteenth century by the Electors of Saxony, see Siebel, *Glory of Baroque Dresden*.
24. Descartes, *Passions de l'âme*, trans. 52. Descartes's term *admiratio* (L.) or *admiration* (Fr.) is difficult to render in English. Fascination is perhaps the best translation, but wonder has been favored in the standard English versions.
25. Another arrangement with positive and negative passions organized symmetrically around love was proposed by Franz Lang in his *Theatrum affectum humanorum* of 1717 (see Leisinger, "Affections, Rhetoric, and Musical Expression," 191).
26. Huret, *Optique de portraiture et peinture* (Paris, 1670) trans. from Montagu, *Expression of the Passions*, 79.
27. Further discussed in Montagu, *Expression of the Passions*, 30.
28. André Félibien, *Les Reines de Perse aux pieds d'Alexandre*, trans., 15.
29. Ibid., 17.
30. Ibid., 19.
31. Juslin, "From Mimesis to Catharsis," 92.
32. Wilson, *Roger North on Music*, 139–40.
33. Buelow, "Johann Mattheson and the Invention of the Affektenlehre."
34. Mattheson, *Vollkommene Capellmeister*, 1, ch. 3 § 60–83.
35. Ibid., 1, ch. 3 § 60.
36. Ibid., 1, ch. 3 § 66.
37. Ratner, *Classic Music*, 9–27.
38. *Plaine & Easie Introduction*, 147.
39. Mattheson, *Neu-eröffnete Orchestre*, 231–53.
40. Quantz, *Versuch*, ch. 14 §6.
41. Türk argued that the frequent transpositions made necessary by pitch differences showed that specific key characteristics did not exist (*Klavierschule*, 381–82). For further details on the pitch levels used by J.S. Bach, see Haynes, *The History of Performing Pitch*.
42. Lehmann, "Bach's Extraordinary Temperament."
43. See Siegele, *Kompositionsweise und Bearbeitungstechnik*, 118–21.
44. Moroney, "Listening to and Playing *The Well-Tempered Clavier*," Cal Performances, program notes, 24 October 2009, 25.
45. On the evolving definition of modulation, see Ranum, *The Harmonic Orator*, 14–18, and Verba, "Rameau's View on *Modulation*," 470–72.
46. Heinichen, *Der General-Bass*, 84
47. Burmeister, *Musica Poetica*, quoted in Tarling, *Weapons*, 192.
48. Bartel, *Musica Poetica*, viii.
49. Buelow, "Rhetoric and Music," *NGD*, Buelow "Johann Mattheson and the invention of the Affektenlehre."
50. Our approach is supported by Vickers, *Rhetorica*, 1–44.

Chapter 3: Bach's Expressive Universe

1. Quoted in David, Mendel, and Wolff, *The New Bach Reader*, 336.
2. *Zufällige Gedanken von der Kirchen-Music*. Trans. as "Random Thoughts about Church Music," in Baron, *Bach's Changing World*, 233.
3. Paris, 1694, s.v. "Expression"; online version at University of Chicago ARTFL Project.
4. Quoted in Palisca, *Music and Ideas*, 59; trans. from Strunk, *Source Readings*, 28–29.
5. *L'art de parler*, trans., 2:134.
6. See, for instance Jensen, *Signs and Meaning*, 32–33.
7. Schweitzer, *J. S. Bach*, 2:4.
8. Ibid., 2:50.
9. Ibid., 2:3ff, 46; Spitta, *Johann Sebastian Bach*.
10. Schweitzer, *J. S. Bach*, 2:26.

11. Ibid., 2:122.
12. Rameau, *Traité de l'harmonie*, 162–63.
13. David, Mendel, and Wolff, *New Bach Reader*, 18.
14. Bartel, *Musica Poetica*.
15. Schweitzer, *J. S. Bach* 2:17.
16. Adapted from David, Mendel, and Wolff, *New Bach Reader*, 16–17.
17. This argument is made by Marrissen in *Social and Religious Designs*.
18. Leaver, "Religion and Religious Currents," 133.
19. Gottfried Ephraim Scheibel, *Zufällige Gedanken*, quoted in Baron, *Bach's Changing World*, 232.
20. The striking similarities in the facial expressions in images in sacred and secular subjects has been noted by Montagu in *The Expression of the Passions*.
21. See report of his altercation with the bassoonist Johann Heinrich Geyersbach in David, Mendel, and Wolff, *New Bach Reader*, 43–46, and Gardiner, *Bach*, 172–74.
22. See Brown, "Tumultuous Philosophers," 41.
23. Both Mattheson and Scheibel advocated using female singers in church, see Baron, *Bach's Changing World*, 118.
24. McClary has discussed this cantata in "The Blasphemy of Talking Politics during Bach Year."
25. In the earliest known version of this aria (BWV 36c/7, 1725) Bach specified viola d'amore in place of violin as the obbligato instrument. Even without the indication of being muted, the viola d'amore was thought of as appropriately muted and weak, as Bach routinely substituted violin *con sordino* for it (see also various versions of mvts. 20, 21 in the St. John Passion). For another version dating from 1735 (BWV 36b) with a new parody text "Mit zarten und vergnügten Trieben" (With tender and delighted impulses), Bach replaced the muted violin with a solo flute.
26. Dürr, *Cantatas of J. S. Bach*, 335.
27. Bacilly, *L'art de bien chanter*, 59; Dubos, *Réflexions critiques* 1:43; trans. 1:168.
28. Batteux, *Les Beaux-Arts*, 266, trans. 1:182.
29. Gardiner, *Bach*, 122.
30. Wilson, *Roger North on Music*, 113.
31. Ibid.
32. *Critica Musica* (Hamburg, 1725), 368, quoted in trans. in Stauffer, "Bach and the Big City," 248–49.
33. Dubos, *Réflexions critiques*, 1:45, trans. 1:373–74.

Chapter 4: Bach's Inner World

1. *Musicalische Patriot*, trans. from Irwin, "Bach in the Midst of Religious Transition," 119.
2. Batteux, *Cours de belles letttres*, 4:46; trans. 4:45.
3. Cf. Kelly, who affirms the one-affect theory in *Early Music*, 50–51.
4. Quantz, *Versuch*, ch. 11 §15.
5. C. G. Körner, "Über Charakterdarstellung in der Musik," *Die Hören* 5 (1795): 99, quoted in Treitler, *Music and the Historical Imagination*, 183.
6. Discussed in Montagu, *Expression of the Passions*, 82.
7. Dammann, *Der Musikbegriff im deutschen Barock* (Cologne: A. Volk, 1967) quoted in Bartel, *Musica Poetica*, 38.
8. Vogt, *Conclave thesauri magnae artis musicae* (Prague: G. Labaun, 1719): 144, trans. from Bartel, *Musica Poetica*, 128.
9. *Critica Musica* (Hamburg: the author, 1722–25): 104, quoted in translation in Leisinger, "Affections, Rhetoric, and Musical Expression," 188.
10. Rousseau, *Dictionnaire*, s.v. "Air."
11. Mattheson *Vollkomene Capellmeister*, 1, ch. 3 § 71.
12. See Leaver, *J. S. Bach and Scripture*.
13. See Moens-Haenen, "Holzbläservibrato," 2; Harnoncourt, *Baroque Music Today*, 128. Cf. the "slurred tremolo" in Boyden, *History*, 266–68.
14. Adopted from Tisch-Wackernagel, "Baroque," 1:35.
15. Ibid.

16. Scherer, "Temporal and Eternal Realities," 158.
17. Published posthumously in *Flemings Teutsche Poemata*, 1:32–3.
18. Schweitzer, *J. S. Bach*, 2:113. For more on the *corta*, see Bartel, *Musica Poetica*, 234. Some theorists distinguished *recta* and *inversa* varieties of *corta*, this being the former.
19. Mattheson, *Veritophili Deutliche Beweis-Gründe Worauf*, trans. from Irwin, *Foretastes of Heaven*, 33–34.
20. Gardiner, *Bach*, 321.
21. Quantz, *Versuch*, ch. 17, 7 §13.
22. For more on the relationship between overture and demon dances, see Burgess, "A l'ouverture des enfers."

Chapter 5: Enhancing Eloquence

1. *Reflexions historiques et critiques*, trans., 3.
2. *De Oratoria*, 11.3.5. trans. Russell.
3. Quantz, *Versuch*, ch. 17 §1.
4. Mattheson, *Vollkommene Capellmeister*, 2, ch. 4 § 62.
5. Kuijken, *The Notation is not the Music*, 10.
6. Quantz, *Versuch*, ch. 17 §2.
7. Schuller, *The Compleat Conductor*.
8. Leech-Wilkinson, *Changing Sound of Music*, ch. 2, para. 30.
9. On this point, see ibid., para. 32.
10. Quantz, *Versuch*, ch. 11 § 2.
11. Bach, *Versuch*, 1, ch. 3 §2; trans. p. 148. Our translation. The page numbers to Mitchell's translation are provided as a guide to English readers wanting to contextualize the quotations.
12. Diderot, *Paradoxe*, 111.
13. Leech-Wilkinson, *Changing Sound*, ch. 6, para. 26.
14. Wimsatt and Beardsley, "The Intentional Fallacy," 468.
15. "The Death of the Author" is the title of Barthes's article published in *Aspen*, 1967.
16. Fénelon, *Dialogues*, trans. 72.
17. Vickers, "Rhetorical and Anti-Rhetorical Tropes," 108.
18. Praetorius, *Syntagma musicum*, 3:231, trans. 215–16.
19. Mace, *Musick's Monument*, 130–32. We have adopted Mace's usage where "humour" refers to character or temperament, and "humor" is used to mean comedy or amusement.
20. Rémond de Saint-Albine, *Le comédien*, 32.
21. Mace, *Musick's Monument*, 130–32.
22. Trans. based on Le Guin available at http://epub.library.ucla.edu/leguin/Boccherini/contents.htm (accessed 9 September 2013). "Sonate, que me veux-tu?" makes reference to a touchstone of expression in eighteenth-century France attributed to Bernard Le Bovier de Fontenelle (1657–1757) that encapsulated the French attitude to the empty expression of Italian instrumental music.
23. Vial (*The Art of Musical Phrasing*, 142) and Le Guin (*Boccherini's Body*) discuss the discrepancies between Cambini's interpretation and expectations based on early music training in greater detail.
24. Le Guin, *Boccherini's Body*, 87.
25. Haydn's tune was published with this text in ca. 1784 as *A Prelude to Auld Robin Gray: Jemmy and Jenny's farewell!*
26. Le Moine, *Romance du Fat dupé*, 1787.
27. Praetorius, *Syntagma musicum*, 3:112, trans. from Bartel, *Musica Poetica*, 47.
28. See Bartel, *Musica Poetica*, 47, and Dammann, *Der Musikbegriff im deutschen Baroque*, 310.
29. Mattheson, *Vollkommene Capellmeister*, 2, ch. 12 §34.
30. Bacilly, *L'art de bien chanter*, 200–201.
31. Wentz, "Gesture, Affect, and Rhythmic Freedom," 78.
32. Grimarest, quoted in Chaouche, *Sept Traités*, 356.
33. See Fuller, "The Performer as Composer," 120.
34. Mattheson, *Vollkommene Capellmeister*, 2, ch. 12 §32.
35. Quantz, *Versuch*, ch. 17, vii §58.

36. Ibid., ch. 14 §22.
37. Quintilian, *De Oratoria*, 11, ch. 3.
38. Le Faucheur, *Traité de l'action de l'orateur*, 82–83.
39. Mace, *Musick's Monument*, 130–32.
40. Ibid., 147.
41. Ibid., 133.

Chapter 6: Figures: Spinning Straw into Gold

1. This anonymous inscription appears over a portal leading into one of the buildings of the University of Amsterdam.
2. "C. P. E. Bach's Aesthetic," 63.
3. Elizabeth Tolbert writes about the Karelian women's lament in "The Voice of Lament."
4. See Bowen, "Finding the Music in Musicology," 428–30.
5. Bach, *Versuch*, 1, ch. 3 §13, trans., 152.
6. Darbellay, "C. P. E. Bach's Aesthetic," 54.
7. Seymour, "Oratory and Performance," 919.
8. Bacilly, *L'art de bien chanter*, 253.
9. *OED*; see also *Dictionnaire de L'Académie française*, 1st ed., 196. Cf. Chaouche ed. *Sept traités*, 823, and Tarling, *Weapons*, 10.
10. d'Aubignac, *La Pratique du théâtre* (Amsterdam: Bernard, 1715): 443, cited in Montagu, *Expression of the Passions*, 53.
11. Dubos, *Réflexions critiques*, 1:42, trans. 1:341.
12. Ibid., 1:33; trans. 1:229.
13. Longfellow, *Poems of Places*, France, 1:183.
14. De Brosses, *Lettres d'Italie*, 58:497 (1739–40), trans. by Scholes in his edition of Burney, *Present State of Music*, 1:58.
15. See Haynes, *Music for Oboe*, "Bessozzi."
16. Fénelon, *Dialogues*, trans. 78.
17. Quantz, *Versuch*, ch. 11 § 18, § 15.
18. Mattheson, *Vollkommene Capellmesiter*, 2, ch. 3 §20ff; see Donington, *Interpretation*, ch. 7 for a discussion of the performer's responsibilities when adding ornaments.
19. Gjerdingen, *Music in the Galant Style*.
20. Beaussant, *Lully ou le musicien du soleil*, 198.
21. Bacilly, *L'art de bien chanter*, 135.
22. L. Mozart, *Versuch*, ch. 9 §1; Eng. trans., 166.
23. Wilson, *Roger North on Music*, 150.
24. Mattheson, *Vollkommene Capellmeister*, 2, ch. 3 § 8.
25. Neumann referred to the "Platonic ideal" of each ornament—the essence of each grace that lies behind the variations of execution ("Introduction," *Ornamentation*, 10).
26. MS quoted in Donington, *Interpretation of Early Music*, 155.
27. Couperin, *L'art de toucher le clavecin*, 23.
28. Montéclair, *Principes de musique*, 78.
29. In 1678 Printz treated figures and graces as identical. See Bartel, *Musica Poetica*, 121.
30. Fielding, *Tom Jones* (1749), Book 18, ch. 3. Cited in *OED* as a noteworthy use of "expression" in this sense.
31. Cf. Palisca, *Music and Ideas*, 227.
32. Tarling cites a striking example published by Erasmus in 1523–26 of two hundred figurative variations on a simple statement (*Weapons*, 194–95).
33. Marshall, *Compositional Process of J. S. Bach*, 1:171.
34. Letter, January 1738. Quoted in *Bach Dokumente*, 2:304, trans. from David, Mendel, and Wolff, *New Bach Reader*, 343.
35. See Bartel, *Musica Poetica*, 113.
36. Quoted in in Palisca, *Music and Ideas*, 228.
37. Printz, *Musica modulatoria vocalis* (Schweidnitz: C. Okel, 1678): 42, quoted in Butt, *Bach Interpretation*, 17.

38. One of the definitions of "figure" in the *OED* is "a form of expression deviating from the normal arrangement or use of words, which are adopted in order to give beauty, variety, or force."
39. Quantz, *Versuch*, ch. 17, vi § 12.
40. Ibid., 17, vi § 15. This is discussed more extensively in Haynes, *End of Early Music*, 196–99, which also reproduces Quantz's Adagio with detailed dynamics.
41. Bach, *Versuch*, 1, ch. 3 § 7; trans., 150.
42. Quantz, *Versuch*, ch. 18 § 11
43. Darbellay, "C. P. E. Bach's Aesthetic as Reflected in his Notation," 52.
44. Bacilly, *L'art de bien chanter*, article 5, 199–204. Bacilly used the term *agrémens* to refer not only to ornaments shown with symbols—both essential and non-essential, but also certain particular techniques that give expression to vocal declamation through special techniques such as prolonged consonants, exaggerated voicing of vowels, etc.
45. Quantz, *Versuch*, ch. 11 § 15
46. Geminiani, *Art of Playing on the Violin*, 6–8.
47. Stowell described Geminiani's close shake as "essentially a continuous vibrato in the approved modern fashion" ("Strings," 245).
48. Geminiani, *Art of Playing on the Violin*, 8. The italicized passage was omitted in later printings of the book.
49. See Hickman, "The Censored Publications," 73.
50. Kuijken has questioned the assumption that vibrato was used on a regular basis to enhance the *messa di voce*, but brings only one piece of evidence to support his case (*Notation is not the Music*, 57, 79).
51. Ellen Harris's and Will Crutchfield's contributions to Brown and Sadie, *Performance Practice: Music after 1600*, provide excellent summaries of historical evidence (104–5, 295–96, 453).
52. The account of Farinelli's performance comes from Burney, as quoted in Heriot, *Castrati in Opera*, 96–97.
53. Quantz, *Versuch*, ch. 13 § 2.
54. Darbellay, "C. P. E. Bach's Aesthetic," 53.
55. Printz, *Musica modulatoria vocali*, quoted in Bartel, *Musica Poetica*, 120.
56. Darbellay, "C. P. E. Bach's Aesthetic," 52.
57. Bach, *Versuch*, "Vom Vortrage" (On Expression), § 31.
58. See Zaslaw, "Ornaments for Corelli's Violin Sonatas, op. 5."
59. In 1923 Lauschmann presented the work in c minor, in line with an early manuscript copy of the oboe version, and most oboists came to know it in that key, along with anomalous a♭s and piquant augmented seconds resulting from a misunderstanding of the original key signature of two flats. The first commercially available edition with an accurate transcription of Bach's ornaments edited by H. Voxman is no longer in print, but Hugo Ruf's edition, based on the 1716 Roger print also supplies Bach's ornaments, and is currently available from Schott.
60. See Scheibe, *Critische Musicus* (Hamburg, 1737), trans. David, Mendel, and Wolff, *New Bach Reader*, 338. See also J. A. Birnbaum's defense of Bach's practice, which justified it on the basis that so few performers possessed the requisite knowledge and taste to ornament his music without spoiling it (*New Bach Reader*, 347).

Chapter 7: The Expressive Gesture

1. *Rule of the Metaphor*, 220.
2. "The Actor's Epitome," [2].
3. *Musick's Monument*, 130.
4. Quintilian, *De Oratoria*, 11.3.33–35; trans. adapted from Dunn, *Outlaw Rhetoric*, 62. Emphasis added.
5. Rice, *Introduction to the Art of Reading*, 236. The caesuras Jefferson marked in his prose and speeches and their relationship to musical notation is discussed by Fliegelman in "Jefferson's Pauses," in *Declaring Independence*, ch. 1.
6. Grimarest, *Traité du recitatif*, 46–47, 71.

7. Schoenberg used *Schrpechstimme* most famously in *Pierrot Lunaire* (1912), a melodrama written for Albertine Zehme who was an actress—not a singer
8. Also see Kuijken's comments on the differences between everyday speech and theatrical declamation in *The Notation is not the Music*, 52–53, where he comments: "I am not sure that modern actors would necessarily be good models for composers."
9. Frescobaldi, *Toccate e partite d'intavolatura di cimbalo . . . libro primo*, trans. from Dolmetsch, *Interpretation*, 5.
10. Mace, *Musick's Monument*, 109 (original spelling and italics).
11. See Darnton, *The Great Cat Massacre*, 225.
12. These terms are difficult to render in English. In the standard English translation of Quantz, Reilly settled on "phrase" for *Sin*. This however conveys a somewhat different meaning from the original that literally means "something that makes sense." The problem of equating Quantz's terminology with "phrase" is discussed in the following paragraphs.
13. Quantz, *Versuch*, ch. 17, 6 §33.
14. According to the *OED*, "motif" identifies "a motivating, dominant, or regulating idea, *esp.* a recurrent or pervasive one."
15. Quantz, *Versuch*, ch. 17, 7 §26, ch. 17, 11 §16; Introduction §17.
16. Ibid., ch. 7 §4.
17. Barnett, *Art of Gesture*, 18.
18. Oudart de Richesource, *L'Eloquence de la Chaire*, 2:175.
19. Saint-Lambert, *Principes*, trans., 32.
20. Telemann, *Forsetzung des Harmonischen Gottesdienstes*.
21. Mason, *An Essay*, 22.
22. Discussed in Donington, *Interpretation*, 661–64.
23. Grimarest, *Traité du Récitatif*, 47 and 70.
24. Marpurg, *Kritische Briefe*, 1759–64. The second and third parts of Marpurg's publication are translated in Appendix 1 of Vial, *Art of Musical Phrasing*, 232–59.
25. Bach, *Versuch* 2:29 § 20, 375.
26. NB. Reilly's translation gives "phrase" in place of "gesture."
27. Quantz, *Versuch*, ch. 7 §10.
28. Ibid., ch. 7 §3.
29. C. R. Brijon, *Réflexions sur la Musique*, 17.
30. First elaborated in Riemann's *Musikalische Dynamik und Agogik*. Cf. Thiemel, "Agogic," *NGD*.
31. The recorder is only capable of limited dynamic contrasts through finger shading and leaking. See Haynes's "The Accommodating Recorder," 124.
32. Cockin, *Art of Delivering Written Language*, 33–35, quoted in Tarling, *Weapons*, 120.
33. Fénelon, *Dialogues*, trans., 89.
34. Mattheson, *Vollkommene Capellmeister*, 2, ch. 9 §1. This portion of the treatise originally appeared in the *Kern melodischer Wissenschaft* of 1737 (71–92). References to *diastolica* permeate later eighteenth-century performance manuals including those by Leopold Mozart and Daniel Gottlob Türk.
35. Ibid., 2, ch.9.
36. Ibid., 2, ch. 13 §82.
37. Kelly takes a contrary position and equates Baroque phraseology with prose (*Early Music*, 53). This may be true of some seventeenth-century music with irregular and unpredictable phraseology, and fantasy genres that do not follow a standard formal design, but most eighteenth-century instrumental movements based on dance forms are closer to poetry than prose.
38. Saint-Lambert, *Principes*, ch. 8. trans., 32, where an explanation of our use of "phrase" in place of *cadence* is given.
39. Corri, *Singer's Preceptor*, 73; cited in Toft "The Expressive Pause," 231.
40. Hill, "The Actor's Epitome."
41. Marpurg, *Der critische Musicus* (Berlin, 1750), quoted in C. P. E. Bach, *Versuch*, trans., 81 n4.
42. Mattheson, *Vollkommene Capellmestier*, 2, ch. 12 §30.
43. Quantz, *Versuch*, ch. 12 §25.
44. Ibid., ch. 11 §16.
45. Ibid., ch. 12 §24.

46. Ibid., ch. 17, 7 §25
47. Mace, *Musick's Monument*, 130.
48. Ibid., 131 (italics original). Mace describes his "stinging grace" on 109.
49. See Moroney, "The 'Parodies' of François Couperin's Harpsichord Pieces." For another parody of a piece by Couperin, see ch. 8, Ex. 8.7.
50. Grimarest discusses this in his *Traité du Récitatif*, 62f.
51. The *calotte* was a floppy beret that was the regiment's mock insignia.
52. Kirnberger, *Kunst des reinen Satzes in der Musik* (1774); Riepel, *Anfangsgründe zur musicalischen Setzkunst* (1752–68).
53. Burney, *Present State of Music*, 2:158.
54. Quantz, *Versuch*, ch. 14 §20, and §11.
55. Letter to Leopold Mozart, Vienna, 27 June 1781, quoted in trans. in Marshall, *Mozart Speaks*, 218.
56. L. Mozart, *Versuch*, ch. 5 §14.
57. Stendahl, *Vie de Rossini*, 326; trans., 344.
58. Brod, *Méthode pour le hautbois*, 10.
59. Haynes, *End of Early Music*. The title of ch. 11 is "The Rainbow and the Kaleidoscope: Romantic Phrasing Compared with Baroque."
60. This point is made by Milsom and Peres da Costa in "Expressiveness in Historical Perspective," 81.
61. Leech-Wilkinson, "The Changing Sound of Music," ch. 6, para. 54.
62. Wistreich, "Reconstructing Pre-Romantic Singing Technique," 179–80.
63. Leech-Wilkinson, "The Changing Sound of Music," ch. 6, para. 57.

Chapter 8: Kairos: Expressive Timing

1. *Traité du récitatif*, 356.
2. It remains unclear what type of bells were heard in the original performance of this work. The most likely possibility is that they were operated by the organ and, like clock-tower chimes in Germany, were relatively small and sounded in treble register despite the part being notated on a bass staff.
3. Reported in the *Lute Society of America Quarterly* 25 no.4 (Nov. 1990): 24–26, quoted in Hudson, *Stolen Time*, 439n11.
4. Leech-Wilkinson, *The Changing Sound of Music*, ch. 4, para. 44.
5. "Der Ausdruck in der Musik," *Sammlung Musicalische Vorträge* 50 (1884): 55, quoted in Milsom and Peres da Costa, "Expressiveness in Historical Perspective," 83.
6. Hill, "Overcoming Romanticism," 42–43.
7. The term was first introduced by Adam von Fulda (*De musica*, 1490), see Brown, "Tactus," NGD.
8. *Versuch*, ch. 17, 7 §46, §55. See Reilly's discussion in trans., 268n1.
9. Ibid., ch. 17, 7 §35.
10. Bach, *Versuch*, 1, ch. 3 § 28, trans., 161.
11. Wilson, *Roger North on Music*, 184n18.
12. Diderot, "Projet d'un nouvel Orgue sur lequel on peut jouer toute piece sans sçavoir de Musique, avec quelques observations sur les Chronomètres," in *Mémoires*, 193–94; trans. from Wentz, "Freedom of Expression," 2; Loulié voiced a similar opinion (*Elements*, 85–88).
13. See Fallows, "Metronome," NGD.
14. Bach, *Versuch* 1, ch. 3 § 8.
15. Tosi, *Opinioni*, Gaillard's trans., 156.
16. Quantz, *Versuch*, ch. 17, 6 § 7.
17. Ibid.
18. Diderot, *Mémoires*, 193–94.
19. Quantz, *Versuch*, ch. 17, 4 § 7.
20. Corrette, *Méthode théorique et pratique*, ch. 16.
21. Ibid.
22. Rousseau, *Encyclopédie*, 3:401.
23. Mace, *Musick's Monument*, 81.

24. Mersenne, *Harmonie universelle*, 2:324v.
25. Vicentino, *Antica musica*, trans., 301.
26. This is proposed by Razzi in "Polyphony of the seconda prattica."
27. Praetorius, *Syntagma musicum*, 3:112, trans., 122.
28. Hudson lists other sources on the same subject (*Stolen Time*, 6n12 and 13).
29. Caccini, *Nuove Musiche*, trans. from Playford, *Breefe Introduction*, 12th ed. (1694):1:32.
30. Ibid., 1:43.
31. Bach, *Versuch*, 1, ch. 3 §15; trans., 153.
32. Quantz, *Versuch*, ch. 17, 7 § 59.
33. MS supplement to the *Eléments*, see trans., 64.
34. See Marshall, "Bach's Tempo Ordinario."
35. Referred to in Moroney, "Prélude non-mesuré," *GDM*.
36. Couperin, *L'art du toucher*, 33.
37. Bach, *Versuch*, 1, ch. 3 § 15; trans., 153.
38. Examples include the completely composed-out Fantasy, K475 and the incomplete K Anh 32.
39. Garnier, *Méthode raisonnée pour le hautbois*.
40. Bach, *Versuch*, 1, ch. 3 §8, trans. 151 (the passage appears only in the 1787 edition).
41. Quantz, *Versuch*, ch. 15 § 16.
42. Heinrich Christoph Koch, *Musikalisches Lexikon* (Frankfurt, 1802), quoted in Rosenblum, *Performance Practices*, 368.
43. See Bach, *Versuch*, 3 §28; trans. 161.
44. This style of accompaniment with *Zwischenspielen* persisted into the nineteenth century and was brought to Lutheran communities in the United States. See, for example, G. F. Landenberger's edition of chorales, published in Philadelphia in 1861.
45. See Corrette's comments in *Méthode théorique et pratique*, ch. 16.
46. Mattheson, *Vollkommene Capellmeister*, 3, ch. 26 § 13.
47. Tosi, *Opinioni*, 99, trans. 156; cited in Wilson, *Roger North on Music*, 154n.
48. Wilson, *Roger North on Music*, 151–52.
49. *Opinioni*, Galliard trans., 156n.
50. Borrowed time was mentioned or described by many writers of the period, including Tosi, Dubos, Giuseppe Tartini, Johann Friedrich Agricola, Leopold Mozart, Franz Benda, Friedrich Wilhelm Marpurg, Johann Adam Hiller, and Francseco Galeazzi; for further details see Hudson, *Stolen Time*.
51. Wilson, *Roger North on Music*, 194–95.
52. For a succinct discussion of borrowed time in Chopin, see Jonathan Bellman, "Chopin and the Cantabile Style."
53. Bach, *Versuch*, 3 §28, trans., 161.
54. Letter of 23 October 1777 to his father, quoted in Hudson, *Stolen Time*, 113.
55. Quantz, *Lebenslauf* (1755) trans. from Nettl, *Forgotten Musicians*, 292. Santa Stella Lotti (née Scarabelli, ca. 1686–1759) was married to the composer Antonio Lotti
56. Monteverdi, preface, Eighth Book of Madrigals.
57. Wilson, *Roger North on Music*, 105.
58. Mattheson, *Vollkommene Capellmeister*, 1, ch. 10 § 93.
59. Quantz, *Versuch*, ch. 17, 7 § 37.
60. Ibid., ch. 17, 6 § 7.
61. L. Riccoboni, *Réflexions historiques*, trans., 15.
62. The *suspension* is discussed in Troeger, *Technique and Interpretation*, 134–37.
63. Couperin, *L'Art de toucher*, 14.
64. Wilson, *Roger North on Music*, 172, 27–28, 105, 151–53.
65. See Hudson, *Stolen Time*, 102–03.
66. Bach, *Versuch*, 1, ch. 3 § 28.
67. Caccini, *Nuove Musiche*, Playford trans. quoted in Dolmetsch, *Interpretation*, 4.
68. Fénelon, *Dialogues sur l'éloquence*, trans., 24.
69. Batteux, *Les Beaux-Arts*, 3 §3 ch. 2, trans. 1:178.
70. Harris-Warrick, "Interpreting Pendulum Markings" includes a valuable chart giving tempi from all known sources.
71. Diderot, *Mémoires*, 194.

72. Bacilly, *Remarques curieuses sur l'Art de bien chanter*, 106–07.
73. See Harris-Warrick's cautionary remarks on the accuracy of this source by M. La Chapelle in "Interpreting Pendulum Markings," 10.
74. Rémond de Sainte-Mard, *Reflexions sur l'opéra*, 59.
75. For bowings and texts see Mather, *Dance Rhythms*, 291–99, and Ranum, "Audible Rhetoric."

Chapter 9: To Kindle the Heart

1. *Dictionnaire de Musique*, s.v. "Execution."
2. Fénelon, *Dialogues*, trans. 1750 ed., 83.
3. Quantz, *Versuch*, ch.16 § 20.
4. Quintilian, *De Oratoria*, 12.8.15.
5. Mattheson, *Vollkommene Capellmeister*, 2, ch. 2 § 67.
6. This point is makde by Tarling in *Weapons*, 48.
7. Small, *Musicking*, 28.
8. Wilson, *Roger North on Music*, 135; see also 303n49.
9. Weber, "Wagner, Wagnerism," 30.
10. On Bach's audiences, see Kevorkian, *Baroque Piety*.
11. Hanning, "Iconography of a Salon Concert."
12. Johnson, *Listening in Paris*.
13. *Der Jüngling*, 8th issue, (1747–48): 108–23, quoted in Gardiner, *Bach*, 274–75.
14. Mozart, *Briefe*, 2:378–79; *Letters* 2:817–18 (= 2:552–53), trans. from Zaslaw, *Mozart's Symphonies*, 310–11.
15. Harnoncourt, *Baroque Music Today*, 197–98.
16. Parke, *Musical Memoirs*, 1:215.
17. Broughton, *Court and Private Life*, 231. The effect of Fischer's shake, probably resembled Clementi's use of the octave trill (nowadays called a *tremolo*) on the piano, reported in 1784 (see Williams, *Bach, Handel, Scarlatti*, 62).
18. Kivy, *Fine Art of Repetition*, 233.
19. *Musirgia universalis*, 2:142 (bk. 8, § 2), trans. from Palisca, *Music and Ideas*, 227.
20. Dubos, *Réflexions critiques*, 1:3, trans. I:25–26.
21. Paraphrased from Rosenfield, "Rhetorical Criticism," 172.
22. *OED* s.v. "Sympathy".
23. Dubos, *Réflexions critiques*, 1:4, trans. 1:32–33.
24. *OED* dates the first use of "empathy" to the turn of the twentieth century.
25. Report on research by Dr. Marina Davila Ross (University of Portsmouth) and Professor Elke Zimmermann (University of Veterinary Medicine in Hanover, Germany), *BBC News*, 2 January 2008, "'Laughs' not exclusive to humans," http://news.bbc.co.uk/2/hi/science/nature/7167878.stm, accessed 25 November 2014.
26. Hutcheson, *An Inquiry*, 77–78.
27. *Vollkommene Capellmeister*, 1, ch.6 §6.
28. Aristotle, *Rhetorica*, 1.2.4, 2.1.
29. Batteux, *Les Beaux-Arts*, 254–55; trans. 1:173n.
30. Quintilian, *De Oratoria*, 11.3.
31. Ibid.
32. Mattheson, *Vollkommene Capellmeister*, 1, ch.6 § 11.
33. Hotteterre, *Principes*, trans., 2. The conventional use of this pose is confirmed by Franciscus Lang's *Abhandlung über die Schauspielkunst* (Munich, 1727, 18–19), quoted in English in Barnett, *Art of Gesture*, 114–15.
34. Tomlinson, *Art of Dancing*, 3–4.
35. Mattheson, *Vollkommene Capellmeister*, 1, § 12, § 15.
36. Ibid., 1, ch. 6 § 45.
37. Le Guin, "One says that one weeps," 247.
38. Bayly, *Practical Treatise on Singing*, 24.
39. Lang, *Abhandlung*, 40–41, quoted in trans. in Barnett, *Art of Gesture*, 36.
40. Quantz, *Versuch*, ch. 11 § 13. Similar advice is found in Bayly, *Practical Treatise*, 42.

41. Couperin, *L'Art de toucher*, 5–6.
42. Reilly, *On Playing the Flute*, xxxvii.
43. Neither of these parallels was noted in Reilly, *Quantz and his "Versuch"*. Quantz's ideas on *Vortrag* reflect the thoughts of other writers of his day including C. P. E. Bach, Mozart, and Gottsched's guide to orators, *Ausführliche Redekunst*.
44. As *Essai d'une méthode pour apprendre à jouer de la Flûte Traversière*.
45. Mitford, *Frederick the Great*, 20, 205.
46. Reilly, *On Playing the Flute*, xxxv.
47. See Quantz, *Versuch*, ch. 17, 7 § 10, and § 14.
48. Quoted in Bartel, *Musica Poetica*, 34n11.
49. Mace, *Musick's Monument*, 19.
50. Dubos, *Réflexions critiques*, 1:45, trans. 1:366. The reference is to instrumental music (symphonies) in Lully's operas.
51. Cusick, *Francesca Caccini*, 63, citing Cristoforo Bronzini, *Della dignità e nobiltà delle donne*. According to Cusick, Bronzini praised the virtuosa Adriana Basile in ca. 1627 for her "performances of distilled sadness or joy [that] left listeners 'stunned, almost out of themselves.'"
52. Rousseau, *Dictionnaire*, 403 (trans., 336–37) where Tartini's original is quoted.
53. J. F. Reichardt, *Musikalisches Kunstmagazin*, 2:40, cited in Oleskiewicz, "Quantz and the Flute," 403.
54. "Under-interpretation" is Gardiner's term (*Bach*, 10n).
55. De Pure, *Idée des spectacles*, 210. Ménestrier used a similar metaphor in *Des Ballets* (153); Cahusac, *Encyclopédie* s.v. "Ballet."
56. *Ode de la Danse*, as quoted in Bourdelot and Bonnet, *Histoire générale de la danse*, 143.
57. For sources see Schneider, "Die Funktion des Divertissement und des Ballet."
58. Ménestrier, *Des representations*, 101–2.
59. For suggestions, see Pierce, "Choreographic Structure," in Nevile, *Dance Spectacle, and the Body Politick*, 182–208.
60. Templeri, *Rhétorique de l'honnête homme* (Amsterdam, 1699): 88, cited in Grear, "A Background to Diderot's Paradoxe," 229. Also see Rousseau, *Dictionnaire*, 4.
61. *Ad Herennium*, 3.15.27 (ca. 90 BCE), formerly thought to be the work of Cicero. See also Mersenne, *Harmonie universelle*, 12:92–93, Dubos, *Réflexions critiques*, 1:33.
62. Horace, *Ars Poetica*, v. 102; Lamy, *L'Art de parler*, 80 (emphasis added), quoted in Montagu, *Expression of the Passions*, 51.
63. Matteis in North, *Musical Grammarian*, 271. Corelli in a footnote added by the translator (J. E. Galliard?) in Raguenet's *Paralèle des Italiens et des François*, 21.
64. Burney, *Present State of Music in Germany*, 2:270.
65. Bach, *Versuch*, 3, ch. 13. Trans. from Donington, *Interpretation*, 51–52.
66. Mattheson *Vollkommene Capellmeister*, 2, ch.2 § 64. Aaron Hill also spoke of the actor using his own particular associations and memories to induce a given passion (*Art of Acting*, 11).
67. Batteux, *Cours de belles lettres*, 3:9; trans. 3:8–9.
68. *Encyclopèdie* s.v. "Enthousiasme."
69. Quantz, *Versuch*, ch. 14 § 5; see also ch. 10 § 22.
70. Ibid. ch. 17 vii § 17.
71. Ibid.
72. Quintilian, *Institutio Oratoria*, 11.3.
73. Printz, *Musicus magnanimous, oder Pancalus*, quoted in Zohn, "Die vornehmste Hof-Tugend." Stephen Rose also points out that Printz saw dissembling as inimical to honest German manners ("Musician Novels of the German Baroque," 184).
74. Batteux, *Les Beaux-Arts*, 260–61; trans. 1:179.
75. Diderot, *Paradoxe*, 45.
76. Rameau, *Traité de l'harmonie*, trans. Phillip Gossett, 156, quoted in Bartel, *Musica Poetica*, 60.
77. Quantz, *Versuch*, ch. 11 § 16.
78. Diderot, *Paradoxe*, 119.
79. F. Riccoboni, *L'Art du théâtre*, 41.
80. *Hamlet*, act 1 scene.3.
81. Quantz, *Versuch*, ch. 10 § 22.

82. Quantz, *Versuch*, ch. 11 § 17.
83. *OED* s.v. "fiction."
84. See discussion in Kelly, "Mimesis," 234.
85. Dubos, *Réflexions critiques*, 1:28, trans. 1:201. "*Vraisemblance*" appears in the 4th ed. of the *Dictionnaire de L'Académie française* (1762), defined as "*apparence de vérité* (semblance of truth)."
86. Poisson, *Réflexions sur l'art de parler*, 34, trans. in Barnett, *Art of Gesture*, 14.
87. F. Riccoboni, *L'art du théâtre*, 37, partially quoted in Montagu, *Expression of the Passions*, 53.
88. See Diderot, *Paradoxe*, 42.

Chapter 10: Analysing Expression

1. Two are by Telemann, and one by Hertel. A♭-major is nonexistent. Note that I am talking about *fingered* tonalities, since the hautbois d'amour and the oboe da caccia are both transposing instruments. "Zerfließe, mein Herze" in the St. John Passion (BWV245/35), for instance, is written in f minor and played in that key on the traverso, but since the oboe da caccia sounds in F, written f minor is fingered c minor.
2. *OED*, s.v. "Agony" is anguish of mind, sore trouble or distress, a paroxysm of grief.
3. Dürr, *Cantatas of J. S. Bach*, 489.
4. Quantz, *Versuch*, ch. 17, 4 § 7.
5. Batteux, *Les Beaux-Arts*, 3 §3 ch. 3, trans. 1:179.
6. Rousseau, *Dictionnaire*, 164.
7. Quantz, *Versuch*, ch. 11 § 21.

GENERAL BIBLIOGRAPHY

Reference works

Bach, Johann Sebastian. *Neue Asugabe sämtliche Werke.* Kassel: Bärenreiter, 1954-2011.
Bach-Dokumente. Supplement zu Johann Sebastian Bach Neue Ausgabe sämtlicher Werke. Kassel: Bärenreiter, 1963–.
Dictionnaire de L'Académie française. 1st ed. Paris: J. B. Coignard, 1694. Available online at ARTFL Project, University of Chicago, 2001.
Encyclopedia Britannica. 15th ed. Chicago: Encyclopaedia Britannica, 1992.
Encyclopédie, ou Dictionnaire raisonné des sciences, arts et métiers. Edited by Denis Diderot and J. Le Rond d'Alembert. Lausanne and Berne, 1751–72; suppls.1776–77, 1780. Available online at ARTFL Project, University of Chicago.
New Grove Dictionary of Music and Musicians (NGD). New York: Grove. (Most content transferred to Grove Music Online, 2001).
Oxford English Dictionary (OED). 2nd. ed. Oxford: Oxford University Press, 1989.

Books, Articles, and Music

Abrams, M. H. *The Mirror and the Lamp: Romantic Theory and the Critical Tradition.* New York: Oxford University Press, 1953.
Abravaya, Ido. *On Bach's Rhythm and Tempo.* Kassel: Bärenreiter, 2006.
Agawu. Kofi. *Playing with Signs: A Semiotic Interpretation of Classic Music.* Princeton, NJ: Princeton University Press, 1991.
Agricola, Johann Friedrich. *Anleitung zur Singkunst.* Berlin: G. L. Winter, 1757. [Ger. trans. with commentary of Tosi, *Opinioni*, qv.] English translation by J. Baird as *Introduction to the Art of Singing by Johann Friedrich Agricola.* New York: Cambridge University Press, 1995.
Ameln, Konrad. "Die Fermate im evangelischen Kirchenlied." *Jahrbuch für Liturgik und Hymnologie* 33 (1991): 95–110.
Anon. "'Laughs' not Exclusive to Humans." *BBC News*, 2 January 2008. http://news.bbc.co.uk/2/hi/science/nature/7167878.stm, accessed 25 November 2014.
Anon. ca.90 BCE; formerly attr. to Marcus Tullius Cicero. *Ad Herennium/Rhetorica ad Herennium/Silva Rhetoricae.* Translated by Harry Caplan www.rhetorica.byu.edu, 2001.
Anon./Ballard. *Parodies nouvelles et vaudevilles inconnus.* 2 vols. Paris: Ballard 1730–31.
Aristotle. *Rhetorica* (fourth century BCE). Translated by W. R. Roberts in *The Works of Aristotle.* Vol. 11. Oxford: Clarendon Press, 1954.
Arnold, Franck Thomas. *The Art of Accompaniment from a Thorough-Bass as Practiced in the XVIIth and XVIIIth Centuries.* 2 vols. New York: Dover, 1965.

Aubignac, François Hedelin d'. *Pratique du theatre*. Paris: A. de Sommaville, 1657.
Auerbach, Erich. *Mimesis: The Representation of Reality in Western Literature*. Translated by W. R. Trask. Princeton, NJ: Princeton University Press, 1953.
Avison, Charles. *An Essay on Musical Expression*, 2nd ed. London: C. Davis, 1753. Reprint, New York: Broude, 1967.
Babell, William. *XII Solos for a VIOLIN or HAUTBOY with a BASS figur'd for the HARPSICHORD With proper Graces adapted to each Adagio, by the Author*. London: Walsh, ca.1725.
Babitz, Sol. "Concerning the Length of Time that Every Note Must be Held," *The Music Review* 28 (1968): 21-37.
Bach, Carl Philipp Emanuel. *Versuch über die wahre Art das Clavier zu spielen*. Berlin, 1753. English translation by William J. Mitchell as *Essay on the True Art of Playing Keyboard Instruments*. New York: W. W. Norton, 1949.
Bacilly, Bénigne de. *Remarques curieuses sur l'Art de bien chanter*. Paris: the author and Ballard, 1668. Translated by Austin B. Caswell as *A Commentary upon the Art of Proper Singing*. New York: Institute for Mediaeval Music, 1968.
Baillot, Pierre Marie François de Sales. *Méthode de violoncelle et de l'accomagnement*. Paris: Imprimerie du Conservatoire, 1804. Reprint, Geneva: Minkoff, 1974.
Barnett, Dene. With the assistance of Jeanette Massy-Westropp. *The Art of Gesture: The Practices and Principles of Eighteenth-Century Acting*. Heidelberg: C. Winter Universitätsverlag, 1987.
Baron, Carol K., ed. *Bach's Changing World: Voices in the Community*. Rochester, NY: Rochester University Press, 2006.
———. "Tumultuous Philosophers, Pious Rebels, Revolutionary Teachers, Pedantic Clerics, Vengeful Bureaucrats, Threatened Tyrants, Worldly Mystics: The Religious World Bach Inherited." In *Bach's Changing World*, 35–85.
Bartel, Dietrich. *Musica Poetica: Musical-Rhetorical Figures in German Baroque Music*. Lincoln: University of Nebraska Press, 1997.
Barthes, Roland. "The Death of the Author." *Aspen* (1967): 5–6. Reprint in *Image-Music-Text*, translated by S. Heath. New York: Hill & Wang, 1977.
Batteux, Charles. *Les Beaux-Arts reduits à un même principe*. Paris: Durand, 1746. Translated by Miller as *A Course of the Belles Lettres or the Principles of Literature*. London: Printed for B. Law and Co., T. Caslon, J. Coote, S. Hooper, G. Kearsly, and A. Morley, 1761.
———. *Cours de belles-lettres ou principes de la littérature*. (orig. published 1747–48). Paris: Desaint and Saillet, and Durand, 1753. Paris: Durand, 1746. Translated by Miller as *A Course of the Belles Lettres or the Principles of Literature*.
Bayly, Anselm. *A Practical Treatise on Singing and Playing with Just Expression and Real Elegance*. London: printed for J. Ridley, 1771.
Beaussant, Philippe. *Lully ou le musicien du soleil*. Paris: Gallimard, 1992.
Beghin, Tom. *The Virtual Haydn: Paradox of a Twenty-first Century Keyboardist*. Chicago: University of Chicago Press, 2015.
Beghin, Tom and Sander M. Goldberg. *Haydn and the Performance of Rhetoric*. Chicago: Chicago University Press, 2007.
Behrens, Samuel Rudolph. *Maître de danse Anleitung zu ein wohlgegründeten Tanz-Kunst*. Leipzig: C. Heydler, 1703.
Bellman, Jonathan. "Chopin and the Cantabile Style." *Historical Performance: Journal of Early Music America* 2 (1989): 63–71.
Blavet, Michel. *Troisième livre de sonates pour la flûte traversière avec la basse*. Paris: the author, 1740.
Boismortier, Joseph Bodin de. *Sonates pour un Clavecin et une flute traversiere*, op. 91. Paris: the author, n.d.; facsimile Vienna: Universal Editions, 1984.
Bonds, Mark Evan. *Wordless Rhetoric: Musical Form and the Metaphor of the Oration*. Cambridge, MA: Harvard University Press, 1991.
Bourdelot and Bonnet. *Histoire générale de la danse*. Paris: d'Houey, 1724.

Bowen, José A. "Finding the Music in Musicology: Performance History and Musical Works." In *Rethinking music*, edited by N. Cook and M. Everist, 424–51. Oxford: Oxford University Press, 1999.

Boyden, David D. *The History of Violin Playing*. Oxford: Oxford University Press, 1965.

Brijon, C. R. *Réflexions sur la Musique, et la vraie maniére de l'exécuter sur le violon*. Paris: the author, 1763. Reprint Geneva: Minkoff, 1974

Brod, Henri. *Méthode pour le hautbois* [2 parts]. Paris, Schonenberger, 1826, ca. 1830.

Brosses, Charles de. *Lettres d'Italie* (1739–40). Reprint, Paris: Mercure de France, 1986.

Broughton, Augusta Mary Anne. *Court and Private Life in the Time of Queen Charlotte, being the Journals of Mrs Papendiek*. London: Bentley, 1887.

Brown, Clive. "Historical Performance, Metronome Marks and Tempo in Beethoven's Symphonies." *Early Music* (1991): 247–58.

Brown, Howard Mayer, and Stanley Sadie, eds. *Performance Practice: Music after 1600*. Norton/Grove Handbooks in Music. London: Norton, 1989.

Brüggen, Frans. Interview in *American Recorder* 15/3 (1975): 73.

Buelow, George J. "Johann Mattheson and the Invention of the Affektenlehre." In *New Mattheson Studies*, edited by George J. Buelow and Hans Joachim Marx, 393–407. Cambridge: Cambridge University Press, 1983.

——. *History of Baroque Music*. Bloomington: Indiana University Press, 2004.

Burgess, Geoffrey. "À l'Ouverture des Enfers." In *Coll' astuzia, col giudizio: Essays in Honor of Neal Zaslaw*, edited by Cliff Eisen, 1–30. Ann Arbor: Steglein, 2009.

——. *"The Premier Oboist of Europe": A Portrait of Gustave Vogt*. Lanham, MD: Scarecrow Press, 2003.

——. "Vibrato Awareness." *Double Reed* 24/2 (2002): 127–35.

Burgess, Geoffrey, and Bruce Haynes. *The Oboe*. New Haven: Yale University Press, 2004.

Burkholder, J. Peter. "Rule-breaking as a Rhetorical Sign." In *Festa musicologica: Essays in Honor of George J. Buelow*, edited by Thomas J. Mathiesen and Benito V. Rivera, 369–89. Stuyvesant, NY: Pendragon Press, 1995.

Burmeister, Joachim. *Musica Poetica*. Rostock: n.p., 1606. Translated by Benito V. Rivera as *Musical Poetics*. New Haven: Yale University Press, 1993.

Burney, Charles. *A General History of Music from the Earliest Ages to the Present Period . . .* London: Printed for the author and sold by T. Becket, J. Robson, and G. Robinson, 1776–89.

——. *The Present State of Music in Germany, the Netherlands, and the United Provinces*. 2 vols. London: T. Becket & G. Robinson, 1773. Edited by P. Scholes as *Dr. Burney's Musical Tours in Europe*. 2 vols. Oxford: Oxford University Press, 1959.

Butt, John. *Bach Interpretation: Articulation Marks in Primary Sources of J. S. Bach*. Cambridge: Cambridge University Press, 1990.

——. *Bach's Dialogue with Modernity: Perspectives on the Passions*. New York: Cambridge University Press, 2010.

——. *Music Education and the Art of Performance in the German Baroque*. Cambridge: Cambridge University Press, 1994.

Caccini, Giulio. *Le nuove musiche* (Florence, 1602) Translated in Playford, *A Breefe Introduction*.

Chafe, Eric. *J. S. Bach's Johannine Theology: The "St. John Passion" and the Cantatas for Spring 1725* New York: Oxford University Press, 2014.

——. *Tonal Allegory in the Vocal Music of J. S. Bach*. Berkeley: University of California Press, 1991.

Chaouche, Sabine. *Sept traités sur le jeu du comédien et autres textes*. Paris: Honoré Champion, 2001.

Clark, Jane, and Derek Connon. *The Mirror of Human Life: Reflections on François Couperin's "Pièces de clavecin."* Huntingdon, UK: King's Music, 2002.

Cleland, John. *Memoirs of Fanny Hill*. (1st ed. London, 1748) Paris: I. Liseux, 1888.

Collingwood, R. G. *The Principles of Art*. Oxford: Clarendon Press, 1938.

Cook, Nicholas, and Mark Everist. "Analysing Performance and Performing Analysis." In *Rethinking Music*, edited by N. Cook and M. Everist, 239–61. Oxford: Oxford University Press, 1999.

Corelli, Arcangelo. *Sonatas op. 5* (Rome 1700). London: Walsh, 1740.
Corrette, Michel. *Méthode théorique et pratique pour apprendre en peu de temps le violoncelle dans sa perfection*. Paris: the author, 1741. Reprint, Geneva: Minkoff, 1972.
Corri, Domenico. *The Singer's Preceptor*. London: Chappell & Co., 1810.
Couperin, François. *Concerts royaux*. Paris, Couperin, Boivin, Le Clerc, 1722.
———. *L'Art de toucher le clavecin*. Paris: the author & Foucault, 1717.
———. *Les Gouts réünis*. Paris: the author & Boivin, 1724.
———. *Troisième Livre de pièces de clavecin*. Paris: the author, 1722.
Cox, Howard H., ed. *The Calov Bible of J. S. Bach*. Ann Arbor: UMI Research Press, 1985.
Crescentini, Girolamo. *Raccolta di Esercizj per il canto all'uso del Vocalizzo con discorso preliminare del Signor Girolamo Crescentini/ Recueill d'exercices pour la vocalization musicale avec un discours préliminaire par M. Jérôme Crescentini*. Paris: Imbault, ca.1810
Cusick, Suzanne G. *Francesca Caccini at the Medici Court: Music and the Circulation of Power*. Chicago: University of Chicago Press, 2009.
Cumming, Naomi. *The Sonic Self: Musical Subjectivity and Signification*. Bloomington: Indiana University Press, 2000.
Dahlhaus, Carl. *Grundlagen der Musikgeschichte* (1977). Translated by J. B. Robinson as *Foundations of Music History*. Cambridge: Cambridge University Press, 1983.
———. *Die Idee der absoluten Musik* (1978). Translated by R. Lustig as *The Idea of Absolute Music*. Chicago: University of Chicago Press, 1989.
———. *Musikästhetik* (1967). Translated by William W. Austin as *Esthetics of Music*. Cambridge: Cambridge University Press, 1982.
Dammann, Rolf. *Der Musikbegriff im deutschen Barock*. Cologne: A Volk, 1967.
Dannreuther, Edward. *Musical Ornamentation*. 2 vols. London: Novello, 1893–5.
Darbellay, Étienne "C. P. E. Bach's Aesthetic as Reflected in his Notation." In *C. P. E. Bach Studies*, edited by Stephen L. Clark, 43–63. Oxford: Oxford University Press, 1988.
Darnton, Robert. *The Great Cat Massacre and other Episodes in French Cultural History*. New York: Basic Books, 1984.
David, Hans T., Arthur Mendel, and Christoph Wolff, eds. *The New Bach Reader: A Life of Johann Sebastian Bach in Letters and Documents*. New York: W. W. Norton, 1998.
Descartes, René. *Les passions de l'âme*. Paris: H. Le Gras, 1649. Translated by Stephen Voss as *The Passions of the Soul*. Indianapolis: Hackett Pub. Co., 1989.
Diderot, Denis. *Mémoires sur différens sujets de mathématiques*. Paris: Durant & Pissot, 1748.
———. *Paradoxe sur le comédien* (1773). Edited by R. Abirached, with dossier compiled by Jean Bardet. Paris: Gallimard, Folio, 2009.
Dolmetsch, Arnold. *The Interpretation of the Music of the XVII and XVIII Centuries*. London: Novello and Co., 1915.
Donington, Robert. *The Interpretation of Early Music*. London: Faber & Faber, 1963.
Dubos, Abbé Jean-Baptiste. *Réflexions critiques sur la poësie et sur la peinture*. Paris: J. Mariette, 1719. Translated by Thomas Nugent as *Critical Reflections on Poetry, Painting and Music*. London: printed for J. Nourse, 1748.
Duffin, Ross. *How Equal Temperament Ruined Harmony (and Why You Should Care)*. New York: W. W. Norton, 2007.
Dunn, J. *Outlaw Rhetoric*. Ithaca, NY: Cornell University Press, 2012.
Dürr, Alfred. *The Cantatas of J. S. Bach*. Revised English translation of *Die Kantaten von J. S. Bach* (1971) by Richard D. P. Jones. Oxford: Oxford University Press, 2005.
Earlom, Richard. *Liber veritatis, or, A collection of prints, after the original designs of Claude le Lorrain in the collection of His Grace the Duke of Devonshire*. 3 vols, London: Boydell et Co., 1777, 1819.
Feldman, Martha. *Opera and Sovereignty: Transforming Myths in Eighteenth-century Italy*. Chicago: University of Chicago Press, 2007.
Félibien, André. *Les Reines de Perse aux pieds d'Alexandre, peinture au Cabinet du Roi*. Paris: P. Le Petit, 1663. Translated by William Parsons as *The Tent of Darius Explain'd: Or the Queens of Persia at the Feet of Alexander*. London: various, 1704.

Fénelon, François de Salignac de La Mothe. *Dialogues sur l'éloquence en général et sur celle de la chaire en particulier, avec une Lettre écrite à l'Académie françoise* (1674). Paris: F. Delaulne, 1718. Translated by William Stevenson as *Dialogues Concerning Eloquence in General; and Particularly, that Kind which is Fit for the Pulpit*. London: Printed by T. Wood, for J. Walthoe, Jun., 1722.

Fielding, Henry. *The History of Tom Jones, a Foundling*. London: printed for A. Millar, 1749.

Fliegelman, Jay. *Declaring Independence: Jefferson, Natural Language and the Culture of Performance*. Stanford: Stanford University Press, 1993.

Fleming, Paul. *Paul Flemings teutsche Poemata*. Lubeck: Jauch, 1642. Reprint, Hildelsheim: G. Olms, 1969.

Forkel, Johann Nikolaus. *Allgemeine Geschichte der Musik*. Vol. 1. Leipzig: Schwickert, 1788. English translation by Doris B. Powers as "Johann Nikolaus Forkel's Philosophy of Music in the Einleitung to Volume One of his *Allgemeine Geschichte der Musik* (1788): A Translation and Commentary with a Glossary of Eighteenth-Century Terms." PhD diss., University of North Carolina, Chapel Hill, 1995.

Franklin, Don. "The Fermata as Notational Convention in the Music of J. S. Bach." In *Convention in Eighteenth- and Nineteenth-Century Music: Essays in Honor of Leonard G. Ratner*, edited by Wye J. Allanbrook, Janet M. Levy, and William P. Mahrt, 345–81. Stuyvesant, NY: Pendragon Press, 1992.

Fuller, David. "The Performer as Composer." In *Performance Practice: Music after 1600*, edited by H. M. Brown and S. Sadie, 117–46. New York: W. W. Norton, 1990.

Gable, Frederick. "Some Observations Concerning Baroque and Modern Vibrato." *Performance Practice Review* 5 (1992): 90–102.

Ganassi, Sylvestro. *Opera intitulata Fontegara*. Florence, 1535. *Opera intitulata Fontegara: Venice 1535: A Treatise on the Art of Playing the Recorder and of Free Ornamentation*. English translation of the German edition by Dorothy Swainson. Berlin-Lichterfelde: R. Lienau, 1959.

Galilei, Vincenzo. *Dialogo della musica antica et della moderna*. Florence, 1581. Translated by C. Palisca as *Dialogue on Ancient and Modern Music*. New Haven: Yale University Press, 2003.

Gardiner, John Eliot. *Bach: Music in the Castle of Heaven*. New York: Knopf, 2013.

Garnier, François-Joseph. *Méthode raisonnée pour le hautbois*. Paris: Pleyel, ca. 1802.

Gay, Peter. *The Enlightenment: An Interpretation/The Rise of Modern Paganism*. New York: Knopf, 1966.

Gebauer, Gunter, and Christopher Wulf. *Mimesis: Kultur, Kunst, Gesellschaft*. Translated by D. Reneau as *Mimesis: Culture–Art–Society*. Reinbek bei Hamburg: Rowohlt, 1992; Berkeley: University of California Press, 1995.

Geminiani, Francesco. *The Art of Playing on the Violin*. London: Printed for the author by J. Johnson, 1751. Reprint edited by D. Boyden. Oxford University Press, [n.d.].

Geringer, Karl. "Symbolism in the Music of J. S. Bach." Lecture delivered at the Library of Congress, Washington DC, 1955.

Gjerdingen, Robert. *Music in the Galant Style*. New York: Oxford University Press, 2007.

Göner, Rüdiger. "Die Sprache in der Musiktheorie Jérôme-Joseph de Momignys." In *Logos musicae: Festschrift für Albert Palm*. Wiesbaden: Steiner, 1982, 100–109.

Goethe, Johann Wolfgang von. *Torquato Tasso: Ein Schauspiel*. Leipzig: G. J. Goschen, 1790.

Gottsched, Johann Christoph. *Ausführliche Redekunst*. Leipzig: B.C. Breitkopf, 1728. Reprint, Hildesheim: G. Olms, 1973.

Grant, Roger Mathew. *Beating Time and Measuring Music in the Early Modern Era*. New York: Oxford University Press, 2014.

Grear, Allison. "A Background to Diderot's *Paradoxe sur le Comédien*: The Role of the Imagination in Spoken Expression of Emotion, 1600–1750." *Forum for Modern Language Studies* 31/3 (1985): 225–38.

Grimarest, Jean Léonor Le Gallois sieur de. *Traité du Récitatif dans la lecture, dans l'action publique, dans la déclamation et dans le chant, avec un traité des accens, de la quantité et de la punctuation*. Paris: J. Le Fèvre, 1707. Reprint in Chaouche, *Sept Traités*. Paris: Honoré Champion, 2001.

Grimm, Jacob, and Wilhelm Grimm. *Kinder- und Hausmärchen*, 1812. Translated by M. Hunt as *Household Tales*. London: G. Bell & Sons, 1884.

Hampson, Christopher. "Pausing for Reflection: Re-evaluating Bach's Use of the Fermata." MMus diss., University of Glasgow, 2007.

Hanning, Barbara Russano. "The Iconography of a Salon Concert: A Reappraisal." In *French Musical Thought, 1600–1800*, edited by Georgia Cowart, 129–48. Ann Arbor: UMI Research Press, 1989.

Harding, Rosamond. *Origins of Musical Time and Expression*. Oxford: Oxford University Press, 1938.

Harnoncourt, Nikolaus. *Musik als Klangrede, wege zu einem neuen Musikverständnis*. Salzburg: Residenz Verlag, 1982. Translated by R. Pauly as *Baroque Music Today: Music as Speech: Ways to a New Understanding of Music*. Portland, OR: Amadeus, 1988.

———. *Der musikalische Dialog: Gedanken zu Monteverdi, Bach und Mozart*. Salzurg: Residenz Verlag, 1984. Translated by R. Pauly as *The Musical Dialogue: Thoughts on Monteverdi, Bach, and Mozart*. Portland, OR: Amadeus, 1989.

Harris-Warrick, Rebecca. "Interpreting Pendulum Markings for French Baroque Dances." *Historical Performance* 6 (1993): 9–22.

Hatten, Robert S. *Interpreting Musical Gestures, Topics, and Tropes: Mozart, Beethoven, Schubert*. Bloomington: Indiana University Press, 2004.

Haydn, Joseph. *A Prelude to Auld Robin Gray: Jemmy and Jenny's Farewell! A New Dialogue and Duett Adapted to the Principal Movement in Haydn's Favorite Overture Performed at Messrs. Bach and Abel's Concerts*. London: Bland & Weller, ca. 1784.

Haynes, Bruce. "The Accommodating Recorder." In *Recorders Based on Historical Models: Fred Morgan, Writings and Memories*, compiled by Gisela Rothe, 119–27. Fulda: Mollenhauer, 2007.

———. "Beyond Temperament: Non-keyboard Intonation in the Seventeenth and Eighteenth Centuries." *Early Music* 19 (1991): 357–81.

———. *The Eloquent Oboe: A History of the Hautboy from 1640 to 1760*. Oxford: Oxford Univeristy Press, 2001.

———. *The End of Early Music: A Period Performer's History of Music for the Twenty-First Century*. New York: Oxford University Press, 2007.

———. *The History of Performing Pitch: The Story of "A."* Lanham, MD: Scarecrow Press.

———. *Music for Oboe: A Bibliography*. 2nd ed. Berkeley, CA: Fallen Leaf Press, 1992.

Heinichen, Johann David. *Der General-Bass in der Composition*. Dresden, 1728. Translated by G. Buelow as *Thorough-bass Accompaniment According to Johann David Heinichen*. Berkeley: University of California Press, 1966.

Heriot, Angus. *The Castrati in Opera*. London: Secker & Warburg, 1956. Reprint, New York: Da Capo, 1975.

Hickman, Roger. "The Censored Publications of *The Art of Playing on the Violin*, or Geminiani Unshaken." *Early Music* 11 (1983): 73–77.

Hill, Aaron. "The Actor's Epitome." *Prompter* 113 (9 December 1735): 2.

———. *The Art of Acting*. London: J. Osborn, 1746.

Hill, Robert. "Overcoming Romanticism: On the Modernization of Twentieth-Century Performance Practice." In *Music and Performance During the Weimar Republic*, edited by Bryan R. Gilliam, 37–58. Cambridge: Cambridge University Press, 1994.

Hilse, Walter. "The Treatises of Christoph Bernhard." *Music Forum* 3 (1973): 1–196.

Horace. *Odes and Epodes*. Translated by N. Rudd. Cambridge, MA: Harvard University Press, 2004.

———. *Ars Poetica*, ca. 18 BCE. In *Satires, Epistles and Ars Poetica*. Translated by H. R. Fairclough. Loeb Classical Library. Cambridge, MA: Harvard University Press, 1926.

Hotteterre, Jacques-Martin. *Principes de la flûte traversiere ou flûte d'allemagne, de la flûte à bec ou flûte douce et du haut-bois*. Paris: C. Ballard, 1707. Reprint, Kassel, Bärenreiter, 1982; Partial translation as *The Rudiments or Principles of the German Flute*. London: Walsh, 1729.

Hudson, Richard. *Stolen Time: The History of Tempo Rubato*. Oxford: Oxford University Press, 1994.

Hummel, Johann Nepomuk. *Ausführliche theoretisch-practische Anweisung zum Piano-Forte-Spiel.* Vienna: T. Haslinger, 1827. Translated as *A Complete Theoretical and Practical Course of Instructions on the Art of Playing the Piano Forte.* London: Boosey, 1828.

Huret, Grégoire. *Optique de portraiture et peinture.* Paris: C. de Sercy, 1670.

Hutcheson, Francis. *An Inquiry into the Original of Our Ideas of Beauty and Virtue.* London: s.n., 1726.

Irwin, Joyce L. "Bach in the Midst of Religious Transition." In Baron, *Bach's Changing World,* 108–26.

——. *Foretastes of Heaven in Lutheran Church Music Tradition.* Lanham, MD: Rowman & Littlefield, 2015.

Isherwood, Robert M. *Music in the Service of the King.* Ithaca, NY: Cornell University Press, 1973.

Jensen, H. James. *Signs and Meaning in Eighteenth-Century Art: Epistemology, Rhetoric, Painting, Poesy, Music, Dramatic Performance, and G. F. Handel.* New York: P. Lang, 1997.

Joachim, Johann, and Andreas Moser. *Violinschule,* 3 vols. Berlin: Simrock, 1902–5.

Johnson, James. *Listening in Paris: A Cultural History.* Berkeley: University of California Press, 1995.

Juslin, Patrik N. "From Mimesis to Catharsis: Expression, Perception, and Induction of Emotion in Music." In *Musical Communication,* edited by D. Miell, R. MacDonald, and D. J. Hargreaves, 85–115. New York: Oxford University Press, 2005.

Kelly, Michael, ed. "Mimesis," *The Encyclopedia of Aesthetics, vol. 3.* Oxford: Oxford University Press, 1998.

Kelly, Thomas F. *Early Music: A Very Short Introduction.* New York: Oxford University Press, 2009.

Kevorkian, Tanya. *Baroque Piety: Religion, Society, and Music in Leipzig, 1650–1750.* Aldershot: Ashgate, 2007.

Kirnberger, Johann Philip. *Kunst des reinen Satzes in der Musik.* Berlin: Decker, 1774. Reprint, Hildesheim: G. Olms, 1968.

Kivy, Peter. *The Fine Art of Repetition: Essays in the Philosophy of Music.* Cambridge: Cambridge University Press, 1993.

Koch, Heinrich Christoph. *Versuch einer Anleitung zur Composition.* Leipzig: Böhme, 1782–93. Reprint, Hildesheim: G. Olms, 1969.

Kuijken, Barthold. *The Notation is not the Music: Reflections on Early Music Practice and Performance.* Bloomington: Indiana University Press, 2013.

Lamy, Bernard. *De l'art de parler.* Paris: A. Pralard, 1675. Anonymously translated as *The Art of Speaking.* London: W. Godbid, 1676.

La Bruyère, Jean de. *Les caractères de Théophraste traduits du grec avec les Caractères ou les Mœurs de ce siècle.* Lyon: T. Amaoulry, 1688. Modern critical edition Paris: GF-Flammarion, 1965.

Lancelot, Francine. *La Belle danse: catalogue raisonné fait en l'an 1995.* Paris: V. Dieren, 1996.

Landenberger, G. F., ed. *Choral-Buch für die Orgel mit Zwischenspielen versehen und für den vierstimmigen Gesang eingerichtet.* Philadelphia: J. Kohler, Reformirte Kirchen Buchhandlung, 1861.

Le Faucheur, Michel. *Traité de l'action de l'orateur. Ou de la prononciation et du geste.* Paris: A. Courbé, 1676. Anonymously translated as *An Essay upon the Action of an Orator.* London: N. Cox, 1680.

Le Guin, Elisabeth. *Boccherini's Body: An Essay in Carnal Musicology.* Berkeley: University of California Press, 2006.

——. "'One Says that One Weeps, but One Does not Weep': Sensible, Grotesque, and Mechanical Embodiments in Boccherini's Chamber Music." *Journal of the American Musicological Society* 55 (2002): 207–54.

Le Moine. *Romance du Fat dupé.* Paris: Imbault, [1787] F:Pn Vm7.1957(8).

Leaver, Robin A. *J. S. Bach and Scripture: Glosses from the Calov Bible Commentary.* St. Louis: Concordia, 1985.

——. "Religion and Religious Currents." In *The Worlds of Johann Sebastian Bach: An Aston Magna Academy Book,* edited by Raymond Erickson, 105–40. New York: Amadeus Press (Hal Leonard), 2009.

Le Brun, Charles. *Conférence sur l'expression générale et particulière* (*Méthode pour apprendre à dessiner les passions*), MS 1668; 1st pub. Amsterdam: F. van der Plaats, 1702. Translated in Montagu, *Expression*.

Leech-Wilkinson, Daniel, *The Changing Sound of Music: Approaches to Studying Recorded Musical Performance*. London: CHARM, 2009. Available at www.charm.rhul.ac.uk

Lehman, Bradley. "Bach's Extraordinary Temperament: Our Rosetta Stone," Parts 1 and 2. *Early Music* 33/1 (2005): 3–23, and 33/2 (2005): 211–26.

Leisinger, Ulrich. "Affections, Rhetoric, and Musical Expression." In *The World of the Bach Cantatas; Johann Sebastian Bach's Early Sacred Cantatas,* edited by Christoph Wolff, 185–97. New York: W. W. Norton, 1995.

Leppert, Richard. *Music and Image: Domesticity, Ideology, and Socio-cultural Formation in Eighteenth-Century England*. New York: Cambridge University Press, 1988.

———. *The Sight of Sound: Music, Representation, and the History of the Body*. Berkeley: University of California Press, 1993.

Lévi-Strauss, Claude. *Mythologies: Le cru et le cuit*. Paris: Plon, 1964. Translated by J. and D. Weightman as *The Raw and the Cooked*. London: Cape, 1970.

Lewis, Clive Staples. *Oxford History of English Literature: English Literature in the Sixteenth Century, Excluding Drama*. Oxford: Clarendon Press, 1962.

Lindley, Mark. "Bach-style Keyboard Tuning." *Early Music* 34 (2006): 613–23.

Little, Meredith, and Carol Marsh. *La Danse noble: An Inventory of Dances and Sources*. Williamstown, MA: Broude Brothers, 1992.

Longfellow, Henry Wadsorth. *Poems of Places: An Anthology*. Boston: J. R. Osgood and Co., 1876–79.

Loulié, Étienne. *Eléments ou principes de musique*. Paris: C. Ballard, 1696. Translated by A. Cohen as *Elements or Principles of Music*. New York: Institute of Mediaeval Music, 1965.

McClure, Theron. "Making the Music Speak: *Silences d'articulation*." *American Recorder* 29 (1988): 53–55.

Mace, Thomas. *Musick's Monument*. London: Printed by T. Ratclisse and N. Thompson, 1676. Reprint, New York: Broude, 1966. Facsimile with commentary by Jean Jacquot and André Souris. Paris: Éditions du Centre National de la Recherche Scientifique, 1958–66.

Machy, Le Sieur de. *Pieces de violle en musique et en tablature . . .* Paris: the author, 1685. Reprint, Paris: Minkoff, 1973.

Marcello, Alessandro. *Concerto 2*. In *Concerti a cinque*. Amsterdam: Roger, 1716.

———. *Concerto für Oboe, 2 Violinen, Viola, Basso, und Cembalo, C-Moll*. Edited by Richard Lauschmann. Bonn: R. Forberg, 1923.

———. *Konzert für Oboe, Streicher und Basso continuo d-Moll*. Edited by Hugo Ruf. Mainz: Schott, 1985.

———. *Concerto in d minor (c minor) with Bach's Ornaments*. Edited by Himie Voxman. London: Musica Rara, 1977.

Marissen, Michael. "On the Musical Theology in J. S. Bach's Church Cantatas." *Lutheran Quarterly* 16 (2002): 48–64.

———. *The Social and Religious Designs of J. S. Bach's Brandenburg Concertos*. Princeton, NJ: Princeton University Press, 1995.

Marpurg, Friedrich Wilhelm. *Kritische Briefe über die Tonkunst*. Berlin: W. F. Birstiel, 1759–64. Reprint, Hildesheim: G. Olms, 1974.

Marshall, Robert L. "Bach's Tempo Ordinario: A Plaine and Easie Introduction to the System," *Performance Practice Review* 13/1 (2008) available at http://scholarship.clarement.edu/ppr/vol13/iss1/5: Updates the section in Marshall, *The Music of Johann Sebastian Bach: The Sources, the Style, the Significance*, 255–70. New York: Schirmer, 1989.

———. *The Compositional Process of J. S. Bach*. Princeton, NJ: Princeton University Press, 1972.

———. *Mozart Speaks: Views on Music, Musicians, and the World Drawn from the Letters of Wolfgang Amadeus Mozart and other Early Accounts*. New York: Schirmer Books, 1991.

Mason, John. *An Essay on Elocution and Pronunciation.* London: M. Cooper, 1748.
Mather, Betty Bang. *Dance Rhythms of the French Baroque.* Bloomington: Indiana University Press, 1987.
Mattheson, Johann. *Der Musicalische Patriot.* Hamburg: s.n., 1728.
———. *Das Neu-eröffnete Orchestre.* Hamburg: s.n., 1713. Reprint, New York: G. Olms, 1993.
———. *Veritophili Deutliche Beweis-Gründe Worauf der rechte Gebrach der Music, beydes in den Kirchen als ausser denselben beruhet . . .* (Hamburg: B. Schiller, 1717). Translated by J. Irwin as *A Truth Lover's Clear Reasonings on which the Correct Use of Music Is Based, both Within the Church and Outside It*. In Joyce L. Irwin, *Foretastes of Heaven in Lutheran Church Music Tradition*. Lanham, MD: Rowman & Littlefield, 2015.
———. *Der Vollkommene Capellmeister.* Hamburg: C. Herold, 1739. Translated by Ernest C. Harriss as *Johann Mattheson's "Der Vollkommene Capellmeister": A Revised Translation with Critical Commentary*. Ann Arbor: UMI Research Press, 1981.
Mattick, Paul Jr., ed. *Eighteenth-Century Aesthetics and the Reconstruction of Art.* Cambridge: Cambridge University Press, 1993.
McClary, Susan. "The Blasphemy of Talking Politics during Bach Year." In *Music and Society: The Politics of Composition, Performance, and Reception*, edited by Richard Leppert and Susan McClary, 13–62. Cambridge: Cambridge University Press, 1987.
Mellers, Wilfred. *Bach and the Dance of God.* Boston: Faber & Faber, 1980.
Ménestrier, Claude-François. *Des ballets anciens et modernes.* Paris: R. Guignard. Reprint, Geneva: Minkoff, 1972.
———. *Des représentations en musique anciennes et modernes.* Paris: R. Guignard, 1681, 1685.
Mersenne, Marin. *Harmonie universelle.* Paris: S. Cramoisy, 1636. Reprint, Paris: Centre National de la Recherche Scientifique, 1963. Partial English translation in Edward A. Lippman, *Musical Aesthetics: A Historical Reader.* Vol. 1, *From Antiquity to the Eighteenth Century.* New York: Pendragon, 1986.
Meyer, Richard. "Introduction: The Problem of the Passions." In *Representing the Passions: Histories, Bodies, Visions*, edited by Richard Meyer, 1–11. Los Angeles: Getty Research Institute, 2003.
Milson, David, and Neal Peres da Costa. "Expressiveness in Historical Perspective: 19th-Century Ideals and Practices." In *Expressiveness in Music Performance: Empirical Approaches across Styles and Cultures*, edited by Dorottya Fabian, Renee Timmers, and Emery Schubert, 80–97. Oxford: Oxford University Press, 2014.
Mitford, Nancy. *Frederick the Great.* London: Hamilton, 1970.
Moens-Haenen, Greta. "Holzbläservibrato im Barock." *Brussels Museum of Musical Instruments Bulletin* 14/1 (1984): 1–59.
———. *Das Vibrato in der Musik des Barock.* Graz: Akademische Druck- und Verlagsanstalt, 1988.
Monelle, Raymond. *The Sense of Music: Semiotic Essays.* Princeton, NJ: Princeton University Press, 2000.
Montagu, Jennifer. *The Expression of the Passions: The Origin and Influence of Charles Le Brun's "Conférence sur l'expression générale et particulière."* New Haven: Yale University Press, 2006.
Montéclair, Michel Pignolet de. *Principes de musique.* Paris: Vve Boivin. Reprint, Geneva: Minkoff, 1972.
Moroney, Davitt. "Listening To and Playing *The Well-Tempered Clavier*." Berkeley: Cal Performances, program notes, 24 October 2009.
———. "The "Parodies" of François Couperin's Harpsichord Pieces." In *"L'esprit français" und die Musik Europas: Enstehung, Einfluss und Grenzen einer ästhetischen Doktrin—Festschrift für Herbert Schneider / "L'esprit français" et la musique en Europe: Émergence, influence et limites d'une doctrine esthétique*, edited by Michelle Biget-Mainfroy and Rainer Schmusch, 608–33. Hildesheim: G. Olms, 2007.
Mozart, Leopold. *Versuch einer gründlichen Violinschule.* Augsburg: J. J. Lotter, 1756. Translated by Editha Knocker as *A Treatise on the Fundamental Principles of Violin Playing.* New York: Oxford University Press, 1951.

Nettl, Paul. *Forgotten Musicians*. New York: Philosophical Library, 1951.
Neubauer, John. *The Emancipation of Music from Language: Departure from Mimesis in Eighteenth-Century Aesthetics*. New Haven: Yale University Press, 1986.
Neumann, Frederick. "Authenticity and the Vocal Vibrato." *American Choral Review* 26 (1987): 13–18.
———. *Ornamentation in Baroque and Post-Baroque Music, with Special Emphasis on J. S. Bach*. Princeton, NJ: Princeton University Press, 1978.
———. "The Use of Baroque Treatises on Musical Performance." *Music and Letters* 48 (1967): 315–24.
Nevile, Jennifer. *Dance, Spectacle, and the Body Politick, 1250–1750*. Bloomington: Indiana University Press, 2008.
North, Roger. *The Musical Grammarian*. MS ca.1728. Edited by Mary Chan and Jamie Kassler. Cambridge: Cambridge University Press, 1990.
O'Donnell, John. "Bach's Temperament, Occam's Razor, and the Neidhardt Factor." *Early Music* 34 (2006): 625–33.
Oleskiewicz, Mary A. "Quantz and the Flute at Dresden: His Instruments, His Repertory and Their Significance for the *Versuch* and the Bach Circle." PhD diss., Duke University, 1998.
Ong, Walter J. *Orality and Literacy: The Technologizing of the Word*. London: Routledge, 2002.
———. *Rhetoric Romance and Technology: Studies in the Interaction of Expression and Culture*. Ithaca, NY: Cornell University Press, 1971.
Ortiz, Diego. *Trattado de Glosas*. Rome: V. and L. Dorico, 1553.
Ossi, Massimo. *Divining the Oracle: Monteverdi's Secundo Prattica*. Chicago: University of Chicago Press, 2003.
Palisca, Claude V. *The Florentine Camerata: Documentary Studies and Translations*. New Haven: Yale University Press, 1989.
———. *Music and Ideas in the Sixteenth and Seventeenth Centuries*. Chicago: University of Chicago Press, 2006.
Parke, William Thomas. *Musical Memoirs*. London: H. Colburn & R. Bentley, 1830. Reprint, New York: Da Capo, 1970.
Pater, Walter. *The Renaissance: Studies in Art and Poetry*. London: Macmillan & Co, 1922. Reprint, Luton: Andrews, 2011.
Peacham, Henry. *The Garden of Eloquence*. London: H. Jackson, 1577; Facsimile, Gainesville, FL: Scholars' Facsimiles & Reprints, 1954. Available online at http://rhetoric.byu.edu/primary texts/Peacham.htm.
Pepys, Samuel. *Diary* [1660–69]: Selections in *The Illustrated Pepys*. Edited by R. Latham. Berkeley: University of California Press, 1978.
Peres da Costa, Neal. *Off the Record*. New York: Oxford University Press, 2012.
Philidor, Pierre. *Suittes*, Opp.1–3. Paris: Foucault, 1717–18. Reprint, New York: Performers' Facsimiles, 2007.
Plebuch, Tobias. "Dark Fantasies and the Dawn of the Self: Gerstenberg's Monologues for C. P. E. Bach's C-minor Fantasia." In *C. P .E. Bach Studies*, 25–66. Cambridge: Cambridge University Press, 2006.
Playford, John. *A Breefe Introduction to the Skill of Musick* [1654]. 12th ed. London: E. Jones for H. Playford, 1694.
Poisson, Jean. *Réflexions sur l'art de parler en public*. n.p., 1717. Reprint in Chaouche, *Sept Traités*. Paris: Honoré Champion, 2001.
Pope, Alexander. *An Essay on Criticism*. London: printed for W. Lewis, 1711.
Praetorius, Michael. *Syntagma musicum tomus tertius*. Wolfenbüttel, 1618. Edited and translated by Jeffrey Kite-Powell. Oxford: Oxford University Press, 2004.
Printz, Wolfgang Caspar. *Musica modulatoria vocalis*. Schweidnitz: C. Okel, 1678.
Pure, abbé Michel de. *Idée des spectacles anciens et nouveaux*. Paris: M. Brunet. Reprint, Geneva: Minkoff, 1972.

Quantz, Johann Joachim. "Herrn Johann Joachim Quantzens Lebenslauf, von ihm selbst entworfen." In *Historisch-kritische Beyträge zur Aufnahme der Musik*. 1/3 197–250, edited by F. W. Marpurg. Berlin, 1754; English translation in Paul Nettl, *Forgotten Musicians*, 280–319.

———. *Versuch einer Anweisung die Flöte traversiere zu Spielen* Berlin: Voss, 1752. French version *Essai d'une méthode pour apprendre à jouer de la Flûte Traversière*. Berlin: Voss, 1752. English translation by E. R. Reilly as *On Playing the Flute*. London: Faber & Faber, 1971.

Quintilianus, Marcus Fabius. *Institutio Oratoria*, 95 AD, Books 1–12. Translated by William Guthrie as *Quinctilian's Institutes of Eloquence: Or, The Art of Speaking in Public*. London: T. Waller, 1756. Translated by Donal Russell as *The Orator's Education*. Cambridge, MA: Harvard University Press, 2001.

Raguenet, François. *Paralèle des Italiens et des François en ce qui regarde la musique et les opera*. Paris: J. Moreau, 1702. Reprint Geneva: Minkoff, 1976.

Rameau, Jean Philippe. *Erreurs sur la musique dans l'Encyclopédie*. Paris: S. Jorry, 1755. Reprinted in Jacobi, *Complete Theoretical Writings of Jean-Philippe Rameau*. Middleton, WI: American Institute of Musicology, 1967–72.

———. *Observations sur notre instinct pour la musique*. Paris: Prault fils, 1754. Reprinted in Jacobi, *Complete Theoretical Writings of Jean-Philippe Rameau*. Middleton, WI: American Institute of Musicology, 1967–72. Partial English translation in Edward A. Lippman, *Musical Aesthetics: A Historical Reader*. Vol. 1, *From Antiquity to the Eighteenth Century*. New York: Pendragon, 1986.

———. *Pieces de clavecin en concerts avec un violon ou une flute, et une viole ou un deuxième violon*. Paris: the author, Vve Boivin, and Le Clair, 1741.

———. *Traité de l'harmonie reduite à ses principes naturels*. Paris: Ballard, 1722. Translated by Philip Gosset as *Treatise on Harmony*. New York: Dover, 1971.

Rameau, Pierre. *Le Maître à danser, qui enseigne la manière de faire tous les différens pas de danse dans toute la régularité de l'art*. Paris: J. Villette, 1725. Reprint, New York: Broude, 1967.

Ranum, Patricia M. "Audible Rhetoric and Mute Rhetoric: The Seventeenth-Century French Sarabande." *Early Music* 14 (1986): 22–39.

———. *The Harmonic Orator: The Phrasing and Rhetoric of the Melody in French Baroque Airs*. Hillsdale, NY: Pendragon, 2001.

Ratner, Leonard. *Classic Music: Expression, Form, and Style*. New York: Schirmer, 1980.

Razzi, Fausto. "Polyphony of the *Seconda Prattica*." *Early Music* 8/3 (1980): 298–311.

Reilly, Edward R. *Quantz and his "Versuch": Three Studies*. New York: American Musicological Society, 1971.

Rémond de Sainte-Albine, Pierre. *Le comédien*. Paris: Desaint & Saillant, 1747. Reprint, Geneva: Slatkine, 1971.

Rémond de Sainte-Mard, Toussaint. *Reflexions sur l'opéra*. The Hague: Neaulme, 1741. Reprint, Geneva: Minkoff, 1972.

Reynolds, Joshua. "Discourse no. 2," December 11, 1769. *Seven Discourses on Art*. Edited by D. Price, 1:28. London: Cassell & Col.

Riccoboni, François. *L'Art du théâtre*. Paris: C. F. Simon, 1750.

Riccoboni, Luigi. *Pensées sur la declamation*. In *Reflexions historiques et critiques sur les differens theatres de l'Europe*. Paris: J. Guerin, 1738. Anonymously translated as *Reflections upon Declamation: An Essay on Action or the Art of Speaking in Public in an Historical and Critical Account of the Theatres in Europe*. London: T. Waller, 1741.

Rice, John. *Introduction to the Art of Reading with Energy and Propriety*. London: printed for J. & P. Tonson, 1765.

Richesource, Oudart de [Jean de la Sourdière]. *L'éloquence de la chaire, ou Rhétorique des prédicateurs*. Paris: the author, 1665.

Ricœur, Paul. *Rule of the Metaphor: Multi-disciplinary Studies of the Creation of Meaning in Language*. Toronto: Toronto University Press, 1977.

Riemann, Hugo. *Musikalische Dynamik und Agogik: Lehrbuch der musikalischen Phrasirung*. ... Hamburg: D. Rahter, 1884.

Riepel, Joseph. *Anfangsgründe zur musicalischen Setzkunst*. Various locations, 1752–86.

Rink, John. "Translating Musical Meaning: The Nineteenth-Century Performer as Narrator." In *Rethinking Music*, edited by N. Cook and M. Everest, 217–38. Oxford: Oxford University Press, 1999.

Rooley, Anthony. "Renaissance Attitudes to Performance: A Contemporary Application." In *Companion to Contemporary Musical Thought*, edited by J. Paynter et al., 948–60. London: Routledge, 1992.

Rose, Stephen. "Musician-Novels of the German Baroque." In *The Worlds of Johann Sebastian Bach: An Aston Magna Academy Book*, edited by Raymond Erickson, 175–90. New York: Amadeus Press (Hal Leonard), 2009.

Rosenblum, Sandra. *Performance Practices in Classic Piano Music: Their Principles and Applications*. Bloomington: Indiana University Press, 1988.

Rosenfield, Lawrence W. "Rhetorical Criticism and an Aristotelian Notion of Process." *Speech Monographs* 33/1 (1966): 1–14.

Rousseau, Jean-Jacques. *Dictionnaire de musique*. Paris: Duschene, 1768. Reprint, Hildesheim: G. Olms, 1969. Translated by W. Waring as *A Dictionary of Music*. London: Printed for J. French, 1771.

Saint-Lambert, M. de. *Les principes de clavecin contenant une explication exacte de tout ce qui concerne la tablature & le clavier*. Paris: Ballard, 1702. Translated by R. Harris-Warrick as *Principles of the Harpsichord*. Cambridge: Cambridge University Press, 1984.

Sainte-Colombe M. de. *Recueil de pièces pour basse de viole seule*, MS, ca. 1690. Facsimile, Paris: Minkoff, 1998.

Salmen, Walter, ed. *The Social Status of the Professional Musician from the Middle Ages to the Nineteenth Century*. English translation by H. Kaufman and B. Reisner of *Der Sozialstatus des Berufsmusikers vom 17. bis 19. Jahrhundert*. New York: Pendragon Press, 1983.

Scherer, William. "Temporal and Eternal Realities in German Baroque Homiletics." *Modern Language Quarterly* 32 (1971): 158–67.

Schmitter, Amy M. "17th and 18th Century Theories of Emotions." In *The Stanford Encyclopedia of Philosophy*, edited by Edward N. Zalta (Summer 2006 edition). Available at http://plato.stanford.edu/archives/sum2006/entries/emotions-17th18th.

Schneider, Herbert. "Die Funktion des Divertissement und des Ballet." In *La Musique et le Rite sacré et Profane: Actes du XIIIe Congrès de la Société Internationale de Musicologie, 1982*. Strasbourg: Association des Publications près des Universités de Strasbourg, 1986, 2:433–63.

Schoenberg, Arnold. *Style and Idea: Selected Writings of Arnold Schoenberg*. New York: Philosophical Library, 1950.

Schulenberg, David. "Musical Expression and Musical Rhetoric in the Keyboard Works of J. S. Bach." In *Johann Sebastian Bach: A Tercentenary Celebration*, edited by S. Benstock, 95–109. Westport, CT: Greenwood Press, 1994.

Schuller, Gunther. *The Compleat Conductor*. New York: Oxford University Press, 1998.

Schweitzer, Albert. *J. S. Bach*. Translated by Ernest Newman. London: Breitkopf & Härtel, 1911.

Seymour, Peter. "Oratory and Performance." In *Companion to Contemporary Musical Thought*, edited by John Paynter, 913–19. London: Routledge, 1992.

Sherman, Bernard D. *Inside Early Music: Conversations with Performers*. New York: Oxford University Press, 1997.

Siebel, Sabine, ed. *The Glory of Baroque Dresden*. Jackson: Mississippi Commission for International Cultural Exchange; Dresden: State Art Collections Dresden, 2004.

Siegele, Ulrich. *Kompositionsweise und Bearbeitungstechnik in der Instrumentalmusik Johann Sebastian Bachs*. Neuhausen-Stuttgart: Hänssler, 1975.

Sipiora, Baumlin. *Rhetoric and Kairos: Essays in History, Theory, and Praxis*. Albany: SUNY Press, 2002.

Small, Christopher. *Musicking: The Meanings of Performing and Listening.* Hanover, NH: University Press of New England, 1998.

Smith, Anne. *The Performance of Sixteenth-Century Music: Learning from the Theorists.* Oxford: Oxford University Press, 2011.

Spitta, J. A. P. *Johann Sebastian Bach.* Leipzig: Breitkopf & Härtel, 1873–80/5. Translated by Clara Bell and J. A. Fuller-Maitland as *Johann Sebastian Bach: His Work and Influence on the Music of Germany, 1658–1750.* London: Novello, 1951.

Stauffer, George B. "Bach and the Lure of the Big City." In *The Worlds of Johann Sebastian Bach: An Aston Magna Academy Book,* edited by Raymond Erickson, 243–66. New York: Amadeus Press (Hal Leonard), 2009.

Steblin, Rita. *A History of Key Characteristics in the Eighteenth and Early Nineteenth Centuries.* Ann Arbor: UMI Research Press, 1983.

Stendhal, Henry Beyle. *Vie de Rossini.* Paris: Boulland, 1824. Translated by N. Coe as *Life of Rossini.* New York: Criterion Books, 1957.

Stravinsky, Igor. *Autobiography.* New York: Simon & Schuster, 1936.

Strunk, Oliver. *Source Readings in Music History.* New York: W. W. Norton, 1950.

Sulzer, J. G. *Allgemeine Theorie der schönen Künste.* Leipzig: Weidmann, 1771–74. Reprint, Hildesheim, G. Olms, 1967.

Tarling, Judy. *The Weapons of Rhetoric.* St. Albans Hartfordshire: Corda Music, 2004.

Tartini, Giuseppe. *Trattato di musica.* Padua: G. Manfré, 1754.

Taruskin, Richard. *Text and Act: Essays on Music and Performance.* New York: Oxford University Press, 1995.

Tatlow, Ruth. *Bach and the Riddle of the Number Alphabet.* Cambridge: Cambridge University Press, 1991.

———. *Bach's Numbers.* Cambridge: Cambridge University Press, 2015.

Taubert, Gottfried. *Rechtschaffener Tanzmeister, oder gründliche Erklärung der Französischen Tanz-Kunst.* 3 vols. Leipzig: Friedrich Lanckischs Erben, 1717.

Telemann, Georg Philipp. *Der Harmonische Gottesdienst.* Hamburg: the author, 1731.

Thurmond, James Morgan. *Note Grouping: A Method for Achieving Expression and Style in Musical Performance.* Camp Hill, PA: JMT Publications, 1982.

Tidhar, Dan, Simon Dixon, Emmanouil Benetos, and Tillman Weyde. "The Temperament Police." *Early Music* 42 (2014): 579–90.

Tilney, Colin. *The Art of the Unmeasured Prelude for Harpsichord.* London: Schott, 1991.

Tisch-Wackernagel, Johannes Hermann. "Baroque." In *Periods in German Literature,* edited by J. M. Ritchie. London: Wolff 1966.

Toft, Robert. "The Expressive Pause: Punctuation, Rests, and Breathing in England, 1770–1850." *Performance Practice Review* 7 (1994): 1–32, 199–232.

———. *Tune Thy Musicke to Thy Hart: The Art of Eloquent Singing in England, 1597–1622.* Toronto: University of Toronto Press, 1993.

Tolbert, Elizabeth. "The Voice of Lament: Female Vocality and Performative Efficacy in the Finnish-Karelian Itkuvirsi." In *Embodied Voices: Representing Female Vocality in Western Culture,* edited by Leslie C. Dunn and Nancy Jones, 179–94. Cambridge: Cambridge University Press, 1994.

Tomlinson, Kellom. *The Art of Dancing Explained by Figures.* London: the author, 1735.

Tosi, Pier Francesco. *Opinioni de' cantori antichi e moderni.* Bologna: L. dalla Volpe, 1723. Translated by J. E. Galliard as *Observations on the Florid Song.* London: Printed for J. Wilcox, 1742; German translation by Agricola as *Anleitung zur Singkunst.*

Treitler, Leo. *Music and the Historical Imagination.* Cambridge, MA: Harvard University Press, 1989.

Troeger, Richard. *Technique and Interpretation on the Harpsichord and Clavichord.* Bloomington: Indiana University Press, 1987.

Tromlitz, *Ausführlicher und gründlicher Unterricht die Flöte zu spielen*. Leipzig: A. Böhme, 1791. Translated by Ardal Powell as *The Virtuoso Flute-Player*. Cambridge: Cambridge University Press, 1991

Türk, Daniel Gottlob. *Klavierschule oder Anweisung zum Klavierspielen für Lehrer und Lernende*. Leipzig: Auf Kosten des Verfassers, in Kommission bey Schwickert, 1789.

Verba, E. Cynthia. "The Development of Rameau's Thoughts on Modulation and Chromatics." *Journal of the American Musicological Society* 26 (1973): 69–91.

Vial, Stephanie D. *The Art of Musical Phrasing in the Eighteenth Century: Punctuating the Classical "Period."* Rochester, NY: University of Rochester Press, 2008.

Vicentino, Nicola. *Antica musica ridotta alla moderna prattica*. 1555. Translated by Maria Rika Maniates as *Ancient Music Adapted to Modern Practice*. New Haven: Yale University Press, 1996.

Vickers, Brian. "Rhetorical and Anti-Rhetorical Tropes: On Writing the History of Elocution." In *Comparative Criticism: A Yearbook* 3, edited by E. S. Shaffer, 105–32. Cambridge: Cambridge University Press, 1981.

Vogt, Gustave. *Vocalises de Crescentini, transcrites pour le hautbois. . .avec accompagnement de piano par A. Bourdeau*. Paris: S. Richault, ca. 1860.

Vogt, Moritz Johann. *Conclave thesauri magnae artis musicae*. Prague: G. Labaun, 1719.

Walker, Daniel Pickering. "Musical Humanism in the Sixteenth and Early Seventeenth Centuries" (1941–42). Reprinted in *Music, Spirit and Language in the Renaissance*, edited by Penelope Gouk. London: Variorum Reprints, 1985.

Walls, Peter. "'Ill-compliments and Arbitrary Taste'? Geminiani's Directions for Performers." *Early Music* 14 (1986): 221–35.

Walther, Johann. *Musikalisches Lexikon oder Musikalische Bibliothek*. Leipzig: W. Deer, 1732.

Weber, William. "Wagner, Wagnerism and Musical Idealism." In *Wagnerism in European Culture and Politics*, edited by D. C. Large and W. Weber, 28–71. Ithaca, NY: Cornell University Press, 1984.

Weigel, Johann Christoph. *Musikalisches Theatrum*. Nuremberg: Weigel, ca. 1720

Wentz, Jed. "Freedom of Expression: A Right to 'Mutilate the Meter.'" *Traverso: Historical Flute Newsletter* 12/2 (2000): 1–3.

———. "The Relationship between Gesture, Affect, and Rhythmic Freedom in the Performance of French Tragic Opera from Lully to Rameau." PhD diss., Leiden University, 2010.

Wessel, Frederick. "The Affektenlehre in the Eighteenth Century." PhD diss., University of Indiana, Bloomington, 1955.

Williams, Peter. *Figured Bass Accompaniment*. Edinburgh: Edinburgh University Press, 1970.

Williams, Peter, ed. *Bach, Handel, Scarlatti: Tercentenary Essays*. Cambridge: Cambridge University Press, 1985.

Wilson, John, ed. *Roger North on Music*. London: Novello, 1959.

Wimsatt, William K., and Munroe C. Beardsley. "The Intentional Fallacy." *Sewanee Review* 54 (1946): 468–88.

Winn, James Anderson. *Unsuspected Eloquence: A History of the Relations between Poetry and Music*. New Haven: Yale University Press, 1981.

Wistreich, Richard. "Reconstructing Pre-Romantic Singing Technique." In *The Cambridge Companion to Singing*, edited by John Potter, 178–91. Cambridge: Cambridge University Press, 2000.

Wragg, J. *The Oboe Preceptor; or the Art of Playing the Oboe. . .* London, the author, 1792.

Zaslaw, Neal. *Mozart's Symphonies: Context, Performance Practice, Reception*. Oxford: Oxford University Press, 1989.

———. "Ornaments for Corelli's Violin Sonatas, op. 5." *Early Music* 24 (1996): 95–115.

INDEX

Page numbers in italics refer to musical examples and figures. Numbers followed by an "a" refer to audio examples; often the subject of the entry is discussed on the same page.

a battuta, 215
Abrams, M. H., 37
Abravaya, Ido, 232
absolute music, 25, 28–29, 31–32, 33–34, 37, 69–70, 207
acting, 4, 53, 69, 91
   craft of, 170
   manuals, 117, 142, 246–247, 173, 258
   in opera, 10
   voice distinguished from everyday, 142
Adams, Piers, 166
Æsthetics, 13, 17, 28–29
affect, 4, 7. *See also* passions
   contrasting, 92–93, 106, 126, 148, 152, 212
   and keys, 59–65
   in music, 13, 18, 23, 117, 140
   musical parameters defining, 188–189, 194
   and ornaments, 155, 156, 214, 226
   or passions, 8, 12, 17, 25, 91, 241
   in performance, 10, 13, 20, 68, 125, 127, 175, 225, 259, 273
   real and false, 256
   in recitative, 215
   single, 91, 187
   in speech, 169–70
   and tempo, 134–7
   and texts, 71
   of *tremolo*, 99–100
Agawu, Kofi, 66
agogics, 181–183, 201, 208, 221, 226
   defined, 181, 228, 233
Albani, Francesco, 27
Alembert, Jean-Henri d', 11, 215
Alessandrini, Rinaldo, 5, 223, 224a
Amadeus (motion picture), 29
Ameln, Konrad, 233

Amsterdam Baroque Orchestra
   BWV 74/7, 114a
   BWV 155/4, 124a
   BWV 154, 125a
   BWV 127/3, 264
anabasis, 102
Anglebert, Jean-Henri d', 215
antithesis, 88, 100–105, 111, 113, 190, 217
appoggiaturas, 96, 149–151, 155–156, 197, 203, 212
arias, 23
arioso, 196, 215
Aristotle, definition of rhetoric, 3, 17, 23, 259
   on artistic subjects, 30
   and *ethos*, 244
   on imitation, 68
Arnold, Frank Thomas, 167
Arnold, Samuel, 133
art for art's sake, 31–33, 235. *See also* absolute music
articulation, 110, 127, 130, 132, 169, 188,
   agogic, 171–181, 226, 228
   in dance, 254
   Baroque and Romantic styles compared, 195–199
   markings, 103, 178–181, 190, 199
   of musical structures, 40, 133, 171–181, 187, 194, 221, 229
   and silence, 186, 226, 228 (*see also* silence d'articulation)
aspiration, 226, 231
Aubignac, François Hédelin abbé d', 142
audiences and authentic ears, 234–240, 261
Auerbach, Erich, 17, 90
Auernhammer, Josepha, 196
Auld Robin Gray, 133
autonomous music, *see* absolute music
Avison, Charles, 31, 43, 44

Babell, William, 161, 163, *164*
Babitz, Sol, 233
Bach Collegium Japan, 263
 BWV 101/1, 109, 110a
 BWV 127/3, 264a
 BWV 143/4, 129a
 BWV 150/6, 76a
 BWV 154/1, 125a
Bach revival in 1950s, xiv
Bach, Carl Philipp Emanuel, 16, 123, 160
 on articulation breaks, 172, 176, 199, 227
 on borrowed time, 223, 227, *227*
 education, 24
 on fantasies and improvisation, 140, 216–217, 255
 on performance, 154, 155
 on recitative, 214
 Sanguineus and Melancholicus, 59a, 145, 146a
 sonatas with varied repeats, 160–161, *161*, 165
 on tempo, 206, 207, 212a
 Versuch, xxiv, 17, 283n5
 on *Vortrag*, 249
Bach, Johann Sebastian,
 character, 80
 dramatic characterizations, 86–87
 education, 24
 fermatas in chorales, 217–19
 as Fifth Evangelist, 9
 as musical rhetorician, 25
 musical symbolism, 65–67, 100
 as painter of passions, 9, 72
 portrait by Haussmann, 50
 and religion, 72–73, 80
 sacred and secular works, 73
 scoring for woodwinds, 81–83
 and tempo, 206, 207, 210
 use of chorale tunes, 94, 107, 109–111, 217–219, 233
 use of figures, 65, 70–72, 101–103
Bach, J. S., works by (by title):
 Ach wie flüchtig, ach wie nichtig, 44, 89, *89–90*
 Ach, Herr, mich armen Sünder, 144, 145a
 "Air on a G String," 68
 Ascension Oratorio, 71, 94
 Aus der Tiefen, xi
 Aus tiefer Not, 113, *113*
 Brandenburg Concertos, xiv, 81, 173 174a
 Capriccio sopra la lontananza del fratello dilettissimo, 43
 Cello Suites, *see* Suites for violoncello
 Christus, der ist mein Leben, 200, *201*, *202*, 217
 Christmas Oratorio, 81, 94, 115, 215
 Chromatic Fantasy and Fugue, 182a
 Coffee Cantata, 86
 Concertos for harpsichord, 63, 162
  transcribed for oboe d'amore, 225a
 Concertos for violin, 63
 Der Himmel lacht, die Erde jubilieret, 80–81, *81*, 94
 Du Friedefürst, Herr Jesu Christ, 96–97, *98*
 Easter Oratorio, 94, 115, 215
 Erforsche mich Gott, und erfahre mein Herz, 270–72, *272*
 Erbauliche Gedanken eines Tobakrauchers, xxi–xxv
 Erhalt uns, Herr, bei dienem Wort, 267–68, *267*
 Es reisset euch ein schrecklich Ende, 94
 Es wartet alles auf dich, 71
 Goldberg Variations, 62
 Gott fahret auf mit Jauchzen, 83, *83*, 176, *177*
 Gott, wie dein Name, 209a, 268–69, *268*
 Gottlob! Nun geht das Jahr zu Ende, 94
 Herr Christ, der einge Gottessohn, 74, 75
 Herr Jesu Christ, wahr' Mensche und Gott, 264a
 Herr, deine Augen sehen, 265–66, *265*
 Herr, gehe nicht ins Gericht, 269–70, *269*
 Herr, wie du willst, 111–13, *112*
 Ich elender Mensch, wer wird mich erlösen, 47
 Ich glaube, lieber Herr, 94, 95
 Ich habe genug, 162a, *162*
 Ich hatte viel Bekümmernis, 88, 93
 Ich will den Kreutzstab gerne tragen, 46
 Ihr Menschen, rühmet Gottes Liebe, 94
 Ihr werdet weinen und heulen, 47, 101, *102*
 In allen meinen taten, 101
 Italian Concerto, 225a
 Jesus schläft, was soll ich hoffen? 86, 86a
 Komm, du süße Todesstunde, 78, 79
 Lobet den Herrn, meine Seele, 129a
 Lutheran Mass in g minor, 71, 265a
 Mass in B minor, 29, 68, 103, *103–104*
 Mein Gott, wie lang, ach lange, 124a
 Mein Herz schwimmt in Blut, 104
 Mein liebster Jesus ist verloren, 125a
 Meine Säufzer, meine Tränen, 105, *105*, 113
 Nach dir, Herr, verlanget mich, 75–78, 76–77, 75a
 Nimm von uns, Herr, du treuer Gott, 108, *109–110*, 110a
 Nun ist das Heil und die Kraft, 102–03, *102*
 Nun komm, der Heiden Heiland, 74
 O Ewigkeit, du Donnerwort, 116
 Orchestral Suites, *see* Suites for Orchestra
 Passion settings, xii, 74. *See also* St. John Passion, St. Matthew Passion
 Preise, Jerusalem, den Herrn, 115–16
 St. John Passion, 65, 74, 75, 87, 96, 97, 99a, 218, 219a
 St. Matthew Passion, 29, 74, 78, 111, 20a, 218, *218*, 265
 Schlage doch, gewünschte Stunde, 202n
 Schweigt stille, plaudert nicht, 86
 Streit zwischen Phoebus und Pan, Die 115

Suites for orchestra, 68, 71, 116;
Suites for violoncello, 228
Tritt auf die Glaubensbahn, xi
Unser Mund sei voll Lachens, 71, 80, 82, 94, 264a
Von Himmel Hoch, 219a
Wachet auf, 80
Wachet! betet! 99a, 107
Wedding Cantata, 104
Weichet nur, 104
Weinen, Klagen, Sorgen, Zagen, 71
Well-Tempered Clavier (WTC), 62–63, 63a, 216
Wer mich liebet, 114, 114a, *115*
Wer weiß, wie nah emir mein Ende? 29
Wir müssen durch viel Trübsal, 71
Wohl dem, der sich auf seinen Gott, 105–06, *106–07*
Wohltemperierte Klavier, Das, see *Well-Tempered Clavier*

Bach, J. S., works by (by BWV number):
BWV 11, 71, 94
BWV 12, 71
BWV 13, 101, 105, *105*, 113
BWV 20, 116
BWV 21, 88, 93
BWV 26, 44, 89, *89–90*
BWV 27, 29
BWV 28, 94
BWV 31, 80–81, *82*, 94
BWV 33, 265–66
BWV 38, 113, *113*
BWV 43, 176, *177*
BWV 43, 83, *83*
BWV 44, 101
BWV 46, 100
BWV 48, 47, *47*
BWV 50, 102–03, *102*
BWV 53, 202n
BWV 56, 46, *46*
BWV 60, 100
BWV 61, 116
BWV 61, 74
BWV 70, 99, 99a, 107
BWV 73, 111–13, *112*
BWV 74, 114, 114a, *115*
BWV 81, 86a
BWV 82, 165a, *165*
BWV 95, 200, *201*, 202, 218
BWV 96, 74, *75*
BWV 97, 101
BWV 101, 108, *109–110*, 110a
BWV 102, 265–66, *265*
BWV 103, 101, *102*
BWV 103, 47, *47*
BWV 109, 94, *95*
BWV 110, 71, 80, *81*, 94, 116, 214a
BWV 114, 100
BWV 116, 96–97, *98*
BWV 119, 115–16
BWV 124, 100
BWV 126, 267–68, *267*
BWV 127, 264, 264a
BWV 131, ix
BWV 135, 144, 145a
BWV 136, 270–72, *272*
BWV 139, 105–06, *106–07*
BWV 140, 80
BWV 143, 129a
BWV 146, 71
BWV 150, 75–78, *76–77*, 76a
BWV 152, ix
BWV 154, 125a
BWV 155, 124a
BWV 161, 78, *79*
BWV 164, 78
BWV 167, 94
BWV 171, 209a
BWV 171, 268–69, *268*
BWV 187, 71
BWV 190, 94
BWV 199, 104
BWV 201, 115
BWV 202, 104
BWV 211, 86
BWV 235, 71
BWV 248, 81, 94
BWV 248, 94, 115, 215
BWV 249, 115
BWV 515, xix–xxiii
BWV 715, 218
BWV 722, 218
BWV 732, 218
BWV 903, 182a
BWV 971, 224, 225a
BWV 974, 162
BWV 992, 43
BWV 998, 62, 62a
BWV 1009, 228
BWV 1041, 63
BWV 1042, 63
BWV 1043, 63
BWV 1047, 173, 174a
BWV 1049, 63
BWV 105, 269–70, *269*
BWV 1053, 225, 225a
BWV 1054, 63
BWV 1057, 63
BWV 1058, 63
BWV 1062, 63
BWV 1068, 69
BWV 1069, 71
Bach–Lehmann temperament, 62, 63a
Bach, Wilhelm Friedemann, 15, 24

Bacilly, Benigne de, 84
  Art de bien chanter, 17
  on dances, 230
  on ornaments, 149, 155
  on tempo, 135
  on theatrical speech, 141
Baillot, Pierre, 26–27, 33–34, 227
Bang Mather, Betty, 138
Barnett, Dene, 117, 173
Bartel, Dietrich, xix, 45, 47–48, 66, 72
Barthe, Roland, 126
Bartoli, Cecilia, 158a
basso continuo, 21, 148–149, 159, 176, 207–209, 211
Batteux, Charles,
  Les Beaux arts reduits à un meme principe, 17
  on dance and gesture, 229, 244
  on imitation, 84
  on inspiration, 256
  on meaning in music, 12, 42–44, 267
  on moving an audience, 7, 35
  on persuasion and passions, 6–7, 8, 31, 35, 91
  on punctuation, 169
  on theatrical show, 257
Bayly, Anselm, 248
Beardsley, Monroe, 126
beating time, 204–207, 220. *See also* conductor
Beauchamp, Pierre, 229
beauty, aesthetic of, xxii, 28–29, 224, 270–271
Bebung, 156
Beerbohm Tree, Herbert, 142a, 171
Beethoven, Ludwig van, 207, 232
Beghin, Tom, 66, 262
Behrens, Samuel Rudolph, 229
Bernhard Christoph, 154, 22
Bernini, Gian Lorenzo, 92, 92
Bertini, Rossana, 224, 224a
Besozzi, Alessandro, 145
Biber, Heinrich, 74
Birnbaum, Johann Abraham, 24, 153
Blavet, Michel, 178
Blaze, Robin, 114a
body language, *see* deportment and body language
Boccherini, Luigi, 27, 34, 130, 132, 138
Boismortier, Joseph Bodin de, 151
Bonds, Mark Evan, xix, 42
borrowed time, 201, 211, 221–225, 293n50
Boulanger, Nadia, 223, 224a
Boulez, Pierre, 122,
Bienemann, Kasper, 111
Boyden, David, xvii
Branagh, Kenneth, 171a
breaking with time, 210–211
Bremner, Robert, 156
Brijon, C. R., 178
Brod, Henri, 197

Bronzini, Cristoforo, 251
Brown, Clive, 232
Brüggen, Frans, xi, xii, xv, xix, xxv, 5, 6, 164a
Buelow, George, xix, 16, 65–66
Burgess, Geoffrey, 157a, 164a, 167
Burkholder, John, 33
Burmeister, Joachim, 65
Burney, Charles, 15, 195, 197, 255
Burton, Richard, 142a
Butt, John, 36, 90, 199
Buxtehude, Dieterich, 183a
Bylsma, Anner, 228a

Caccini, Giulio, 214, 228, 233
cadence, 253
cadenzas, 161, 214, 216–217, 217, 218, 219a, 240
Cahusac, Louis de, 253, 256
Calmeta, Vincenzo, 20
Calottinne, La, parody, 190–194
Calov Bible, 93, 117
Calovius, Abraham, 117
Cambini, Giuseppe Maria, 26, 130–133, 145
Canal, Giovanni Antonio (Canaletto), 236, 237
cantar recitando, 21
carpe diem, 200
Carter, Elliott, 123
Casals, Pablo, 228a
catabasis, 102, *102*
Cavalieri, Emelio de', 21
Cavalli, Francesca, 251
Chafe, Eric, 67
character, 58. *See also ethopoeia*, and key characteristics
Charles, J. A. C., 207
Charpentier, Marc Antoine, 60, 61, Table 2.2
  Médée 64–65, 64a
Chaulieu, Guillaume Amfrye de, 144
chorale tunes, 39, 107, 111
  fermatas in, 217–219
  interstrophic improvisations in, 218, 293n44
  use by J. S. Bach, 94, 107, 109–111, 217–219, 233
choreography, 247, 253–254. *See also* dance notation, 254
Christie, William, 5, 64a, 129a
chromaticism, 97, 104, 105, 108, 208
  as expressive figure, 22, 74, 87, 102
chronomètre, 207, 209, 229
chronos, 200–205, 207, 210, 232
Cicero, Marcus Tullius, 9, 17
  on eloquence, 127, 255, 260
Clairon, La (Claire Josèphe Hippolyte Léris de La Tude), 123, 261
Clark and Connon, 67
Cleland, John, 7
close shake, 156–157

Cockin, William, 182
composers and performers, 11–12, 34, 42
    respective responsibilities, 12–13
Concentus Musicus Wien, 263
    BWV 74/7, 114a, 264a
    BWV 101/1, 110a
    BWV 110/1, 264a
    BWV 154, 125a
    BWV 155/4, 124a
    BWV 171/4, 209a
    Monteverdi, 223, 224a
    St. John Passion, 219a
conclusio, xviii, xx, 41
conductor, 40, 204, 209, 220–221, *220*, 247
confirmatio, 12, 24, 41, 84
confutatio, 12, 24, 41, 84, 93, 104
contagion, emotional, 243, 252
conversational style, 145–147, 146a
Corelli, Arcangelo, 161, 163, 255
Corneille, Pierre, 24, 251
Corrette, Michel, 146a, 209
Corri, Domenico, 186
corta, 102
counterpoint, 23, 124. *See also* polyphony
Couperin, François, 17
    L'Apothéose de Corelli, 255
    L'Art de toucher le clavecin, 182, *182*, 215–216
    "Les Calotins," 190–194
    commas, 178–181, *179*, 190, *191*, 194
    on gestures in performance, 248
    Les Goûts réunis, *179*, 179a, 184, *185*
    Livre de pièces, 178, 190
    his music parodied, 190–194
    ornaments, 151, 226
    pièces de caractère, 59, 67
    on rhythm and tempo, 135, 150, 215–216
    sarabandes by, 231–232, *231*, *232*
Couperin, Louis, 215
Couvay, Jean, 78
Cox, Howard, 117
Coypel, Antoine, 78, 79
Cramer, Johann Andreas, 239
creativity in Romantic art, 33–35
Crescentini, Girolamo, 197–198, *198*
Critique du genre humain, parody, 190–194
cross, image of the, 46, 71
Curtis, Alan, xi

da capo, xviii, 24, 84, 93, 104, 106, 138, 271
    ornamented, 160–161
Dahlhaus, Carl, 31–32, 37
dance as poetry, 252–254
dance tempos, 135–138, 228–232
dance topics, 58, 135–138
Daniels, David, 157, 158a
Dannreuther, Edward, 167
Darbellay, Étienne, 139, 155, 160

David, Hans, 72
declamation in speech, 141–143, 146, 197, 213
decorum, 38, 39, 44
deportment and body language, 29, 41, 52, 234, 243–244, 262
Descartes, René, 51–52, 55, 56
dialectics, 6
diastolica, 168, 291n34
Dictionaire de l'Académie française, 45, 49, 68
Diderot, Dénis, 123
    on tempo, 207, 208, 209, 211, 229
    Paradoxe sur le comedien, 257, 258, 261, 262
dispositio, 11–12, 24, 42, 121, 124
    definition, 38, 39–40
    in contrast to *elaboratio*, 147–151, 153, 159, 160, 211, 212
dissonance, affective use of, 21, 30, 46, 96, 108–110, 188, 266
    in figures, 47, 147, 149, 153–154,
    at fermatas, 218
    and temperament, 62
    treatment of, 22, 116, 127, 147, 149, 153–154
divine praise, music composed for, 73, 93–94, 219, 269
Dolmetsch, Arnold, 167
Dresden, 14–15, 50, 165, 223, 260
Dryden, John, 21, 38
Dubos, abbé Jean Baptiste,
    on credibility, 242, 251, 259
    on elevated speech, 143
    on figures, 49, 88–89, 143
    on *mimesis*, 9–10, 84
    and parallels in the arts, 10
    Reflexions critiques, 17
    and sincerity, 254, 259
    on sympathy, 242–243
Duffin, Ross, 67
Dürr, Alfred, 90, 266
"Dutch bulge," 128
Dutch early music school, xii, xix
dynamics, and articulation, 180, 196–197, *198*
    to define form, 113
    notation of, 122, 212
    as ornament, 155, 156
    use in "humouring," 130, 132–133, 137, 188, 196, 264

Earlom, Richard, 85
Einschnitt, 172, *172*
elocutio, in rhetorical process, 11, 12, 15–16, 24, 38
    and *actio*, 41
    contrast in, 137
    defined, 40
    distinguished from *inventio* and *dispositio*, 103, 148, 212, 250
    as ornamentation, 146
    as performance practice, 121, 127–128

eloquence, 4, 6, 8, 12, 42
　in 19th-century music, 29
　essential to a performance's success, 12, 13, 38, 121–130, 234, 242
　and feigning, 255
　figures essential to, 44, 49, 66, 74
　and judgment of a performance, 249, 260, 263
　and ornamentation, 146
　in Rhetorical music, 12, 36, 73, 169
　and truth, 3
Eloquent style, xiv
English Baroque Soloists and Monteverdi Choir, 263
　BWV 70/9, 99a
　BWV 74/7, 114a
　BWV 81/3, 86a
　BWV 101/1, 109, 110a
　BWV 127/3, 264a
　BWV 155/4, 124a, 125
　St. John Passion, 219a
Enlightenment, 24, 39, 256, 257
Ensemble Caprice, 174a
equal temperament, 62a, 67
Equiluz, Kurt, 129a
Erickson, Raymond, 90
essential graces, 146, 149–151, 155, 159, 166–167
ethopoeia, 58–59, 71, 86
etiquette, 50, 252, 257
　concert, 238, 241–242
Everest, Mark, 138
exclamatio, 128
exordium, 12, 24, 41, 104, 105
expression, individual, 28, 33–35, 39, 68–69

fantasies, 214–216, 221
　C. P. E. Bach on, 140, 154, 216
Farinelli (motion picture), 158a
Fat dupé, Le, 133
feigning, 165, 255–259
Feldman, Martha, 261
Félibien, André, 53, 56
female singers, 80, 287n24
Fénelon, François de,
　definition of persuasion, 3–4
　on expression, 35, 49–50, 127, 146, 229
　on performance, 234, 235
　on timing, 183
fermatas,
　as cadenzas, 217–218
　in chorales, 217–219, 233
Feuillet notation, 229, 254
Feuillet, Raoul-Auger, 229
Fielding, Henry, *Tom Jones*, 152, 289n30
Figurenlehre, 65–66
figures, 23, 26, 44–49, 60, 65. See also hypotyposis, pathopoeia
　in Bach's music, 69–72
　difficulty of defining, 47, 48, 65–66, 69, 152
　as *elaboratio*, 45, 139–141, 143–144
　and gestures, 172
　as gloss, 146–149
　meaning of, 46, 50
　as ornaments, 146–149, 152–154
　in Rhetorical music, 6, 19, 41
　specific examples, 46, 66, 101-103 (*see also corta*, cross, knot untied, *passus duriusculus, pianto*, symbols)
　of speech, 22, 44–45, 152, 165
Fischer, Johann Christian, 240–241
flattement, 156, 180, 211. See also virbato
Fleming, Paul, 100–101
Florentine academies, 21, 23, 36
Fontenelle, Bernard Le Bovier de, 288n22
formal analysis, 33
Forqueray, Jean-Baptiste, 182a
Francesco da Milano, 20, 29
Frank, Salomon, 88
Franklin, Don, 233
Frederick the Great, King of Prussia, 14–15, 249, 252, 256
French overture, 71, 115–117

Gable, Frederick, 167
Galilei, Vincenzo, 3, 36
Galliard, Johann Ernst, 222
Ganassi, Sylvestro, 20
Gardiner, Sir John Eliot, xviii, 90, 109a, 110a, 114a, 263
　BWV 70/9, 99a
　BWV 74/7, 114a
　BWV 81/3, 86a
　BWV 101/1, 109, 110a
　BWV 127/3, 264a
　BWV 155/4, 124a, 125
　on *kairos*, 232
　St. John Passion, 219a
Gebauer, Gunter, 90
Geminiani, Francesco, ornaments of expression, 143, 155–156, 167
Geringer, Karl, 67
German Baroque poetry, 100–101, 117
gestures
　in acting, 117
　musical, compared with phrasing, 195–199
　musical, defined, 171–172
　musical, and figures, 172
　in musical performance, 241, 247–248
　in Rhetorical music, 44–45, 168, 169
Gielgud, Sir John, 171a
Gjerdingen, Robert, 147–148, 167
gloss, 88
　ornaments as, 146–147, 151–153, 161, 164
Gluck, Christoph Willibald, 34

Goebel, Reinhardt, 5
Goethe, Johann Wolfgang, 32, 129a, 254, 260
Goldberg, Sander, 66
Goossens, Léon, 162–163, 164a
Gottsched, Johann Christoph, 45
Greek drama, 21, 23
Gessner, Salomon, 27
Grimarest, Jean Lénor Le Gallois sieur de, 135, 169, 174, 200
Grimm brothers, 139, 140
Großes Concert, Leipzig, 239

Haas, Arthur, 182a
Hamburg, 16, 88
Hampson, Christopher, 233
Handel, Georg Frideric, xiv, 8, 74, 91, 122, *148*
   Alexander's Feast, 21
   concertos, 163
   Giulio Cesare, 78–80
   "Lascia la spina," 158a
   Laudate pueri, 157a
   Messiah, xiii, 44, 161, 170, 194, 215
   his notation, 122
   "Ombra mai fù," 158a
   and personal expression, 8, 35
   his revisions, 125
   tempos, 206
   transpositions, 63
   Zadok the Priest, 151a
Hanning, Barbara Russano, 261
Hantaï, Pierre, 62a
Harding, Rosamond, 232
harmonic schemata, 39, 147–148, 154
Harnoncourt, Nikolaus, xv, xix, 5, 17, 35–36, 110, 263
   Monteverdi, 223, 224a
   Mozart, 240
   BWV 74/7, 114a, 264a
   BWV 101/1, 110a
   BWV 110/1, 264a
   BWV 154, 125a
   BWV 155/4, 124a
   BWV 171/4, 209a
   St. John Passion, 219a
harpsichord technique, 180, 181, 182a, *182*, 183a
Harris-Warrick, Rebecca, 138, 233, 293n70
Hatten, Robert, 67
Haussmann, Elias Gottlob, 50
hautboy, xi, xii,
   technique, 81, 99, 266, 296n1
Haydn, Joseph, 34, 44, 130–133, *133*, 204–205, 238
Haynes, Bruce,
   Althea of Tarsis, xiv
   character, xxi, xxii, xvi–xvii
   recordings by, 164a, 179a, 225a
Hebenstrreit, Pantaleon, 254

Heinichen, Johann David, 24, 91, 167
   and key characteristics, 64, 66
   on passions, 18
Henrici, Christian Friedrich, 194
Hickman, Roger, 167
Hill, Aaron, 168, 186, 295n66
Hill, Robert, 204
HIP (Historically Inspired Performance), 159, 164, 244
   characteristics, 157, 202
   movement, xiii, xxiii–xxiv, 35, 127, 166
Hippocratic medicine, 59, 128
Hippocrene source, 155
Hitler, Adolf, 142
Hoffmann, Melchior, 202
homophony, 23
Horace, 200, 254, 255
Hotteterre, Jacques, 246
Hudson, Richard, 232
Humanism, 6, 36
   and Rhetorical ethos, 18–25
Hume, David, 242
Hummel, Johann Nepomuk, 26
humor in the music of Bach, 65, 80, 114–117
"humouring," 40, 128–134, 138, 169, 187, 188–189, 264
humours, theory of, 26, 58–59, 87, 128, 134, 145
Huret, Grégoire, 30, 52
Hutcheson, Francis, 243
hypotyposis, 49–50, 71–75, 88, 285n17

iconography, musical, 236–237, 239
imitation, 9–10, 19, 25, 41. *See also mimesis*, and representation
   and Bach, 9, 35, 71–74, 80–84, 85–86, 99, 106, 270
   of character, 59
   and expression, 39–40, 69, 72, 85–86, 89–90
   in music, 42–44, 55, 58, 134
   of nature, 52, 68–74, 91–92, 242
   and painting, 10, 36, 49, 84–87
   and rhetoric, 156–157, 173–174, 214
   in Romantic art, 26–27, 33
   and studied passions, 254–259
improvisation, 65, 140, 180, 183, 212–216
   as *memoria*, 38, 40, 41
improvised ornamentation, 146–147, 152, 155–159, 161–165, 167, 218, 255
inspiration in art, 33–34, 38–39, 72, 140, 160, 165, 256. *See also inventio*
intention, 126, 130–133, 138, 148, 156, 159, 254
intentional fallacy, 121–126
inventio, 11, 12, 42, 44, 117, 121, 266
   defined, 38–40, 211
   as catalyst for musical creation, 66, 49, 111, 147, 160

Jacobs, René, 144, 145a
Jefferson, Thomas, 169
Jensen, James, 17, 34, 37
Joachim, Joseph, 194
Johnson, James, 239, 261
Johnstone, James, 219a
Jonas, Justus, 111
Jukes, Francis, 236
Juslin, Patrik, 55, 90

kairos, 139, 200–202, 210, 225–228, 232
Karelian lament, 139–140
Kelly, Michael, 259
Kennedy, Nigel, 244
key characteristics, 59–65, 67
King, Martin Luther, 142a
Kircher, Athanasius, 19, 241, 250
Kirkby, Emma, 157a, 223, 224a
Kirkpatrick, Ralph, 62a
Kirnberger, Johann Philipp, 195, 199
Kivy, Peter, 241
knot untied, 46–47
Koch, Heinrich Christoph, 195, 217
Koninklijk Conservatorium Den Haag, xi
Koopman, Ton, and Amsterdam Baroque Orchestra, 263
    BWV 74/7, 114a
    BWV 155/4, 124a
    BWV 154, 125a
    BWV 127/3, 264a
Körner, C. G., 92
Kuhnau, Johann, 59
Kuijken brothers, xv
Kuijken, Barthold, xix, 138, 179a, 180–181, 291n8

La Bruyère, Jean de, 50, 58–59
laments, 53, 135, 166, 199
    by Bach, 43, 101, 266
    Karelian, 139–140
    by Monteverdi, 223, 224
    musical attributes, 42–43, 43, 60–61, 102, 155–156
Lamy, Bernard, 68, 255
Lancelot, Francine, 262
landscape painting, 84–85, 85, 87
Lang Lang, 244
Lang, Franciscus, 248
Lassus, Orlando di, 20
laughter, 71, 80–81, 88, 94, 114–115, 243, 264a, 294n25
Lauschmann, Richard, 162, 290n59
Le Brun, Charles, 55
    Conférence sur l'expression, 50–52, *51*
    historical painting, 52–54, *54*
    on emotion in painting, 76, *76*, 77, 90, 92
Le Faucheur, Michel, 137

Le Guin, Elisabeth, 138, 247, 288n23
Leaver, Robin, 73, 117
Lebègue, Nicholas, 215
Leech-Wilknison, Daniel, 124, 138, 198–199, 203
Lehmann, Bradley, 63, 67, 224, 225a
Leipzig, 14–15, 24, 153
    dance culture, 229
    listening practices in, 239
    theater in, 24
    town council, 115–116
Leisinger, Ulrich, 17
Leonhardt, Gustav, xi, xiv, xix, 127, 263
    and Leonhardt Consort:
        BWV 127/3, 264a
        BWV 135/4, 145a
        BWV 143/4, 129a
        BWV 903, 181, 182a
Leppert, Richard, 37, 261
Leusink, Pieter Jan, 263
    BWV 101/1, 110a
Lévi-Strauss, Claude, 34, 38
Lewis, Clive Staples, 3
Liebesstrahl, 76–78, *76*, *77*
Lindley, Mark, 67
listening practices, 30–31, 37, 236–239, 241–243, 261
Liszt, Franz, 232
Little, Meredith, 262
Locatelli, Pietro, 29
London pleasure gardens, 236–239
long-line phrasing, 195, 197–198
Longfellow, Hendry Wadsworth, 144
Lorrain, Claude, 84, *85*
Lotti, Santa Stella, 223
Louis XIV, 3, 50, 53
Loulié, Étienne, 135, 215
Lully, Jean-Baptiste, xiv, 23, 254
Luther, Martin, 73, 109, 117
Lutheran cantatas, reforms, 88
Lutheranism, 23, 73, 80, 88, 100–101, 107, 115
lyre, 20–21

Mace, Thomas,
    and articulation, 168, 170, 171–172
    describes ecstatic state induced by music, 32, 250–251
    dynamics, 137–138, *137*
    and "humouring," 12, 128, 129–130, 170, 188–189, *189*
    on musical drudges, 12–13
    Musick's Monument, 17
    on timing, 210—211
Machy, Le Sieur de, 215
mad scenes, 87
Maetzel, Johann Nepomuk, 207
Mahler, Gustav, 122, 140

Marais, Marin, 86a, 116a
Marcello, Alessandro, 42, 162–163, *163*, 164a, 290n59
Marenzio, 22
Marissen, Michael, 9, 117
Marpurg, Friedrich Wilhelm, 174, 187, 199
Marsh, Carol, 262
Marshall, Robert, 39, 152
Mason, John, 174, 185
Matteis, Nocla, 255
Mattheson, Johann,
   analyses da capo aria, 24, 42
   on bodily gestures, 243, 245, 247
   on chorales, 107
   on inspiration, 39, 255
   and key characteristics, 60–63, Table 2.2, 67, 96
   list of figures, 147
   Das neu-eröffnete Orchester, 61
   on meaning in music, 12, 30, 31, 92–93
   and the passions appropriate to music, 55–57, Table 2.1, 66, 92–94
   on performance, 91, 122, 150, 235
   on punctuation, 183–184, *184*, 187
   as style coach, 16
   on tempo and tempo markings, 134–135, 136, 221, 225
   Der Vollkommene Capellmesiter, 17
Malas-Gollewska, Ewa, 158a
McCreesh, Paul, 203a, 204, 219a
McGill University, xiv
Mei, Girolamo, 21
Mellers, Wilfred, 67
memoria, 11, 38, 40
Mendel, Arthur, 72
Mendelssohn-Bartholdy, Felix, 32
Ménestrier, Claude-François, 253
Mengelberg, Willem, 203a, 204, 210, 221
Mersenne, Marin, 23, 207, 212
messa di voce, 128, 156, 158, 166, 196–197, 226, 290n50. *See also* "Dutch buldge"
Messerschmidt, Franz Xavier, 262
mesure, 135–137, 178, 180, 182, 207, 209–210, 215, 216–217
metabasis, 46
metronome, 202, 205, 206–207, 232
Metropolitan Opera, 157
Meyer, Richard, 90
mimesis, 9, 34–35, 90. *See also* imitation
modulation, 63–64, 75–77, 76, 286n45
Moens-Haenen, Greta, 117, 167
Moissi, Alexander, 129a, 171a
Momigny, Jérôme-Joseph, 199
Monnet, Jean, 133
Monody, 21–23
Montagu, Jennifer, 90
Montéclair, Michel Pignolet de, 151

Monteverdi Choir, *see* English Baroque Soloists and Monteverdi Choir
Monteverdi, Claudio, xiv, 5, 123
   Lamento della Ninfa, 223–224, 224a
   Madrigals, 19–20, 22, 223–224
   Orfeo, 224
   and *seconda prattica*, 19–20
   and text setting, 18, 33
Morley, Thomas, 59
Moroney, Davitt, 67, 286n44
Mortensen, Lars Ulrik, 182a
Moser, Andreas, 194
mouvement, 135–137, 216, 229
Mozart, Leopold, 149, 196–197
Mozart, Wolfgang Amadeus, on *cantabile*, 196
   on improvisation, 161, 216, 217, 293n38
   and the musical sublime, 29, 31, 33
   in Paris, 239–240, 261
   the performer as composer, 11
   and rubato, 223
   and text setting, 18, 33, 199
Murray, Ann, 223, 224a
music and language, 32, 35–36, 66, 72. *See also* rhetoric
musicians as servants, 34, 237, 256–257

Napper, Susie, xiv, 146a, 179a
narratio, 12, 24, 41
nature, artistic imitation of, 9–10, 52, 68, 74, 84, 91
Netherlands Bach Collegium, 263
   BWV 101/1, 110a
Neuberin, Caroline, 24
Neumann, Frederick, 17, 167
Neumeister, Erdmann, 88
Nevile, Jennifer, 262
New Brandenburg Concertos, xiv, 281
Newman, Ernest, 90
Norman, Jessye, 129a
Norrington, Sir Roger, 158a
North, Roger, xxiii
   on "borrowed time," 222–224, 227
   discusses ornamentation, 149, 150
   on improvisation, 40l
   on musical expression, 55
   on music and painting, 30–31, 87–88
   and professional musicians, 237
   on tempo, 206–207, 222
notation, 12, 40, 117, 122–124, 215
   of articulation and punctuation, 178–179, *178*, *184*, *191*, 199, 233
   of ornaments, 150–151, 163–164, 166–167, 224, 226–227
   proscriptive, 134, 138, 140
   in recitative, 174
   of choreography, 229, 254
notes inégales, 227

Obama, Barack, 143
obbligatos, instrumental, 81, 246, 266, 287n25
O'Dette, Paul, 202
O'Donnell, John, 67
offices of rhetoric, 38–41
Olliver, Michel-Barthelémy, 261
one-to-a-part performance, 87
Ong, Walter, 4, 16, 67
onomatopoeia, 43, 80–81
opera singers as actors, 91, 246–247
opera, 10, 18, 73, 190, 194
   arias in, 104
   audience response to, 239, 240, 261, 236
   by Charpentier, 64
   conductors, 220
   dance in, 229, 253
   expressive performance of, 86, 115, 214, 250, 251, 252
   by Handel, 63, 74, 80, 125, 158a
   instrumental sections in, 116
   by Marais, 86a, 116a
   by Mattheson, 16
   by Monteverdi, 22
   origins and dissemination of, 23
   and passions, 21, 91, 144, 267
   Romantic, 32, 157, 199
   and sacred music, 73, 78
   and *seconda prattica*, 22–23
   text setting in, 18
   tonality in, 62, 64
organ, 15, 63, 98–99, 107, 181, 198
organists, 16, 202, 218–219, 247
Orchestra of the Age of Enlightenment, 158a
Orchestra of the Eighteenth Century, xii
ornamentation, 167
   agogic, 226
   and dissonance, 153
   extempore, 40, 160, 203
   and figures, 44, 45, 47, 66, 140
   as gloss, 146–153, *153*
   as heightened expression, 143, 154–157, 166–167
   and "humouring," 130
   influencing tempo, 206, 221, 250
   Italian style, 159, 160–166, *163, 164, 165* (*see also* passaggi)
   memorized, 41, 165
   and structure, 147, 152, 155, 159, 160–165, 224, 271
"ornaments of expression," Geminiani's, 155–156
Orpheus myth, 21, 252
Ortiz, Diego, 152
Ossi, Massimo, 36
Ovid, 21

painting emotions in Rhetorical art, 36, 49–50, 91
Palisca, Claude, 36
Papendiek, Mrs, 240, 294n17
Paris Opéra, 220, 239, 261
Parke, William Thomas, 240–241
parodies, 59, 67, 116, 133–134, 190–195, 199, 229, 287n25
Parrott, Andrew, 138
   St. John Passion, 219a
partimento, 147–148, *147, 148*
passaggi, 38, 146, 159, 160–166. *See also* ornamentation
passion constellations, 53, 57, Table 2.1, 58, 66, 71, 94–96
passions. *See also* affect
   constantly changing, 91, 187, 257
   joyous, 57, 71, 93–94
   negative, 29–30, 71
   single, theory of, 91–92
   stable, 52, 91, 187
passus duriusculus, 102
Pater, Walter, 32
pathetic, 8
pathetick, definition of, 7
pathopoeia, 50–57, 71, 86, 285n17
Pavarotti, Luciano, 157, 244
Peacham, Henry, 8, 44
Pepys, Samuel, 28, 284n22
Peres da Costa, Neal, 233
performers and composers
   division of labor, 11–12
   responsibilities, 12–13
Peri, Jacopo, 21
Periode, 195
peroratio, 12, 24
persuasion, art of, 3, 6
   in music, 6–7, 68, 242
Philidor, Pierre, 178
phrases and phrasing, 195,
   compared with gestures, 195–199, 291n12
pianto, 42–43, 44, 46, 55, 80
Picander (Christian Friedrich Henrici), 194
pièces de caractère, 59, 60
Pietism, 73
Pinnock, Trevor, 173, 174a
Pisendel, Johann Georg, 165
pitch, xiii, 60, 62a, 63a, 67, 83, 129, 183
   oscillation, 156–157
Plato, 4, 13, 234, 263
Platonic ideal, 124, 126
Playford, Henry, 233
Plebuch, Tobias, 199
Podger, Rachel, 145, 146a
poetic parodies, *see* parodies
poetic models for music, 183–185, 189–194
poetry as heightened speech, 143–144,

point d'orgue, 216
Poisson, Jean, 260
political rhetoric, 26, 142
polyphony of passions, 105–113, 165
polyphony, 22, 23, 105–113. *See also* counterpoint
Pontus de Tyard, 20, 29
Pope, Alexander, 150
portamento, 203
Positivism, 126, 166
Postmodernism, 126, 166
posture, 244, *245*, 246. *See also* deportment and body language
Poulenard, Isabelle, 166a, 167
Poussin, Nicholas, 84
Praetorius, Michael, 128, 134, 213
preludes, 214, unaccompanied, 215, 233
Prima prattica, 19, 22
principal passion, 88, 89, 92, 155. *See also* affect
Printz, Wolfgang Caspar, 154, 160, 256
Prohaska, Felix, 174a
Promnitz, Balthasar Erdmann von, 256
pronuntiatio, xviii, 11, 23, 38
propositio, 12, 41
Puccini, Giacomo, 199
pulse, as guide to tempo, 205–206
punctuation, 168–170, 171a, 174, 186, 199, 218
and breath, 175–176
Purcell, Henry, xiv, *Dido and Aeneas*, 129a, *King Arthur*, 44, 151
Pure, Michel de, 252–253

Quantz, Johann Joachim, 14
advice on feigning, 256
on accompaniment, 266
on cadenzas, 217
on comic effects in performance, 115
on dance characters, 136–137
defines *Einschnitt*, 172, *172*, 215
discusses key characteristics, 60
and "humouring," 187–188
on musical rhetoric, 7, 12
his ornamentation, 146, 152, *153*, 159
on performance, 8, 13, 187, 121, 235, 248, 258, 269
on punctuation, 177, 183
and theory of changing passions in music, 91–92, 257
on tempo, 207–208, 215, 225
his use of dynamics, 195–197, *196*, 208
Versuch, 249
Vortrag, 249–250
Quickelberg, Samuel, 20
Quinault, Philippe, 23
Quintilianus, Marcus Fabius, 17, 35, 121
on decorum, 244, 246
and false emotions, 256

on performance, 235, 260
on punctuation, 168, 180
on *elocutio*, 137

Racine, Jean, 24, 251
Ragin, Derek Lee, 158a
Rameau, Jean-Philippe, 17, 59, 70, 125, 239
on engagement in performance, 257
on key characteristics, 60–61, Table 2.2
Pièces de clavecin en concert, 226–227
use of *aspiration* and *suspension*, 226, 227
Rameau, Pierre, 246
Ranelagh Rotunda, 236, 237
Ranum, Patricia, 199, 233
Raphael, 30
Rebel, Jean-Féry, 44
received pronunciation, 142
recitative, 23, 104, 210, 214, 215, 251
French and Italian styles compared, 174
recorder technique, 181, 291n31
recording industry, 159–160
Red Priest, 166a
rehearsals, 13, 41, 66
Reichardt, J. F., 252
religion and spirituality, 72–73
representation, 68–70, 74. *See also* imitation, and *mimesis*
Reynolds, Joshua, 40
rhetoric as used by politicians, 142–143
rhetoric,
its demise in 19th century, 5, 17, 25, 26, 141
in education, 4–5, 24–25
offices of, 11, 19, 38–42, 121, 250
revival in 20th century, 5
and science, 4, 25
and truth, 3–4
Rhetorical music, defined, 6
differences with modern performance aesthetics, 14, 36–37
rhetorical structure, 24, 41–42
Riccoboni, François, 260
Riccoboni, Luigi, 121, 225
Richesource, Oudart de [Jean de la Sourdière], 173
Richter, Jean Paul, 32
Ricœur, Paul, 168
Riemann, Hugo, 181, 203
Riepel, Joseph, 195
Rifkin, Joshua, xxv, 42
Rink, John, 232
Romanesca, 147–148, *147–148*, 153
Romantic aesthetics, 8, 28, 55, 203. *See also* Æsthetics
Romantic phrasing, 195, 197–199. *See also* long-line phrasing
Romantic Revolution, xxii, 25–26
Rooley, Anthony, 224a, 233

Rosenblum, Sandra, 233
Rousseau, Jean-Jacques, 135, 210
    defines *air*, 93
    Le Devin du village, 132, 133
    on *inventio*, 13
    on performance, 210, 234, 251, 267
Rousseau, Jean, 60, 61, Table 2.2
Rowlandson, Thomas, 236
Roy, Pierre Charles, 253
rubato, 203, 211–212, 223–225, 232–233
Russell, Lucy, 145

Saint-Albine, Rémond de, 128
Saint-Lambert, M. de, 173, 184
Sainte-Colombe, M. de, 215
Salieri, Antonio, 29
sarabande, 136, 230–233, *231*, *232*
Saxony, artistic taste in, 50
Scarlatti, Domenico, 123
Scheibe, Johann Adolph, 24–25, 164, 287n23, 290n60
Scheibel, G., 68
Schelhase, Leon, 183a
schemata, harmonic, *see* harmonic schemata
Schlegel, Friedrich, 32
Schmitter, Amy, 17
Schneider, Herbert, 262
Schoenberg, Arnold, 122, 177, 291n7
Schubert, Franz, *Erlkönig*, 129a
Schulenberg, David, 67
Schuller, Gunther, 122
Schulz and Sulzer, 199
Schweitzer, Albert, 69–70, 72, 90, 102, 263
seconda prattica, 11, 19–24, 36, 213, 214
Seymour, Peter, 140
Shakespeare, William, 100, 104, 167
    Hamlet, 142a, 171a, 258
    Richard III, 45
silence d'articulation, 180
Silvestre, Louis de, 50
simultaneous interpretation, 165–166
Sipiora, Baumlin, 232
Small, Christopher, 236–237, 262
Smith, Anne, 36
sorrowful passions, 71, 80, 96–99, 101, 113, 140, 155. *See also* laments
Spitta, Phillip, 69
sprezzatura, 213–214, 221, 233
Steblin, Rita, 67
stile rappresentativo, or *stile recitativo*, 21, 22
stinging grace, 189, *189*
Stokowski, Leopold, 174a
storm at sea, 42, 85–86, 86a
Stravinsky, Igor, 33, 123
Streisand, Barbra, 158, 159a
Strozzi, Barbara, 166–167, 166a
stylus fantasticus, 215

sublime, 139
    beauty, 224, 270
    in Romantic art, 29,
    in Rhetorical art, 31–32, 69, 136, 151, 163, 187, 257
Susenbrotus, Johannes, 49
suspension, 183, 226–227, *227*
Sutherland, Dame Joan, 157
Suzuki, Masaaki, 263
    BWV 101/1, 109, 110a
    BWV 127/3, 264a
    BWV 143/4, 129a
    BWV 150/6, 76a
    BWV 154/1, 125a
sympathy, 43, 234–235, 242–244, 252, 254
synonymy, 10, 247

tactus, 205–206, 217, 225
Tagliavini, Luigi Ferdinando, xv
Tarling, Judy, xix, 16–17, 61
Tartini, Giuseppe, 251
Taruskin, Richard, xiii, 232
taste
    as arbiter, xvii, xxiv, 30, 235, 238
    of audiences, 13, 34, 50, 178, 235, 238
    bad, 21, 31, 137, 149, 166, 167
    based on experience, 188, 222, 229
    based on musical details, 208, 210
    changes over time, 15, 27, 28, 126, 174, 216
    essential to eloquence, 155, 159, 222
    and moderation, 128, 161, 166, 270
    Romantic, 133
Tatlow, Ruth, 67
Taubert, Gottfried, 229
Telemann, Georg Philipp, 24, 59, 91
    Methodische Sonaten, 161
    on punctuation, 174, 185
    Tafelmusik, 238
    Wassermusik, 116
temperament and tuning, 60, 62–64, 67, 83
temperament, or humour, 235, 259. *See also* humours
Templeri, Joseph de, 254–255
tempo and affect, 134–137
tempo fluctuation, 206, 208, 210, 211–214, 215, 223–228, 232–233
tempo giusto, 206, 215
tempo in dance music, 136–147
tempo ordinario, 206
text fidelity, 40–41, 122–123, 140, 159
text setting, 18, 22, 33, 71, 84–85, 87–88
Theophrastus, 58
Thurmond, James Morgan, 199
Tidhar and Dixon, 67
Tieck, Ludwig, 27, 32
tierce coulée, 180
Tilney, Colin, 233

timepieces and musical time, 202, 205, 207, 292n2
timing, 200–205
    in dance music, 228–232
    at fermatas, 218–219
    and musical structure, 221
    in oratory and recitative, 214
    and passionate expression, 135, 223
Timotheus, myth of, 20–21, 284n8
Tisch-Wackernagel, Johannes Hermann, 100, 117
Toft, Robert, 36, 199
Tomlinson, Kellom, 246
topics, 23, 26, 44, 57–58, 60, 66
Tosi, Pier Francesco, 221–222, 224
trait de liaison, 194
transgresso, 46
"transparent" performance, 13, 126, 252
transposition, 60–62, 63, 266
tremblement étouffé, 155
tremolo, 98–100, 99a, 117, 143, 157
    on 18th-century organs, 99
trill, 13, 96, 155, 157, 167
    an essential grace, 149–151
    performance and effect, 47, 155, 249
Tritto, Giacomo, *147*
Tromlitz, Johann Georg, 152
tropes, 44, 66, 70. *See also* figures
trumpet, use of by Bach, 83–84, *83*, 107
tuning, 83, 123, 266. *See also* pitch, temperament and tuning.
Türk, Daniel Gottlob, 199
Türk, Gerd, 129a

unmeasured preludes, 163, 215–216, 233
ut pictura poesis, 9–10, 49

"Vater unser im Himmelreich," 109, *110*
Vauxhall Gardens, 236, *236*

verisimilitude, 23, 44, 259, 296n85
verismo, 157, 203, 223
Vial, Stephanie, 199, 288n23
vibrato, 117, 156–158, 167, 189
    as used in modern performance, 99, 128, 158, 199
Vickers, Brian, 65
Villeneuve, Alexandre de, 145
Vincentino, Nicola, 213
Visse, Dominique, 129a
Vivaldi, Antonio, xiv, 166
    Four Seasons, 44, 74, 116, 151
    La Notte, 176a, *175*, 176
Vogt, Gustave, 197, *198*
Vogt, Mauritius Johann, 50, 92
Voltaire, 123
Vortrag, 38, 41, 146
    defined, 249–250, 252

Wagner, Richard, 199
Walls, Peter, 167
Walther, Johann G., 92
Watchorn, Peter, 63a
Weber, William, 238
Weigel, Johann Christoph, *245*
Wentz, Jed, 135, 233
Werckmeister, Andreas, 92, 134
Wimsatt, William K., 126, 138
Wistreich, Richard, 167
wonderment, 51–52, 75–77
woodwind instruments and tonality, 64, 81–82, 266, 296n1
word painting, 47, 72, 74, 84, 87–88, *113*
Wragg, J., 216, *217*
Wulf, Christopher, 90

Zarlino, Gioseffo, 22
Ziegler, J. G., 68

Printed in the USA/Agawam, MA
December 20, 2019

745864.016